# REVOLUTIONARY COUNCIL TO
# Military Dictatorship

## KYI WIN SEIN
## (Malcolm)

SEQUEL TO 'ME AND THE GENERALS
OF THE REVOLUTIONARY COUNCIL'

First published in Great Britain as a softback original in 2018

Copyright © Kyi Win Sein (Malcolm) 2018

The moral right of this author has been asserted.

All rights reserved.

No part of this publication may be reproduced, stored in a retrieval system, or transmitted, in any form or by any means, without the prior permission in writing of the publisher, nor be otherwise circulated in any form of binding or cover other than that in which it is published and without a similar condition including this condition being imposed on the subsequent purchaser.

Typeset in Minion Pro & Patua One

Editing, design and publishing by UK Book Publishing

UK Book Publishing is a trading name of Consilience Media

www.ukbookpublishing.com

ISBN: 978-1-912183-43-2

# FOREWORD BY MAUNG NYO

I have known U Kyi Win Sein since I was a cadet at the Defense Services Academy together with his young twin brothers Captain Tin Htoo Sein (Master Mariner) and Tin Htet Sein (Electronics Engineer). When he and his family came to Maymyo (now Pyin-Oo-Lwin) in April 1970 I was a staff officer at the Academy and had the opportunity to give a guided tour of the campus and its facilities. Again, when I was assigned to the Ministry of Defense and resided at Yankin township I frequently visited U Kyi Win Sein's home in Pyidaw-Aye Avenue on Kaba-Aye Road.

During WWII Japanese occupation when the entire country was suffering his mother gave birth on Christmas day of 1943 to twin boys at a small village on the bank of the Myitnge river, under deprived and impoverished conditions of malnutrition, no medical facilities, just under the care of an 80 year-old village midwife. Unable to breastfeed the newly born babies, the elder three brothers had to get cow's milk from two miles away on foot through thick forest canopy every day. It helped the mother and the twin boys to survive and regain normal health.

After the war U Kyi Win Sein's father U Sein resumed his service in the Excise Department that enabled him and his siblings to attend regular school at Saint Albert's English High School in Maymyo (now Pyin-Oo-Lwin). With accelerated double promotions combined with sports activities in football (soccer), track and field, boxing and golf in High School years, he successfully matriculated and was admitted to the University of Rangoon (now Yangon) in 1953-54 Academic year and pursued his Intermediate of Arts higher education.

During his final year in High School he was befriended by Colonel Thaung Kyi, Irrawaddy Region Brigade Commander who recruited and inducted him into the Intelligence training program at the Brigade Headquarters in Bassein (now Pathein). The Senior Colonel was his mentor throughout his career and long professional service as Legal Adviser in the Ministry of Defense.

While studying at the University of Rangoon he was selected to study International Law in Japan as a State Scholar by the then Deputy Prime Minister Bo Khin Maung Galay. It was during that time (1955) in Tokyo that he met General Ne Win together with General Aung Gyi, Army Chief of Staff and Vice Chief of General Staff, General Tommy Clift, Chief of Staff of Burma Air Force and Admiral Than Phay, Chief of Staff of Burma Navy. It was the beginning of his long relationship with the top leaders and founders of the modern Burmese Military establishment, the Tatmadaw as it is known today.

On his return from Japan (in 1959) with degrees in International Law from University of Tokyo and Waseda University, General Ne Win, Commander-in-Chief and then Caretaker Prime Minister, appointed him with a direct Commission in the Judge Advocate General's Office in the Ministry of Defense where he soon became the General Counsel and Legal Adviser.

He was one of the very few and exceptional persons to survive the serious disobedience of not reporting to Officer Training Camp and despite that appointed by the Deputy Prime Minister of the Caretaker Government in the Burma Oil Company (BOC) as Regional Marketing Officer of South Burma. The youngest person (at age 23) to serve in that Senior Executive Position in the British-Burma Government Joint Venture Petroleum / Energy Corporation.

His very early relations and involvement at a young age with the Myanmar Military (Tatmadaw) in its efforts to eliminate foreign domination of the country's economy, commerce and trade for many decades since the colonial period makes him eminently qualified to enlighten the people of Myanmar as to what actually transpired at the very top of the seat of power of our country. He was one of the very few civilians that was entrusted and assigned to lead Overseas and International Economic, Commercial, Trade, Financial and banking projects by the Caretaker and later by the Revolutionary Council Government led by General Ne Win.

I am very pleased, happy and privileged to be invited to write this FOREWORD for the SEQUEL TO ME AND THE GENERALS OF THE REVOLUTIONARY COUNCIL.

MAUNG NYO, MAJOR-GENERAL (RETIRED)
FORMER VICE ADJUTANT GENERAL (MINISTRY OF DEFENSE).
MYANMAR TATMADAW

# PREFACE

At the time my memoir was published in the UK two years ago it was a great relief of a huge burden that I had been carrying for nearly 30 years taken off my aging shoulders. There was absolutely no intention nor desire on my part to take on another writing task in the years left for me in this incarnation. In fact I was reflecting on the past immediate two years it took to complete the memoir from start to finish. In November 2012 I visited Myanmar for the first time in 41 years just a year after inception of President Thein Sein's "Civilian Government".

I was now free to begin writing my memoir because the last original member of the Revolutionary Council, General Aung Gyi, had passed on in September 2012, and he was among the many who had asked me to write my memoir "only after they had passed on to their next incarnation". I mention a few most adamant that they need to be gone from this world when their direct involvement in the affairs of State are disclosed to the people of Myanmar by one that worked closely with them and the Burmese Military Establishment from his High School days in 1952.

(General Aung Gyi, General San Yu, General Tommy Clift, Senior General Saw Maung, General Maung Maung, Colonel Thaung Kyi, Colonel Maung Lwin (Moustache), Colonel Khin Nyo, Colonel Chit Khin, Colonel Kyi Maung – Zat-Laik, and Colonel Aung Din. Their more than normal high regard and innate fear of General Ne Win, the Dictator, paranoia and insecurity was such that their common request to the only young Civilian Japanese educated Lawyer was "If ever you write a book of your memoirs make sure that we are dead and gone".

This sequel, or more appropriately supplement to the original memoir, was written in response to the request of surviving associates and friends who enthusiastically welcomed the original memoir but took exception that I had, for reasons of my own, omitted many of the most critical innermost personal conflicts and blunders of the Ne Win Regime and implored me to put them on record for people and country and especially those in the "Seat of Power, both Politicians and Military" to learn from those errors of judgment, mistakes, petty personal conflicts and outright ignorance made worse by Bo Ne Win's embrace of extreme leftist daydreams of socialist utopia borrowed lock stock and barrel from Aung San's BLUEPRINT FOR INDEPENDENT BURMA, an assignment given to him by General Suzuki (Bo Moegyo) while staying at his residence in Hamamatsu, Japan.

The title of this sequel emerged from the many and varied reactions to the original memoir, especially from my contemporaries and associates with close personal links to the present Military establishment – with one common question they raised: "Why do you think General Ne Win was feared so much by the Generals and Colonels of the Revolutionary Council?" For me that question has been lingering in my head since the very first reluctant encounter with him at age 19 in the Presidential Suite of the Imperial Hotel Tokyo in late September 1955, six months after my arrival in Japan as a State Scholar, unhappy, miserable and unwillingly studying International Law (a subject chosen for me by Burma State Scholarship Board Chairman) at the University of Tokyo Faculty of Law. I was at a very low point in my young life, sent off to a foreign land with absolutely no say in determining my future. As a matter of fact when the First Secretary of the Burmese Embassy, U Hla Aung, called and instructed that I must go to the Imperial Hotel because "a VIP from Burma wanted to meet you", I refused since he did not tell me who it was. But Ambassador U Myat Tun himself called later and asked me to be there at 8:00 AM. So here I am in the lobby.

Colonel Maung Lwin (Moustache), Military Intelligence Service, and Colonel Hla Myint, Commanding Officer of Artillery and Armor, came down to the Main Lobby where I was waiting and escorted me to the huge and well-appointed suite. In the corridor we ran into U Myat Tun, the Burmese Ambassador. Upon entry to the suite I noted that Gen. Ne Win was seated alone on a large sofa, on the right Gen. Aung Gyi was seated alone on a sofa and on the left sofa Admiral Than Phay and Gen. Tommy Clift were sitting together. Gen. Ne Win waved his hand pointing to the right next to him and said 'sit here'. To my surprise and amazement the two Colonels were standing at the entry door and the Ambassador was never asked to come in. It dawned on me then and there that here is a man quite at ease to have Colonels standing at the door and the Burmese Ambassador out in the corridor.

I also noted that the four Generals were very much relaxed and then all attention was on me when Gen. Ne Win was upset when I responded to his question "how are you getting along?" that I was unhappy in Japan and wanted to return home to Burma. Gen. Aung Gyi was very understanding and quick to jump in to clarify and explain things calmly to the nervous young student. Bo Ne Win's demeanor and language was crude, rough and abusive but it was quite clear to me that was his regular communication style, similar to our journalist uncle Hanthawaddy U Sein – every second word is swearing or cursing. Once the initial brow-beating was over Bo Ne Win was the typical Burmese elder brother / uncle inquiring if I had eaten breakfast, telling Bo Lwin to "feed him, give him money to buy warm clothes and some pocket money and have him come see me before we leave Tokyo". He definitely noticed my extreme discomfort and unhappiness.

Then his tone changed, wrapping his arms around my shoulder, saying, "Don't worry, everything will turn out OK, and if you need any help contact Bo Aung Gyi or Bo Lwin. Make sure to tell him how to contact you fellows." He took very seriously Bo Khin Maung Galay's request to check on and take care of the student he sent to Japan despite his objections to pursue studies in International Law at Japan's top Tokyo University. I later learned that Gen. Ne Win was impressed that a young Burmese was studying at Japan's most prestigious university, recalling that all the instructors of the 30 Comrades at the Imperial General Staff were graduates of that university especially at the elite Advanced Intelligence Training School at Nakano where the infamous and feared Japanese Ken-Pei-Tai Security Operatives were trained. The Japanese Imperial Staff selected Bo Setkya, Bo Zeya, Bo Yan Naing, Bo Kyaw Zaw, Bo Ne Win and Bo Letya for special Intelligence training. I was too unhappy and naïve to understand and appreciate the rare once-in-a-lifetime opportunity to be studying at Japan's #1 University.

After the overthrow of the elected Government of Prime Minister U Nu in 1962, detaining the President, the Speakers of the Lower and Upper Houses of

Parliament and the entire Cabinet, General Ne Win assumed the four major posts in the hierarchy of the Armed Forces and the Command and Control channeled down from Chairman of the Revolutionary Council, Council of Ministers, the Ministry of Defense and the Chief of General Staff. With all the State and Military powers held by the Revolutionary Council Government, it was the Chairman himself that assumed all the authority. As such the path towards a Military Dictatorship was paved from the very inception of the Revolutionary Council on March 02, 1962. That was perhaps why Gen. Aung Gyi, the Vice Chief of General Staff, was deliberately kept out of the loop when Ne Win was planning the Coup.

This is perhaps the appropriate time and forum to remind all concerned in Myanmar that General Suzuki (Bo Moegyo), Commander-in-Chief of the Burma Independence Army (BIA) and his Chief of Staff General Aung San who selected Bo Ne Win to lead the newly formed battalions and battle groups into Burma (1941-1942) from Siam (now Thailand). In real historical perspective that was the time Burma's supreme Military Commander was ordained by the Japanese Imperial Army Minami Kikan Burma Operation and leader of the 30 Comrades, Bo Aung San. That selection was again confirmed in the immediate post WWII 1946-1948 period when Aung San shed his uniform to lead the (AFPFL) political party and asked Bo Ne Win (Colonel) to remain in the Army as 4th Battalion Commander under General Smith Dun, Commander-in-Chief of Burma Army.

However, Aung San asked Bo Ne Win to release Bo Aung Gyi (Lt. Colonel), Deputy Commander of 4th Battalion to stand for Constituent Assembly election as AFPFL Candidate in his native Paungde in Prome (now Pyay) that he won handily. When the Burma Communist Party (BCP) opposed Aung San's "Independence Policy Manifesto as being Weak, Subservient and Lackey of the British", and 3 battalions commanded by 30 Comrade-members Zeya, Zin Yaw and Yan Aung went underground and defected to the BCP in 1947. Bo Ne Win's 4th was the only one battalion left on the side of Aung San's AFPFL Party with him as Governor Hubert Rance's Prime Minister. The rest of Burma Army at that time were Karens, Kachins, Gurkhas (Nepalese), Chins and remnants of

British Military Mission for Ordinance, Signals, Logistics, Naval and Air Force Maintenance and Training.

Therefore his consolidation of power and authority over the Burmese Armed Forces was from its very inception and when the process of integration with some elements of the various "out of control militias" was initiated he asked Bo Aung Gyi to return to the Army as Vice Chief of General Staff with the rank of Brigadier-General. It was in fact a demotion for Aung Gyi because he was serving as Parliamentary Secretary of the Defense Ministry, a Cabinet Rank of Deputy Minister Senior to the Commander-in-Chief of the Armed Forces. In the Ministry of Defense where "Rank and Status" trumps everything, Bo Aung Gyi and Bo Maung Maung were exceptions and stand out prominently because both served in General Aung San's Headquarters as his Aides and then in 4th Battalion under Bo Ne Win. The two could pick up the phone and speak to him any time and walk into his office any time and get his attention. Before Bo Maung Maung was ousted, he had the notoriety of barging into the Chief of Staff's Office and sitting on the corner of his desk, asking or raising questions and Bo Ne Win did not think it was such a big deal as Maung Maung was just being himself. Their relations go back to Rangoon University days, the agitation and underground movement and the fight for independence from colonial rule. He was a friend more than a subordinate officer serving under his Command. Aung Gyi on the other hand was a "soldier politician" as well as a friend highly respected by the "political elite" because of his seniority, having served as Parliamentary Secretary of Defense in Aung San's Cabinet in the final days of British Colonial Governor Sir Hubert Rance (1945-1948).

But for other officers even of the same rank it was a different story entirely. Getting an appointment would be difficult, let alone walking in. Officers with confirmed appointments were checked by a Security Major in the waiting room. Bo Maung Maung, Bo Aung Gyi, Navy Chief and Air Force Chief, were the only ones that had direct secure phone lines to Bo Ne Win's desk, mobile signal box and his private residence. These very few handful of personal friends and senior officers practically carried him on their shoulders and helped modernize and build the Burmese Military that enabled Ne Win to take over the reins of the country in 1962 in an almost bloodless coup. His reliance and confidence in these top few officers was such that after the Prime Minister and his Cabinet was locked up, he simply telephoned Aung Gyi and said, "We have taken over the country so proceed with setting up the Government and all that is necessary."

He did not even mention from where he was calling. We later learned that Bo Maung Lwin (Moustache) who was with him called all Generals and Senior Colonels to report to Bo Aung Gyi in Dagon House, his Official Residence and private office at the entrance to the Ministry of Defense. Colonel Khin Nyo called me around 6:30 AM saying he was on his way to the Ministry and soon calls from Gen. Clift and Admiral Than Phay instructing me to proceed to the Export-Import Bank and standby there for further instructions. The important factor here to note was that Ne Win did not even bother to show up to set up the Government Apparatus to manage the affairs of the country he had just taken over, but simply left everything in the hands of Aung Gyi to take the leadership role in organizing the Revolutionary Council Government.

Bo Aung Gyi had been through this same process in 1958 when Bo Ne Win asked him to set up the Caretaker Government that was dubbed by the media as "A Soft Coup", which was engineered by the Commander-in-Chief ordering Aung Gyi and Maung Maung to pressure the then Prime Minister U Nu to hand over State Power to the Army through the Parliament. According to Gen. Tommy Clift, the only guidance from Gen. Ne Win was to include "a few" Civilians in the Cabinet. We all remember that a highly respected senior politician and colleague of Aung San U Lunn Baw was appointed Deputy Prime Minister to run the day-to-day affairs of the Government together with Bo Aung Gyi as Minister of Trade and Commerce.

The important modus operandi to note here was that Bo Ne Win's delegation of power to those in his inner circle was almost total without reservations, which to his critics was tantamount to negligence and running the affairs of State through surrogates by remote control. In any event he was not a "Hands-On Manager", but to the surprise of all, the results and outcome of the Caretaker Government was very popular with the general population because the improvements in infrastructures could be seen and daily lives improved – by the Circular Railways under Colonel Khin Nyo's leadership and moving the "slums to new satellite towns of North and South Okkalapa by Colonel Tun Sein the Mayor of Rangoon. Making slum-dwellers new land and home owners almost overnight.

The author has attempted to highlight the developments and events described in this sequel that is a far cry from the performance and achievements of the Caretaker Government of General Ne Win from 1958-1960 and his complete isolation from the true condition of the country and the suffering people in 1988 when he and his seriously ill Ex-President San Yu were told by the Military Intelligence that the Country's Economic Decline and the people's suffering was much worse than what Aung Gyi has written to him, and both of them were shocked and at a loss what to do. The country was at an abyss, absolute chaos in all major cities taken over by mobs and dead bodies hanging from utility poles. The aging Dictator and his sick Ex-President procrastinated and hesitated to ask Senior General Saw Maung to take over and stabilize the situation. When finally President San Yu in desperation consulted his next-door neighbor Bo Khin Nyo, he was advised that only the Army could save the country. San Yu, suffering from kidney failure and on dialysis in a special room in his house, asked his attending Doctor to take him off the machine and pleaded with his close friend Bo Khin Nyo to accompany him and rushed to call on their boss Ne Win, telling him that only Bo Saw Maung could now restore Law and Order to the Country. Bo Khin Nyo when revealing this particular event to me in California became very emotional because Bo San Yu's life was on the line because the doctor had told him that his heart and major organs would fail within an hour but to no avail. Bo San Yu calmly said he was prepared to leave this world after delivering the most critical message to Bogyoke (General) together with his friend, next-door neighbor and comrade Bo Khin Nyo. The only other person who knew about this was Mrs. Khin Nyo who was admonished a million times not to reveal to anyone.

When Ne Win did ask the Army to intervene immediately it was too late but Senior General Saw Maung resolutely took the hard and difficult task and restored law and order on September 18, 1988 and inevitably the country paid a very heavy price in lives lost. History will vindicate Bo Saw Maung and the Myanmar Military in saving the country from falling off the cliff in 1988. Foreign Powers with ulterior motives and neo-imperialistic agenda were already at the door-step of Myanmar with their lackeys inside ready to do the bidding of their foreign masters. In 1825 the ignorant, naïve and isolated Burmese Kingdom at Ava got entangled between the British and falsely expecting the French to be on its side but they went on to Indo-China for easier pickings. The Burmese were alone fighting three wars with the British, losing half the country first and then in 1825 King Thibaw was captured like a little mouse in his huge Palace in Mandalay and taken away to India. The peoples of Myanmar must never allow that to happen again and must make every effort to remain united, especially with the border regions and the Armed Forces to protect the Sovereignty and Territorial Integrity of the Country. That was at stake in 1988 and the Armed Forces under Senior General Saw Maung resolutely stepped up to the plate and averted the disaster about to happen. When push comes to shove and the country is faced with existential threat, only the Armed Forces will deter the potential aggressor from testing its resolve and determination to defend the sovereignty, territorial integrity and freedom of the Myanmar peoples. After 70 years of Independence it is still a challenge in 2018.

# DEDICATION

I dedicate this book to my deceased father U Sein Galay and his cousin brother Hanthawaddy U Sein (Pen-Name: Naphetchun), both of Zeebyuthaung Village, on the Eastern bank of Sit-Taung River, Htantabin Township, Taungoo District, Myanmar.

And to my beloved family: Wife: Kazuko Ueda Sein, Son: Robert Thiha Sein, Daughter-in-Law: Samhee Park Sein, Daughter: Sayoko Sein Chiba, Son-in-Law: Kimiaki Chiba, Grandson: Hale Zeya Hayato Chiba and Granddaughter: Hana Maykyi Chiba.

# ACKNOWLEDGMENTS

I am greatly indebted to my beloved wife Kazuko for her persistent encouragement to write my memoir while physical condition and mental faculties are functioning normally. The urgency to embark on the memoir writing became imperative during my first visit to Myanmar after being away for 41 years. When I called on the surviving family of the late Gen. Aung Gyi (who had passed away two months before my arrival in Yangon), his wife Daw MuMu (who passed away April 2015) told me how much he had wanted to talk to me about the important political, national and Army matters that he could not write about himself and wanted me to include them in my memoir. Fortunately I had survived all of them in good health and it was my responsibility to honor and complete the task assigned to me by my peers before their transition to the next incarnation.

I also wish to acknowledge the invaluable help, guidance and support from the persons (all deceased) named hereunder that changed and shaped the course of my life and destiny:

Colonel Thaung Kyi, the Irrawaddy Region Military Commander, who befriended the young High School student (age 16) on the Pathein Golf Course (in 1952), nurtured and introduced him to the world of "undercover operations" working for the Military Intelligence Service.

Colonel Maung Lwin (Moustache), Chief of Military Intelligence (MIS), who from our first meeting at Colonel Thaung Kyi's residence (in 1952) took me under his wings and impressed upon me the importance of "discipline, loyalty to country, confidence in yourself, strength of character and to defend foreign interference in domestic affairs".

The late Bo Khin Maung Galay, Deputy Prime Minister, Finance Minister and Chairman of Foreign State Scholarship Selection Board. At the interview in early March 1955, he ordered me to study International Law in Japan because Burma had signed a Treaty of Peace, Friendship, Cooperation and War Reparations. I pleaded that I did not want to study in Japan as the language was difficult and the Japanese had mistreated us during the War. He rejected my plea outright, gave me no other option but to study in Japan as the first Government State Scholar under the provisions of the newly signed Treaty of Peace. Within six weeks I was in Tokyo on May 05, 1955 after a long flight via Bangkok and Manila, for the first time out of the country and away from family at age 18, terribly lonely and lost, not speaking nor understanding a word of Japanese. My life was turned upside-down. In September of that year, four months after my arrival, my life was again remotely manipulated by the Deputy Prime Minister. He requested that Gen. Ne Win, who was leading a Military Mission to Japan, check on the young State Scholar he had ordered to study in that country. I was summoned to the Presidential Suite in the Imperial Hotel by the Burmese Ambassador in Tokyo, His Excellency U Myat Tun.

I was received in the Imperial Hotel main lobby by Colonel Maung Lwin (Moustache), the Military Intelligence Chief who escorted me to the General's suite. There, I met for the first time, Gen. Ne Win, the Commander-in-Chief, Gen. Aung Gyi, the Vice Chief of General Staff (VCGS), Gen. Tommy Clift, Air Force Chief of Staff and Vice Admiral Than Phay, Navy Chief of Staff – the four (4) most powerful men of the Burmese Military. Gen. Ne Win asked me to sit next to him on the sofa and said, "Ko Lay requested that I check how you are getting along here." I had no clue who he was talking about. Gen. Aung Gyi came to my rescue and explained that Bo Khin Maung Galay, the Finance Minister, had invited the mission members to his residence for dinner before their departure from Rangoon and mentioned the student he had sent to Japan – and requested the General to look you up.

Then suddenly, the tone of the conversation abruptly changed because I told the General that my life in Japan was miserable, I was unhappy and wanted to return home to Burma. Instead of getting understanding and sympathy for my plight, he abused me ("you little SOB"), "we didn't send you here to be happy, we sent you to study, do you understand? You are not going back to Burma until you finish your studies here. If you have any problems here contact these fellows," pointing to Gen. Aung Gyi and Colonel Maung Lwin. "I have a busy schedule here but come see me again before I leave. By the way have you eaten this morning?". Then, he turned to Colonel Maung Lwin. "Feed him and give money to buy warm clothing and pocket money." Then to me: "We are sending a Military Attaché here, and I will instruct him to contact you to get help with the language." Looking back 60 years, my future was determined at that meeting in the Presidential Suite of the Imperial Hotel in Tokyo.

My sincere thanks, appreciation and gratitude to the late Gen. Aung Gyi, the Vice Chief of General Staff (VCGS) and deceased Colonel Khin Nyo, the Director of Military Training (DMT) for their unwavering trust and confidence in me personally and my ability to assume responsibility and leadership of the projects, unfailing support and guidance in the implementation of sensitive and delicate covert domestic / foreign projects and operations, achieving very exceptional level of success and desired outcomes for the country's economy, finance, banking, trade and commerce.

My thanks and appreciation to: U Kyaw Lwin Nyo (wife ChoCho) for the search and collection of Bo Khin Maung Galay's (his uncle) and his father's photos, the late Dr. Htay Lwin Nyo for his invaluable help and insight in the review of military archive documents on loan from Senior General Saw Maung in 1989. The late Daw MuMu Thein (Mrs. Aung Gyi), Dr. Pandora Aung Gyi (husband U Ye Myint), Daw Thin New Aung, U Aung Myo Khine (Ko Tha Chit) for providing many photos of General Aung Gyi for this book.

# REVOLUTIONARY COUNCIL TO
# Military Dictatorship

### SEQUEL TO 'ME AND THE GENERALS OF THE REVOLUTIONARY COUNCIL'

# REVOLUTION DEVOURS ITS OWN SONS

A year after the bloodless coup of March 02, 1962 the cohesion and unity within the ruling Revolutionary Council started to crack at the very top between General (Bo) Ne Win, the Chief of General Staff and General (Bo) Aung Gyi, the Vice Chief of General Staff. The irony was they were very close personal friends and their relationship went far back to the days of student uprising and agitation against the British colonial Government of Burma. Both hailed from the same Prome (Pyay) district of Paungdele and Paungde townships.

Their paths crossed in the Students' Union activities at the vernacular High Schools and Rangoon University where the Thakin Party was aggressively recruiting students especially the Union leaders. (The Thakin party came about as a direct challenge to the British colonial rulers that required – "more correctly forced" – the natives to address all white British as "thakin" or master). Almost all student union leaders joined the party. The most prominent of course were Thakin Nu (U Nu), Thakin Aung San (General Aung San), Thakin Shu Maung (General Ne Win), Thakin Aung Gyi (General Aung Gyi), Thakin Mya, Thakin Ba Sein and many more.

Notwithstanding that close and long comradeship and being the closest aides to Aung San throughout the struggles against the British and the Japanese occupiers, Bo Ne Win and Bo Aung Gyi found themselves in early 1963 with divergent views and vision for the future of the country. Here, it must be stressed that Bo Ne Win, with the intensive indoctrination at the Japanese Imperial Army Intelligence School that "your worst enemies are most often closest to you", now that ultimate power was in his hands, his top priority and preoccupation was to protect and preserve that power at all cost and to eliminate all threats and challenges from all sources and quarters. That mindset rendered him vulnerable to rumors and fabricated disinformation by "factions within the military" as well as the National United Front (NUF) above ground communists allied with Ne Win and in control of the country's finances and economy – with U Ba Nyain appointed as "Finance and Economic Advisor" to the Revolutionary Council.

At that time (end of Summer 1962) the day-to-day administration of the Revolutionary Government was almost entirely left in the hands of Bo Aung Gyi, assisted by senior Generals and Colonels trusted by Bo Ne Win – Bo Khin Nyo, Chairman of Burma Economic Development Corporation, Chairman of Burma Railways Board of Directors and Deputy Chairman of Burma Oil Corporation; Vice Admiral Than Phay, Chief of Naval Staff and Minister of Health and Education; General Tommy Clift, Chief of Air Staff and Minister of Communications; Colonel Thaung Kyi, Adjutant General, Ministry of Defense; General San Yu, Commander North Burma Region; General Sein Win, Commander South Burma Region; Colonel Than Sein, Colonel General Staff Ministry of Defense and Chairman of Central Security and Administrative Committee; Colonel Kyaw Soe, Military Appointment Secretary, Ministry of Defense and Minister of Home Affairs; and U Thi Han Minister of Foreign Affairs, the lone civilian.

This was clear evidence that the entire Cabinet was entrusted to report to and work with Bo Aung Gyi. Bo Tin Phay, the Minister of Agriculture and Forests, for health reasons was only involved "on a need to and policy matters". Looking back with the benefit of hindsight, this special consideration extended to him by Bo Ne Win himself and Bo Aung Gyi was hugely misconstrued by Bo Tin Phay as being deliberately marginalized by Aung Gyi keeping him out of the loop and in the dark. He had conveniently forgotten (or deliberate selective amnesia) that it was Bo Aung Gyi who interceded and appealed to Ne Win when the Military Medical Board Certified Colonel Tin Phay medically unfit for Active Military service. The Chief of Staff (Ne Win) was flabbergasted and asked Aung Gyi "Are you out of your mind? Are you telling me to reject out of hand the professional verdict of the top doctors of our Military Medical Corps?"

Bo Aung Gyi pleaded to keep Tin Pe as Quarter Master General (QMG), the department with light duties. Bo Aung Gyi in fact had to plead with the Medical Board Members: Colonel (Dr.) Hla Han, Colonel (Dr.) Maung Lwin, Colonel (Dr. Ko Ko Gyi) and Dr. Ba Than (Ne Win's father-in-law) to amend the Medical Certification with the condition that he was "only qualified for light duties". This unprecedented act by Aung Gyi not only helped Tin Phay to continue his military service but was promoted because the QMG position was a Brig-Gen. Post.

I mention this event here again as an extraordinary event in the early history of the Tatmadaw's top leadership affairs and the consequences (outcome) of such personal and emotional interventions against the "rule" instituted by Aung San himself that "there must be no intervention to overrule or circumvent the decision of Another Department". The consequences for the Military and the ultimate outcome for Aung Gyi personally, was the man (Tin Phay) he went out of his way against customary rule to save, schemed and plotted his (Aung Gyi's) ouster from the Revolutionary Council and the Military. Decades later, Bo Khin Nyo, Bo Maung Lwin (Moustache) MIS Chief, Bo Chit Khin MIS Chief, and Bo Kyi Maung (Zat-Laik) Colonel General Staff related to me that "it was the height of ungratefulness ever" by one senior officer against another and the perpetrator got off lightly. I leave this record for the benefit of current and future leaders of the country, especially the Tatmadaw and the Political Parties.

# THE GOOD, THE BAD AND THE UGLY

As the belief and saying in Burma goes, the good, the bad and the evil all come together at the same time. For the Military Regime leaders at the top, the country was stable and under control domestically and in its relations with the rest of the world. Bo Ne Win was confident and felt secure to leave the country under the care of Bo Aung Gyi, and he took a flight to London with his wife Katy and his entourage for rest, recreation and medical care. For Bo Aung Gyi and his group, the country's economy, trade and commerce was progressing in the planned direction under his leadership and approved and with full support of the maximum leader whose Action Plan was successfully implemented in London. The buy-back of stock from foreign joint venture companies was completed and the financial and cash assets of BEDC REPRESENTATIVE OFFICE IN UK (BURTRADE) bank accounts and CREDIT STANDING (AAA++) the highest ever for an Asian developing country. All imports "paid cash against documents in London". This was the good achievement that Bo Ne Win acknowledged and conveyed his satisfaction with and congratulations to us through Bo Khin Nyo and Bo Lwin (Moustache).

The bad and the evil was the conspiracy and plot led by Ba Nyain, Tin Phay, Tan Yu Saing (brother-in-law of Tin Phay), Kyaw Soe, Tha Gyaw, San Win and above ground Communist National United Front's Thein Phay Myint to oust Bo Aung Gyi and the BEDC group from the Revolutionary Council and Government. Rumors and a disinformation campaign was that with the huge mountain of money in UK and European banks controlled by Kyi Win Sein, Aung Gyi was opposing Bo Ne Win's State controlled economy and Nationalization Plans using the money to destabilize the country and to overthrow Ne Win from power. Oblivious to Bo Tin Phay and his cohorts was the "Action Plan in the UK" – Bo Ne Win's covert project entrusted to Bo

Aung Gyi for implementation assisted by Bo Khin Nyo and Bo Maung Lwin (Moustache) the Military Intelligence Chief. They misconstrued it as being BEDC plan to move and control funds, financing and banking overseas and usurp Bo Ne Win's hold on power.

Lt-Col. Aung Din (Air Force), who was serving as Executive Director in the BEDC Joint Venture Oppenheimer-Jones Company in London after early retirement from his last post as Assistant Defense Services Attaché at the Embassy, was nominated by the Action Plan Committee to lead the implementation team in London by General Tommy Clift who was a Committee member. Bo Ne Win rejected that proposal and Bo Aung Gyi was asked "where is our Japanese educated young fellow (in Judge Advocate General Office) who successfully completed the Middle East Project with Egypt and Yugoslavia?" – "He is currently assigned to set up the Export-Import Bank project." – "Who sent him there? Call him back and send him to London at the earliest possible date to lead the implementation of the Action Plan in London. "The Yugoslav President's Office was very impressed with his performance with their highly trained professional team of International Covert Operators."

It was quite apparent to Bo Aung Gyi that Ne Win's memory was not what it used to be because he was instructed to assign me to implement the establishment of the Export-Import Bank and buy back all stock held by the Jews in the JV Ava Bank. Bo Ne Win's penchant for secrecy required that my Official Position of Legal Advisor in the Ministry of Defense and to the BEDC Chairman in the Prime Minister's Office was kept "Under Cover". There were clear and unmistakable signs that the aging clock has caught up with Bo Ne Win – very short attention span, hair trigger temper and short term memory loss. At the Revolutionary Council and Cabinet sessions only Bo Aung Gyi and a few others like Bo Than Phay, Bo Khin Nyo, Bo Thaung Kyi would speak up. Others would remain silent, even senior generals Bo San Yu, Bo Sein Win, Tommy Clift and Bo Tin Phay. More often than not, Bo Ne Win would suddenly get up and walk out, asking (ordering) Bo Aung Gyi to carry on with the sessions. As such, there was tremendous envy, jealousy and prejudice against Bo Aung Gyi, especially by the above ground communist party and the Tin Phay faction within the Army. It was an urgent imperative for them to drive a wedge between Ne Win and Aung Gyi, failing which there was all possibility that Ne Win would delegate more power and authority to Aung Gyi to manage and run the Revolutionary Government of Burma.

# THREAT TO REGIME FROM WITHIN DISCOVERED

While the Tin Phay faction and the communist financial advisor pushed ahead with their State Controlled Economy scheme based on Aung San's "Blueprint for Independent Burma" knowing full well that Bo Ne Win was keen to implement the "utopian extreme leftist" document that young Aung San penned while staying at Colonel Suzuki's home in Hamamatsu waiting for final approval of the Imperial General Staff to train and set up the Burmese Army that would fight alongside the Japanese Imperial invasion forces to drive out the British and declaration of independence for Burma.

It was discovered that Colonel Kyi Maung, Commander of South West Region in Bassein (now Pathein), was contacted by Karen National Union (KNU) senior level elements with links to the Christian Organizations in the U.K. and the U.S. These Christian entities in the West work in tandem with or often for intelligence agencies to set up "sleeping cells, moles and outright subvert, bribe, trap and plot to destabilize a country and attempt to change the regime from within". The alarming development was it went well beyond the S.W. Region; it was taking place in the South East Region in Moulmein (Maw-la-myaing) under Colonel Lun Tin (who later defected).

Bo Kyi Maung was sent to Japan for officer training in 1943 and completed the course in 1945 and was posted to No. 5 Burma Rifles upon return to Burma. He was also sent to the U.S. for further training between 1955 and 1956 when he was already a Battalion Commander. The intel- discovery further revealed that personnel involved in the "training program" in the U.S. at that time in American bases are now posted at the U.S. Embassy in Rangoon and Bangkok as civilian diplomats. (Years later the same was true in the case of spectacle General Tin Oo who was sacked and imprisoned.) We must remember that

Bo Maung Maung's liaison with British and American intelligence while held prisoner by the KNU. America's foreign policy of "Regime Change" since the removal of Mohammed Mosadekh of Iran in 1953 was attempted several times in Burma to oust Ne Win but all were detected early and foiled.

The status of relations between Burma and the U.S. was rather normal or stable in early 1963 but still the American politicians and the government's interventionist foreign policy was pursued despite the fact that almost all the outcomes over the world were disasters. Moderate officers like Bo Aung Gyi, Bo Than Phay, Bo Thaung Kyi, Bo Maung Lwin (Moustache) the intelligence Chief and U Thi Han the lone civilian in the cabinet were concerned that relations with Thailand and their U.S. supporters would worsen and advocated to contain the situation locally, and Bo Ne Win ever keen to avoid conflict and confrontation with "foreign powers" went along with the "moderates".

Bo Kyi Maung was dismissed from the Army and the Revolutionary Council with a statement (for public consumption) that he disagreed with the leaders of the council regarding the Military's role in politics and government. He was kept under close scrutiny and his indiscretions continued, and General Ne Win ordered his detention later in 1963 and the second time in 1987. Bo Saw Maung sent him to prison again from 1990 to 1995 and he was released when Bo Than Shwe took over state power. He was sent to prison four times by successive military regimes for a total jail time of 12 years. He was founder of NLD with Bo Aung Gyi and Suu Kyi and sided with her and the communists (saved by Bo Ne Win from certain death during the height of the Cultural Revolution of the Burma Communist Party in the mountains along the Chinese border) to oust Bo Aung Gyi and his group from the NLD. On May 30, 1990, NLD's landslide election victory, Bo Kyi Maung proclaimed that the first order of the new government would be to set up a tribunal to prosecute Bo Saw Maung and SLORC members for brutally suppressing the uprising in 1988. One must remember that in 1990, he was NLD leader because Suu Kyi was placed under house arrest. Subsequently he fell out with Suu Kyi herself and quit the NLD.

It is very important for the current military leaders, politicians and the general Myanmar public to know and understand these events of the past that had serious and dire consequences for the entire country and lives of the people for many decades. The investigation and interrogation of Bo Kyi Maung himself (while in prison) and those involved lasted several years and the discoveries, revelations, insinuations and implications went far and wide. In some of the deposition documents that Bo Saw Maung sent me through Bo Khin Nyo to California we (myself, Dr. Htay Lwin Nyo and Bo Khin Nyo) were astounded that he insinuated and implicated many of his closest comrades, fellow officers and politicians of all stripes. Among the most prominent and well known was Bo Aung Gyi, U Nu, Thakin Tha Khin, Bo Kyaw Zaw and Bo Set Kya. This was confirmed by U Kyaw Nyein, when I met him for the last time in California, who said: "He caused more harm and suffering to many people than one can imagine". Bo Ne Win told U Kyaw Nyein that Kyi Maung implicated Bo Aung Gyi in the plot, which later proved to be a deliberate lie.

# RIVALRY AT THE TOP FOR LEADERSHIP AND CONTROL OF THE MILITARY HIERRACHY

When the aging old General Ne Win appointed Tin Oo (Spectacle) to the powerful and much feared post of Military Intelligence Service (MIS) Chief, there was great shock and widespread misgivings and unhappiness, particularly within the Officer Corps of the Regional Commands, especially the Combat Divisions.

Tin Oo, now the MIS Chief with a rank of Full General, had reached that position without ever serving in any combat unit since the rank of Captain. The reason was that his two older brothers had died in the early days of the insurgencies and his parents requested General Ne Win to protect the third son's life. When Bo Ne Win entered the Mon State at the spearhead of the BIA, Tin Oo's father, a staunch nationalist supporter of the country's independence from British rule, offered his three sons to the BIA entrusting them to Bo Ne Win. With that heavy burden on his shoulders, after the two elder brothers fell in battle, he issued a special Order that Tin Oo be strictly confined to non-combat positions in the Army. He was always deskbound and became the butt of joke among the Army top brass, to protect and preserve the adopted son of Ne Win.

He refers to him as his big Daddy (A-Phay-Gyi) especially after a few drinks. I can never forget upsetting him beyond imagination when I burst out laughing when he referred to "A-Phay-Gyi". It was my meeting him for the first time in Tokyo by introduction of Colonel Maung Lwin (Moustache), MIS Chief, his boss. He was a Captain at that time and on his way to Okinawa, Saipan and Guam for covert training with U.S. Defense Intelligence and CIA Operation Centers for the Pacific and Asia. He was staying with me at the International

Student House for a few days as advised by his boss. If not for that he would have manhandled me for making fun of him. He was a very tall man (well over 6ft) 160-170lbs and I was merely 5'-5" and just over 100lbs. Almost in anger he stared at me and asked, "What the hell is so funny about what I said?"

I was not intimidated at all and told him frankly "Ko Tin Oo, Bogyoke Ne Win is famous for being a womanizer with so many wives and it struck me that you are much older to be his son" and moreover I have not come across anyone using the that term. He then blurted out "now I know why my boss (Moustache) cautioned me not to be fooled by your appearance of youth and small size". From that encounter and incident I could see that despite his size he could not handle alcohol too well or perhaps he forgot the advice of his boss. He was also at a loss as to why the Defense Attaché Col. (Dr.) Maung Lwin and Major Aye Kyaw were very friendly and polite in their overall relations with me which he observed during his one week's stay in Tokyo. Then our paths crossed many times in the course of my assignments in the Ministry of Defense but none in the same project because he was moved around to other Commands because Lt. Col. Charlie Thein Shwe and Major Lay Maung were serving MIS Chief Bo Lwin (Moustache) as his deputies. I was officially posted as General Counsel (Legal Advisor) to Gen. Aung Gyi, Vice Chief of General Staff and Chairman of Burma Economic Development Corporation.

# THE SUDDEN AND MYSTERIOUS DEMISE OF A PROMINENT SENIOR COLONEL

When General Tin Oo reached the pinnacle of ultimate power by the patronage, support and blessing of his big Daddy (A-Phay-Gyi), he was anointed as the successor to be the next Dictator after Bo Ne Win, who was still pulling the strings from behind his puppets in the Military establishment, the BSPP Party and the Government led by President San Yu. The country had descended to the level of a Banana Republic, an economic basket case classified as the least developed country by the UN and other World Bodies. Tin Oo, the Military Intelligence Service (MIS) Director, was touted as #1.5 immediately after #1 Ne Win. Tin Oo would proudly boast to other Generals that his "A-Phay-Gyi" invites him several times a week to share his favorite Dimple Scotch whisky and have dinner with him. It was his self-proclamation of being the Crown Prince and a clear intimidating message to potential challengers to back off or else.

However, as we all know very well the saying "man proposes and God disposes", the karma and personal circumstances of those in the seat of power took an abrupt turn for the worse. First, President San Yu, officially the Commander-In-Chief of the Tatmadaw as Chairman of the BSPP Polit-Bureau Military Committee, who was under medical treatment for kidney failure, would now have to be on dialysis. This deterioration of Bo San Yu's state of health and incapacity to function fully put an urgent imperative on Bo Ne Win to name his replacement or as a stop-gap measure assign a Senior Army Officer to assume a major portion of the critical and heavy responsibilities now on the sick man's shoulders. True to his character and instincts (6th sense) Bo Ne Win's modus operandi was utilizing his own human assets within the Military Establishment (referred to as his own personal Intelligence Resource) to sound out the true grassroots thinking of the rank and file, non-commission officers and the officer corps.

Tin Oo, the self-proclaimed Crown Prince and #1.5, was aghast when he got wind of what was taking place under his nose at the behest of his very own "A-Phay-Gyi". To add insult to injury the name that emerged and floated widely among the BSPP Big-Wigs and the Military's Elite Top leadership and the Regional Commands was Colonel Thaung Kyi, a tough disciplinarian straight arrow, but well liked and highly respected by many including Bo Ne Win himself, as evidenced by appointing him to oversee the Burma Navy Command above the Chief of Naval Staff. Thaung Kyi was a very conservative, soft-spoken and considerate person but very FIRM. Do I know that very well? Yes indeed, I do. He picked me up in my high teens, a naïve High School Final student, gently nurtured and guided me into the world of National Security and the Intelligence World by having me attend the Special Intelligence Courses together with the officers of his Brigade in the Irrawaddy Region Command and personally introduced me to the Military Intelligence Chief, Colonel Maung Lwin (Moustache), in 1952.

There were many rumors and speculations emanating from the inner circle of Bo Ne Win that Colonel Thaung Kyi was about to be promoted to the rank of General and Deputy Chairman of the BSPP Central Military Commission to relieve San Yu of the very heavy burden he was carrying and to have enough time to be on dialysis for his failing kidneys. Such rumors speculating on an impending elevation of someone to such a high National Status, tantamount almost to the transfer of political power, did not materialize in a timely fashion that was well noted by the stakeholders as well as the rank and file in the Military especially the Army. It could very well be attributed to the procrastination of the aging Bo Ne Win or it could be his cunning strategy to "force the hand of someone with an ambitious agenda"? I trust that it was the latter. But one must always bear in mind that obsession and thirst for ultimate political power will blind the human mind to commit the most heinous and barbarous, unthinkable crimes.

Bo Thaung Kyi loved the game of golf and greatly enjoyed playing very early in the morning before the weather warms up and was especially someone who was at ease and comfortable to associate and spend quality time with at such early hours of the day. As if ordained by the confluence of the constellations and stars above, I became his next-door neighbor in Bassein (now Pathein) early 1952 after serious personal conflicts and great setbacks the previous year. To recover, reset and regain my mental balance I would get up early and walk over to the Irrawaddy Golf Club driving range with a few clubs and hit the odd ball at sunrise, retrieve them since I only had about a dozen and repeat the procedure until my hands and feet got sore because I was hitting and walking in bare feet. Oblivious to me the next-door Colonel was observing my daily routine. After about a month of seeing the young fellow walk past in front of his house carrying a few golf clubs he decided (unsolicited) to join this young student.

## FOUL PLAY AND DELIBERATE POLITICAL ASSASINATION SUSPECTED

On the unfortunate and fateful day of his demise, Colonel Thaung Kyi played golf at the Army Golf Course and after the game was having his favorite drink of "shandy" (Fresh Lime juice with soda, sugar and beer) which was the first drink he always took after a round of golf since his days in Bassein (Pathein) as Irrawaddy Delta Region Brigade Commander when he seriously took up the game. But this shandy drink he took at the Army Golf Club House contained something else. Within less than ten minutes of having the drink he went into a massive cardiac arrest and collapsed. He was rushed to the Military Hospital nearby but was lifeless on arrival and could not be revived.

From the personal account related to me by retired Colonel Khin Nyo when he came to California as Special Envoy of Sr. Gen. Saw Maung and stayed at my residence, the immediate family and Gen. Ne Win were informed at about the same time and both parties wanted to ascertain the cause of Col. Thaung Kyi's sudden death at the Army Golf Club. The family of course was devastated and in a state of shock as well as Bo Ne Win who summoned the Head of the Military Medical Directorate and ordered an autopsy to be conducted on the remains by the best Forensic Pathologists in the country and to submit their findings directly to him ONLY. According to Colonel Khin Nyo and his close colleagues and associates, since the #1 ordered the autopsy, one can rule out any foul play emanating from the top. Additionally, Regional Army Commanders close to the Seat of Power were already in the know of Bo Ne Win's intent to have Col. Thaung Kyi replace San Yu. Therefore his sudden demise was a deliberate elimination by one that felt threatened and considered him the rival.

That can only mean one who was touted to be the "successor" to the Seat of Power (The Dictator) and the BSPP Party. The territorial or regional Commanders held ultimate raw power in their hands and the rumors, accusations and finger-pointing going on in Rangoon was reminiscent of the old AFPFL Political leaders at each other's throats, but this tragic incident taking place at the very top of the Military hierarchy was most disturbing especially to young and fast-rising Officer Corps. Despite the secrecy under which the autopsy was conducted, leakage of information was almost immediate from the very source as well as from the surviving family. The talk of the town was that the corpse of the dead colonel had turned "black", unmistakable evidence of the deceased dying by ingestion of a lethal poison. There were even specific pathologic details of the stomach and major organs being eaten away by the poison and disintegrating. As such there was serious concern that the perpetrator may not stop with one perceived rival and continue with this barbaric act of eliminating those others perceived to be rivals in his quest for ultimate Military and Political power of the country.

# RETRIBUTION COMES VERY SWIFTLY IN THIS LIFE

The aging and scheming old Dictator Gen. Ne Win was still very much aware of the risks involved in giving more than necessary "Free-Hand" to subordinates, especially to those in the Military Intelligence Services and in the feedback from his own "Intel-Assets within the Establishment", there were excesses committed by his Intelligence Chief Gen. Tin Oo (Spectacle) especially in his "personal relations and dealings with foreign Intelligence Agencies – like the Thais, Indians, U.S., British, Singapore, etc". The wedding reception of his son in Rangoon, Mon State as well as in Bangkok was extraordinarily lavish and scandalous to the extent that some "Influential Factions within the Thai Intelligence" deliberately leaked out all the dirty stuff on their colleagues as well as on Tin Oo, which damaged his standing within the Burmese Intelligence Community.

He was a brash, proud and arrogant person and took all those affronts personally, which led him down the path of irrational thinking, judgment errors and ultimately prey to foreign intelligence manipulation touting him as the next "Strongman Ruler of Burma" as a true friend of the WEST. All of that turned out to be delusional and led to his catastrophic downfall and practically the entire MIS Organization under his control. It was a typical and classic case of "false overconfidence in one's power to topple the #1Ruler of the Country to whom you owe everything" like your very own father. As always in such cases one forgets that "to seize power from a King, you must slay him first". Regardless of such a precautionary note, Tin Oo was going to pursue his quest for power his own way. Unbeknownst to him there were foreign elements at play to create serious doubt and mistrust in the Country's Seat of Power "as to his absolute loyalty".

The rivalry and competition within the Thai Intelligence Factions manipulated by Western Intelligence Moles started their wishful thinking plot and scheme of Regime change in Burma. Elements within Thai Intelligence friendly to the Burmese got wind of the plot and for reasons of their own tipped off Japanese Intelligence to warn "your Burmese Friend Dictator" that his closest and most trusted General was plotting with the WEST to overthrow his regime. At first it was dismissed as bizarre because of the strange route it came through using the 5 Japanese most trusted by the Burma Army and they were used to carry messages to the Burmese Generals from Japanese Seat of Power. Despite the serious initial doubt and dismissal, the message kept coming in various guises and clues that it could no longer be ignored because it also revealed that several Regional Commanders along the China/Burma/Thai border had become aware of the Regime Change Plot through their own Operational Undercover Contacts and Assets.

That situation raised red flags and alarm bells rang within Ne Win's inner circle. The BSPP Central Commission Military Committee (of which Tin Oo was a member), set up a Special Secret Committee of - Vice Chief of General Staff, Chief of Staff (Air), and Chief of Navy with General Operations Officer (G-1) as Committee Secretary to thoroughly investigate the "Foreign Intelligence Input" to monitor closely the activities of the MIS Chief. The surveillance and intercept operations were raised to the highest "critical threat level". The discoveries and findings shocked all concerned because they corroborated the information from the Thais relayed by the Japanese. The most disturbing was several of the "handlers" assigned to specifically program and guide the training of Tin Oo during his training in Okinawa, Saipan and Guam, were now at the U.S. Embassy in Rangoon working in nondescript positions. There was also confirmation that off and on there had been clandestine meetings and liaison with Tin Oo under very elaborate arrangements at unsuspecting locations and in disguise.

Thorough scrutiny of Tin Oo's biodata and his entire personal and family profile brought to the fore the "strong and intense Anti-Burmese sentiments holed up inside" biding the time for revenge and apparently the Americans had exploited the hard historical grievances of the Mons and giving false hopes to the naïve Tin Oo of their support. In fact it was history repeating itself in a way. When the

Mon Kingdom in Pegu (Bago) defied the Burmese King Alaungpaya because Portugese DeBritto, the ruler of Syriam, promised his support. The Burmese conquered Pegu and DeBritto ended up skewered on the spear and left to dry in the sun. I clearly remember Tin Oo bitterly complain to me about this long past historical incident after a few pegs of whisky when he stayed with me at the Tokyo International Student House on his way to Okinawa in 1956.

Bo Ne Win's pre-emptive action was swift and thorough as always. Oblivious to Tin Oo, he and his entire Military Intelligence apparatus, especially the core pillars of his assets, were in the cross-hairs to be dismantled instantly having no clue of what had hit them. One afternoon when Tin Oo returned home, he received a phone call to immediately report on the double to his big Daddy (Ah-Phay-Gyi's) office. He probably thought there was some urgent matter #1 wanted to tell him with the last thing he imagined being that he was on his final trip to his patron and father-like boss since being a teenager. As his car left the house, the contingent moved in and put the family under house arrest and the compound was sealed off. Simultaneously all the Military Intelligence units, Officers and other ranks were disarmed and taken away under heavy armed escort to prearranged camps. Tin Oo entered the office of #1, saluted and stood at attention.

Ne Win looked him in the eyes and said "Get out of the Army". As he got out the door, he was arrested and taken away to the detention location. It would be many years before he saw his wife and family again. He was released when Than Shwe took over from Saw Maung and declared a General Amnesty.

I would like to state here for the record and have the reading public understand and accept the fact that a large part of the information surrounding the unexpected and sudden demise of Colonel Thaung Kyi was related to the Author by the late Colonel Khin Nyo when he visited U.S.A., Japan and Thailand as Special Envoy of Senior General Saw Maung, Chairman of State Law and Order Restoration Committee (SLORC) in late or early Autumn of 1989. He, his wife and son Dr. Htay Lwin Nyo, a professor at University of California Davis, stayed in my house for 3 months. The Military Archive in Rangoon did not have any File Record of the General Tin Oo Official Investigation. Under the Ministry of Defense Administration and Operational Manual, all such Matters and Official

Actions are to be investigated by a Panel or Committee set up by the Chief of General Staff and recorded and archived for the Mandated Time Period, unless the Chief of General Staff deemed it necessary and appropriate to exercise his discretionary authority to dispense with the Mandated Investigation itself and/or destroy the findings/results of the investigations. In the case of General Maung Maung, Bo Ne Win exercised that authority. He appointed Bo Khin Nyo to be the "One man Investigation and submit to him in 60 days". On receipt of the Investigation Report, he asked Bo Aung Gyi to review it and immediately thereafter to destroy it together with Bo Khin Nyo. Apparently he ordered the same in Tin Oo's case or perhaps retained it in his files.

Looking back with the benefit of hindsight, the two Generals personally very close to Bo Ne Win were in fact given special treatment, protected and saved from Court Martial for deliberate acts of treason, sedition and attempts to seize State Power but in the case of young Captain Ohn Kyaw Myint and accomplices, the harshest capital punishment was meted out to the leader of the group. The lesson for the present Myanmar Military leaders, politicians and the general public is acknowledge such disparities of treatment and injustice took place at the very top in the recent past and to incorporate the much needed institutional safeguards to ensure that future generation political and military leaders will not repeat the same mistakes of destroying "Official Investigation Findings".

The circumstantial evidence surrounding the sudden death of Colonel Thaung Kyi which was rendered more ugly and questionable was the heavily redacted Autopsy Results that made the surviving immediate family, relatives, close friends and colleagues' suffering and sadness unbearable. Then there was the leaks, rumors and speculations (intentional or otherwise, we don't know), some supposedly from members of the forensic team of pathologists who conducted the autopsy on the corpse of the deceased colonel. The talk within the medical community was the pathologists found clear and definitive evidence of ingesting a lethal chemical drug/substance/poison inducing immediate irreversible cardiac-seizure. The specific substance was not named for obvious reasons.

The highly trained specialists at the adjoining Forensic Laboratory were under orders to keep their findings sealed. Such lethal and dangerous drugs/chemicals/poisons are only in the hands of the "top handful of Military

Intelligence Officers", usually referred to as "Designer Pills/Capsules" given to "Moles and Undercover Operatives Overseas" as a last resort measure not to be captured alive, a normal and universal practice of every country's elite Intelligence organization. Then the MIS committed the most despicable act of adding insult to injury by the disinformation campaign of the possibility of suicide, and that it could not be completely ruled out. It was the height of immorality on the part of the Military Intelligence and it backfired on them big time. The perception of the general public was "Guilty Conscience of the MIS". It remains a huge black mark on the image of the Military Establishment, especially the hated and feared Intelligence Service.

I have included this sad and unfortunate event during the period of the country's catastrophic economic decline under the Burma Socialist Program Party of aging Ne Win, forced to pre-emptively remove his aggressive and arrogant Intelligence Chief scheming with external collaborators to oust his big Daddy (Ah-Phay-Gyi). A short time before this sweeping purge of the Intelligence apparatus there was overwhelming circumstantial evidence of its involvement in the sudden death of Colonel Thaung Kyi by lethal poisoning confirmed by the forensic pathology report which was heavily redacted by the authorities. The immediate surviving family, relatives, colleagues in the Military and friends were devastated at the lack of transparency and an authoritative official cause of the sudden death made worse by the appearance of a "cover up and silence at the top". For personal reasons of my own relations with the deceased since my high teens in 1952, I requested of Senior General Saw Maung for the "Official Investigation Report" from the Military Archives to be included in the documents (On Loan) to be carried by Ex-Colonel Khin Nyo on his visit to the U.S.A. as the Senior General's Personal Envoy. The Senior General asked Bo Khin Nyo to inform me that "No such report could be located in the Archives, as well as the one regarding Gen. Maung Maung's Coup attempt".

However, by strange coincidence of events and very old friends of Bo Ne Win since his early days with the 30 Comrades and the Japanese Imperial Army Intelligence Operatives attached to the Burma Independence Army (BIA), in my last get-together meeting with elderly Okuda, Yamada and Takahashi in Tokyo some unexpected information came out from one of them on the conversation he had had with Ne Win during his recent visit to Yangon. The conversation concerns how close they were to leaving this world and Bo Ne Win revealed that he needed to prepare the Documents, Official Reports and Private Communications to be in the Custody of the Military Archives before he died or have his survivors hand them over after he passed away "is what he is struggling with". So, Yamada and Takahashi, the frequent visitors, offered their advice to do it ASAP especially the "Official Reports". But Ne Win in his "off guard" moment with old friends said "things like Tin Oo, Thaung Kyi cases" must only be on record after I am gone. As such there is every likelihood that the Military Archives have them now.

# FROM NO. 2 GENERAL OF MILITARY TO TEA SHOP VENDOR

U Kyaw Nyein told me that he had asked Bo Ne Win directly why he had treated Bo Aung Gyi so harshly, keeping him in prison for so many years. The response was that Bo Kyi Maung had implicated him and after many reviews and cross checking it was found to be completely false many years later. Bo Ne Win immediately ordered his release from Mandalay prison and sent Bo Chit Khin to Maymyo (Pyin-Oo-Lwin) in late 1969, offering Ambassadorship to Washington. Bo Aung Gyi declined. I went up again in April 1970 when Bo Chit Khin and Bo Than Sein asked me to repeat Bo Ne Win's offer of Ambassador to America but I was not successful. He told me that his conscience would not allow him to represent a regime and its policies that he opposed for which he had been imprisoned for seven and a half years. Unlike Bo Maung Maung, Bo Aung Shwe, Bo Chit Myaing meekly accepted ambassador posts and colonels like Aye Maung gratefully served in exile as Defense Attaché practically discarded from the Army.

Bo Aung Gyi was not going to accept such an undignified fate imposed on his life by Bo Ne Win. Moral values and principles are more important in life than material things and social status. Perhaps that was attributable to being a bachelor officer and daily meditation practice – he was mild mannered, soft spoken and never hesitated to admit not knowing certain things (particularly specialized professional tasks and duties) that "it is a subject matter he knows very little of and would not attempt to comment or suggest alterations to professional conclusions submitted to him for approval and onward transmission to the Chairman of the Revolutionary Council and the Cabinet". I found that to be a valuable learning experience.

On my return to Rangoon (Yangon) I told Bo Chit Khin and Bo Than Sein about my discussion with Bo Aung Gyi in Maymyo and both of them were truly saddened and concerned about the present and future economic well-being of Bo Aung Gyi, now with his new wife and a baby girl. I told them that he indicated a plan to start a bakery and tea shop business. The two powerful colonels are visibly shaken and uttered that it was beneath the dignity of one who was the #2 general of the Military and the Revolutionary Government. Early the next morning at the end of his briefing session with Bo Ne Win, Bo Chit Khin reported to the boss my discussion with Bo Aung Gyi and he was greatly distressed and remarked "I did not know he was this hardheaded and stubborn. Give him all the help possible to start his business". Bo Chit Khin and Bo Than Sein, as ordered, extended help and the business was a huge success first in Maymyo, then Mandalay and Rangoon, expanding to restaurants and he became very famous with customers lining up to be seated at tables served by the ex-general himself. Bo Aung Gyi appreciated the help and acknowledged this in his memoirs. The restaurant and bakery operation prospered and he was able to provide for the family started rather late in life from scratch (soon after release from Mandalay prison) with Mu Mu Thein, after suffering several imprisonments under Bo Ne Win's regime for a total of seven and a half years.

# OPEN LETTERS TO NE WIN TO CHANGE COURSE

At this juncture in the country's path to a democratic multi-party political system the Tatmadaw and the political parties must remember that it was Bo Aung Gyi's many open letters to Bo Ne Win telling him in plain but strong terms that the people of Myanmar had been reduced to living in abject poverty under his Burmese way to socialism party rule and that he (Bo Ne Win) was out of touch with the true situation of the country. It was those open letters that first irritated and angered Ne Win according to the account of Bo Khin Nyo related to me when he came to California on a special mission for Bo Saw Maung. However, after receiving several more Bo San Yu (neighbor of Bo Khin Nyo who was in poor health already) was called in by the beleaguered Dictator to check and confirm if the situation was as dire as described in Bo Aung Gyi's letters. The sick and ailing Bo San Yu, in desperation, privately discussed this with his good friend and neighbor Bo Khin Nyo, who was incredulous and aghast that the two most powerful men in the country were hopelessly isolated, misinformed and out of touch with the real plight and suffering of the people they ruled over.

Bo Khin Nyo said that about a week later, he was asked by Bo San Yu to come over to his house where he was informed that the Military Intelligence investigated the assertions in Bo Aung Gyi's letter and found out that the economic situation in the country was a lot worse than described in the letters. Bo San Yu also mentioned that Bo Ne Win was in a state of shock, dejected and depressed. But he also firmly said changes must be made quickly. However, the "quick change" options available to him at that time within the political realm were almost none as he had lost all confidence in BSPP, the devil of his own creation. The Military was the only institution with disciplined professional leadership at the top but with eroding morale issues. At that time of national crisis, Bo Ne Win could only rely on Bo San Yu who was notorious for not having an opinion or if he had one never expressing it to, or in the presence of, his boss. Quite apparently he was utilizing Bo Khin Nyo as a "sounding board" to get a perspective from a comrade fellow Ex-Army officer and conveniently living next door.

## COUP D'ÉTAT OPTION CONSIDERED

The most surprising and crucial revelation of the private discussions between Bo San Yu and Bo Khin Nyo in Ching Tsong Estate of Gaba Aye Road was that Bo Ne Win preferred the option of having Bo Saw Maung, the Chief Of General Staff, take over the country from the BSPP in the Spring of 1988. There was procrastination on the part of the desperate Dictator left with the most obedient soldier San Yu, who never failed to carry out orders but was not one to offer alternative options or even an opinion. It did not even reach the stage of bringing the Chief of General Staff into the deliberations because of the procrastination and the huge generation gap. Ne Win was already a General when Bo Saw Maung joined the Army and his Commission Appointment Certificate was signed by Bo Khin Nyo, who was Military Secretary (Military Appointment Secretary today) of the Ministry of Defense. In any event Ne Win gave up the idea on his own without any input from anyone, but years later he told Okuda at their reconciliation meeting in Rangoon that he had made a mistake not ordering Military takeover earlier in 1988. He joked to Okuda (Atama Karapo) "my head is empty". That is typical Japanese superior (professor) scolding a subordinate or student (you empty head). All absolute rulers and dictators sooner rather than later reach the stage of "isolation surrounded by incompetent yes-men" and Ne Win reached that point early when he alienated Aung Gyi (barely a year and a half after the coup), his true friend, comrade, trustworthy colleague, principled and with a rational realistic approach to the political and economic development of the country. Looking back with the benefit of hindsight, it was the biggest and most damaging judgment error of Ne Win's political and military career, with catastrophic consequences for the entire country and its population.

# HANDOVER TO MILITARY IN EARLY 1988 WOULD HAVE SAVED MANY LIVES

Bo Ne Win's public speech telling the gathering that the Army was trained to shoot straight and not into the air was a blunt warning to all, especially the instigators of mass uprising and riots, to be fully aware of the catastrophic consequences in the event of the Army being ordered to restore law and order. However, despite this public warning he procrastinated because there were many senior Military Officers, many retired but a large number of active senior officers serving in BSPP top party positions. He was seriously concerned that the Military would split like the AFPFL had done and the situation would deteriorate out of control. All of this desperate search to change course was going on between Ne Win and San Yu, who in turn was relating them to Bo Khin Nyo, his neighbor.

It was quite apparent that Ne Win was a prisoner of his own schemes, unsure of himself and further, even his hand-picked Central Committee of the BSPP had rejected his proposal for reversion to a Multi-Party Democratic System of Governance. He resigned and Sein Lwin, whose army career began as a private and Ne Win's "bed-man" was appointed Party Boss and President as San Yu was in poor health. The above ground communists, sensing a power vacuum, started their agitation and mobilized all sectors of Burmese society and the mobs took over Rangoon and several major cities such as Mandalay, Bassein, Moulmein, Shwebo, Taungoo, Pegu, etc. Even some elements of the Navy, Air Force, Police, Civil Service, Teachers participated and Anarchy reigned and Law and Order collapsed throughout the country. Revenge, vendetta and murder was rampant and corpses hung from telephone poles in Rangoon, Mandalay, Baseein, Moulmein, Etc.

President Sein Lwin resigned and Dr. Maung Maung was appointed President of Burma. The Military, under the Command of Bo Saw Maung, was alarmed that the lower and other ranks from within would join the mobs, revolt and disobey orders from above, which would be the end for all. That eventuality would happen quickly if the Military personnel was not paid. To prevent that and to safeguard the Military, Bo Saw Maung demanded that President Maung Maung immediately release six months' salary and expenses for the entire Military in cash and move them to a safe location under Army control. He now had the money to pay his forces and run the defense establishment for at least half a year.

The anarchy and mob rule went on for more than six weeks and by early August 1988, the neighboring countries began taking precautionary measures, fearing that Burma was at the abyss and on the verge of becoming a failed State. The Burmese Military recognized that borders need to be secured with adequate forces and have them on highest combat readiness. In the evaluation and analysis it turned out that "risks of outside intervention", especially from neighbors, was "remote" but could not be "ruled out". However, the intimidation and intervention from a "world power from the Sea was real" and that assessment was on target as the U.S. Navy Carrier Group from the Pacific Fleet ports in Japan, Taiwan and Okinawa were lurking just outside Burmese territorial waters and several were already "within a few hours from Rangoon". It was at this juncture that all intelligence assets and resources had to be brought into play in key locations and countries – such as the U.N. Security Council.

It was the appropriate time to establish contact (communicate) with Military Attachés of Embassies in Rangoon and assure them that "law and order will be restored as soon as practically possible ON OUR OWN". It is a common diplomatic practice to inform diplomatic missions that "interference in domestic affairs would not be tolerated under any circumstances". Burmese Embassies abroad were directed to inform host countries. However, with neighboring countries like Thailand, India, Singapore, Malaysia, etc. where "intelligence to intelligence" exchanges take place on a normal "need to know basis" "a firm and clear message" would be given to "stay out and not contemplate any interference". No country would ignore such a message from the Military Intelligence Service or duly accredited diplomatic mission.

# HANDOVER TO MILITARY IN EARLY 1988 WOULD HAVE SAVED MANY LIVES

The mob rule of the major cities in Burma escalated to unacceptable levels and in early September 1988 Ne Win summoned Bo Saw Maung, the Chief of General Staff, to his Ady Road residence and instructed him to "restore law and order and set up a Military Government". Saw Maung raised the inevitable casualties in crushing the large numbers in the streets and he was reminded that as Commander-in-Chief of the Armed Forces of the Country, it was his Official Duty to protect and preserve the safety and welfare of the people that no longer exists and that those mobs that have taken over the country must be removed at the earliest, at whatever cost.

# COUP D'ÉTAT BY GENERAL SAW MAUNG

On September 18, 1988, Bo Saw Maung ordered his troops to remove the mobs from all major cities and regained control of all within a matter of hours. The troops ordered the mobs to disperse and return home but the "agitators within the crowds" ridiculed the soldiers and dared them to open fire and to their horror bullets rained on them and there was pandemonium, and those not hit ran helter-skelter when the troops were ordered to "hold fire". Only those confronting the troops were fired upon and after several such bursts it all ceased. Only the dead and the wounded lay on the ground and the evacuation and cleaning teams went to work with the fire trucks hosing down the streets. According to the "battle operation reports", "Law and Order/Peace was restored within a matter of six hours" (from start to finish). The country paid a very heavy price in blood but in statistical terms, it was light considering the large number of people in the streets who had defied and disobeyed the order of the troops to disperse and return home. Bo Saw Maung proved to be a true professional soldier and saved the country from disintegration and possible foreign intervention.

Bo Saw Maung went on national TV and Radio and announced the Military take-over of the country and establishment of the STATE LAW AND ORDER RESTORATION COMMITTEE (SLORC) with him as its Chairman, Head of Government and Head of State. The people of Burma, the neighboring countries and the world was horror-struck at the brutal suppression. That public and international reaction was understandable, but for the people of Myanmar, especially for the present Military leaders and the politicians, it is critically important to take serious note that Bo Ne Win's isolation, procrastination and the huge generation gap with the Commander-in-Chief of the Armed Forces in not transferring State Power to the Army in early August 1988, that Bo Saw

Maung was then forced to take extreme measures to save the country from mob rule and anarchy. Only at the eleventh hour when the situation was totally out of control and there was an existential threat to the country did Ne Win turn to Saw Maung for the Military to take over the country.

In hindsight he should have transferred power to Saw Maung in early August 1988 like U Nu did in 1958. These are the lessons that present and future generations of Myanmar need to learn to ensure that the country will not have to suffer such a traumatic event in the future. History and future generations of Myanmar will remember Bo Saw Maung as a very courageous Commander-in-Chief of the Tatmadaw who did not shirk from the heavy responsibility placed upon his shoulders at the critical time of existential threat to the country. On the same token, I wish to put on record here that Bo Than Shwe and Bo Maung Aye deserve credit and respect for "electing retirement together" and selecting the next generation Military Chief (Min Aung Hlaing) and putting the country on the "path to democracy" under Thein Sein. Regardless of the past, the people of Myanmar need to recognize, acknowledge and extend due credit, respect and regard to those named herein for their courageous efforts in bringing the country to what it is today (2018) sharing State Power with the populist Party under the leadership of Aung San's daughter but jointly founded originally with Bo Aung Gyi, Bo Khin Nyo, Bo Maung Shwe, Etc.

# MILITARY ELIMINATES FOREIGN ECONOMIC AND TRADE DOMINATION

In 1958 when U Nu, the Prime Minister, transferred State Power (under pressure from the Army), the Caretaker Government of Bo Ne Win came to the stark realization that Burma's economy, trade and commerce were firmly in the hands of the British; Chinese, Indians, Anglos and the Burmese merely were subsisting on their handouts. The 85% peasant class was landless and at the mercy of the money lender Chettia Indians. The new Burmese politicians that ruled the country for ten years (1948-1958) were bought, paid for and in the pockets of these foreign businesses in the country and their overseas connections. The bureaucracy under the politicians were made up of remnants of the British Colonial Administrations and resisted every effort of the U Nu Cabinet for change. It carried on and functioned as if nothing had changed except the white British (Thakins) had left and the Burmese Thakins had taken their places. The lot of the common Burmese to all intents and purposes were worse off than colonial times for the entire country. The monumental task of regaining control of the country's economy from these entities was assigned to Bo Aung Gyi, the Vice Chief of General Staff.

As Minister of Trade and Commerce, Bo Aung Gyi set up a Special Advisory Panel (Task Force) to evaluate and explore the key sectors of the country's economy (essential and critical services) that must be under State Control and management as a matter of top priority. The members of the National Economic Restructuring Panel were:

- B-General Aung Gyi, Chairman
- Vice Admiral Than Phay, Deputy Chairman
- B-General Tin Phay (Minister of Agriculture & Forests)

- B-General T. Clift, Member (Minister of Transportation)
- Colonel Khin Nyo, Member (Chairman of Burma Railways Board)
- Colonel Thaung Kyi (Adjutant General Ministry of Defense)
- Colonel Htun Sein, Member ( Rangoon City Mayor)
- Colonel Maung Lwin (Moustache), Chief of Military Intelligence
- U Maung Maung, Permanent Secretary, Ministry of Defense
- U Thi Han (Director of Defense Procurement)

# TOP PRIORITY ECONOMIC SECTORS AND ESSENTIAL SERVICES

1. National Food Sufficiency
2. National Health
3. National Energy Sufficiency (Oil Exploration, Production, Refining, Etc.)
4. Transport and Communications
5. National Education
6. Agriculture, Industry and Forests
7. Domestic Commerce, Exports, Imports and Overseas Trade
8. Finance, Banking, Insurance and International Shipping
9. Domestic Industry Development (Cottage, Medium and Heavy Manufacturing)
10. Cross-Border Trade and Commerce

The Military Institution, at the time of accepting the transfer of State Power from Prime Minister U Nu, approved by Parliament, was the most well organized and disciplined organization in Burma. Whereas the Party of Aung San (the AFPFL) was on the verge of splitting, and the politicians were engaged in petty squabbles, and the wives of the leaders were gossiping and spreading rumors of who was wearing diamonds of what size and who owned land in which part of Rangoon.

Bo Ne Win's Caretaker Government went about the business of governing the country in a real business-like manner and the Committee under Bo Aung Gyi quickly decided on the top priorities to be implemented under the direction and leadership of the members. Significant and notable even today was Colonel Htun Sein, the Rangoon Mayor at that time, moving the squatters out of the slums and building new cities, Okklapa (North & South), Thaketa and Yankin extension that today (2017) are major extensions of Yangon. The next is the Circular Railway under Colonel Khin Nyo's leadership which Burma Railways built. Vice Admiral Than Phay was tasked with the establishment of Burma's first International Shipping Line (Burma Five Star Line and Burma Fisheries Industry that is still running today). Colonel Thaung Kyi and U Thi Han established the Defense Services Industry (Burma Garment Factory, Burma Shoe Factory, Burma Milk Factory) first to supply the Military, the Police, Forest Services, Inland Waterways Services and then the general public.

With strong and dedicated leadership these new enterprises took off very rapidly with a huge ready market starved of such domestically produced products. Bo Ne Win's Caretaker Government proved its worth by the successful implementation of these National Developments that Aung San's AFPFL Government of U Nu was unable to do in ten years of their governing the country. The people of Burma enthusiastically welcomed such national progress and economic achievements, and applauded the Military Government. One can say with confidence that the Military's credibility and popularity was at its apex. It would not reach that height ever again up to the time of this writing (2018).

# ARMY TAKES ON BOC, THE BIGGEST BRITISH INTEREST IN BURMA

In early 1959 when I returned to Rangoon after four years of study at Japan's four top universities; the Caretaker Government was in the throes of implementing the policy to eliminate foreign domination of the country's economy, trade and export-import businesses. One early morning, two days after arriving in Rangoon, I called on General Clift, Chief of Air Staff, at his official residence on Prome Road and he heartily welcomed me back home and invited me to join him for breakfast. During the meal he thanked me profusely for taking care of him during his many official missions to Japan and now it was his turn to reciprocate. However, he hastily added with the reality of the "pecking order of the day" that the "greens call all the shots" and the "khaki and whites" (Air Force and Navy) have to play second and third fiddle, if at all.

I was amazed at his brutally honest admission of his official status. "For you there is no need for any worry or concern since the 'top dog' of the country know you personally and all the senior officers of the Ministry of Defense have been taking care of you under direct order from General Ne Win who is now the Prime Minister." He went to the adjoining room and called Gen. Aung Gyi on the phone and reported that "our Yebaw in Tokyo" is back in Rangoon and he would be escorting me to his office that morning. We were driven to the Ministry of Defense in his official car and arrived at the very large estate like a university campus with armed soldiers stationed at strategic locations outside as well as in the wide corridors. The two generals exchanged salutes and to the surprise of his staff officers Bo Aung Gyi came forward and gave me a big "welcome home hug" and said Bo (Saya) Lwin, the Defense Attaché in Tokyo, had sent a telex message that I was on my way back to Rangoon. He ordered tea for both of us but Gen. Clift left for his office saying "you are in good hands".

While having tea in his private office Gen. Aung Gyi brought me up to date on the current state of affairs of the country under the Caretaker Government of Gen. Ne Win, the Prime Minister. The workload was heavy for all officers and staff in the Ministry of Defense as most of the other Ministries were reporting to the Deputy Prime Minister U Lun Baw who coordinates with General Aung Gyi on National Policy issues for submission to Prime Minister General Ne Win for approval. Therefore under present circumstances "you must submit a written report to Bogyoke (general) following your successful completion of studies in Japan and arrival back in Rangoon with a Degree from Tokyo University".

He pulled out some letterhead stationery of his Office and was very considerate to dictate the body of the official letter addressed to the Chief of General Staff and Prime Minister. The core of the arrival report stated that "I, Kyi Win Sein, had returned to Burma after successful completion of my studies at the University of Tokyo and Waseda University School of Law and was awarded the degrees of Bachelor of Arts (B.A.) and Bachelor of Laws (LL.B) in International Law. I respectfully request employment in appropriate Government Department. Respectfully, (Signed) Kyi Win Sein". On the letter General Aung Gyi wrote: "Onward submission to Chief of General Staff and Prime Minister (Signed) Bo Aung Gyi. He then called out to his Personal Staff Officer (PSO – a Captain) asking him to escort me to the War Room where General Ne Win was in conference with senior officers. It was a short walk along a wide corridor with armed security guards every ten feet apart on both sides. Gen. Aung Gyi said he would call ahead to say that I was on my way.

At the entry door sat a Captain behind a desk. The two exchanged salutes, opened the huge solid teak door, stood to attention and reported "U Kyi Win Sein is here, Sir". It was a very large room with a long one-slab teak table. Gen Ne Win looked up and yelled in his peculiar 'squeakish voice' "Hey you rotten short Japanese when did you get back? Come here, come here, what do you have in your hand?" I approached his chair gingerly and was made to stand beside it. He read my arrival report and within a few seconds looked up to my face with a grin saying "you received a degree from Tokyo University in International Law?" – "yes, Sir" – "That is very good, you are the first young Burmese to graduate from that top Japanese University." He then told the officers with him "all the instructors of the 30 Comrades were graduates of Tokyo University". He continued "you did very well" and wrote on the arrival report "to be given direct commission in JAG (Judge Advocate General's Office)" (Signed) Bo Ne Win. "Now go back to Bo Aung Gyi's office and he will take care of the rest." Before leaving I whispered in his ear, "I also got married." "What? You got yourself a Japanese wife?"

I later learned that the officers with him at that time were: Gen San You, Colonel Khin Nyo, Colonel Ba Ni, Colonel Thein Maung (Shorty) and Colonel Maung Lwin (Moustache) Chief of Military Intelligence who walked me back to Gen Aung Gyi's office telling me on the way that Col. Dr. Maung Lwin, the Defense Attaché in Tokyo, had sent him a telex that I was on my way back to Rangoon. He reported to Bo Aung Gyi that the "Boss" was happy that a young Burmese under his charge had returned from Japan with a law degree from Tokyo University. With a broad smile Bo Aung Gyi said to me "Ko Kyi Win Sein, everything is in order now, welcome to the Burma Army". I sat in front of him as in a daze without a word to his kind remarks. He asked, "Are you not happy? The Commander-in-Chief and Prime Minister gave you a direct commission in the Judge Advocate General's Office, Ministry of Defense."

I apologized for not understanding the significance of what had just taken place. He then wrote on the arrival report: "Military Secretary, please follow up and complete the appointment procedures" (Signed Bo Aung Gyi, Vice Chief of General Staff). "Now, my PSO will take you to Colonel Kyaw Soe's office and I will phone and brief him on the background and to expect you." The Colonel was slender and appeared to be rather sickly and exhausted. He asked me to sit down and reviewed the arrival report with several "notations" on it. Then he stared at me and asked, "Do you know what we call people like you?" "No, Sir, I do not know." "Golden person that drops from the sky (Mo-Kya-Shwe-Ko). As Military Secretary I have not come across any one given direct Commission by the number 1 and #2 Generals of the Army." I was surprised and taken aback by his sarcastic remarks and did not know what to make of it.

Then with abrupt change in his demeanor, he said "since it is almost lunchtime" and he would order some meat puffs, samosas and tea for both of us. "The direct Commission appointment papers needed to be completed today before

3 PM" and he would send me to Slim Lines Basic Officer Training Camp on Prome Road to be outfitted with uniforms and other Officer paraphernalia by the Camp tailor and check into my quarters where I would be resident for three months. As of that moment he announced that I was (a Full) Army Lieutenant and he would address me as such. "You are no longer a civilian and do bear that in mind at all times." While he was lecturing me, his Personal Staff Officer came in to report that Colonel Thaung Kyi, the Adjutant General, was on his way to this office. Soon thereafter Col. Thaung Kyi barged into the Office, shook my hands and gave me a hug saying "welcome home". Bo Lwin informed me that you were with "Bo Aung Gyi and the Chief of Staff." Bo Kyaw Soe was wide-eyed and said, "You know each other from before?" Col. Thaung Kyi explained that "he is our 'Yebaw' since his High School days in Bassein and now he is officially inducted into the Ministry of Defense by the Commander-in-Chief". After that the Military Secretary's attitude and demeanor changed noticeably. He carefully chose his words in speaking to me and was curious to find out what my close relations were with the top brass of the Military hierarchy. While the paperwork was being completed he asked one of his staff officers to escort me to the office of Colonel Solomon, the Judge Advocate General, with a copy of the arrival report. A tall, dark skinned Anglo Indian man greeted me very politely and after reviewing the arrival report said "welcome to JAG" and introduced me to the officers of the department, one Major, five Captains and two were women. Colonel Solomon said he was familiar with Tokyo University's academic reputation and felt honored that the Chief of Staff was assigning me to his Department. He followed that welcome speech with a sarcastic remark – "you will soon be sitting in this chair". I was taken aback by his unwelcome remark and lost for words. I assumed it was the psyche of being an Anglo-Indian in the Burmese Army.

# MY NARROW ESCAPE FROM ADOPTION BY MATERNAL ANGLO FAMILY

Our mother Daw Hnin (Rose) was the eldest adopted daughter of Ivan Nicholson, husband of Daw Nu, elder sister of Daw Pu, our grandmother. Mom started school as Rose Nicholson in a Christian Missionary school together with Mike Nicholson, and Mary Beecher, her first cousin and daughter of her father's younger sister. As such, our immediate family was dominated and under the influence of two white English men married to our grandfather's sister and his sister-in-law and their issues (Anglo-Burmans) by having been fathered by white men enjoyed a status accepted and recognized as being superior to the native Burmese. However, our mother the eldest daughter (adopted) of Ivan Nicholson was considered equal to her Anglo cousins and that was a big deal in the colonial era. I was made to understand that fact very early in life.

Rose Nicholson having a special social status where the one hundred percent British whites were at the top, Anglo-Burmese at the second tier, the Anglo-Indians, Anglo-Chinese in the third, followed by the mixed bloods with the frontier area Hill Tribes. But WWII dismantled that social structure of nearly a century in a very profound way, especially for all the Anglos of Burma. In 1945 soon after the end of the war our Dad and Mom with nine children settled in Maymyo (now Pyin-Oo-Lwin) with Dad reappointed Inspector of Excise for that Sub-Division and the children back in schools – four boys in St. Alberts Catholic Missionary School and the two girls in the Catholic Missionary Convent. And a year later were joined by Trevor Masters, the only son of Mary Beecher (Mom's first cousin) and Sonny Masters just returned from India. Sonny Masters resumed his old job of Works Manager at Burma Railways Carriage Factory at Myitnge between Mandalay and Paleik, our Mom's ancestral village.

## MY NARROW ESCAPE FROM ADOPTION BY MATERNAL ANGLO FAMILY

We lived in a small one-story wooden bungalow on stilts and Trevor was the 10th child to join the large family of Harry Maung Sein and Daw Hnin (Rose Nicholson) and all the boys (now 5) walked to St. Alberts every morning. Despite the cramped living space and having to share food with 9 others that he had never done before in his entire life, Trevor was happy because he was now part of a family having brothers and sisters. Unfortunately and regretfully for Trevor it did not last very long. Every two weeks his parents and Aunty Kyi (Mom's youngest sister) who lived with them would drive up to Maymyo bringing things and to be with their only son, within conditions of the cramped small wooden bungalow with 9 other kids. She found an ex-catholic nun school teacher living alone through the Catholic Church of Maymyo and Trevor was moved to that house where he had his own bedroom, study table and full attention of the spinster school teacher at St. Alberts and horse-drawn carriage transport every day to and back from school. Sonny Masters, the father, was aghast but was totally hapless against the domineering wife. Poor Trevor was devastated beyond description at being ripped away from his newly found brothers and sisters, Aunty Hnin (Rose) and Uncle Harry, who consoled him saying that he was always welcome to this house anytime and to come join us for meals on weekends and holidays. Trevor left our place looking miserable and hardly able to hold back tears. That attempt by the mother to arbitrarily impose and control the life of the son in total disregard of his personal preference and happiness had an irreparable impact on Trevor's attitude towards his mother for the rest of his life.

Perhaps Aunty Mary realized the negative outcome of her well intentioned arrangement for Trevor's schooling in Maymyo – her interpretation of the situation was that her son needed companion like a brother and what could be better than to ask Hnin (Rose) for Malcolm to be adopted by Sonny and Mary Masters and give Trevor a younger brother. It would also be killing two birds with one stone, doing a great favor to the struggling family of her first cousin with seven sons. It was all done hush hush between the cousin sisters and during the long summer school break we all visited Myitnge and I was talked into spending the holidays with Trevor in Myitnge. At first it looked like a good idea and before I could say yes or no, they took off in the big Government provided truck for Maymyo and I was left behind in Myitnge. I could clearly see that Trevor was excited and happy to have someone to play with during the long holidays. As I remember it, I had just received my second double promotion from third grade to fifth (my 1st was from first to third grade). But I was not happy to be left behind in Myitnge.

I felt abandoned by the family because this was not the first time my mother succumbed to manipulation to give up her third son. It had happened in Paleik during the war. Our grandfather (Pho-Pho Gyi) was a very close friend of the richest man (U Chan) in that village and he had no children. He pleaded with Pho Pho Gyi to persuade his daughter (Hnin-Zi) Rose given to Nicholson for adoption, to give up (Myet-Pyu) big eyes to U Chan who would legally declare him as heir to his fortune. I clearly remember U Chan telling me that he would buy me a "one man racing bullock cart" which in those days was the "convertible sports car" of the times. To a kid of 8 or 9 it was quite appealing. But Dad was adamant and felt insulted that the richest man of the village felt his riches could buy someone's child. He felt insulted and angry at his beloved wife for talking such rubbish with her father who had given up his eldest daughter because she was Saturday-born (a bad omen / superstition). He put his foot down and forbid her never to even think about such nonsense. That was the end of it.

Now in Myitnge, I started to wonder why Dad agreed to leave me behind. While in that state of mind, I had my first taste of control and manipulation of Aunty Mary. Her strategy was to use Aunty Kyi, Mom's youngest sister, who was practically the Maid of the Master's household. She was "invited" to live with cousin Mary just before Trevor was born and it was quite obvious what the intent was behind the invitation (to serve as the baby's maid). Aunty Kyi started to tell me that this house is "not the same as the wooden bungalow in Maymyo" and there are things I am not allowed to do without "Aunty Mary's or her permission". Even to a young fifth grader it was like being told that your poor living behavior and habits will not do in this house. I am not sure what but something prompted me to tell Aunty Kyi that I wanted to go home. She stared at me with an expression of disbelief and said that was not possible because they (my parents) would only be coming a month later to get me. I learned later that it was a trial period to see if the plan to adopt Malcolm the third son of Rose Nicholson as a brother for Trevor Masters would go well.

Somehow in my mind I felt strongly that being obedient and following all their rules would prolong my stay with them and I would never get to be with my family again. Without any hesitation or qualms I would not listen to what I was told and more often than not do the opposite or simply ignore and shut them out. I did enjoy playing with Trevor despite the "unequal treatment" I was receiving from Aunty Kyi and Mary. During all this time Uncle Sonny was simply an observer and had no say in the matter at all. Another thing I remember clearly was Trevor was always humming or actually singing Indian love songs like (Mera Bull-Bull, Sora-Hai-Hair) "my little baby bird soaring in the air". After about ten days the two Aunts had had enough of the headstrong unruly kid ignoring their rules of conduct and simply being stubborn. Aunty Kyi wrote to Mom telling her that things are not working out as I had a mind of my own and would not listen to them. Dad sent his truck driver Ko Kyaw Ya in the family jeep to get me and we drove up to Maymyo.

Trevor wanted to come along to spend the hot days up in the Hill Station but Aunty Mary said no. That was the end of the scheme cooked up by the two cousin sisters (Rose Nicholson Sein and Mary Beecher Masters) to have me adopted by Mary and Sonny Masters. This was the second time I narrowly escaped the fate of adoption by the unwavering strong principle of Dad that he would not under any circumstances give up any of his beloved children. He was determined to keep the family together and he did. If the scheme of the cousin sisters had succeeded, I would have become Malcolm Masters, a second or third class member of an Anglo family and most probably ended up working as an Apprentice in Myitnge Workshop after the 7th or 8th grade. All of my encounters with our Anglo relatives flashed through my head while reporting to Colonel Solomon, an Anglo-Indian and the Lawyer Officers in the Judge Advocate Generals Office.

I was shocked and amazed by how the insecurity factor as well as the intimidation these senior officers demonstrated. To make matters worse for the JAG Colonel and his staff, Col. Moustache Maung Lwin walked in and asked if Col. Thaung Kyi has caught up with me and told me to drop by his office after I was done here. He briefly explained to Col. Solomon that "our association goes back to the days when he was a High School student in Bassein and Col. Thaung Kyi was Delta Region Brigade Commander". It dawned on me that I had accepted the order of Bo Khin Maung Galay, the Deputy Prime Minister and Chairman of the Foreign State Scholar Board, to study International Law in Japan because the only other option available for me at that time was to apply for Army Officer Training School (OTS). After four years of hard struggle in Japan I still ended up in the Army on my return to Burma. What a fate, I thought to myself.

One of the JAG officers escorted me to the Intelligence Department where Col. Moustache Maung Lwin and his staff officers, Major Thein Shwe (Charlie) who was a few classes ahead of me at St. Alberts in Maymyo, Captain Kyaw Zwa Myint (Johnny Lears) class mate at St. Peters at Mandalay and Major Lay Maung whom I had met at Col. Thaung Kyi's home in Bassein, awaited for a reunion with tea and cakes. I was rather tired after a day of going through a stressful reporting to the Military ruler of the country and his senior officers and now with four Intelligence Officers already scheming to have me transferred to their Department after my three months' basic training. In the midst of the reunion tea party, the Military Secretary called and informed Col. Maung Lwin that his PSO was waiting to escort me to Slim Lines and the Commandant was expecting me there by 4 PM. Apparently he was determined to get me off his hands and ensure that I was safely encamped at the Officer Training Command in Rangoon.

On hearing that plan I naively replied that there was no way for me to report today as I had arrived back in Rangoon just 48 hours earlier after being away in Japan for over 4 years. I was put on the phone to explain the situation directly to Col. Kyaw Soe, who repeated his earlier lecture: "Bo Kyi Win Sein, you are no longer a civilian and there is no option for you to choose your convenient time to report for duty." I pleaded for him to understand my desire to spend time with my family. He relented and said he would grant me ten days' special leave. I had the distinct feeling that he did not want the matter to go further than his office. Looking back in hindsight, the events of that entire day in the Ministry of Defense escorted from one office to another led my mind to conclude that I must find a way to wiggle out of this predicament I had got myself into. I was fully aware of the risk factors involved that would influence my entire future in the country.

Bo Lwin dropped me off in late afternoon at my parents' home in Yankin. I was exhausted on arrival at the two room apartment where my Dad, Mom, elder brother Ivan and brother-in-law Ko Tin Tun eagerly awaited to hear what had transpired at the Ministry of Defense. I explained the events of the day and that I had been given direct Commission in JAG; there was a sigh of relief by all with a remark from Mom that "nothing to be surprised at, it is a Military Government, recruiting you into the Army is the easiest thing for Ne Win to do". Without thinking I blurted out that I was not too happy about being a Lieutenant in JAG. Mom retorted, "Then why did you accept it?" I admitted that I was afraid and too intimidated by their high ranks and offices and did not have the courage to reject their arrangements for my career in Government. Brother-in-law Tin Tun, a Lieutenant-Commander in the Navy commended that it was the appropriate and correct decision to accept, as refusal would have serious consequences. Ivan said it is all done now and there is no other alternative for you but to follow orders. He was a 2nd-Lieutenant in the University Training Corps and it was no surprise coming from him to take orders from above.

That night I was too exhausted to contemplate what had happened to me on a personal level and my future career in Burma. On awakening the next morning, it became quite clear in my mind that being inducted into a Military career by the top Generals would entail official responsibilities and personal obligations my entire life without having any other option of my own choice. I was going to have to find, on my own, a way to circumvent this predicament. I had no idea nor clue how but aware that it was going to take more than the ten days, after which the Military was going to come after me for not showing up for duty at the Officer Training Camp. I told my parents I was going to visit friends and not to worry if I did not come back for a few days. I needed time and space to figure out a resolution with minimum risk and repercussions.

As I had expected after the expiry of ten days' special leave a despatcher from the Ministry of Defense came to my parents' home every other day and delivered notices, warnings and demands for Lt. Kyi Win Sein to report for duty at Slim Lines Officer Training Camp immediately. After one month of ignoring the written demands the Military Secretary's Office issued to the Rangoon City Police Commissioner a "warrant for the arrest of Lt. Kyi Win Sein for being away without leave (AWOL) and desertion from the Army". Yankin Town

Police Station officer showed up at my parents' apartment and served the arrest warrant. Dad and Mom were aghast and freaked out, asking my eldest brother Ivan and brother-in-law Tin Tun to search for this reckless and irresponsible son of theirs and escort him to the Officer Training Camp.

I returned home, and apologized for causing the family great trouble, concern and worry. I assured all that I would take care and resolve the problem, to which there was serious reservations and skepticism as to the veracity of my assurance as well as my capability of finding a resolution. The next morning I drove the family jeep to the residence of Bo Khin Maung Galay, the Ex-Deputy Prime Minister and Chairman of State Scholarship Board. I was questioned by the security at the gate but after a lengthy explanation of who I was and why I was there conveyed by phone to the house, I was permitted to drive up to the big teak mansion where the Ex-Minister awaited at the car porch. He ushered me to his private office and called out to his wife (Ma Ma Thein) and her father (a retired District Commissioner in the British colonial government) to join us.

After updating him on our last encounter at the State Scholar selection interview, he remembered forcing me to study International Law in Japan as well as asking Bo Ne Win to check how I was getting along in Japan and to extend necessary assistance. He was very frank and said he was no longer a Minister and practically powerless. On hearing my predicament, Ma Ma Thein said, "Since Ne Win is running the country it is quite natural to put you in uniform." Exactly what my Mom had said. However, Bo Khin Maung Galay, characteristic of an Ex-High School Principal before entering the independence movement and politics was understanding and sympathetic towards the plight of the young student he had personally selected and ordered to study in Japan against his will. He asked what other jobs I had in mind. I replied, "Any private or Government-Private Corporation like the Burma Oil Company (BOC)." He took out a letterhead stationery pad from his desk drawer and started writing a letter with his fountain pen while Ma Ma Thein served me tea, cakes and some biscuits and I chatted with her elderly father. Bo Khin Maung Galay handed the letter to the old man who reviewed it, said "perfect" and passed it on to me. It was addressed to U Lun Baw, Deputy Prime Minister, Government of the Union of Burma:

"This is to introduce U Kyi Win Sein, a State Scholar who has recently returned after successfully completing studies in International Law at Tokyo University. I would be obliged if you would kindly find employment for him in any Private-Government Joint Business Corporation such as Burma Oil Company. Thanking you for your help, Yours Sincerely (Signed Khin Maung Galay)". He carefully folded and inserted the letter in his printed envelope, sealed it and said, "Now proceed to the Old Secretariat Deputy Prime Minister's Office and hand it to him personally. I wish you all the best and keep me posted at all times." I said, "Thank you very much Minister, Sir" and he replied, "Don't call me that, just call me as others in the family do (Ko Lay)".

I was received by the Office Superintendent (Administrator) of the Deputy Prime Minister's Office and was ushered to the reception room where he served me tea, mutton patties and cakes. Apparently the Administrator had served Bo Khin Maung Galay who had held that office in the previous government and therefore extended to me the courtesy and help. After about an hour's wait, U Lun Baw returned to his office accompanied by aides and security detail. The Administrator escorted me to the Deputy Prime Minister's adjoining office and I handed him the letter. He immediately opened the envelope and reviewed the letter. Then he looked at me with a smile and said "bagairoo" (fool) which he had learned from Japanese soldiers during the war years. It was the ice-breaker and we briefly chatted about the Japanese higher education system and their universities. He had been a High School Principal before taking part in the independence movement.

On the Official Letterhead: Office of the Deputy Prime Minister, Government of the Union of Burma he wrote in long hand: To, the Managing Director, Burma Oil Company, Rangoon Head Office; The bearer of this letter is U Kyi Win Sein, a State Scholar who has recently returned after receiving his Bachelor of Laws Degree in International Law from Tokyo University. I would like to nominate U Kyi Win Sein for an appropriate position in BOC Head Office. Please accept my thanks and appreciation for your cooperation in this matter. Signed (Lun Baw) Deputy Prime Minister. He folded the letter and sealed it in the official envelope of his office. "Now proceed to the Office of Mr. Strain, the BOC Managing Director, and keep me (and Bo Khin Maung Galay) posted of the result and your progress at all times."

At the BOC Managing Director's office, the Secretary (an Anglo woman) coldly told me to first get an appointment and then come back tomorrow. I handed her the envelope and told her, "give this letter to Mr. Strain and he will see me now." She stared at the envelope and her eyes almost popped out and she rushed into the office. Within minutes, an English man with a thin moustache rushed out and on seeing me extended his hand saying "How do you do, I am Strain, welcome to BOC, U Kyi Win Sein". He ushered me to his well-appointed office and politely pulled out a chair in front of his huge executive teak desk. I could clearly see that the British executive, red faced, was in a state of shock, intimidated and lost for words but made every effort to remain calm and collected. Then, somewhat regaining his composure he said, "To be honest and frank, one does not receive a handwritten official letter from the Deputy Prime Minister of the country in one's entire career, if at all.

You must excuse me for being flustered and lost for words." I assured him it was not a problem and there was no need for any excuse. He probably felt much better and asked, "When can you join us, U Kyi Win Sein?" "I am ready right now." Again he was taken aback and explained that the office is about to close today at 4 PM. He asked for my residence address saying that a car would come tomorrow morning at 8 AM to pick me up. We both looked at our watches and it was 10 minutes to 4 PM. He stood up and shook my hands saying "welcome to BOC and I look forward to us working together" and walked me to his office door. I learned later that after I left Mr. Strain asked all the senior managers to come to his office for an emergency conference – General Manager U San Cho (Stanley), Deputy General Manager U Khin Hlaing, Sales Manager U Myo Nyunt and Barrister U Maung Gyee, the Company Legal Department Head and a close relative of Sir Maung Gyee.

# MANAGEMENT CAUGHT OFF-GUARD FACED HUGE DILEMMA

Their primary concern centered on the BOC being a Joint Venture Corporation owned 51% by the Government of Burma now under the Military Prime Minister General Ne Win. The letter to Strain was from his Deputy Prime Minister U Lun Baw, the trusted civilian in the Caretaker Government. They surmised or rather speculated that since the nominee was educated in Japan there was a high probability that it was General Ne Win using the civilian in his Cabinet to "place their man in BOC Head Office". The British Managing Director went as far as to tell the Burmese Managers that "perhaps this is the first bold step by the nationalistic Burmese Army goal to take over foreign commercial interests in Burma".

One of the Burmese Managers at that meeting revealed to me later that "they were totally taken by surprise and were in a state of shock" especially Stanley Cho who first came to know my name from his father U Cho who had met me in Bassein (Pathein) where I introduced him to Colonel Thaung Kyi, the Delta Region Commander, on the golf course and we played a threesome nine holes early in the morning and later had breakfast at the Club House. Apparently U Cho was quite impressed, so much so that he related the unexpected encounter with a young High School student with a lot of self-confidence. When Strain raised the question of "what position to be given to the Military Government nominee", the Burmese Managers kept silent as if to tell the English man, "you will have to decide that on your own as well as the consequences that come with it". The Burmese Managers were all from the ruling class of Burma's social order, and were not going to stick their necks out, knowing full well Burma Army's attitude towards that aristocratic upper class society. However, Strain closed the meeting with "we will give him South Burma Region". The North Burma Region Manager was the son of Sir Ba U, Ex-President of Burma.

What transpired next at that meeting was most interesting revealing the innate bias and prejudice of those educated in the East compounded by the 30 Comrades trained in Japan, one of whom was now Prime Minister running the Caretaker Government of Burma. Barrister U Maung Gyee (a member of the Rangoon University Law Faculty) reminded his colleagues that the University of Tokyo before WWII was Imperial University No. (1), Kyoto University No. (2) and Hokkaido University N0. (3). The LLB (Bachelor of Laws) is a postgraduate degree like in the UK and Europe. After WWII Japan adopted the U.S. system of "major and minor" subjects in pursuing higher academic degree courses and as indicated in the Deputy Prime Minister's letter he must have majored in International Law. A very special and unique subject to be selected for and approved by the Ministry of Education and the State Scholarship Board to study abroad especially in Japan. This is clear evidence of his connection to the Burma Army, the creation of the Imperial Japanese Army.

I arrived back home quite exhausted where Dad, Mom, eldest brother Ivan and brother-in-law Tin Tun anxiously awaited to hear what had transpired that day. I related to them in detail the day's events culminating in BOC Managing Director Strain's office showing his business card as evidence. Dad commented that only sons of the very top elite are employed by BOC – "are you sure they are going to really give you a job?" He was definitely skeptical but Mom was more willing to give me the benefit of the doubt and said, "Let us wait and see if a car comes tomorrow morning to pick him up." Yes indeed, at 8 the next morning there was a knock on the apartment door and the driver said, "I have come to pick up U Kyi Win Sein." My parents gave me a broad smile and waved me off.

On arrival at BOC Head Office, the Anglo Secretary who had first told me to come back the next day, was waiting at the main entry car porch and greeted me with "good morning, U Kyi Win Sein, Mr. Strain is waiting for you in the Board Room" and escorted me there on the 3rd Floor. Strain greeted me at the entry door to the large Board Room where there were a dozen or so men, some in trousers and tie, and some in traditional Burmese longyi (sarong) and jackets. I was introduced to each one of them, starting with Stanley Cho who said, "I have heard a lot about you from my father". After the formal introductions I was made to sit next to the Managing Director, who stood up and announced,

"Gentlemen, please welcome U Kyi Win Sein, our new Regional Marketing Manager (RMO) for South Burma. He was nominated by the Deputy Prime Minister U Lun Baw to serve in BOC Head Office. U Kyi Win Sein, please say a few words to our Management Team." I stood up and addressed the gathering: "Mr. Strain, Gentlemen, I wish to thank you for welcoming me to BOC and I look forward to working together with all of you and receiving your cooperation and guidance in carrying out my assigned responsibilities of my office. Thank you very much." We moved to the Executive Dining Room where tea/coffee/cold drinks were served and a standing free "get to know you chatting" went on for about fifteen minutes.

One man had the audacity to ask "who is your father?". I looked into his eyes and said "you would not know even if I told you" and turned to chat with others in the room. One can imagine the innate bias of the Burmese lackeys of the British. That quick retort established my reputation – "this young fellow is not intimidated and very self-confident". Mr. Strain escorted me to his private office and briefed me on the orientation program for me on the entire BOC Operations in Burma from: exploration, drilling, extraction, storage, refining, production of gasoline, diesel, kerosene, lubricants, petro-chemicals, candles, aviation fuel, distribution, marketing, sales, transportation by road, rail, water, air, tanker, etc, etc.

After that he personally escorted me to my Department and officially introduced me to the Managerial Heads and the General Staff, in total more than fifty. I came to the stark realization that I was the youngest (officially 23 but real birth age 26). There was no time for any second thoughts, reflection or procrastination but to take on the challenge that were placed in front of me. I was later told by BOC old-timers that "no Manager under 40 years of age got to that position". I was too young and naïve to allow that to stand in my way and was determined to give it my best shot no matter what. It turned out that my experience with International Student Unions, dealings with Japanese Government, political leaders, Ambassadors, Ministries, Ministers, Ambassadors and Diplomatic Missions were of great help.

In fact I learned later that Managing Director Strain and his Burmese Management team had serious reservations and some expressed doubts whether a very young man just graduated from university had the necessary maturity, the capacity and capability to shoulder the responsibilities of a major petroleum corporation at the 2nd tier of management, running the marketing of the entire Southern half of Burma. However, those concerns vanished quickly when the Deputy Managers, Assistant Managers and General Staff were amazed with my frank, open and straightforward attitude without any pretenses or self-importance. I assured all in the Department that "I am here to learn and work with you and my office will be open to all without any artificial or bureaucratic barriers". Within a matter of a month and a half on the job there was chatter and gossip of the young Japun pyan (returnee from Japan) being "a quick learner and straight talker" without any pretensions of his position in the company or social status and mature beyond his age.

Both the refineries and related industrial and production facilities were in the Southern region, Chauk in central Burma and Syriam across the Rangoon River. I had to read all available documented history of the world petroleum industry and the British role in its development in the Middle East, Asia, South America and the North Sea. After about two months on the job, Mr. Strain asked me to attend a meeting in the Board Room. As I walked into the room, I noted that Stanley Cho and Strain were in conversation with General Aung Gyi, seated at the head of a long teak table. He looked up and stared at me like he had just seen a ghost and my heart almost stopped. Then, regaining his composure and realizing that other directors had arrived, he asked the others to leave the room as "I need to discuss with U Kyi Win Sein for a few minutes".

"Well, Ko Kyi Win Sein, please tell me what has been going on and why are you here to attend the Board of Directors' Meeting of BOC?" He was taken aback and besides himself when he saw me because he instinctively thought that I had been sent by General Ne Win. I pleaded that I would explain everything after the meeting but he rejected that and said he wanted to know right now. Having no escape I told him how I had ended up in BOC through Bo Khin Maung Galay and U Lun Baw, the Deputy Prime Minister. I noted that he was relieved but raised the question of the arrest warrant issued by Colonel Kyaw Soe, the Military Secretary. I said I was going to need his help but he rejected that too and said, "I and Bogyoke himself signed your direct Commission appointment to JAG and there is no way for me to undo it." In desperation I said I would make a request to Colonel Maung Lwin (Moustache) to help find a resolution. "That is a better idea and follow up quickly, don't delay." "Yes, Sir." "Now let us get on with this meeting." He made me sit next to him.

Strain and the Directors, most of them were Permanent Secretaries of Ministries. General Aung Gyi apologized for having them leave the room as "I needed to discuss some urgent matters with U Kyi Win Sein". All eyes were on me and wondering "who is this young fellow that the No. 2 General of the Army made us leave the room for him to discuss urgent matters?". At the end of the meeting Gen. Aung Gyi asked me to accompany him to the Ministry of Defense. Strain, however, gathered all the Burmese Managers in his office and related to them what he had witnessed in the Board Room and said, "There is no doubt whatsoever that U Kyi Win Sein is the Army's man in our midst." To make matters worse, a week or so later, General Aung Gyi asked me to accompany him to Chauk Refinery together with Strain, U Khin Hlaing, Deputy GM, and Barrister U Maung Gyee in the executive aircraft of BOC. On arrival at Chauk airfield, my old golf nemesis Colonel Aung Zin was leading the welcome party and on seeing me he grinned from ear to ear and lifted me off the ground like I was a toddler to the laughter of all.

The next morning after our return from the Chauk refinery I went to see Col. Maung Lwin (Moustache) the Chief of Military Intelligence and requested his help in resolving the arrest warrant issued by the Military Secretary's Office. He told me that Gen. Aung Gyi had informed him about our meeting in the BOC Board Room. He scratched his head saying that he would have to lean on Col. Kyaw Soe to quietly withdraw the arrest warrant with the cooperation and understanding from the Rangoon Police Commissioner assuring him that the matter had been "resolved internally by the Ministry of Defense". What actually transpired was that all top Army brass did not want the matter to reach "Gen. Ne Win's ears" at any cost. In the event the big boss found out I was in BOC, Gen. Aung Gyi and Col. Maung Lwin (Moustache) would simply say that the Deputy Prime Minister U Lun Baw assigned me there, which is in fact what happened. However, the big boss always held the impression that I was serving in Judge Advocate General's Department and sent to BOC as well as later to Export-Import Bank as Officer on Special Duty (OSD). That proved to be true when we met "face-to-face" at London Heathrow's Royal Lounge when he asked "when did you leave the Army?" and Col. Khin Nyo and Col. Maung Lwin (Moustache) freaked out, meekly pleading "we will explain everything later about him".

The big boss said, "There is no need for you fellows to explain anything; I knew him since he was a student in Japan and entrusted into my care by Ko Lay." Col. Khin Nyo had no clue who Ko Lay was and asked me in a whisper "which Lay?" but the boss overheard that and said "hey Bo Khin Nyo, it is your brother". In the drive back to the office I had an earful of complaints from Bo Khin Nyo in the presence of Ambassador U Hla Maung – "why in the world did you not tell me that my own elder brother sent you to Japan and entrusted you to the care of Bogyoke (General)?" The Ambassador said he was a class mate of Bo Khin Maung Galay at Rangoon University. These events and instances of the Revolutionary Council Chairman's visit to London at the end of 1962 created media interest and hype, rumors and gossip among the Embassy staff from where the large Burmese expatriate community would get the information and all kinds of speculations would begin. The most shocking and disturbing were the manufactured stories based on hearsay regarding the Military Regime's young man dismantling the country's established business and commercial enterprises in the UK, Europe and the U.S.

Soon after my arrest warrant for desertion from the Army Officer Training Camp was resolved I looked around for a place for us to settle down. As luck would have it I was on an inspection tour of the Tannaserim Division in Maulmein (Maulamyine) where BOC had a big depot, and I was required to officially call on the Commissioner and the Deputy Commissioner (DC) to report and discuss pending issues of BOC products being smuggled across the border to Thailand and by sea pirates to Singapore and Malaya. The Commissioner had invited the Karen and Kayah State Governments to attend the meeting. There I ran into U Sein, the Parliamentary Secretary of Kayah State, with whom I had become friends in Tokyo helping Sao Wunna, the Kayah State Minister, on his many business visits to Japan to spend the reparations money allotted to that State's development, the biggest of which was the Lawpita Dam Hydro Electric Plant.

At lunch hosted by the Commissioner, U Sein sat next to me and during our conversation he asked when "the wife from Tokyo" was coming. I told him about looking for a place and he immediately offered the Kayah State Guest House in Rangoon (now the Governor's Hotel) with all the facilities and to feel free to stay until a suitable place was found. It was very kind and considerate of U Sein (the same name as my father) and truly a godsend lucky break for me. Having said that, in all fairness I must mention here that when BOC Management learned that I was looking for a place, the Estate and Housing Manager offered to accommodate my needs but as I had already accepted the Kayah State offer, I declined. BOC housing estate is only a few blocks from the Guest House and was a much desired place of residence, fully furnished and equipped with all household electric appliances. Looking back with the benefit of hindsight, the BOC offer would have been a better choice for me as it was permanent as long as I was with the Company. Perhaps the other reason I rejected their offer was my gut feeling that it was not sincere on their part as being looked upon as the "Military's plant" for the purpose of upsetting the apple cart and taking away their gravy train. I became the only Head Office officer that refused BOC housing in the long history of the Company in Burma. Behind my back Rangoon society sneered "what an arrogant young fool". With their colonial mindset and disdain for the Military that is the natural and only way to interpret the attitude and behavior of this Japanese educated young Burmese.

# FAMILIES OF COMRADES WANT SHARE OF BOC MONOPOLY BUSINESS

One early morning I received a phone call from the personal aide of Gen. Aung Gyi to drop by at Dagon House (his residence at the entrance to the Ministry of Defense) after work. When I arrived there late in the afternoon he was in his longyi (sarong) and having noodles with Gen. San Yu and Col. Maung Lwin (Moustache) in the dining room. He told me that at the meeting the previous day with Bogyoke (Gen. Ne Win), he was told about the family of deceased infamous Bo Sein Hman who had died while dropping an improvised bomb by hand from an Air Force plane on Karen insurgents. At that time there were no bombs nor dropping system and the bomb that Bo Sein Hman attempted to drop exploded prematurely and all on that unfortunate plane perished. The surviving family had exhausted the properties in Rangoon granted by the U Nu Government and on pleading assistance from him to help them in any possible way, Bo Maung Lwin contacted the family and learned that it would greatly help if BOC products sales agency for their town (Thonze / Tharawaddy) could be had. Since it was in my Region, "do try and help the family out". Bo Maung Lwin gave me the names and address of the family.

Since the message emanated from the then Prime Minister and Commander-in-Chief, relating to his Comrade who had lost his life in fighting the Karen insurgency, it was a matter that must be attended to with utmost urgency and speed. The very next day I asked my Secretary and Senior Deputy Manager to set up my itinerary to Prome (Pyay) where BOC had a large Full Regional Depot, with stops at Thonze and Tharawaddy. Next, I confidentially consulted with the Sales Manager U Myo Nyunt telling him that the request came from Gen. Aung Gyi, BOC Chairman. He was wide eyed and suggested that I take up the matter with Stanley Cho, the GM, but I told him that the appropriate procedure was for him to inform the "Top Management". I clearly noticed that he was concerned and uncomfortable because we had long established agents in those towns and of being left with the task to inform those at the very top.

He indicated without being specific that his brother (Retired Ex-Ambassador to U.S., U Soe Nyunt, ICS) had a relationship with that family. I also informed him that I would be touring the Prome Region within the next few days and a copy of my itinerary would be forwarded to his desk. I was meticulously following Company procedures. Clearly he did not want to be the one to deliver the message to top Management that their long established "Agency arrangements are targeted for change". I requested from him the relevant Agency Contract Files for me to review and he suggested that I get them directly from Barrister U Maung Gyee, the Head of Legal Department. By now he was visibly disturbed that I was pursuing the matter aggressively with utmost speed and there was a look of resignation on his face.

I advised Gen. Aung Gyi and Col. Maung Lwin of my itinerary and both said all the Civil, Army and Police authorities should be notified to extend any assistance I might need on the long drive from Rangoon. Col. Maung Lwin told me (in fact ordered) that he was sending a plain clothes armed guard from his unit along and for me to carry my side arm as well. Our first stop was Thonze after a leisurely drive in the Company Land Rover. At the entrance to the town a police Inspector's car awaited and introduced themselves and escorted us to the BOC Agent's office and adjoining warehouse. The Agent, a Sino-Burmese man with refined features, was taken aback and looked rather shaken by the unannounced arrival of the Police followed by the unmarked Land Rover from which an armed guard and a young man emerged carrying a side arm in his belt. I extended my hand and introduced myself and he became more relaxed and apologized for not coming earlier to Rangoon to meet the new Regional Marketing Manager. I told him that no apologies were needed and it was my duty to visit all the Agents in South Burma. I thanked the Police Inspector and asked him about the security situation in the town and its vicinity. He said it was stable but that he had orders to escort us into Town. He said he would return to his Office and to call him when we were ready to leave here and took off. I had a very frank and open discussion with the Agent and learned that he had inherited the Agency from his father who had succeeded his grandfather.

The Agency has been in the family for several generations and apparently the entire "clan was well to do" and in fact considered rich by local standards. All local Town Agencies were "Non-Exclusive" but for those with long years of association with BOC, the Agency could be terminated by three-six months or a year's advance notice on the length / history of the Agency and the recommendation of the Prome Region Depot Manager. As such, each Agency had an ironclad market monopoly in the Town and the villages in its vicinity. It was and is even today a very profitable business. The Agency owner in his late forties was visibly concerned that he would completely lose the franchise for the town. I assured him that I was here not to take away his business and the livelihood of his family but to restructure the "marketing arrangements" with his cooperation to meet the changed circumstances of the times. He was greatly relieved and thanked me profusely. He told me that a few days previously he was in Prome and the Depot Manager had not mentioned anything about such changes (it was a loaded question). I informed him that I would be informing him when I got to Prome. I was fully aware that Agents always have to be in "the good book of the Depot Manager" and more often than not "work in cahoots".

When told to whom I was giving the 2nd Agency for the Town, he said Bo Sein Hman was a nationalist leader of the region and he was glad to hear from me that the surviving family would be helped with a BOC Agency and he would fully cooperate with my arrangements and extend any assistance they may need. He asked me if there was anything he could do for me personally and I quickly told him that all I needed was his understanding and cooperation for the new Agency to be set up for the Town. I learned that it was a longstanding custom for all agents to ask that of touring managers from Head Office. A system of give and take (bribery and corruption) that is practiced in business, government and all aspects of human interactions all over the country since colonial days. I was happy and grateful that the Agent recognized and accepted the reality that is characteristic of a Sino-Burmese rational and good businessman and especially his willingness to give up the monopoly of the family for several generations and save whatever was possible. I asked him to inform me immediately of any problems that emerged from the new set up and to feel free to come see me personally in Rangoon. He offered to host us for lunch but I declined and asked him to call the Police Inspector that we were ready to proceed to our next stop.

I requested that the police inspector guide us to the town's restaurant famous for its noodles in fish broth (Mohinga) because I wanted to get his insight of the "ins and outs" of the community's interactions from top to bottom. Police officers have their "ear to the ground" and are tuned in to what is going on where on a daily basis. I learned that the Inspector was a graduate of the Police Training College at Mandalay where his uncle was a senior police officer and instructor and his father was also a career police officer. After graduation his first posting was in Prome as Sub-Inspector and then a few years later he received his promotion to Police Inspector of Thonze. He was familiar with the legendary nationalist hero of the town and the region, his immediate family and the "followers or clan" with close connection to the surviving family members. Those remaining here were his sisters as the wife lived in Rangoon at the substantial property (Residence) given in gratitude for giving his life in serving the country by U Nu the then Prime Minister. Additionally, the Inspector also included the local hero's "rather questionable pursuits" before WWII as the feared gang leader of the region's bad heads, dacoits demanding "protection money" from commercial houses and businesses and more often than not outright extortion.

The inspector quickly added that this aspect of the hero was known to all but since the lucrative businesses, trade and commerce were in the hands of the Indo-Burmese, Sino-Burmese and the wealthy land owners and cronies of the British colonialists, the common Burmese looked upon his illegal actions and pursuits as "resistance and fighting the exploiters of the poor and downtrodden peasant class of the country". Bo Sein Hman survived and lived to see the day when the British left and Independence was gained whereas Saya San was hanged by the British for fighting the cause and liberation of the Burmese peasants. It was really an invaluable insight into the town's true perspective of the man respected and held in high regard to this day. It was indeed a true story and living legend of "yesterday's rebel and today's national hero".

We were received by two middle aged ladies, a man of similar age who did not identify himself, and many others whom I assumed were the extended family members. My first impression was of the fenced large compound (estate) with several wooden buildings and corrugated roofing that only the affluent could afford in those days. I was ushered to the well-furnished living room of the main residence and served plain Burmese tea, pickled tea leaves and ginger with varieties of condiments such as dried shrimp, fried scallions, peanuts, roasted sesame seeds, etc. in a lacquer tray with compartments for each item. Most of the talking was done by the lady who addressed herself as 'Ah-Ma-Gyi' elder / big sister very normal in a Burmese family. She mentioned from the outset that Mrs. Sein Hman lived in her Rangoon residence close to medical facilities as she was in rather poor health. She stressed that despite the free medical services received at the Rangoon General Hospital and Military Hospital, the cost of medicines and other related medical items was very high. It was therefore imperative for the family to have a sustainable steady revenue that would support the entire family. What she revealed next was a bombshell that would haunt BOC for years until the very end when the 49% stock was acquired by the Government in cash.

Apparently their quest for BOC Sales Agency began a few years back going through the normal channels and connections, that is under the management and control of the Regional Depot Manager in Prome, the Administrative Head Quarters of the Division. All their attempts failed because there were numerous intermediaries, each of whom demanded upfront payments (bribes) and the highest hurdle being the BOC Depot Manager who was in cahoots with the Rangoon Head Office final decision makers. No wonder that the National Sales Manager U Myo Nyunt, the Deputy General Manager U Khin Hlaing and the General Manager U San Cho (Stanley) were so upset and uncomfortable when I broached the matter directly informing them frankly and openly where the request came from. The lady said after exhausting whatever they could paying the middlemen and despite all that investment in money and time was rejected by the Depot Manager. She said the entire family was devastated, betrayed, cheated and robbed.

In desperation the family approached Bo Hmu Aung (one of the 30 Comrades), closest friend and associate of Bo Sein Hman, with their predicament and pleaded for his assistance to seek the intervention of Bo Ne Win the Prime Minister who had served under Bo Hmu Aung the Defense Minister in the U Nu Cabinet. I realized then and there that it was no longer a simple matter of an additional sales agency for a sleepy town on the main Rangoon to Prome highway but it was going to unravel the entire sordid business practice of the largest commercial enterprise of the British in Burma for over a century where the native Burman was forced to bribe his/her way through the colonial system without any assurance of success after extortion of the upfront payments (bribes).

I asked her for copies of their application for a Sales Agency submitted to the BOC Depot Manager and the relevant attachments such as upfront Security Deposit Guarantee in the form of Bank / Government Treasury Bonds, Land Titles, Liens and Certificates / Affidavits and Draft Agency Contract from Prome Depot. She gave me several files and I gave her a receipt witnessed by the Police Inspector. I requested the Inspector join me in the meeting as an observer / witness since it was my first time meeting a prominent local family and he was the town's Law Enforcement Officer. I thanked the two ladies for their hospitality and cooperation with the assurance that I would get back to them within a few weeks. The Police Inspector suggested that I drop by the Sub-Division Officer's (SDO) Office to keep him posted of my visit and plans for an additional Sales Agency. Adjoining the SDO's Office was the Office of the Deputy Superintendent of Police (Dy.SP), the Inspector's immediate superior, who was very pleased and thanked me for dropping by his office.

We made a night stop at Tharawaddy, the District Town, and slept the night at the Government Circuit House and place of rest for all officials on tour. The local Military Commander (a Lt. Col) and one of his senior Battalion Commanders (a senior Major) entertained me to dinner at a Chinese restaurant. (The Army station's 3 Battalions in Tharawaddy being a notorious district with multi-colored insurgency including the Red and White Communists.) The Lt. Col. informed me that the section of road to Prome is infested with insurgents as well as badheads (Dacoits / Highway Robbers) and he was asked to provide escort by the Brigade Commander in Prome who had received the request from the Ministry of Defense.

# HEAD OFFICE ABANDONS DEPOT MANAGER TO BE SCAPEGOAT

The Depot Manager U Shwe Hla Phru (Arakanese from Millionaire Square in Sittwe) with many years' seniority and close to retirement with full benefits, was clear evidence of having the right connections (protectors) in Rangoon. The Senior Deputy Depot Manager was Saw Daniel San Dun from one of the prominent Karen families and a relative of General Smith Dun, Army Chief of Staff under British Governor Sir Hubert Rance. Both were surprised and taken aback because I arrived at the Depot with a police escort and the Inspector was responsible for security and law enforcement of that Ward and knew the Depot Manager and his entire staff and the labor force of more than 100. It was a fairly large facility with many brick / concrete buildings for storing inflammables like gasoline, aviation fuel, kerosene, diesel, heavy oil, bunker oil, petro-chemicals and hazardous items like DDT, Dieldrin, Eldrin, lubricants, candles, and many more dedicated buildings for receiving, delivery and repacking. It was very close to the main River Port where BOC had its own Landing Jetty for our low draft River Tankers. The tour of the Facilities and the Port took nearly two hours and we returned to the Main Office for a one-on-one private meeting. It was hot and humid with no air conditioning.

He was noticeably nervous and uncomfortable. I briefed him on the discussions I had had with our Thonze Agent and during the conversation learned that the Agent had practically told him all on the phone. I had expected that and was not surprised at all. However, when I asked him about "Agency applications from Thonze over the past few years" he balked. His excuse was that unsuccessful (rejected) applications were not retained (archived). I also learned from him that all the Townships in the Prome Division had single agents and only District Towns had two Agents and a few permitted to appoint Sub-Agents. The enormous power, discretion and authority of the Depot Manager can be seen in such an arrangement where BOC with total monopoly and its distribution centers throughout the country was a treasure chest and a bottomless gold mine. Faced with a stonewalling and uncooperative Depot Manager, I realized that it would be senseless to pursue the matter with him any further and to avoid unnecessary argument on the matter at the local level. However, I advised him that on return to Rangoon, "Agency Policy for South Burma Region will be restructured to meet the new circumstances" as required by the Government of the day. He was glad to see me leave.

The Police Inspector escorted me to the Commissioner's Office where I also met the District Commissioner (DC) and the District Superintendent of Police (DSP). I briefed the top Administrators of Prome Division on BOC's energy production and distribution status in the Division and our desire to cooperate fully with the Government. All three officials thanked me for calling on them and made a "verbal request" to BOC Head Office to seriously consider their wish to "directly buy their energy needs from BOC Depot instead of from the designated Agents". I assured them that their message would be conveyed to the Top Management of BOC on my arrival back in Rangoon. I could see the writing on the wall and it turned out to be the harbinger of critical policy issues that would be assigned to me for change and restructuring.

Early the next morning around 6:30 our police escort inspector, accompanied by three armed constables, came to the Circuit House and suggested that we have breakfast on our way to Thonze for a brief stopover. Tea shops open very early and by 7 AM all tables are full with people on their way to work that starts at 8 AM. Thanks to the police escort Land Rover leading the way, the Tea Shop manager would set up a table some distance from the crowd. The crew would have the noodles in fish broth with all the toppings (Mohinga) that my stomach could not handle so early in the morning. I ordered nanpya (naan) and boiled peas fried with chopped onions and tomatoes and tea. It is the typical breakfast commonly eaten by the working class Burmese throughout the country. We stopped by briefly at the BOC Agent's office and then proceeded to Bo Sein Hman family residence and were received by the same two ladies we had met a few days ago.

I advised them to submit a formal "Application for a Sales Agency for Thonze to the Depot Manager in Prome" and to follow the procedures, requirements and conditions stipulated in the Official Contract Form reviewed by their lawyer before submission. I advised that on my return to Rangoon necessary structural and relevant policy changes would be effected and the Depot Manager would be officially instructed to implement the new policy and structural changes. They wanted to know the "Agency Territory" (Market Area) and I disclosed to them my discussion with the Commissioner of Prome Division "the Administrative Demarcation of Jurisdictions for Law Enforcement and the Judicial / Courts System". Under present arrangements specifically for Thonze Sub-Division the "Demarcation of Jurisdiction is NORTH AND SOUTH". The criteria and decision for which Jurisdiction Agency will be assigned will be determined by the Prome Depot Manager and submitted to Head Office (Regional Marketing Manager South Burma) for final decision. I took leave of the ladies and the Police Inspector said all the Highway Security Patrol units had been notified on the "Police Channel" to look out for our Land Rover along the way and cautioned the driver not to press too hard on the gas pedal. I thanked him and his Constables for taking care of us for several days. We arrived back safely in Rangoon in the afternoon around 3:30 and I went directly to my office and called Dagon House, Gen. Aung Gyi's residence. He asked me to drop by on my way home and join him for dinner together with Gen. San Yu, the Northern Commander who was in Rangoon and staying with him.

After dictating my Tour Report to the Stenographer I left my office after 5:30 PM and arrived at Dagon House just before 6 PM and was ushered to the dining room, where the two generals and Col. Maung Lwin (Moustache) were working on their drinks and munching on appetizers and waiting for dinner from the food stalls of the Open Air Market that practically is the "Kitchen of the number 2 General of the Burma Army". I reported the state of affairs of BOC distribution and sales operations in Prome Division through the Main Depot and the Agents and Sub-Agents. I related to them my visit with the family of Bo Sein Hman and arranging to have them officially apply for a BOC Sales Agency for Thonze that would be an additional separate entity from the long existing original Agency. Bo Maung Lwin was upset when he heard about the rejection of their first attempt several years ago by the Depot Manager.

Having Police Detective experience before being recruited into Army Service he was familiar with the actual reason for the rejection.

When I conveyed the verbal request of the Prome Division Commissioner for direct off take of BOC petroleum products for all Government Departments, Gen. San Yu said it is about time for such a policy to be enforced by the Government without any more delay. Gen. Aung Gyi said he would inform Gen. Ne Win tomorrow after the Cabinet Meeting about the arrangement I had made for the family of Bo Sein Hman with a visit to Tharawaddy / Thonze and Prome. I said my full written official tour report would be submitted tomorrow and Gen. Aung Gyi instructed me to give "a confidential copy to Gen. San Yu" who joked that it would give him an opportunity to "practice my English reading". This matter would reach the Prime Minister's desk within the next few weeks through the Directorate of Procurement, Ministry of Defense. The Director was U Thi Han and the Defense Minister portfolio was held by Gen. Ne Win. The Army, Navy, Air Force, National Police and the Civil Services under the Home Ministry were all having to buy BOC products through Agents or their Sub-Agents depending on their location. The political Government of U Nu had danced to the tune of BOC since January 04, 1948.

On receipt of my Official Tour Report submitted under Confidential Cover with the Agency Application file received from Bo Sein Hman's family, the National Sales Manager U Myo Nyunt freaked out. He immediately forwarded the report to U Khin Hlaing, the Deputy General Manager, who forwarded it to U San Cho (Stanley Cho) the General Manager asking for "guidance, instructions and orders for further official action". The three Senior Burmese Managers huddled together to find a way to "soften the impact" on Strain, the British Managing Director and the consequences on the Company's Distribution, Marketing and Sales Policies. They asked Barrister U Maung Gyee to join the discussions considering the fact that I had reviewed the Agency Contract Files of Prome Division before embarking on the tour. The strong desire to defend and maintain the status quo by the cronies of the British was remarkable. The colonialists, through centuries of occupying other countries and enslaving the entire populace, have practiced the strategy and technique of "divide and rule" to exploit the resources of the country as long as possible. That was exactly what

Burma was going through with the British in 1959. Strain and his Burmese lackeys were in a state of shock.

The country was going through a period of political transition with Gen. Ne Win leading the Caretaker Government assigned with the task of restoring political stability and holding free and fair general elections to hand over State Power back to the Party receiving the majority vote of the people. In managing the affairs of the country, the Military leaders came to the stark realization that the country's economy, resources, trade, commerce and the rudimentary production industries were in the hands of foreign entities and practically controlled by the British, the Indians, Chinese, Anglos, Indo-Burmese, Sino-Burmese and their network of companies abroad. The Burmese were left to serve these commercial enterprises in clerical and menial positions. The Civil Service bureaucrats ruled at the top by the remnants of the Indian Civil Service (ICS) class and the newly minted Burma Civil Service (BCS) and their political superiors who had replaced the British colonial rulers from January 04, 1948. The politicians were totally dependent on the bureaucrats to keep the administrative machinery of the Government functioning and law and order maintained. However, for the first time since independence, the dominance of the bureaucrats in the Ministries, Departments, State Corporations and Enterprises would be abruptly taken away by the Caretaker Government of Gen. Ne Win. Military Officers were assigned to all Ministries and Major Departments as the Officer on Special Duty (OSD) to look over, supervise and manage the bureaucrats along the same lines as in the Military's Chain of Command system.

The Civil Service Officers no longer called the shots, they were reporting to the OSDs and in many cases the Officer's rank was a mere Lieutenant, giving orders to officers in their fifties who were close to retirement. The establishment people in government and their business community collaborators were aghast and in a state of shock and utter disbelief. The thinking behind such a radical and revolutionary move by the top Military Officer assigned by Gen. Ne Win to run the day-to-day Administration of the Government and the Economy of the country Gen. Aung Gyi together with U Lun Baw (a civilian), the Deputy Prime Minister, was to "break the stranglehold of the Bureaucrats and their Business Cronies" on how the "affairs of the country are managed".

It was strongly believed by the Military Caretaker Government that unless and until the bureaucrats in Government and the British, Sino-Burmese, Indo-Burmese and Anglo Business Community were brought to heel quickly the necessary changes in the "National Interest" would not move forward as desired. Therefore, it was an urgent imperative that the Government Machinery and the Business Community be placed firmly under the Management and Control of "Officers on Special Duty appointed by the Military Caretaker Government led by Gen. Ne Win, the prime Minister". By far the most valuable and largest British economic interest in Burma at that time (1959) was their 49% ownership in Burmah Oil Company (1951) Ltd. and Burma Oil Company (BT – Burma Trade) Ltd. Joint ventures with Burma Government holding 51% of both Corporations. Management, Technical, Engineering, Parts and Equipment Support Contracts were included in the Joint Venture Agreements. Managing Director (Strain) at the Head office and other British nationals serving in exploration, extraction, refineries and production facilities came under the terms of these Agreements and Contracts. The Government of Burma reserved the Right to acquire the 49% Shares of the British at Fair Market Value at its discretion.

Pursuant to this "National Policy Objective" envisaged by the Caretaker Government, Gen. Aung Gyi set up a "Task Force" to conduct a thorough in-depth exploration of the critical issues involved, the priorities to be considered and to recommend the official "UK Action Plan". The composition of the "Task Force":

1. Gen. Aung Gyi, Minister of Trade & Commerce (Chairman)
2. Admiral Than Phay, Chief of Naval Staff (Vice Chairman)
3. General T. Clift, Chief of Air Staff (Vice Chairman)
4. Colonel Thaung Kyi, Adjutant General Ministry of Defense (member)
5. Colonel Khin Nyo, Chairman Burma Railways Board (Member)
6. Colonel Maung Lwin, Chief of Military Intelligence (Member)
7. Colonel Hla Han, Head of Military Medical Services (Member)
8. U Thi Han, Director of Procurement, Ministry of Defense (Group Secretary)

9. U Kyi Win Sein, Regional Marketing Manager South Burma, Burma Oil Company (Research Analyst and Legal Adviser to Burma Economic Development Corporation).

The composition of the Task Force was approved by Gen. Ne Win, the Prime Minister, with the order to classify it "Under Cover and Restricted" and report to him directly the Group's discoveries and / or recommendations. He also approved the Security Clearance for the two civilians in the Group. No one outside of the Task Force members had any knowledge of its existence and meetings several times a month were held at Dagon House, the Official Residence of Gen. Aung Gyi, at the entrance to the War Office (Ministry of Defense).

# LEGAL SHACKLES AND IMPEDIMENTS OF THE CARETAKER GOVERNMENT

As far as the memos in my old diaries indicate, the full Task Force met only a few times a month because of their other primary responsibilities as well as the length of time involved in getting the feedback information from the Ministries, Departments, Corporations and the Business Community. The Task Force also came to the stark realization of the Caretaker Government's "time limitation" to hold a free and fair general election and transfer State Power back to the elected party. The Generals and the Colonels also became aware of the fact that the promised General Election must be held in accordance with the flawed Constitution which in the first place led to the transfer of State Power by Parliament to the Military Commander-in-Chief to restore stability in the country. The first "Mandate from Parliament as recommended by Prime Minister U Nu" was to hold elections in six months but it was found to be practically impossible to do so in such a short time and was extended to 18 months by all concerned.

The Generals and the Colonels also realized that the Military's long term agenda was shackled and bound by the Constitution that did not work as envisaged by the AFPFL Party of Aung San. When Gen. Ne Win reviewed the Minutes of this meeting he was flabbergasted and remarked to Bo Aung Gyi, "We ran into their trap. We should have taken over and scrapped the Constitution." That was precisely what he did on March 02, 1962: dismissed Parliament, scrapped the Constitution, detained the entire Cabinet and placed the country under the rule of the Military Revolutionary Council led by him as Commander-in-Chief.

Looking back with the benefit of hindsight, the Caretaker Government was really a prelude and / or preparation for the overthrow and complete takeover of the country from the democratically elected Government of U Nu. However, it is noteworthy for the people of Myanmar and especially historians that none of the Task Force members were involved in "Bo Ne Win's planning of the takeover" (Except Bo Lwin the Intelligence Chief), although all Military Officers were included in the Revolutionary Council and Dr. Maung Maung was proposed for Foreign Minister but rejected by Gen. Ne Win as being "Western educated" and he chose U Thi Han to run the Ministry of Foreign Affairs (the only civilian in the Military Cabinet).

# FORMATION OF REVOLUTIONARY COUNCIL GOVERNMENT

Another noteworthy situation on the morning of the takeover (March 02, 1962) was at Dagon House where Gen. Aung Gyi received a phone call from Gen. Ne Win informing him that the Military had successfully taken over State Power from Prime Minister U Nu and to proceed with the formation of the Revolutionary Council Government and that all senior Ministry of Defense officers had been ordered to immediately report to the Vice Chief of General Staff. Bo Ne Win did not disclose from where he was calling and before hanging up Bo Aung Gyi informed him that Bo Hla Myint (Commander of Artillery & Armor) and Bo Than Sein (Colonel General Staff) were dancing with the troops in celebration, whereupon Bo Ne Win said "order those idiots to stop that nonsense and to return to barracks at once". By about 9 AM most of the senior officers – Admiral Than Phay, Gen. Tommy Clift, Gen. Tin Phay, Gen. SeinWin, Colonel Khin Nyo, Colonel Than Sein, Colonel Ba Ni, Colonel Kyaw Soe, Colonel Saw Myint, Colonel Thaung Kyi, Colonel Tan Yu Saing, Colonel (Dhamika) Ba Than, Colonel Kyi Maung (Rangoon Region Commander) and many others – were at Dagon House.

I was staying at the Kayah State Guest House (now the Governor's Hotel) and was woken at around 6:30 AM by a phone call from Col. Khin Nyo, informing me of the Coup and ordering me to proceed to the Export-Import Bank in downtown Rangoon to check the situation and to ensure its security, and to standby for further instructions. I was stopped on Prome Road and on seeing my Ministry of Defense Official ID the Captain commanding the troops of that location said he would escort me to the Bank in his car, leading the way as no civilian traffic is permitted on the roads. In front of the Bank there were combat-ready troops all over and another Captain came over to the two cars and I was escorted by the officers to enter the Bank premises. At around 9:30

AM I received a phone call from Col. Khin Nyo to come over to Dagon House and when told about the "No Civilian Traffic Order", he said an Army car would be sent to pick me up.

When I arrived at Dagon House the place was swarming with Generals and Colonels and the Conference Room was overflowing with the top brass going in and coming out. In the adjoining living (reception) room was a "working group" of Colonels Thaung Kyi, Khin Nyo, Dhamika Ba Than, Thein Maung and Saw Myint, who were standing in a corner engaged in discussing something serious. When they saw me Bo Khin Nyo said "you have showed up at the right time". Before I was able to gather my thoughts and figure out what was going on and the reason of their order for me to come over, the Colonels started asking the questions – "What is required under International law for us to do after takeover of State Power?" I said there is a Legal Division in the Ministry of Foreign Affairs and their official opinion would be the most appropriate one to get. I was shocked and taken aback to be told bluntly "those SOBs cannot be trusted" and "that is why we are asking you". I realized the seriousness and gravity of the situation and their mindset.

Without hesitation I said, "An official Statement needs to be issued by the entity (the Military in this case) that State Power has been assumed by the Military due to deteriorating internal domestic political circumstances and that our Foreign Policy of Strict Neutrality Remains Unchanged and further announcements will be made as needed." Bo Khin Nyo went into the Conference Room to tell Bo Aung Gyi of the need to issue an Official Statement ASAP and Bo Aung Gyi said "OK, draft one and bring it to us". I suggested that the Ministry of Foreign Affairs should be instructed to draft the statement under directive for our review and approval. The Ministry of Foreign Affairs until a few hours ago was under Sao Khun Khio, a Shan Saobwa with a British wife. The Permanent Secretary was James Barrington (ICS and an Anglo Burmese). The Secretary was U Tun Shein (BCS Class 1), and the Chief of Legal Division was U Ba Thaung (B.A., B.L., BCS).

Minister Sao Khun Khio was under detention and the Ministry that morning was being run by James Barrington and U Tun Shein. Bo Khin Nyo called Barrington on the phone and asked him to draft the "Statement" to be issued urgently. Within an hour the draft statement was delivered and Dhamika Bo Ba Than first reviewed it and then asked me to review and comment on it. I said it is more than adequate but Bo Ba Than, a very well read and an intellectual in his own right, wanted to be perfectly correct and ordered a Staff Captain to phone the Defense Ministry Library to send the Oxford and Webster's Dictionary to Dagon House Conference Room. After checking both the dictionaries we agreed that the draft statement was acceptable. The Statement was issued as a "Special announcement" by the Burma Broadcasting Service and signed by Colonel Ko Ko, Secretary of the Revolutionary Council.

Bo Aung Gyi very quickly and efficiently set up the Revolutionary Council and the Revolutionary Government. By about noon that day Bo Ne Win was back at his Ady Road Residence and in touch with Bo Aung Gyi on a secure line in Dagon House at the entrance of the Ministry of Defense, practically running the Revolutionary Council and the Revolutionary Government. All Ministries and Regional Military Commands were reporting to the Vice Chief of General Staff. By about 2 PM Bo Lwin (Moustache) showed up and reported to Bo Aung Gyi and conveyed the messages from Bo Ne Win and joined us in the working room. U Thi Han, on being informed that he is the Foreign Minister, came over to report to Bo Aung Gyi later that afternoon and was advised to discuss with the working group important issues of International Law and Diplomatic Protocol to be handled with the Diplomatic Corps in Rangoon.

While we were having tea in the Conference Room with several members of the Revolutionary Council, the Ministry of Foreign Affairs reported that Embassies in Rangoon were calling asking for clarification on the situation and requesting a meeting with the Ministry Officials. Bo Aung Gyi advised U Thi Han to quickly take charge of the Ministry of Foreign Affairs before the day is over and establish control and management of the situation. One could clearly notice that the newly appointed Foreign Minister, a mild mannered civilian, was cowed, uncomfortable at the prospect of grappling with the foreign affairs of the country with the bureaucracy whose Minister has been rudely removed and detained early that morning. However, the poor man had no option but to obey the marching orders from the #2 General of the Revolutionary Council and proceed to the Ministry of Foreign Affairs. Bo Lwin (Moustache), the Chief of Military Intelligence, asked me, "What is the most important requirement in International Law for us to understand and observe?"

Without hesitation I said, "Recognition, Full Fledged Recognition (the Legal Definition is De-Jure Recognition). It is very critical for the Revolutionary Council and the Revolutionary Government to receive early De-Jure Recognition from Major World Powers (Five Permanent Members of the U.N. Security Council) and close neighboring countries." It was therefore urgently imperative for the Ministry of Foreign Affairs to invite the Ambassadors in Rangoon, starting with the Dean of the Diplomatic Corps, and express the desire and wish for continuation of Diplomatic Relations with that country and to instruct our Ambassador in that country to convey that sentiment to the Ministry of Foreign Affairs of the host country. I further explained that it is very unlikely that the Foreign Ambassadors in Rangoon would "respond negatively" as they were requesting an appointment to call on the Ministry of Foreign Affairs as well as the fact that the Revolutionary Council was in "full and complete control of the entire country without any resistance whatsoever". The reality on the ground that Gen. Ne Win, the Commander-in-Chief of the Burmese Military, was in complete control would have already been reported by the Embassies in Rangoon to their Governments soon after the "Official Statement of the Revolutionary Council was broadcast by BBS".

However, there was still insecurity and concern on the part of some Council Members, and Bo Tan Yu Saing who had served as Defense Attaché at the Burmese Embassy in Washington DC asked, "What if an Ambassador responded negatively and raised the question of legitimacy of the Coup? What should be our response?" To firmly ask for closure of their Embassy ASAP. And to instruct our Embassy in their country to close according to Diplomatic Protocol and return ASAP. This is not the time and issue to negotiate as this Ambassador must have received instructions from his Government to challenge the legitimacy of the Revolutionary Council. This is the time to be firm and resolute in letting the rest of the world know that the entire country was firmly and completely under the Revolutionary Council's control. U Thi Han apparently was quite relieved after this briefing and said he had now grasped the immediate urgent issues at stake and how to proceed. Armed with that knowledge and guidance he was escorted to the Ministry of Foreign Affairs by a Staff Officer and a carload of troops. Bo Tan Yu Saing called Permanent Secretary James Barrington on the phone and told him that the Foreign Minister was on his way.

Bo Maung Lwin (Moustache) asked me to accompany him to his office where he wanted me to review some documents in English. It was a good ten minutes' walk from Dagon House to the Ministry of Defense main building complex. I realized that his real purpose was to get me out of the crowd of Revolutionary Council members for a private chat. During the walk followed by the security detail some distance behind, the Intelligence revealed that this Coup is a game changer for all concerned and the Military was in uncharted waters, especially with running the country and dealing with the rest of the world. One could clearly notice that security was tight with soldiers in full combat gear in the huge estate grounds as well as in the corridors of the main building. He revealed to me that the "work of the Action Plan for the UK, Europe and U.S." would be expedited and to be prepared for the important foreign assignment by the RC Chairman. He cautioned me to keep it to myself. I was taken aback, surprised and rather concerned that he did not want others to know when in reality I was serving in several capacities – Export-Import Bank, Burma Economic Development Corporation (BEDC), ACTION PLAN COMMITTEE (Ministry of Defense), RESETTLEMENT COORDINATION (Ministry of Defense) reporting directly to Gen. Aung Gyi, Vice Chief of General Staff, Admiral Than Phay and two other Colonels – Khin Nyo, and Maung Lwin (Moustache). And yet another job is going to be added.

In the Military Intelligence H.Q. we were greeted by Captain Kyaw Zwa Myint (Johnny Lears), Lt. Col. Thein Shwe (Charlie), Lt. Col. Tin Oo (Spectacle) and Major Lay Maung – top aides to the Chief. After a brief tea break in his office, we moved to an adjoining secure room. He ordered Charlie to bring the "intercept file" and to join us. As required I signed the "review register" and Bo Lwin signed the "approving officer column". I went through the file and learned that the Ambassadors of the major powers in Rangoon has been in contact with their respective governments throughout the night. Within a matter of a few hours of the Statement being issued by the Revolutionary Council, most of the Diplomatic Missions and the UN Representative Office in Rangoon had received instructions from their respective governments to call on the Ministry of Foreign Affairs and "Extend Formal Recognition of the Revolutionary Council Government".

I was relieved and happy that the clarifications I had given to the International Law Questions raised by RC Members were right on the money. Bo Maung Lwin congratulated me and shook my hands and said, "You have studied your subject well at Tokyo University and I am very impressed that you responded with confidence to the critical questions raised by the RC Members. No wonder that Bogyoke has such a high impression of 'our young Japun kaung-lay'." It seems that I had passed the most crucial test at the critical juncture of the Military's takeover of State Power on the question of relations with other Nations and allayed the concerns of the Revolutionary Council members with correct and accurate evaluations that were confirmed by the information gleaned from Intelligence assets and resources. Charlie and Bo Tin Oo (Spectacle) were wide eyed and surprised when Bo Maung Lwin (Moustache) remarked, "This young fellow here had figured out what we are seeing in this file. I will report this to Bogyoke and he will be very pleased."

Our review of the intercept file was just about half way through when the working group in Dagon House called for me to return with the staff officer sent to fetch me in a car instead of walking back. It was late afternoon and I could clearly see that a dozen or so Generals and Colonels were exhausted and pushing on with the help of caffeine and willpower. A few were already snoring in the sofas of the reception room. As instructed by Bo Maung Lwin (Moustache) I briefed Bo Aung Gyi, Admiral Than Phay, Gen. Tommy Clift and the working group Colonels – Thaung Kyi, Khin Nyo, Ba Ni, Thein Maung, Saw Myint, Than Sein and Dhamika Ba Than on the "Intercept File" review and the information gleaned from it confirming full-fledged recognition by the permanent members of the UN Security Council. It was a huge step forward for the Military and the Revolutionary Council.

Bo Aung Gyi ordered drinks from the bar and food from China Town Restaurant to be delivered and served in the Conference Room and the reception room buffet style. It was a very somber celebration of exhausted Generals and Colonels without their Commander-in-Chief. Bo Maung Lwin and his officers came to join the celebration. By the time I arrived back in Kayah

State Guest House where I was staying at the time it was past 11 PM. Rangoon was back to normal life except for Armored Personnel carriers patrolling the major streets and strategic locations being guarded by Rangoon Command Troops. There was no time to reflect on the eventful day as I fell asleep as soon as my head hit the pillow and I awoke the next morning at 6:30 with a phone call from Dagon House to come over for a breakfast meeting with the "working group" at 8 AM. Traditional Burmese sweet rice (white & brown), naan with fried peas and Indian Parata was served with coffee and tea. Bo San Yu, the Northern Region Commander, had arrived the previous night by special plane and as usual was staying at Dagon House with Bo Aung Gyi.

The sudden change of circumstances would require job assignments to be readjusted at every level especially those entrusted under Bo Aung Gyi's Management and Control, additional to the Vice Chief of General Staff (VCGS) position in the Ministry of Defense. On that morning (March 03, 1962) Official Orders were issued appointing Bo Khin Nyo Deputy Chairman of Burma Economic Development Corporation (BEDC) and Burma Oil Company (BOC) in addition to Chairman of Burma Railways Board. Bo Aung Gyi could not relinquish his Chairman position in the two organizations because of Legal Restraints. I was officially transferred from Export-Import Bank to BEDC Head Office (Prime Minister's Office) as Legal Adviser concurrently to VCGS Ministry of Defense (UK, EU, U.S. Action Plan Committee) and Burma Oil Company (BOC). The latter being "Covert Operation" of Bo Ne Win it was placed under the Chief of Military Intelligence. It was truly a complicated, confusing act of juggling, working closely with the three powerful officers of the Military establishment and innermost circle of Bo Ne Win's "Seat of Power" of the Revolutionary Council and Government.

The minutes of the meeting were forwarded to Col. Ko Ko, Secretary of the Revolutionary Council as all the changes – appointments and transfers – required Cabinet approval. The meeting ended around 10 AM as Bo Aung Gyi and others needed to take charge of the Ministries assigned to them. I was ordered to accompany Bo Khin Nyo to BOC Head Office to meet the Management and clarify the Revolutionary Government's position and policies on business relations with Joint Ventures with foreign corporations and entities. We were ushered to the Conference Room by Mr. Strain, the British

Managing Director, and later joined by U San Cho (Stanley), the General Manager, U Khin Hlaing, Deputy General Manager, U Myo Nyunt, National Sales Manager, Barrister U Maung Gyee, Chief of Legal Division and Percy the Chief Accountant.

Strain and all his Burmese cohorts were in a state of shock, disbelief and clearly intimidated by the appearance of a member of the Revolutionary Council accompanied by the very person assigned to BOC by the Caretaker Government a few years previously. On the way in the car Bo Khin Nyo asked me for suggestions of what to tell the Management. I advised him to stress the importance of continuing the company operations smoothly as before and as the Executive Deputy Chairman of the Corporation representing the Revolutionary Government, he was always ready to assist the Management in finding resolutions to any problems encountered in the course of running the operations and business activities.

"At this particular time, the Revolutionary Government's policy on such joint ventures with foreign entities remains unchanged. Please do not hesitate to contact U Kyi Win Sein, Legal Adviser to Gen. Aung Gyi (Vice Chief of General Staff, Ministry of Defense), Chairman of BOC and Minister of Trade and Commerce of the Revolutionary Government for any assistance and guidance you may need. He will assist me in carrying out the responsibilities of the Deputy Chairman of the Board of Directors of Burma Oil Company. In this regard I would appreciate your understanding and cooperation." We then proceeded to the Head Office of the Burma Economic Development Corporation and were received by U Soe Myint, Chief Executive Officer and U Ba Thein, Managing Director and U Htun Minn, the Administrative Officer and Chief Financial Officer. Bo Khin Nyo explained the new management set up put in place today (March 03, 1962) by the Revolutionary Council Government as Gen. Aung Gyi had been assigned the heavy responsibility of managing the day-today Administration and Management of the Government in addition to the Ministry of Trade and Commerce.

"The Management of BEDC has been assigned to the Deputy Chairman (Bo khin Nyo) assisted by U Kyi Win Sein, Legal Adviser. However, since this Corporation is legally under the Prime Minister's Office the final approval and authorization must be submitted to the Chairman (Gen. Aung Gyi), the nominee of Gen. Ne Win the Prime Minister to 'Administer BEDC on his behalf'. Please ensure that all the Corporations and their subsidiaries numbering more than 75 continue to operate and function normally." Despite the speed of our move to assure these State owned business enterprises, one could clearly notice the apprehension, fear of uncertainty of their positions and how much trust could be placed in the Army that had just toppled the democratically elected Government of U Nu. Without exception the State owned business enterprises at that time were run by the educated elite technocrats of Burmese society and BEDC Corporations were held in high regard by the domestic business communities as well as the overseas international trading partners in Asia, Europe and the U.S.

It would definitely take a toll on the trust and confidence the international business community had prior to the takeover of the country by the Army. From the silence and body language of the executives, it was quite evident to both of us the urgent need for the Revolutionary Council Government to issue its political economic policy to the country as well as the international community. Bo Khin Nyo expressed his personal concern of the daunting tasks ahead of us but quickly added that with Bo Aung Gyi's business acumen and the high regard and respect accorded to him by the Burmese commercial enterprises and overseas traders and Governments, we would be able to move forward and develop the country's economy. Looking back with the benefit of hindsight, there was a huge gap in the mindset of Bo Ne Win and the "rational thinking" members of the Revolutionary Council such as Bo Aung Gyi, Bo Tommy Clift, Bo Khin Nyo, Dhamika Bo Ba Than, Bo Saw Myint, Bo Lwin (Moustache), Bo Chit Myaing, Bo Thaung Kyi and others.

However, the "yes men" without any clue as to how the country's economy functions went along with Bo Ne Win, also with no knowledge of national economic fundamentals, but bent on experimenting Aung San's flawed "Day Dream Wishful Thinking" document (BLUEPRINT FOR INDEPENDENT BURMA) written while holed up in General Suzuki's home in Hamamatsu awaiting the final decision of the Imperial General Staff to give military training to the 30 Comrades, to establish Burma Army to liberate Burma from British colonial rule. Aung San could not implement his thesis so Bo Ne Win was going to do it regardless of foreseen consequences to the people and country. All those opposing his decision to proceed with this "Blue Print of Aung San" with the name "BURMESE WAY TO SOCIALISM" were removed and detained in prison. Bo Aung Gyi, the No. 2 General of the Military and the one who stood by Bo Ne Win through thick and thin, spent 7.5 years in prison for telling him that it would lead to catastrophic failure and it did. From the Rice Basket of Asia in 1962 to the poorest, least developed nation in the world in 1988.

# THE UNEXPECTED CHALLENGE TO THE REVOLUTIONARY COUNCIL

The situation stabilized quickly and everything returned to business as usual. I was still staying at the Kayah State Guest House off Helpin Road, juggling between several offices including the Export-Import Bank and its subsidiary Ava Insurance as well as Inya Lake Hotel which was placed under BEDC. In early May 1962, after the Action Plan meeting in the "secure room" of the Intelligence Office, Bo Maung Lwin (Moustache) asked me to accompany him to Dagon House where Bo Aung Gyi and Bo Khin Nyo were having a discussion in the Conference Room. Bo Aung Gyi told us that the RC Chairman had ordered him to expedite the "Action Plan Implementation" as he was concerned that the politicians and their business cronies (British, Sino-Burmese, Indo-Burmese) with their hidden financial assets could "destabilize the situation inside the country. It is urgently imperative to retrieve those hidden financial assets and take control ASAP". He also mentioned that Marshal Tito of Yugoslavia would extend cooperation in UK and Europe. This discussion must be confined to the four of us.

"This covert operation will not be easy and must be pursued with great care because it must be implemented in London as a normal BEDC business and commercial project." Bo Aung Gyi looked at me and said "your experience with the Middle East Kalars will be most crucial". I was lost for words and thought it would be best to remain silent, at least for now. As usual the meeting ended with takeout dinner noodles and barbecued pork from the open air market. The next day Bo Maung Lwin (Moustache) revealed to me that some politicians from the deposed party were conspiring with their business associates and foreign cash "to create trouble in the country" and Bogyoke (General) wants to quickly eliminate that threat". I quickly realized that it was a difficult and confusing time for all concerned with so many unrelated and diverse issues raised and thrown at you by those in the seat of power at the same time. There was no way for one to focus on a single issue and tackle it because the priority changes according to the maximum leader's agenda. For the next several weeks the "Action Plan" group meeting was called every day at Dagon House in the evening for Bo Aung Gyi to preside over the deliberations and move the project forward as ordered by the RC Chairman.

The governance and administration of the country was running well, with the civil service bureaucrats cowed into submission and marching to the orders of the uniformed Officers on Special Duty (OSDs) assigned to all Ministries, Departments and Corporations. This was achieved at a rather high cost of the economy slowing down to a snail's pace due to an additional layer of "Red Tape" at the top. Foreign trade, import-export, banking, insurance, transportation, trucking, shipping almost came to a stop. The military officers' learning curve of these specialized professional business practices was steep due to the mediocre education level of High School for most of them. Payments for good and services, money transfers, letters of credit were delayed for weeks. The British, Indian, Chinese, Japanese and European companies began to suffer losses and Ministry of Trade and Commerce under Bo Aung Gyi received a deluge of letters from Commercial Attachés of Foreign Embassies in Rangoon complaining regarding non-payment for goods awaiting shipment at ports all over the world. The situation was serious and immediate resolution was imperative. I witnessed the same situation in Egypt after nationalization of businesses and the banking-insurance industries.

I suggested that day-to-day routine transactions be delegated to "department professionals / specialists" as before and exempted from submission to the OSDs along the lines of the Egyptian Nationalization Committee policy. Military Officers were directed to focus on "General Policy Issues" and to assist the Departments in implementing the policy directives from their respective Ministries. The improvement was dramatic and the backlog was quickly resolved and the morale and productivity of the professionals and specialists in the banks, shipping and insurance companies increased to a very high level. Bo Aung Gyi's understanding and knowledge of the commercial world and willingness to accept and appreciate the advice and counsel of those around him made the difference in this particular case. A serious international trade conflict and diplomatic confrontation was averted by the Minister's decisive action in defining the role of the Military officers assigned to Ministries, Departments and Corporations.

# CONSPIRACY OF POLITICIANS AND CHINESE MAFIA

In the midst of struggling to keep ahead of the ever increasing workload, one late afternoon I received a phone call from Bo Khin Nyo to come over to Dagon House for an important meeting. When I arrived at the Conference Room Admiral Than Phay, Bo San Yu (Finance Minister), Bo Lwin (Moustache), Bo Khin Nyo and U Thi Han were already there. The topic of discussion surprised me at first. Apparently the intelligence discovered that the politicians of the Union Party (U Nu) and some from the Stable AFPFL (Swe-Nyein) had come together for cooperation to survive as political parties. To move towards that goal financial resources had to be acquired quickly from their friends, associates and partners in the business communities that they had helped and nurtured during the time they controlled the Government since January 1948. The time had now come for those business associates and friends to "pay back" in gratitude the riches accumulated here and abroad with our help. The discovery of this conspiracy was a direct challenge and threat to Bo Ne Win and his Revolutionary Council Government. U Nu and his entire Cabinet and President Mahn Win Maung were all locked up from the morning of the Coup and now the politicians plotting with the Chinese had joined the deposed ministers in prison.

Additionally, all the China towns of major cities such as Rangoon, Mandalay, Bassein, Moulmein, Pegu and those in the Shan States were swept clean of the various "Chinese Clans and Factions". The most conspicuous were the Hong Kong, Singapore, Taiwan and Mainland Yunan, Canton, etc. It was executed with such speed and thoroughness that even the Chinese Embassy in Rangoon was caught by complete surprise and shock as all their "human assets" suddenly vanished overnight. The innermost circle around Bo Ne Win – Bo Aung Gyi, Bo San Yu, Bo Lwin (Moustache), Bo Thaung Kyi, Bo Khin Nyo and Bo Ko Ko, Secretary to the Revolutionary Council, were involved in the planning and execution of the operation. The primary objective I later learned was to deny them all possible access to the "ill-gotten money hidden overseas" and to gain time for the "Action Plan" to establish the necessary organization in London and to move forward with the implementation to gain control of the hidden money. Bo Maung Lwin (Moustache), with his training and experience from the British Imperial Police Detective Special Branch, was at his best in infiltration tactics and nurturing moles and sleeping cells in the various racial / ethnic communities with overseas network connections and up to date on developments of "who is doing what" at any given time and place. The foreign connections and State entities were scrambling to determine the true state of affairs as to the intent of the Burmese strong man and how to react to it. It shattered the myth that Burma's Military lacked the will to take on the rich British, Chinese, Indian and the politicians bought and paid for and in their pockets.

In our subsequent discussions of the legal ramifications of detention without trial and / or bail, the Attorney General and the Judge Advocate General of the Ministry of Defense concurred that Section 5 of POPA (Public Order Protection Act) would allow detention of 180 days without presentation to Court for trial. It would give us the crucial time to set up our organization in London and recruit the necessary personnel with experience and expertise supported by the best legal, banking and financial professionals available in the UK and Europe. I was instructed to focus attention on the "organization structure and the immediate operational procedures to quickly achieve the desired outcomes" for submission to Gen. Ne Win for prior approval before my departure for London" as all Ministry of Defense overseas extended covert projects required the prior authorization and approval of the Minister of Defense and the Commander-in-Chief. Under the strict secrecy requirements there was no one I could turn to for help and guidance. Once again in my life I had no other option but to start from scratch for a job I did not go after but was thrust on me by those in the seat of State Power.

The top secret official authorization and approval was issued by Col. Ko Ko, Secretary to the Revolutionary Council with the names of Officers assigned with the task of implementing, managing and supporting the "UK Action Plan Organization in London" – Gen. Aung Gyi, Revolutionary Council Member and Minister of Trade and Commerce, Gen. San Yu, Revolutionary Council Member and Minister of Finance and Revenue, Gen. Tommy Clift, Revolutionary Council Member and Minister of Transport and Communication, Col. Khin Nyo, Revolutionary Council Member and Chairman, Burma Economic Development Corporation (BEDC), Col. Maung Lwin, Chief of Military Intelligence Service (MIS), U Kyi Win Sein, Legal Adviser (BEDC), and Chief Executive Officer (CEO) BEDC Representative Office UK, London. The Revolutionary Council Order was confined and restricted to the five officers only. I was issued with Official Identification Credentials under the Signature of Gen. Aung Gyi, Revolutionary Council Member and Minister of Trade and Commerce and another under the Signature of Col. Khin Nyo, Revolutionary Member and Chairman of (BEDC) Certifying my Official Status in the Government and Accreditation to be Head of the Revolutionary Council Government Trade and Commercial Representative Office in London, UK.

I was staying at the Kayah State Guest House awaiting the return of Kazuko and Bob to Rangoon but with the new developments I thought it would be better for mother and toddler to join me in London and save the hassle of getting her visa and the travel document for the child. However, when I discussed the plan with Bo Maung Lwin (Moustache) he said he would instruct the Ministry of Foreign Affairs to cable the Embassy in Tokyo to immediately issue the visa and the travel document for the child. I requested the BEDC travel agent to wire the air tickets to Tokyo. It took a few weeks for mother and son to prepare for the trip and they arrived back in Rangoon in early June 1962.

*Maung Nyo, Major-General (Retired) Former Vice Adjutant General (Ministry of Defense)*

*General Aung Gyi*

*General Ne Win*

*General San Yu*

*General Aung Gyi in Myanmar attire*

*Senior Gen. Saw Maung*

*Colonel Khin Nyo*

*General Ne Win*

*General Aung Gyi in Tokyo leading Burmese Delegation to signing of Final Reparations Agreement 1963*

*Bo Khin Maung Galay, Burma Independence Army*

*General Ne Win*

*General Aung Gyi, official photo, Ministry of Defense*

*General Aung Gyi at his desk*

*General Ne Win Commander-in-Chief and General Aung Gwi Vice Chief of General Staff*

*General Aung Gwi and General Tommy Clift, Airforce Chief of Staff*

*In student uniform, University of Tokyo Law School 1955*

*Mal Kyi Win Sein, first Burmese State Scholar to University of Tokyo Law School after WWII*

*Mal Sein receiving Golf Championship trophy from Dr Ba Oo, President of Burma for Irrawaddy Division Champion 1953*

*Official wedding portrait: Teruo and Hideko Godo, Mal and Kazuko Ueda Sein, April 16, 1959*

*Group photo of wedding, April 16, 1959*

*Mal Kyi Win Sein and Kazuko Ueda, April 16, 1959*

With best friends standing l-r Major Aye
Kyaw, Assistant Military Attaché, Duwa
Mike Maran Jala, Dr Ko Ko Lay
Sitting: Mal and Kazuko Sein

*Mal Sein and Okuda, collaborator and
friend of Ne Win and Aung San*

*International Students Union and Japanese government leaders conference: Mr Takeo Miki
(2nd from left) and his Education Minister (in Japanese dress) and Foreign Minister. Mal Sein,
founder and President of Union standing behind Education and Foreign Ministers*

*Bo Khin Maung Galay, Deputy Prime Minister with Marshal Tito of Yugoslavia*

*General Aung Gyi with Alan Dulles, US CIA Director and Colonel Saw Myint*

*General Aung Gyi and Admiral Than Phay with Egyptian Ambassador to Burma 1960*

*L-r Mal Sein, Teruo Godo, Mrs Javan, Hideko Godo, Kazuko Sein*

*L-r Robert Sein, Luke Moore, Teruo Godo, Mal Sein and Sasan Javan*

*L-r Luke Moore, Teruo Godo and Mal Sein*

*Colonel Khin Nyo with US representative and Mal Sein*

*Hon. Nakao Eiichi, Minister of Economic Development with Colonel Khin Nyo, Senior General Saw Maung's personal envoy and Mal Sein*

# OVERSEAS FINANCIAL TRANSACTIONS – PAYMENTS AND RECEIPTS

Compiling the list of documents relating to overseas payments in the form of letters of credit, bank transfers by wire, drafts and bankers checks from the Ministry of Trade and Commerce Directorate of Exports and Imports and from the Union Bank of Burma was not only time consuming but stressful due to the bureaucratic "Red Tape" compounded by the "release authorization" rules and regulations. With Bo Aung Gyi being the Minister at the Ministry of Trade and Commerce it was the prerogative of the Minister to waive the rules and regulations and order the Head of the Ministry Archives to release them after proper receipt and registration. However, the Union Bank of Burma under the Ministry of Finance and Revenue made attempts to put up fear factor barriers of sovereign assets and debts, gold reserves, Government to Government Financial Transactions and Agreements and Negative Repercussions from Foreign Governments and Traditional Trading Partners. Gen. San Yu, a very soft and risk averse, mild person, despite being a member of the "Action Plan Group", hesitated to issue the "Waiver Order" within our required time constraints.

Instead he consulted with the four members of the "Support and Management Group" perhaps with the mindset of should things go awry we are all responsible for the decision. Bo Aung Gyi and the three were aghast but Bo San Yu being a close personal friend since their High School days told him that the only option would be to submit the matter to Bo Ne Win. Now, that was the last thing Bo San Yu wanted to do. Bo Aung Gyi understood the over-cautious character and demeanor of his friend and suggested that he ask Bo Maung Lwin (Moustache) to call U San Lin, the Governor of the Union Bank of Burma, to release the requested information and documents to U Kyi Win Sein as soon as practically possible. The next morning Bo San Yu went over to the Intelligence Department and asked the Chief exactly what his friend suggested. Bo Lwin (Moustache) immediately picked up his phone (in the presence of Bo San Yu), asked his aide to get U San Lin on the line and told him what to do and that I would be calling on him soon.

Bo San Yu thanked him and went on to the Ministry of Finance. I was with Bo Khin Nyo at the BEDC Head Office when he conveyed the message to me from the MIS Chief to visit with the Union Bank Governor soon. It was clear evidence that a phone order from the Intelligence Chief supersedes any and all Government Rules and Regulations. Once again the intelligence chief was the one to lean on the senior civil service bureaucrat of the country's central bank to comply ASAP. When I arrived at the Union Bank of Burma the security officer asked for my Ministry of Defense ID and escorted me to the Governor's well-appointed reception room adjoining his office. He greeted me with an incredulous expression on his face, staring at my face for a couple of seconds before extending his hand with the remark "I was expecting someone of my age". I told him that I am now used to that greeting and we both had a laugh. We were joined by the Chief Administrative Officer responsible for "Classified and Confidential Bank Transactions and Documents Archives". I handed U San Lin the 15-20 pages of documents list required and he was visibly shaken by the volume, the categories and depth, going back to the inception of the Central Bank for the newly independent Union of Burma in January 1948.

The Chief Administrative Officer reviewed the list and remarked that it was very well prepared along the lines of the "banking system and operations procedures" but that it would take six weeks to two months for location, duplication and proper recording and special budget allocation to cover the cost. I said they were needed urgently and U San Lin instructed his CAO to deploy extra staff and overtime work to expedite the collection. I requested "secure packing in heavy duty cartons or proper boxes" and to inform Col. Lwin (Moustache), Chief of Military Intelligence in the Ministry of Defense, or Col. Khin Nyo, Chairman of BEDC. As I was leaving U San Lin asked for my business card. I could see that he was surprised and quite taken aback to see "U Kyi Win Sein, Legal Adviser to Chairman (BEDC), Office of the Prime Minister". He escorted me right out to the Bank's entry door to the surprise of the bank staff. In about four weeks' time the Intelligence Chief received a phone call from the Central Bank Governor that the documents were ready.

He sent one staff officer in a pick-up truck to get the 15 boxes to National Defense College Secure Conference Room for our Special Staff to review, sort and pack the documents to be shipped (as Diplomatic Baggage) to the Defense Attaché's Office, London, UK for safekeeping until my arrival. It was a huge monumental undertaking and my experience in the United Arab Republic (UAR) in President Gamal Abdel Nasser's Nationalization of the Banking, Insurance, Export-Import, Shipping Industries and Retrieval of hidden assets and money by King Farouk helped greatly to prepare for the Action Plan in the UK, Europe and the U.S. It is appropriate at this stage to categorically state that the UAR Egyptian Regime under Nasser did honor their promise to Marshal Tito and General Ne Win to open up and allow us access to their innermost working and operational practices in dealing with the hegemonic political and economic policies of the Zionists supported by the WEST and the stolen wealth of the country hidden by the ruling elite in the UK, U.S., Europe and Swiss Banks and Corporations.

It was indeed an eye opener and game changer because without such active support and cooperation the domination of our economic, business and commerce by foreign elements would have prolonged for many more years or even decades. This is the lesson we learned and the knowledge gained that I want to share with the current and future leaders of Myanmar. To engage with the rest of the world but to be on guard always and selective in choosing your friends bearing in mind that "Countries do not have permanent friends only permanent interests".

# POLITICIANS SUCKERED INTO GIVING AWAY COUNTRY'S RESOURCES

When the last British ruler, Governor Hubert Rance, was sent off in the early hours on January 04, 1948, the economy of the country barely three years after the end of WWII was in fairly good health with a few million tons of rice exports bringing in revenues in foreign currencies. However, the trading, commerce, export-import, international banking, cottage and small industries were all in the hands of the British, Indians, Chinese and their cronies. That dismal situation was compounded by the AFPFL Government of Prime Minister U Nu which inherited a plethora of one-sided legally binding business contracts with British, European and Scandinavian corporations practically giving away the rich resources of the country like Oil (energy), Lumber, Minerals, Export of Agricultural products and Import business under the control of the Indians and Chinese. The Prime Minister and his Ministers, drunk with the newly acquired political power, did not have the time or the sense to review these imposed blatantly unfair contracts on the country but went about lining their pockets with bribes from these business parasites.

The Revolutionary Council Government Prime Minister Gen. Ne Win hit the ceiling when he learned that all Teak and Hard Wood lumber export from Burma was exclusively controlled by the Scandinavian Teak and Lumber Federation. At a Cabinet Meeting he asked Gen. Tin Phay, the Minister of Agriculture and Forests, why such a deplorable situation existed and was told that a binding legal contract left the Government with no option. He was incredulous and ordered Bo Aung Gyi and Bo Tin Phay to have the contracts reviewed by the legal specialists and terminate them under any circumstances. Bo Tin Phay freaked out and passed the buck to Bo Aung Gyi, the Trade and Commerce Minister, who in turn leaned on Col. Solomon, the Judge Advocate

General with only a B.L. degree from Rangoon University, where only the bare minimum rudiments of "International Business Contracts" are included in the curriculum of the two year Degree Course.

In the midst of my busy preparations for the imminent move to London, Bo Aung Gyi instructed me to review the Contract between the State Timber Board (STB) and the Scandinavian Teak and Hardwood Federation (STHF) and to discuss the matter with Bo Khin Nyo and Bo Myo Myint, Chairman of STB. I was shocked to learn that the "Exclusive Distribution Rights of all Burma Teak and Hard Products was given to STHF in perpetuity". U Nu, the Prime Minister, and his Minister of Trade and Commerce Minister U Rashid (a Burmese muslim with links to the Bengali community in Maungdaw and Buthidaung in Arakan State) nonchalantly accepted and sat on these Trade Concessions entered into by the British Colonial Government.

I reported my findings to Bo Aung Gyi and Bo Khin Nyo with the explanation of (1) the Fundamental Principle in Jurisprudence States: "imposed unfair Agreements and/or Contracts are NOT BINDING AND UNENFORCEABLE IN A COURT OF LAW" and (2) In all Agreement and/or Contracts between a Government and any State or Private Entity (A Company / Corporation) there is always an UNWRITTEN SOVREIGNTY CLAUSE (3) Therefore all these Contracts can be terminated at the sole discretion of the Sovereign Government of a Country. Bo Aung Gyi, always a considerate person of highest integrity, asked me to touch base with Col. Solomon, the Judge Advocate General, and bring him into the loop. The soldier lawyer was elated and as a true professional he quietly admitted to me that "it was definitely the difference between a two year condensed degree course and a full four years of specialization in the study of Jurisprudence and Relevant Laws". As an Anglo-Indian, I fully sympathized with Col. Solomon's delicate position in the scheme of things of the power structure in the Ministry of Defense.

He was respected and held in high regard by his fellow senior officers but it is an entirely different matter when those in the "innermost circle of the seat of power" officially seek your professional interpretation and clarification of a Legal Contract concluded by the past British Colonial Government of Burma with a Foreign Business Corporation. At that level one could encounter all kinds of unforeseen complications especially if your professional (Legal) opinion is on shaky grounds. It could very well be your last day in office or in the worst case you could be accused of being the lackey of the "Imperial West" and detained for questioning lasting many months or even years. Those were times when the saying "the messenger was killed" becomes very real. The good Col. Solomon thanked me profusely and expressed his appreciation for my due diligent reading of the Relevant Laws and correct interpretation of the "Hidden Tenets of International Law Principles". It definitely saved the day for Gen. Aung Gyi, the Trade and Commerce Minister, and Gen. Tin Phay, the Minister of Agriculture and Forests, who was actually the one in the hot seat.

In the final briefing session with all the members of the Action Plan Committee before my departure for London I was instructed to stop over at Copenhagen and meet the Scandinavian Lumber Federation and serve notice of the Revolutionary Council Government's intention to review the contract with them to revise, amend or terminate if absolutely necessary in the national interest. Lt.Col. Myo Myint, the Chairman of State Timber Board (STB), was also instructed to accompany me up to Copenhagen to participate in the negotiations. Since I was in a hurry to get to London and travelling with the family, I asked the Scandinavians to meet us in our hotel conference room. The Chairman of the Federation, the Managing Director and three attorneys showed up to meet me and the STB Chairman. After an exchange of business cards, one could clearly see that the five white men impeccably attired in three-piece suits were staring at my card and they exchanged words in Danish (I assumed) because it only had on it "U Kyi Win Sein, Legal Adviser, Burma Economic Development Corporation, Office of the Prime Minister, Revolutionary Government of the Union of Burma". I had with me other Official Credentials but the business card served the purpose. Normally, Attorneys would ask for Official Credentials that Certify Full Power and Authority to Represent and Negotiate on behalf of the Sovereign Government of a Country.

The Scandinavian Federation maintained their position and insisted that the Contract they had with the British Colonial Government of Burma (Duly Accepted and Endorsed by the Independent Government of Burma since 1948) was binding on the succeeding Independent Governments of Burma under International Law. I informed them that the Political Government that succeeded the British Colonial Government was OVERTHROWN BY THE MILITARY, "Parliament Dismissed and the Constitution of the Country Abrogated". "The Country is now under the control of the Revolutionary Council headed by the Commander-in-Chief of the Military. The New Revolutionary Government is recognized by a majority of the UN (including all Scandinavian Countries) and all Five Members of the UN Security Council."

I stated firmly that we would not hesitate to "Invoke the Unwritten Sovereignty Clause" to remedy the contents of the contract detrimental to the National Interests of the Country and if necessary terminate it entirely. The three Lawyers said they would take us to Court for abrogation of the Contract. I said "if you elect to go down the litigation path, as a Sovereign Government we will challenge the Jurisdiction and Competency of the Court and reject it outright". The elderly Chairman was visibly shaken by what he heard and said it would be very regrettable and unfortunate for Denmark that has had business with Burma for nearly a century predating the advent of the British colonization. He asked if there was any possibility of continuing the business relations with the Revolutionary Government. I told him that "option" was definitely on the table but "on entirely new terms and conditions compatible with the National Interests of the Country" incorporated in a New Contract.

The Old Contract in question was no longer valid nor relevant as far as the Revolutionary Council was concerned and would be terminated as of this date. The Chairman wanted the assurance of negotiations for a new contract with their Federation to take place in Copenhagen or in London. I said that would not be feasible and the negotiations would have to be in Rangoon within 30 days of the termination of the current Contract. I explained to them that I would dictate the letter of termination to their stenographer in which their Federation would be invited to Rangoon for negotiations on a New Contract. I asked Col. Myo Myint if he brought STB Letterhead Stationery because I wanted him to sign the termination letter. Regretably he did not have any with him. I had a pad of BEDC HEAD OFFICE (OFFICE OF THE PRIME MINISTER) Letterhead stationery and the Official Termination Letter was typed on it and I signed it as Legal Adviser and Col. Myo Myint signed it as Witness. Several "Originals were Executed" and the STHF Chairman signed on three Originals his "Acknowledgment accepting the Termination and the Invitation to negotiate a New Contract in Rangoon".

It was an event of historical significance for both parties but as time was short, I had to fly on to London and Col. Myo Myint return to Rangoon, report to the Government and prepare for the negotiations. On my flight to London, I drafted a detailed report to Gen. Aung Gyi, Minister of Trade and Commerce, and my immediate superior Col. Khin Nyo, Chairman of BEDC, stressing the essential and critical terms and conditions that needed to be in the New Contract. The unshackling of these chains put on the Burmese economy and its rich resources by the British, Europeans, Israelis and the Americans was a high priority on the agenda of Gen. Ne Win who recognized the threat to his regime if left as things were like the politicians had done for fourteen years.

This stark awareness emerged during the Caretaker Government period and immediate attention and efforts were directed by the elite top general staff officers led by Bo Aung Gyi, Bo Maung Maung, Bo Khin Nyo, Bo Aung Shwe, Bo Thaung Kyi, Bo Saw Myint backed by Bo Ne Win. However, their efforts were hampered and held back by their psyche, paranoia, prejudice and disdain of any Burmese educated in the WEST as lacking patriotism and subservience to their Western Masters. That mindset was firmly ingrained in Bo Ne Win, compounded by the only formal regimented training he had received from the Imperial Japanese Military enhanced by the special elite Intelligence Courses at the infamous Nakano Intelligence School (Nakano Gakko).

The first and immediate target was the surrogate of the U.S. hegemonic designs on Burma. The Jews were all over the newly independent country, offering obsolete aircraft (junks) at discount prices, the tabs picked up by so-called American aid. Then training and advising the Army, Air Force and Navy. Before the naïve Burmese knew what was happening, most of the businesses in banking, shipping, insurance and overseas trading were in their hands. However, by early summer of 1962, the Defense Service Industries (DSI) and the Burma Economic Development Corporation (BEDC) had removed the devastating Arab League (22 countries) Economic, Trade Boycott and Blockage of Burmese Flag ships through the Suez Canal with the support of Gamal Abdel Nasser of United Arab Republic (UAR-Egypt/Syria) and Marshal Tito of

Yugoslavia. The Israeli involvement in Burma's economy and overseas trade and commerce was coming to an end and the next priority was the British, European and U.S. "Joint Venture" businesses in the country and the huge amounts of cash and financial assets hidden in the WEST by Burmese politicians and their cronies since independence in January 1948.

# CHALLENGE FROM CHINESE MAFIA

The Revolutionary Council's (RC) Select Committee for the UK ACTION PLAN placed under Bo Aung Gyi and members – Bo San Yu, Bo Thaung Kyi, Bo Khin Nyo, Bo Maung Lwin (Moustache) reported to the Chairman that the preparations for implementation were complete and the designated officer (U Kyi Win Sein, General Counsel and Legal Adviser) to serve as Official Representative of the BEDC in UK, Europe and the USA and report to Bo Khin Nyo, Chairman. Bo Ne Win, the Revolutionary Council Government Prime Minister, approved the arrangements and instructed Bo Ko Ko, the Cabinet Secretary, to restrict the Official Administrative Record to the Action Plan Committee Members Only. True to his characteristic modus operandi, he wanted to keep the other Cabinet Ministers and RC Members excluded from information on the project until the desired objective was achieved. His paranoia and penchant for secrecy was evident to all of us and made things difficult, especially for me as I was by absolute necessity to call on major Ministries to obtain confidential documents, information, data and files relevant to the project.

I was particularly concerned because the Chairman of the State Timber Board was accompanying me and my family up to Copenhagen and would definitely inquire what my mission to London was. He was introduced to me at a meeting in Dagon House with Bo Aung Gyi, Minister of Trade and Bo Tin Phay, Minister of Agriculture and Forests just a few weeks earlier. At that meeting I noted from his demeanor and facial expression surprise and discomfort at being suddenly summoned to the Official Residence of the Military's # 2 General and seeing his immediate superior discussing the STB Contract with the Scandinavians. Bo Aung Gyi, noticing the nervous officer standing stiff at attention, quickly put him at ease saying "come Bo Myo Myimt, sit next to U Kyi Win Sein, our Legal Adviser; Bo Khin Nyo and Bo Lwin will be joining us soon".

In the Military hierarchy at that time one is conscious of the fact that this is actually the "Seat of State Power at work" and there was no room to beat around the bush so you'd better be ready to "give straight answers to questions directed at you". Apparently Bo Myo Myint, a career Army officer newly appointed to take charge of the country's huge National Timber business, was still in the midst of learning the very complex fundamentals as well as the administrative and bureaucratic ropes of the department and was not quite ready to handle the questions thrown at him by the Agriculture and Forestry Minister, his immediate boss.

He was in the hot seat being bullied by his Minister but was saved by the arrival of Bo Khin Nyo, the BEDC Chairman and Bo Lwin (Moustache), the Intelligence Chief. Bo Aung Gyi took over the proceedings, explaining the "Due Diligent Study and Analysis" report of our Legal Adviser on the "Unwritten Sovereignty Clause Principle of International Law" in all Contracts between a Sovereign Country and Private Business Entities, Domestic and/or Foreign. As such, the Revolutionary Government invoking this "Sovereign Right", the Prime Minister has instructed the Minister of Trade and the Minister of Agriculture and Forests to take immediate steps to "Renegotiate the Contract with the STHF the Amendment of the Terms and Conditions in the National Interest and If Necessary to Terminate It Entirely". He then asked me, "What is the First Action for us to take?" I replied, "To send a Cable Immediately Expressing the Revolutionary Government's Firm and Irrevocable Intent to Review and Renegotiate the Terms and Conditions of the Contract at the Earliest Possible Date at a Mutually Acceptable Location."

I had already drafted the Cable and handed it to Bo Aung Gyi, who reviewed it and passed it on to Bo Tin Phay who gave it to Bo Myo Myint in whose name and title (STB Chairman) it needed to be sent. He was instructed to send it immediately and report the response to Bo Khin Nyo, BEDC Chairman. Bo Myo Myint stood up, saluted and rushed back to his office to send the Cable. Bo Aung Gyi, always a hospitable host, ordered drinks to be served and asked his Personal Staff Officer (ADC /PSO) to get food from the nearest Chinese

Restaurant. However, Bo Tin Phay in frail health was exhausted, did not stay for dinner and went home. Bo Lwin (Moustache) revealed to me how much Col. Solomon, the Judge Advocate General, was relieved and appreciated the timely resolution to the Legal Issue that had plagued the Government Judiciary Branches since Independence. "The entire JAG Department was pleased and impressed with your professional competence and that you saved the day (Face) for all of them." I told him that I did not deserve such accolades as I was just doing my job. The next morning the STHF replied, requesting a meeting in Copenhagen. Bo Aung Gyi asked me to stop over in the Danish Capital on my way to London accompanied by the STB Chairman, Bo Myo Myint.

The UK project to retrieve money hidden in accounts of Suppliers and Banks was shifting into high gear while the governance and administration of the country was running well with the Civil Service Bureaucrats cowed into submission and marching to the orders of the Officers on Special Duties (OSDs) placed in all Ministries and Government Departments. It was achieved at a rather high cost with the economy slowing down to snail's pace due to an additional layer of "Red Tape". The Foreign Trade-Import-Export, banking, insurance, transportation and shipping all backed up because the OSDs in uniform were struggling to grasp the fundamentals of the business principle "Time is Money". Their "learning curve" of these highly specialized areas of overseas business was steep and taking time.

Many succumbed to bribery and corruption practices ingrained in the bureaucracy since the days of the British Colonial Government and made worse by the Burmese politicians that came into power with empty pockets. The Army, Navy and Air Force officers were struggling with monthly salaries barely enough to get by on; the offers were just too good (many times their pay checks in cash) to let them go by and they welcomed the windfall without any hesitation. Morality, honesty, integrity and guilt went out the window justifying the abuse of the Official Positions of Power with the typical Buddhist mindset that "Good Karma had brought them luck and good fortune".

Alarmed by the widespread epidemic of bribery and corruption of the Military Officers posted to Civilian jobs, the Regime was confronted by the stark reality that those in uniform were as easy as the politicians to be bought with money. It also dawned on the top brass in the Ministry of Defense that a large percentage of the Officer Corps came from lower and lower middle class families from the Districts in the countryside and who all of a sudden found themselves in positions of power and influence and became easy targets for the moneyed business communities of the British, Chinese, Indians and the Anglos. It was a huge and new problem for the Military Regime and many senior officers expressed serious concern about maintaining discipline and control within the entire Military establishment.

A new class of bureaucracy was emerging in Burma, and the out of power politicians and the wealthy business communities colluded to test the resolve of Bo Ne Win in dealing with dissent, opposition and challenge to his regime's plan to eliminate private enterprises. Intelligence reports indicated large volume of cash movements across the borders to China, Thailand, India, Hong Kong and Singapore as well as seizures at air ports. Business account withdrawals from banks increased exponentially. A great majority of the activities were Chinese, Indians and Sino-Burmese. There were several factions of Chinese – Mainland China, Taiwan, Hong Kong, Singapore and Thailand. The out of power Burmese politicians were complicit in this attempt to "drain the money and destabilize the Regime's economy" first and then proceed to political agitation. It turned out to be an ill-conceived plan and a monumental miscalculation. For the Regime there was an urgent imperative to nip it in the bud.

Bo Ne Win's response was swift, deliberate and sweeping. All the Chinese bigwig clan leaders and their protectors (Mafia) in Rangoon, Mandalay, Bassein, Moulmein, Lashio, Kentung, Myitkyina / Bhamo, Tavoy/Mergui were all rounded up by the Military and the Police and detained under Section (5) of Public Order Protection Act (POPA). All the China Towns throughout the country were "leaderless" and were in a state of awe and shock without any clue as to what had struck them and how to respond. The out of power political leaders complicit in the destabilizing scheme were also detained. There was a "total news black-out" and the public was not aware of what was going on. However, rumors began to spread like wildfire and the Ministry of Foreign Affairs was swamped with inquiries from the Diplomatic Corps in Rangoon. U Thi Han, the civilian Foreign Minister, and the bureaucrats were freaking out and seeking guidance from Gen. Aung Gyi, the number 2 man of the Revolutionary Government and Minister of Trade and Commerce. He immediately reported the situation to Gen. Ne Win who in his characteristic style instructed his #2 to take appropriate action.

Bo Aung Gyi, fully aware that it was a delicate and sensitive "foreign policy issue", convened an emergency meeting of the Action Plan Committee in the Conference Room of Dagon House. Those present were: Gen. Aung Gyi, Gen San. Yu, Gen. Tommy Clift, Col. Thaung Kyi, Col. Khin Nyo, Col. Maung Lwin (Moustache), U Thi Han and U Kyi Win Sein (Legal Adviser). The Foreign Minister reported to the Committee that the Ambassadors of the UK, China, India, Thailand and Singapore were requesting (actually demanding) a meeting with the Head of State Gen. Ne Win. It was very important to respond to their requests ASAP. Bo Lwin (Moustache), looking at me, asked if their requests to see the Head of State was in accordance with the principle of International Law and Diplomatic Practice. I explained that "It is a generally accepted rule that all duly accredited Ambassadors of the Highest Rank do have the Right to Demand Audience with the Head of State and Compliance is Customary and Expected but not always Mandatory especially after WW2, because during the War Adolf Hitler, Mussolini and Emperor Hirohito of Japan (The Axis Powers) rejected all such requests.

"And after the War, Stalin of the Soviet Union and Mao Tse Dong of the People's Republic of China and Charles de Gaulle of France refused to see Ambassadors. As such, with the major world powers flouting International Law, the Ambassadors have the Right to Demand an Audience with the Head of State but more often than not rejected and referred to an Official of Ambassadorial Rank in the Ministry of Foreign Affairs". All the Committee Members were relieved and glad to hear the clarification, especially U Thi Han, the Foreign Minister. He asked who the appropriate Officer in the Ministry to respond and I said it would be the Chief of Protocol or the Head of the Country Desk if there was one. The Committee meeting was adjourned and I went along with Bo Lwin to his Department and dictated the Minutes to the night staff for "Classified and Restricted" Circulation next morning (Committee members only).

This event happened on the eve of my departure for London and coincided with the passing of Admiral Than Phay. The next evening at the Wake I was chatting with Bo Khin Nyo when Gen. Ne Win showed up and we went out to greet him in the front yard. On seeing me he pointed his walking stick and said, "Hey, you Japanese Shorty, why have you not left for London?" "Hey, Bo Khin Nyo send him off quickly". Early next morning I received a call from Bo Aung Gyi's personal aide to drop by at Dagon House. When I got there Bo Lwin and Bo Khin Nyo were in the Conference Room having coffee waiting for the #2 to come down from his second floor modest living quarters. As soon as he entered the room and before taking his seat he wanted to know when I was taking the flight for London. Apparently at the Admiral's Wake last night #1 pushed the UK Action Plan Committee members to get me going ASAP.

I explained that the family's unaccompanied luggage had to be shipped by sea and was taking more time than expected to arrange. Bo Lwin (Moustache) jumped in and suggested "don't waste any more time, just take all of them with you". The airline (BOAC) arranged to air freight the luggage directly to London to await our arrival via Bangkok and Copenhagen. It was critically urgent and important for the Revolutionary Government to lay its hands on the "Hidden Money" before the Politicians.

The detained Chinese business mafia and their cohorts were interrogated and a treasure trove of hitherto unknown information on their modus operandi and the world wide web of their networks. The interrogations also revealed that a large percentage of the Chinese detainees had no identification documents of Burmese citizenship and many were in fact illegal immigrants and some with dual citizenships. It posed a serious problem for the Government to take legal action and prosecute this large number (over 1500) in the Courts, convict and imprison – the prison system would be overwhelmed. The more disturbing revelations of the interrogations were that many of the Chinese gang members had police records of and had admitted to heinous crimes in the China Town Turf Wars Between Clans including but not limited to extortion, fraud, kidnapping and even elimination of rivals (Murder). This state of affairs had been going on in these communities since the days of British colonial rule and it would be impossible for the Government to sort out the mess.

While the Revolutionary Council Government struggled to find a resolution the breakthrough came from the monitoring and intercepts of the communications of the China Towns and their "Clan Connections, Networks Overseas" particularly Taiwan, Hong Kong, Bangkok, Singapore, Yunnan, Canton, Macau, Etc. The Government separated the Clan leaders among the detainees and kept them in isolation with outside contact privilege and visits by immediate family members. The resolution emerged from the monitoring and intercepts of these interactions between clan members and their overseas connections. The Government gave them two options: leave the country for good on their own volition and arrangements, or face Action in accordance with the Laws of the Country and the Justice System of the Courts.

A large percentage (95%) opted to leave the country by their own arrangements without any public fanfare. Private chartered planes from Taiwan, Hong Kong, Singapore, Bangkok, Kuming and Canton were permitted to land according to Government schedule (late evening / night flights) to take them away while the city was asleep. Only a few with serious criminal records remained in detention for their cases to be reviewed / reopened and brought before the Courts for trial and / or disposal. Subsequently more than 120,000 Chinese left Burma. It was a decisive victory of the Revolutionary Government over the Chinese Mafia and a strong message to those contemplating challenging and destabilizing the Military Regime of Gen. Ne Win. However, five years later in 1967, the Chinese problem emerged once again with ugly riots by the public and attacks in China Towns. Troops had to be called in and Martial Law imposed on several major cities. This time the Chinese Communist Party unleashed their mob to demonstrate in front of the Burmese Embassy in Beijing with loud speakers blaring 24/7.

The Burmese Ambassador, Sama Duwa Sinwa Naung, a Kachin Chieftain, freaked out and suffered a nervous breakdown. Diplomatic relations was ruptured for about six months. The negative outcome for Burma was Beijing's blatant support for the Burma Communist Party and the BCP armed insurgents along the Chinese border. A large quantity of heavy arms was given to the Communists as well as advisers from the People's Liberation Army and, to add insult to injury, a BCP Office in Beijing. The Burmese protested but the Chinese responded saying that it was not the Government giving the aid, it was the Chinese Communist Party helping their "fraternal Burmese Communists in their revolution to liberate the country from the reactionary Military Regime".

That double-faced arrogance hardened Bo Ne Win's resolve to expand and update the Military's armaments and combat capability to eliminate the BCP armed insurgents made up of WA Tribesmen equipped and led by Chinese advisers. After several years of brutal combat the Burmese Army prevailed and practically decimated the BCP Armed Faction into oblivion. However, the unintended outcome was the emergence of the WA tribe with all the arms, equipment, and combat capability, not only defending their territory but expanding into Shan State with a de facto Special Administrative Area granted by SLORC under Sr-Gen. Saw Maung.

# UK ACTION PLAN IMPLEMENTATION AND MILITARY POLITICS

I arrived in London with wife Kazuko and baby Bob in early August of 1962, and was staying at our favorite Aunt's home in Cheam Village, Surrey; the Burmese Ambassador was His Excellency U Hla Maung, a close personal friend and colleague of Aung San and U Nu, Prime Minister since independence in 1948 and now overthrown and detained by Bo Ne Win. The Defense Services Attaché was Colonel Aye Maung, exiled to London for involvement in an attempted Coup with deposed Ex-Gen. Maung Maung (Exiled as Ambassador to Israel). And there was retired Air Force Lt. Col. Aung Din (Ex-Deputy Defense Attaché in London) serving as Executive Director in Oppenheimer Jones Corporation, one of many BEDC subsidiaries in the UK joint ventures that I was tasked to dissolve and consolidate into one Umbrella Corporation.

All the above entities, the Ambassador, the exiled Army colonel and the retired Air Force Colonel, were at loggerheads with each other and met only on official occasions. In the briefing sessions with Bo Lwin (Moustache), the Military Intelligence Chief, I was cautioned to maintain good relations with the Ambassador ("He is a close friend of #1") but an arms-length distance from the Embassy staff and a "working relationship" with the exiled Defense Attaché. "With the Air Force man, you will have to fit him into the new organization as you deem appropriate." And the most important of all is "you are the first person closest to the Seat of Power in the Revolutionary Council Government to be officially posted to lead the first BEDC Representative Office in London. Remember that it is under the Prime Minister's Office".

It was indeed a very tall order for one in his mid-twenties. I only had about a day to rest and get reacquainted with Aunty Eve and Uncle Maurice in their quiet home and have Kazuko and baby Bob recover from the jet-lag after the long flight. I was in uncharted waters and eager to get started. The next day early morning I called Bo Aung Din's office number and the first thing he said was, "At long last you have arrived; we have been waiting for months. I will send a car to pick you up." I declined his kind offer telling him, "I need to quickly learn the public transport system, so please give me the nearest station to your office, I will be coming from Cheam village." "Please take the morning express to Waterloo Station and phone me the time of arrival, I will wait for you at the main exit from the platform." "I will have my uncle (Maurice) call your number after he puts me on the train. I will see you soon." I was on the 9:30 AM Express from Cheam Village to Waterloo and was there by 10:10AM. At the main exit I noticed a lean typical Burmese man impeccably dressed in a three piece suit holding a piece of white cardboard with "U Kyi Win Sein" written on it. I could clearly see in his eyes the surprise as he extended his hand and said in Burmese "I am Bo Aung Din, welcome to London" and added "I was expecting a much older man of my age".

I told him that his reaction was a common one that I had become used to for many years. We took a taxi to his office about fifteen minutes from Waterloo Station. He led me to a well-furnished reception room and a secretary served us coffee. He told me that Gen. Tommy Clift, the Air Force Chief of Staff, had written to him about the "BEDC Legal Adviser educated in Japan, who would be coming to London to establish Representative Office and restructure the entire Trade, Commerce and Banking businesses all under one roof and to fully cooperate with him". I told him that was indeed my mission and for that I needed a temporary office in a hotel close by. He suggested Washington Hotel, about ten minutes by taxi. "It is decent 4-Star place with all facilities." I asked his secretary to call the hotel and inquire on the availability of a fully furnished Conference Room for about 8-10 people with reception area partition for lease on a monthly basis. In about thirty minutes, while we were getting acquainted, the secretary informed us that a Conference Room that fitted our needs was available for lease.

We immediately took a taxi to the hotel and got there in under ten minutes. The hotel Manager escorted us to the room that was well furnished with a sliding wall partition with entry door to the Conference Room, conference table for ten with high back executive chairs. The other half as reception / waiting room for six and Secretary Desk with telephone extensions, etc. It was perfect and I asked Bo Aung Din to lease it right away on monthly terms with an option for extensions. He called his Office Manager and the Chief Accountant to take a taxi to the hotel and bring a checkbook to pay the security deposit and the first month's advance lease payment and other incidentals like telephones for the reception desk, Secretary and the Conference Room. After the lease contract was signed and payments made, we asked the hotel Manager to order an appropriate size polished brass Name Plate for the entry door: BURMA ECONOMIC DEVELOPMENT CORPORATION (BEDC)

REPRESENTATIVE OFFICE FOR U.K., EUROPE AND U.S.A.

To check out the facilities of the hotel, we asked his office Manager, Mr. Hari (a Hindu), and his Chief Accountant, Mr. Magol (a Muslim), to join us for lunch at the Coffee Shop in the Main Lobby. In a little more than 48 hours after my arrival in London, our temporary office was in place and functioning at a (4-Star) hotel in the business district of downtown London. It was on the Main Lobby floor with all the facilities. After lunch I and Bo Aung Din continued our discussions in our new office where the hotel management installed the telephones with PBX Extension / Transfer / and Telex / Cable Address features. We requested that Mr. Hari, Office Manager of Oppenheimer Jones Corporation, call employment agencies to send prospective applicants for Secretary / Stenographer for interview as well as purchase the latest electric typewriters, calculators, etc. I gave Mr. Magol a list (Lloyds Bank, Chartered Bank, Westminster Bank, Midland Bank and Barclays Bank) of the banks to invite the Managers to our office for "New Banking and Financial arrangements with BEDC".

I explained to Bo Aung Din the urgent need to hire and retain a reputable Law Firm and Accounting / Audit Firm and he suggested getting a reference and introduction from the Banks and we agreed on that approach. Late afternoon, 3:30, following typical English culture announced that it was "Tea Time". He phoned the hotel coffee shop "Tea Service for 2 with the usual mini-sandwiches and cakes". Within about 15 minutes the tea service was rolled in and it brought back memories of my time in Egypt with the Generals and Admirals trained in Sandhurst and Dartmouth. I found them to be more British than the British themselves and here I was with a middle aged fellow Burmese at tea time in London.

Bo Aung Din had served as Deputy Defense Attaché for more than five years and during that time attended the Royal Air Force Staff College and after early retirement as Executive Director of Oppenheimer Jones Corporation London for the past four years representing BEDC the major share-holder of the joint venture. He had lived in London for more than a decade and was comfortably well settled as a single father raising two beautiful daughters (Blossom and Betty) and only son (Billy). A mild mannered and soft spoken man with impeccable pedigree, excellent academic achievement (B.A., B.L., BCS – Burma Civil Service First Class) and a highly respected leader of the Burmese Baptist Community.

As fate would have it for both of us our careers and life had converged in London under peculiar and extraordinary circumstances of "Abrupt Revolutionary Take-Over of State Power by Gen. Ne Win, the Commander-in-Chief of the Burmese Military". I was enjoying the tea and the snacks that came with it and reflecting on the final briefing by Bo Lwin (Moustache), the Intelligence Chief, that I was the first Credentialed Officer of the Revolutionary Council Government posted to London (four months after the Coup) to lead the restructuring of the Country's Trade, Commerce, Banking and Financial Enterprises in the UK, Europe and the US. "You will in fact be the Official Representative of the BEDC that is directly under the Prime Minister's Office." That perception was conveyed to Bo Aung Din by his immediate superior, Gen. Tommy Clift, in his letter and in the few hours working together on the project his demeanor, attitude and reaction was to play it safe by supporting the "Agenda and Plans" that I had brought with me and approved by the "Powers that be in Rangoon".

After tea I called Colonel Aye Maung and he informed me that many messages for me had been received and a huge volume of boxes had taken up all the space in his office. I told him that the packages would have to remain there but I would like to have the messages soon. I advised him of our temporary office in the Washington Hotel and suggested a breakfast meeting the next day, but he wanted to come right away and bring the messages with him. I gave him the room number and told him to ask the hotel reception desk for directions to BEDC Office. He arrived in about thirty minutes accompanied by Lt.Commander Maung Maung Khin, the Assistant Defense Attaché. Bo Aung Din kindly introduced the two officers to me as it was the first time for me to meet them in person but I had had the opportunity to review their "Bio-Data" courtesy of Bo Maung Lwin (Moustache). Bo Aye Maung, slight of build and stout, typical Army character, high school dropout education, loud in speech with an ego that vanished when caught red-handed in the attempted Coup of exiled Ex-Gen. Maung Maung. In contrast, Maung Maung Khin with a good family pedigree, and a graduate of the Royal Naval Academy at Dartmouth, was well-mannered and very soft spoken. I received the message packages and put them in my briefcase.

Defense Attachés report directly to the Military Intelligence Chief and Bo Aye Maung said he had received information of my posting to London from the Ministry of Defense when the packages arrived by diplomatic shipment with instructions for safe storage until my arrival. I told him that our new office would have sufficient space and facility for the storage and processing. To break the ice, I reminded the three Military officers of the irony of Army, Navy, Air Force and a civilian discussing in a London hotel Conference Room, the restructuring (dismantling) of the joint venture business enterprises with the British and the Europeans and thus eliminate foreign domination of our economy, trade and commerce. I suggested that we order drinks and appetizers from the Main Lobby Bar and later have dinner at the restaurant. Bo Aung Din called the Catering Manager and ordered "a bar on wheels and a tray of assorted appetizers". A bar tender waited on us and kept the drinks coming. Bo Aye Maung, eager to get information on the Coup, told me that Bo Maung Maung (Ambassador to Israel) was in London recently and had mentioned my mission to Egypt and about meeting him "in the safe house in Haifa" arranged by the Yugoslavs and the Egyptians and the high impression he had for the success of the mission.

I had to exercise discretion not to get drawn into talking (gossiping) about those happenings and events and interactions of the senior officers, and also to safeguard the leakage of the implementation plans. In the specific case of

Bo Aye Maung, some of his judgment errors and outright transgressions were very serious and over the line that had to be reported to the Chief of Staff who bent backwards (on compassionate grounds) to save his Military career for the sake of his 10 children. In fact he is only assigned with inconsequential duties in London as his language capability was very limited in every aspect. In the scheme of perceptions in Burmese Military politics, senior officers with "black clouds hanging over their heads" were shunned by fellow officers and usually kept in the dark. It is in fact cruel and unusual punishment.

Fortunately (perhaps lucky is the better term) for me as a civilian personally known to the #1 ruler of the country (since student days) who held in high regard the University of Tokyo because all the instructors and mentors of the 30 Comrades were graduates of that prestigious Japanese Institution; according to Col. Maung Lwin (Moustache), #1 has "a very high impression of you because you are the first Burmese after WW2 that successfully graduated and received a Law Degree from Tokyo University where only less than 1% pass the entrance examination. Additionally, in his mindset Bo Khin Maung Galay entrusted you under his care and he takes that very seriously (remember that was what he told Bo Khin Nyo at Heathrow Airport). I and Gen. Aung Gyi recommended to keep you near him".

He rejected the idea outright saying that "you would be wasted just pushing paper and doing menial errands" and "people will spoil him rotten". "Bo Aung Gyi, keep him with you he has a very good head between his shoulders. Marshal Tito's Ambassador told me that he was admired by all of them for his quick learning ability of Covert Intelligence Operations". That was the state of affairs and the perceptions of the people involved in one way or another in implementing the "Action Plan in London". After dinner Bo Aye Maung dropped me off at Cheam on his way to his residence in Wimbledon. He offered to pick me up the next morning but I declined saying I needed to get used to the public transportation system.

I walked to Cheam Village station next early morning and took the 7:30 AM express and arrived at Waterloo Station 8:00 AM and took a cab to the Washington Hotel where I had breakfast. After that I went through the messages from Rangoon using the "Key". I called Bo Aung Din and requested him to purchase a "Fire Proof Safe" with Secure Combination Lock and to join me for lunch as I was going to visit Rowe & Co. in St. Paul's Church Yard. The place was huge and wide with a maze of side streets and alleys. After some walking around I was able to locate the building with small shops on the ground floor. I had to climb a rather steep squeaky stairs and found Rowe & Co. on the 2nd floor. I knocked on the door and a very fair-skinned Asian man opened it and I could immediately see the resemblance to U Maung Maung, the elder brother, the Permanent Defense Secretary whom I called on before my departure. I extended my hand saying "you must be U Maung Maung Gale, I am Kyi Win Sein". He greeted me warmly but I could see the surprise in his eyes (like thinking my God he is a young fellow).

I noticed that he was sitting at small desk at the entry door. I asked to see Mr. Buchannan, the Managing Director, Mr. Blackstork, the Purchasing Director, and Mr. Smith, the Accounts Director. U M.M. Gale led me along a narrow corridor with three private office rooms. At the far end he knocked on the door and a voice said "come in". He went in and held the door for me to enter and then introduced me to an elderly Englishman impeccably attired in a three piece suit. He stared at me wide eyed like I was an alien from another planet. I walked around the executive desk to where he was standing and extended my hand. "I am Kyi Win Sein." He shook my hands and said he had received a letter from Captain (Navy) Betram Barber, Chairman of Rowe & Co., informing him that the Legal Advisor of BEDC would be coming soon and to fully cooperate with him. The two other elderly men joined us and M.M. Gale was about to leave the room but I asked him to stay.

I gave my business card to each of the elderly men (they all appeared to be in their mid-late sixties) and informed them that I had set up a temporary office at the Washington Hotel and would establish a new Corporation where all BEDC joint venture enterprises and subsidiaries would be consolidated. I requested that Mr. Buchannan have all the "books and accounts of the company audited by Chartered Accounts and Bank Accounts, Deposits, Bonds, Stocks, Notes, Receivables Consolidated and Compiled and that I would have BEDC Law Firm and Accounting / Audit Firm to examine and certify them as required under British Laws. During this transition period, I told them to feel free to call or visit our Washington Hotel office at any time. I also requested of Mr.

Buchannan to permit M. M. Gale to accompany me back to my office. We took a cab back to the hotel and got there in about 15 minutes. I told M. M. Gale about my meeting with his big brother at the request of Gen. Aung Gyi and the conversation I had had with him. I advised him to write a note to his brother informing him of our meeting and working together. He promised to do so.

At 12:00 noon Bo Aung Din joined us and we walked to the Main Lobby Coffee Shop to have lunch. I ordered the typical British lunch of baked beans on toast, with eggs and gammon. Both of them were surprised at my choice and I got a kick out of it when they ordered the same. After lunch we interviewed several candidates for Secretary and Receptionist and I left the selection to them as they knew the local situation a lot better than me. Our temporary office was off and running within a matter of days of my arrival in London and many of the BEDC joint venture corporations in the UK and Europe were informed to communicate with our office.

All the British and European Banks represented by their Senior Management called on our office one after the other and expressed keen interest to work and cooperate fully in providing banking and financial services to BEDC. The Export-Import Bank of Burma and the five British banks established Correspondence Agreements when I was Legal Counsel and Secretary of the Board and the British bankers recalled corresponding with me on many issues concerning the "Bilateral Agreements". It helped greatly to further build trust and confidence now that I was meeting them in person and setting up the Representative Office in London and managing its operations. The UK Action Plan Committee under Gen. Aung Gyi, Revolutionary Council member and Minister of Trade, recognized early on the importance and need for "Initial Upfront Investment in the London Umbrella Corporation" and allocated a "Contingency Budget of £500,000.00 approved by Revolutionary Council Chairman and Prime Minister Gen. Ne Win (Under Ministry of Defense Budget Category: Emergency Overseas Covert Operation). Under UK Banking and Financial Instruments Laws and Ordinances, we opened BEDC Representative Office Current and Savings Accounts in the five London Banks with initial deposits of £100,000.00 in each account.

The Bank of England Certified Checks (Union of Burma Sovereign Funds) and Export-Import Bank of Burma Certified Checks were sent by Diplomatic Pouch to the Defense Attaché's Office. Bo Aung Din and U M.M. Gale with mouths agape looked on with utter disbelief in their eyes. This extraordinary departure from normal or usual procedure was shocking to the two Burmese men acclimatized to the British conservative ways. It was also a manifestation of the Revolutionary Council Government Generals not averse to risks. I asked their consent to be on the Signatory Card of the Accounts; both were not only hesitant but reluctant on flimsy grounds of being out of the country too long and far removed from official Government affairs let alone leaders of the New Military Regime.

My sixth sense of the real reason was the concern of gossip, finger-pointing and innuendo from the large Burmese community wary of the Military Regime that had posted a young Japanese educated lawyer (with a Japanese wife) to dismantle the old business and commercial arrangements in the WEST. That psyche and mindset has been ingrained in that generation (they were contemporaries in University and about the same age). I explained to them frankly that my preference was to build the core management team with expatriate Burmese currently working in BEDC JV Corporations and subsidiaries.

All these JV Corporations in the UK, Europe and USA numbering 50-60 would be restructured by exercising our right to acquire the shares of the minority partners and consolidating all under an Umbrella Corporation established under the UK Company Laws. On hearing my clarification both of them consented to be on the Company Authorized Signatory Card. On our request Midland Bank referred us to Durrant, Cooper and Hambling, a reputable and highly respected Law Firm led by Barrister Sir Guy Hambling (QC), and Lloyds Bank recommended Lloyds Accounting, Auditing and Financial Services, a Chartered Accounting Firm as our Accountants. We now had our Bank Accounts, highly respected Law and Accounting Firms on Annual Retainer Service Contracts renewable at our option.

The City of London Banks, Lawyers and Accountants immediately served as integral partners of BEDC with their Introduction and Endorsement for our

Membership in the UK International Chamber of Commerce and Industry, London. It was in fact the Official Recognition and Acceptance of our BEDC Representative Office by the UK Business and Industrial Communities. Sir Guy Hambling, in recognition of BEDC's Special Importance as a State Owned Corporation, assigned Barrister Templeton Smith and Senior Solicitor Clive Richardson to attend to all our Legal and Related needs. We requested that they expedite the "Incorporation and Registration of our Umbrella Company – BURMA TRADE LIMITED". Our next priority was acquisition of office space in the business district in the City of London. The Washington Hotel Management referred us to their Commercial Real Estate Agent and immediately located available properties in their inventory and recommended Ingersoll House, adjacent to Alexandra House in London City Center, close to the Banking District, the BBC and the Inns of Court.

The entire 6th floor was available for lease or purchase at bargain price because "extensive renovation is required for which substantial price reduction will be considered". We rushed to inspect the property and indeed, extensive renovation was required but the flip side was it could be designed to meet our requirements. The floor space was in excess of 6500 Sq.Ft. with three center elevators (Lifts as the British call them) and one Service Lift in the Rear and two in the underground parking area. The other five floors below had been modernized, renovated and designed by the tenants just a few years ago. I asked U M. M. Gale to proceed with the negotiations and consult with the Real Estate Agent to recommend an Interior Office Designer and the estimated cost. That evening when I returned to our furnished apartment in Twickenham Park in Richmond, I asked my new neighbor Ramsey Short, a licensed interior designer, if he would be interested in designing a brand new office for me in "The City".

He said he liked the idea but would like to see the property first. The next morning he accompanied me to my office and after breakfast he checked out the property and returned to my office quite excited saying it would a great opportunity for him as it is a "Turn Key" project, design, renovation, furnishing, equipment, etc. He would be the Prime Contractor and hire sub-contractors for plumbing, carpentry, painters, office furnishing and equipment. I asked him to submit his bid and proposal ASAP. In the meantime, Bo Aung

Din and M. M. Gale negotiated the lease and purchase price with the owner's broker and I noted that both of them were more concerned and worried about the high costs involved and how the superiors in Rangoon would react to my setting up office in the center of London at such a high cost. They freaked out when I said for our long term interest purchasing it would be the best course to take. Up to that stage the two middle aged Burmese men observing my moving decisively with confidence at breakneck speed were beginning to get "cold feet" and wondering "if this young fellow was given free hand by the Military Regime Generals". I needed to reach a definite goal within a given timeframe and did not have the luxury of procrastination in implementing the "Action Plan". It was time for me to be more specific and direct in articulating the New Government's directives to me.

I said this BEDC Representative Office in London represents the Economy, Trade, Commerce, Banking, Finance and overall "National Interests of The Country" and as such I was instructed to always bear in mind the necessity of hiring the best Law Firm, the best Accounting Firm and not to settle for "Second Best" and "Not to be Penny Wise and Pound Foolish". Therefore, in this specific case, lease or rental fees could never be recovered whereas investing in real property would be better than keeping money in the bank and property value would always increase in value with time, particularly improved and upgraded property in the business center of the City.

I assured them that I had covered all such matters and more with all the Members of the Action Plan Committee. I also assured both men that this is a well thought out project for more than a year and not some one's wishful thinking. I seemed to have laid to rest any doubts lingering in their minds about this young, confident Japanese-educated fellow. However, to allay their concerns, I suggested getting the opinion of our Accounting Firm and the British banks as to whether to lease or purchase. They recommended purchase in writing with offer to finance it with a low interest Mortgage. I also opted to decline the mortgage offer from the banks and paid cash to own the property outright.

Our Balance Sheet at that time was not only on the positive side but Cash Rich because the fully owned companies Rowe & Co, East Asiatic, Bombay-Burma,

British-Burma Pulse and Beans, Oppenheimer Jones Co., Burma Oxygen Ltd., Mawchi (Silver) Mines, Inland Water Transport Corporation (IWTC), Burma Oil Co. (BOC), Mandalay Beer Brewery, Mineral Development Corporation (MDC), State Agricultural Marketing Board (SAMB) Etc on dissolution yielded additional cash from their Current and Savings Accounts as well as interest bearing Savings Bonds, Bank of England Treasury Notes going back six to seven decades.

Many of these Financial Assets and Instruments were "Non-Transferrable / Non-Assignable by Old Security and Debenture Laws and had to be "Cashed out / Converted to Cash" and our bank accounts "swelled to amazing volume" and had to be moved to "Interest bearing Fixed Deposits". This was just from a handful of companies and there were larger ones that were in the pipeline for buyout of minor JV Partners and consolidation into the Umbrella Corporation being incorporated by our Law Firm. Our implementation operation was shifting into high gear and gaining speed every day. We approved the design and layout of the Office Complex and awarded the Renovation Contract to Ramsey Short with a stipulation to utilize quality materials and comply with London City Building Codes and Licensed Sub-Contractors.

In the interim I operated out of the temporary office in the Washington Hotel and retained Offices of several dissolved companies after the managers and staff were settled with severance pay and benefits in accordance with UK Labor Laws and Release Documents Signed. Barrister Templeton Smith and Clive Richardson had to review a maze of Laws and Ordinances governing Foreign State Owned Business Corporations Investing and Incorporating in the UK to Operate Commercial, Banking and General Trading businesses. It took several weeks for Search, Discovery and Verification with the Competent Government Authority, Notary and Disclosure Requirements.

# THE PRINCIPAL HOLDING CORPORATION FOR THE UK, EUROPE AND USA

In late October 1962 after completing all the requirements the Attorneys of the Law Firm successfully registered BURMA TRADE LIMITED with City of London Registrar of Companies and received the Certificate of Incorporation in recognition as British Commercial Corporation, with offices in London. The first Organization Meeting held in the Conference Room of the Law Chambers was presided over by Sir Guy Hambling, Templeton Smith, Clive Richardson, Bo Aung Din, U M. M. Gale, Mr. John Davidson, Accountant of Lloyds Accounting Firm, Mr. George Gates, Senior Managing Director of Midland Bank and myself. The item on the agenda was Authorized and Paid-Up Capital decision by the "Organizers of the Company". The Action Plan approved by the BEDC Board of Directors stipulated that the New Principal Holding Company in the U.K. be "Adequately Capitalized to reflect the National Standing of BEDC representing State Enterprises, Corporations, Quasi-Corporations and Industries".

In compliance with that stipulation and the mandate granted to the Action Plan, Mr. Gates confirmed our prior discussion on the issue that £12,500,000.00 Authorized Capital and the (20%) Legal Mandate of £2,500,000.00 Paid-Up Capital would include Burma Trade Limited in the Exclusive Category of "Adequately Capitalized Private English Company". That was the "yardstick" generally used by major British and European Banks in determining corporations' "Credit Worthy Rating". We accepted and confirmed that Capitalization. All Outstanding Single Category Capital Stock of the Company to be issued in the name of Kyi Win Sein (60%), Export-Import Bank of Burma (20%) and Bo Aung Din (20%). The Law Firm to prepare "Assignment Documents" for the Stocks of Kyi Win Sein and Aung Din for assignment to

U.K. BEDC Representative Office, London. The Law required that the largest stockholders nominated Directors of the Board (1) Bo Aye Maung, Non-Voting Director, (2) Bo Khin Nyo, Director (3) Bo Aung Din, Director (4) U Kyi Win Sein, Director and (5) U M. M. Gale, Director and Secretary to the Board of Directors.

Sir Guy congratulated us and shook hands with the newly elected Directors and declared that Burma Trade Limited had complied with all legal requirements to operate and conduct all businesses permitted under the Law. He called for the traditional champagne bottle to be uncorked for celebration. It was typical conservative British Legal System providing efficient and speedy assistance to foreign enterprises to establish companies in London. We returned to our Washington Hotel Conference Room for the last time and had a celebration dinner in the Main Lobby Restaurant. In just over three months since my arrival in London the "Principal Umbrella Organization" envisaged in the Action Plan was up and running in its own custom-designed new modern "office complex" as good as any in the British Capital. The professional office movers proved their worth with efficiency and knowhow in handling / installation of new equipment / furniture and incredible speed. Well before noon on the Monday of moving in every piece of office paraphernalia from the two companies and all the brand new furniture were in their proper places, tested and working perfectly throughout the 6,500 Sq.Ft new sprawling office complex with plenty of room to expand.

All the officers settled into their assigned individual private office rooms and were pleased to find the state of the art telephone equipment on their Executive Desks and the high-back Executive Chairs. The three Rowe & Co. Managers, the two Oppenheimer Jones Managers and six staff members quickly introduced themselves while the Directors convened the First Board of Directors Meeting in the well-appointed Conference Room adjoining a furnished Lounge Area for entertainment and leading to a Reception Room for guests and visitors. Present for the first meeting – Bo Aye Maung, Bo Aung Din, U Kyi Win Sein, U M. M. Gale and Mr. Clive Richardson from our Law Firm to help in the proceedings to comply with those stipulated in English Corporate Laws. Clive Richardson called the meeting to order. The Law required the directors to elect the Chairman of the Board; Bo Aye Maung was elected Chairman of the Board, accepted and confirmed by unanimous consent. U M. M. Gale was elected to serve as Secretary to the Board of Directors.

Clive Richardson handed over the Bylaws Folder to the New Secretary of the Board for Adoption and approved by the Directors. By unanimous consent, the Bylaws as presented by the Secretary were adopted and approved. "The Board of Directors of Burma Trade Limited is hereby legally instituted. The first order of business for the Board of Directors is to confirm the retention of the Auditors and Lawyers of the Company. By unanimous consent the Directors confirmed the retention of Durrant, Cooper and Hambling as the Company's Legal Counsel and Lloyds Accounting & Audit Co.as the Company's Accountants and Auditors. The next order of business would be to appoint the Officers of the Corporation. By unanimous consent, the following were appointed to the positions described next to their respective names with effect as of this date:

1. U Aung Din.................................................... Senior Managing Director
2. U Kyi Win Sein .................................Director and Chief Executive Officer
3. U Maung Maung Gale ......................... Manager – General Administration
4. H. N. Hari............................. Oppenheimer Jones & Co. Business Division
5. M. A. Magol ...................................................... Treasurer & Chief Accountant
6. S. L. Buchannan ..........Executive Manager, Rowe & Co. Business Division
7. D. K. Blackstock......... Manager, Assets & Accounts, Rowe & Co. Business ................................................................................................................. Division
8. W. J. Smith ........... Manager, Purchasing & Exports, Rowe & Co. Business ................................................................................................................. Division
9. U Ohn Sein.... Senior Executive Manager, Government Liaison Division"

The General Administrator began recruitment of qualified mid-level managers, Clerical and Secretarial Staff. The cartons of files and documents from the Defense Attaché's office were brought to our secure Office Room and I began the tedious work of disclosing the delicate information to Bo Aung Din, U Ohn Sein and U M. M. Gale. All three were surprised by the large number of boxes delivered from Bo Aye Maung's office to our new secure room for safe review of the documents to be utilized as necessary and appropriate in our Action Plan implementation. However, to be on the safe side, I asked for guidance from Bo Khin Nyo, BEDC Chairman, before the "primary objective" of the Action

Plan was implemented under the name of our "umbrella organization" – Burma Trade Limited, London.

The reason being once the action started in London, close coordination and enforcement measures in Rangoon might be necessary by several Law Enforcement Agencies. I received immediate response advising me that the matter was being discussed with Bo Aung Gyi, Trade Minister, and Bo Maung Lwin (Moustache), Chief of Military Intelligence (MIS) and Bureau of Special Investigation (BSI) and to await the "Final Green Light". It was quite obvious that the final go ahead must come from the #1.

On receipt of my request the Action Plan Committee members – Bo Aung Gyi, Bo Thaung Kyi, Bo Khin Nyo and Bo Maung Lwin (Moustache) – reported to the Revolutionary Council Chairman the successful set-up of the principal umbrella organization in London and the imminent initiation of moving forward to the next phase of "Retrieval of Hidden funds and take-over of JV Enterprises". The boss was pleased with the quick progress but was aghast and outraged with his characteristic "which mother F…ing idiot put SOB Aye Maung in the Chairman's post?". All of them freaked out, lost for words.

This exiled Colonel's deep involvement in the failed Coup attempt, his poor judgment, brash bully behavior was known to all in the Military but he had managed to survive this far simply by pleading for the livelihood of his ten children. The powers that be in the Ministry of Defense including the Commander-in-Chief as Buddhists had a soft spot whenever children's survival is invoked. Bo Aung Gyi saved the day by reassuring the boss that he would have Bo Khin Nyo fly to London, pursue all pending issues and resolve them in consultation with Bo Aung Din and U Kyi Win Sein.

I received a short telex advice to await detailed information in the next diplomatic pouch. The Communications Warrant Officer from the Defense Attaché's office delivered sealed packages and the envelopes from Bo Khin Nyo and Bo Maung Lwin, and both stressed the need to remove Bo Aye Maung from the Chairman's post. Also included was the date, time and airline flight number of Bo Khin Nyo's arrival in London and not to disclose the information to anyone outside our circle as a cautionary measure to keep the media away. We reserved a "kitchen attached" suite at the Washington Hotel for the Revolutionary Council Member and Chairman of BEDC and to provide "hotel security" during his stay at their premises. This was the first visit to Britain of (Cabinet Rank) highest level Military Official since the Coup in early March of that year (1962). We were concerned that the Tabloid London Media would get wind of his visit.

A week later we (Bo Aung Din and I) hired a Chauffeur-driven Bentley and went to Heathrow International Airport to meet Bo Khin Nyo's flight. He came through immigration and customs very quickly being a First Class passenger and carrying a diplomatic passport. On the way to the hotel I sat in the front passenger seat and the two of them sat on the back sofa seat. I noted the absence of conversation between the two and Bo Khin Nyo was speaking to me from the back. Apparently he was being careful or was uncomfortable saying things in the presence of a retired Air Force officer in a foreign country whom he'd met casually before only a few times and who now belonged to the innermost circle of the Seat of Power.

I felt sympathy for Bo Aung Din having to endure such an ordeal and the stress that comes with it. No wonder that he was being treated by medical specialists for stress ulcers. At the hotel Bo Khin Nyo was very pleased with the kitchen attached suite, the dining room and the living lounge. He asked for an hour's rest and shower. We waited at the Main Lobby Coffee shop and ordered a light lunch. Bo Aung Din was trying his very best to come to terms with the fact that a Senior Military Regime member was going to be with us for a prolonged period and his Air Force background psyche and complex seemed to bother him.

He frankly expressed his surprise that despite our considerable difference in age the Senior Army Colonel was exceptionally friendly and comfortable and officially correct in his dealings with me like a colleague. I explained that perhaps it was in the mindset of the Regime Leaders (Bo Ne Win, Bo Aung Gyi, Bo Thaung Kyi, Bo Maung Lwin and Bo Khin Nyo) I was the Legal Professional educated in Japan and Involved with the Army since my High School days and throughout my higher studies at Japanese Universities and continuously to this day. As such, they had known me for over a decade and assigned to special tasks in Burma Oil Company (BOC), Covert Multinational Operations in the Middle East, Formation of Export-Import Bank of Burma, Termination of the STB Contract and now the UK Action Plan Operation. To allay his concerns and worries, I assured him that Bo Khin Nyo was here to lend weight, verify and confirm the implementations that have already been authorized and approved by the Revolutionary Council Government prior to my departure from Rangoon.

He appreciated my explanation and seemed to realize that his worries were unfounded. I on my part realized that my relationship with the Army Regime Leadership was quite unique and out of the ordinary for others to fathom. From the perspective of the Action Plan Committee Chairman Gen. Aung Gyi, the primary purpose of sending Bo Khin Nyo to London was to have him personally sort out the appointment of Bo Aye Maung as Chairman of the umbrella organization which had shocked the Commander-in-Chief and he vehemently disapproved. Perhaps it was assumed that the notorious and unscrupulous Army Bully had muscled his way into the project and taken it over. However, Col. Maung Lwin (Moustache) and Col. Thaung Kyi were quite sure that "there must be critical extenuating circumstances for Kyi Win Sein to have made this move" and he is "no push-over" especially with regard to Legal Requirements Governing New Organizations.

Gen. Aung Gyi agreed, saying that Col. Solomon, the Judge Advocate General, as well as the Attorney General had expressed high confidence in his capability to evaluate and interpret the Laws, Ordinances and Legislations of the UK. I fully understood Bo Aung Din's apprehensions as he was a retired Air Force officer stationed in a diplomatic post for a long time, and now having to adjust and learn the complexities of a State owned Economic and commercial Enterprise overseas was taking a heavy toll on him. The situation for him was more complex and delicate having to work with a young Civilian Legal Professional Representing the Generals of the Military Regime authorized to implement, operate and manage the UK, Europe and USA Action Plan Organization. With Col. Khin Nyo, Revolutionary Council member and Chairman of BEDC in London, Bo Aung Din was understandably intimidated and concerned as to how to deal with him for the next several weeks. I told him not to worry because I had known and worked with him for many years since my student days in Japan and had always found him to be considerate, civil and respectful of other's input, opinion and professional expertise. He appeared to be more relaxed after this explanation. The inter-service Military politics is a mine field and one must learn not to step on it but one must not dwell on it because it will always be there.

After a shower and a nap the frail colonel seemed to have recovered from the long flight from Rangoon with a refueling stop in the Persian Gulf. He was eager to get several important things off his chest. I went up to his third floor suite to escort him down to the Main lobby Coffee shop where Bo Aung Din waited for us. In the elevator (Lift) down he told me that Bo Aung Gyi, Bo Tommy Clift and Bo Lwin (Moustache) sent their personal greetings to me with a reminder to take care of my health. He also told me that Bogyoke (Gen. Ne Win) had instructed him to call on the Yugoslav Ambassador in London and discuss the date and itinerary of his official visits to Yugoslavia, Czechoslovakia and Romania. He asked me to call the Yugoslavian Embassy and set up the appointment and to accompany him.

He also revealed that #1 told Bo Aung Gyi and Bo Maung Lwin (Moustache) our fellow (Do-Lu) must be the Head of the New Organization and NOT that Air Force guy. I suggest you reconsider and assume the Chief Executive Officer position of Burma Trade London so as to avoid further negative remarks from the big boss. This is irrefutable evidence of bias, prejudice and innate mistrust of the other services by the Army brass at the very top of the Military establishment. Even a token gesture of deference outside the country is unacceptable. That is the reality.

Apparently he did not want to talk about it in the presence of Bo Aung Din but I wondered why he did not want to involve the Burmese Ambassador in London to set up the meeting with the Yugoslav Ambassador in London. I learned a long time ago to remain silent on such out of the ordinary "odd jobs" assigned to me ad hoc by the various Generals and Senior Colonels on the Official Committees to which I was Assigned as Legal Counsel (Adviser) and more often than not also as Secretary of the Board or Committee. Bo Aung Din ordered "early afternoon tea service" and the Colonel enjoyed the "mini sandwiches, cheese tray and the French pastries". We took a ride to Ingersoll

House in the Bentley. Bo Khin Nyo was very impressed and pleased with Burma Trade Office arrangements and the State of the Art modern furniture and the appointments and the highly polished brass name plate as soon as he stepped off the elevator (Lift) on the 6th Floor. We gave him a guided tour of the entire sixth floor office complex and introduced him to the Managers and Staff. We settled in the Reception Lounge adjacent to the Board Room and refreshments were served from the Wet Bar.

We moved to the Board Room and had a meeting with the Colonel in the Chair and were joined by U M. M. Gale. He immediately brought up the matter of why Bo Aye Maung had been appointed Chairman of Burma Trade and the negative reaction from Gen. Ne Win. However, he stressed that Bo Aung Gyi, the Chairman, and all the Members of the Action Plan Committee recognized the "project's critical importance" and its successful implementation. And should the appointment be necessitated by special extenuating circumstances the action to reverse it needed to be considered carefully so as not to cause any undesirable effect on the Operation of the Burma Trade Limited, the Umbrella Organization.

I explained the Legal and Political perceptions of UK Corporate and Commercial Registration Laws and Ordinances Governing Foreign State Owned Enterprises like Burma Economic Development Corporation (BEDC) which is in fact directly under the Prime Minister's Office of Burma. Burma Trade Limited was the Official Representative of BEDC in the UK and Burma was currently ruled by the Military. Therefore, the Attorneys of our Law Firm recommended that to reflect that Political and Legal Reality of Burma its Defense Attaché in London appointed as "Symbolic Chairman" (Non-Voting, Non-Share Holding, without any Executive or Financial Powers) would be the most "appropriate option under the Present Circumstances".

We accepted the Law Firm's judgment and their recommendation. Notwithstanding the above, the appointment could be terminated by the Board of Directors and/or the Share Holders at any time. I submitted all the Legal Documents and suggested that our Legal Counsel in Rangoon, Barrister U Than Aung, review and translate them for submission to Gen. Ne Win, the Prime Minister. Bo Khin Nyo was relieved to hear the explanation and suggested that I draft a letter to Gen. Aung Gyi and forward the documents by Diplomatic Pouch ASAP.

He was following the Military Chain of Command Procedure by reporting to the Vice Chief of General Staff to officially submit his "findings" to the Chief of General Staff as Col. Aye Maung was in active Service. There is a very good possibility that he might relent and accept our arrangement in London. Under ordinary conditions and circumstances it was very likely that Bo Aye Maung would be replaced by one acceptable to the Commander-in-Chief. We noticed that the jet lag was having an effect on the old soldier and I suggested that he return to the hotel to get some sleep. I accompanied him back to the hotel and made sure that he was safely back in his suite and left phone numbers for him to call us on waking up and should he be up to going for an Indian dinner at the restaurant in the Indian High Commissioner's Office where we had an account for reservation of a private room.

He said that was the kind of food he needed to regain his full strength. I returned to the office to review the letters and documents from Bo Aung Gyi, Bo Lwin (Moustache) and U Maung Maung, the Defense Ministry Permanent Secretary (thanking me for looking up his long lost younger brother and appointing him to a key managerial position in the Umbrella Organization. All three conveyed the good news that the Revolutionary Council Chairman was very pleased and happy with the speedy progress of the Action Plan in London.

At about the time we were winding up for the day, the Colonel called and said he had slept for a few hours and would like to take up our suggestion of going to the Indian dinner. Three of us went to the hotel to pick up the Colonel in the Bentley and then to the Indian High Commissioner's Office Restaurant and ordered a full menu of South Indian food to be served in a private room with a fully stocked bar and bar tender. The food was exquisite with spices prepared to taste. After a few drinks the atmosphere became more relaxed and Bo Khin Nyo was comfortable enough to tell us that the situation had stabilized to the extent that the boss would be leaving the country in the hands of Bo Aung Gyi and coming to London with wife Katy, his doctor and personal cook Rajoo for rest and recreation and to visit Marshal Tito of Yugoslavia to consult on the State Controlled Command Economy and at his suggestion visit Czechoslovakia and

Romania. Apparently the above ground Communist Financial Adviser U Ba Nyain's theoretical preaching to the "yes men" in the Revolutionary Council was beginning to push them in the direction of a State Controlled Command Economy and wholesale Nationalization.

The good friend Marshal Tito would send his private jet to pick him up and his entourage which would include Bo Maung Lwin (Moustache), Bo Khin Nyo and U Thi Han, the Civilian Foreign Minister. "You will accompany me to meet the Yugoslavia Ambassador here in London and discuss the date and itinerary." He cautioned us not to reveal this information to anyone. The private dinner concluded after 10 PM and we all returned home in a private taxi service arranged by the restaurant. It was a long and exhausting day for all especially the middle aged men. The next morning I was at the hotel by 8 AM and we had a leisurely room service breakfast and he brought me up to date on the state of affairs within the ruling Revolutionary Council and the worrisome socialist ideology aggressively promoted by the above ground Communist of the National United Front (NUF) through their Financial Adviser U Ba Nyain. By that very early stage (late 1962) the NUF's agenda and top priority was to lure Bo Ne Win into National Socialist Economic and Political Ideology where his grasp, perceptions and understanding were highly suspect and superficial at best like themselves.

However, to validate and establish relevance to the Country's Independence Struggle led by Aung San, they relied heavily on his BLUE PRINT FOR INDEPENDENT BURMA as the ROAD MAP for the Military to embrace it as a POLICY GUIDE. This document was written while Aung San was staying at Col. Suzuki's home in Hamamatsu, Japan while the Japanese Army Imperial General Staff was considering whether to accept Col. Suzuki's recommendation to support Aung San's request for help to drive out the British from Burma. In the diary of Suzuki he noted that Aung San's request for Books in English put him in a very difficult situation because anyone caught reading anything in English would be detained by the Military Intelligence (Ken-Pei-Tai) for questioning.

Aung San requested books on the U.S., Soviet and Yugoslavia Constitutions, Mein Kampf, Das Kapital and Keynsian Economics. Suzuki got them from the

Imperial Army Central Library and actually lied to the librarian to officially release them for use at the Imperial General Staff (Shirei-Bu) Command Center. Suzuki could not take any chances, so whatever Aung San wrote he made duplicates and had them translated into Japanese and submitted to his superiors and the Ken-Pei-Tai. His diary also noted "here is a young (in his twenties) Burmese nationalist day dreaming of establishing a "UTOPIA" that the world has not seen thus far".

"It is a luxury only a young twenty something can have". It was indeed a fatherly notation and as things turned out later, Suzuki (Bo Mogyo) in fact became the father-figure of the Thirty Comrades and actually the Burma Army. The Imperial General Staff was not pleased with such a relationship and recalled Suzuki back to Tokyo after only a few years in Rangoon. Col. Tagami's diary also recorded this state of affairs regarding Suzuki's bias on the side of Aung San and the Burmese Army. Now after Bo Ne Win's take-over of the country, the wishful daydreaming dissertation of his comrade-in-arms was about to become his and the country's "Achilles Heel".

We continued our conversation in the short ride to Burma Trade in Ingersoll House and it was clear to me that the Revolutionary Council's cohesion and unity of purpose and the direction to be pursued was being tested by the above ground Communist National United Front (NUF). Despite this worrisome trend, Bo Khin Nyo seemed to be putting his faith in Bo Aung Gyi's rational and balanced economic and trade policies at home and overseas that had produced excellent outcomes for the country and the people. With our UK, Europe, USA Action Plan in full operation and shifting into high gear with acquisition of all the stocks from JV partners, the Commercial Enterprises were now fully owned by BEDC. Foreign elements were legally and gently eliminated without resort to wholesale Nationalization that would have brought on retaliation from the International Business Community.

On the contrary, Burma Trade London was welcomed by the key Commercial, Trade and Banking Communities of the world including the International Monetary Fund, World Bank, Bank of Settlements and Organization for Economic Cooperation and Development (OECD). This Recognition and Acceptance by the leading World Bodies was a monumental achievement and in "welcoming Burma Trade to the London Chamber of Commerce and Industry the Chamber President announced 'Burma has arrived on the World's Trade and Commercial Stage and the Country's Economic Take Off is Imminent.'" Bo Khin Nyo as Chairman of BEDC was delighted beyond words for this "reputable and good standing" that would help greatly in our next step of retrieving the "hidden funds of the Burmese Politicians and their Cronies held by Corporations and Banks in the UK, Switzerland and Europe".

It was definitely one of the overriding priorities of Bo Ne Win for these funds to be retrieved and under his control out of reach of the politicians and the opposition elements plotting to remove him from power. Bo Maung Lwin (Moustache) in his letter to me sent through Bo Khin Nyo indicated that "intelligence sources" indicated that the influential British Conservative Party Burma Lobby Members of Parliament had been approached by the out of power politicians to support their "opposition movement" in alliance with ethnic armed insurgents along the Thai and China borders – the Karen National Union (KNU), the Mon National Front (MNF), the Kachin Independence Organization (KIO).

The British Christian Missionaries and the Churchill Conservatives had covertly assisted these ethnic insurgencies since independence in 1948. Now, in the fall of 1962 it was urgently imperative that we move with dispatch to get these hidden funds in the UK, Europe, Switzerland and the U.S. into our bank accounts that had already reached AAA+ in the UK and the International Bank for Settlements based in Geneva, Switzerland. The stock buy back from the joint venture corporations brought with it substantial volumes of interest bearing Treasury Bonds, City of London Development Bonds going back many decades to early 20th century. It was clearly the result of Bo Aung Gyi's business acumen and vision in setting up joint ventures with long established British companies in Burma first with Defense Services Industries (DSI) and later with Burma Economic Development Corporation. Outright Nationalization would have alienated long established foreign businesses in Burma and brought diplomatic retaliation from the WEST especially as the country was still in the Sterling Area Currency.

# BRITISH BOARD OF TRADE (MINISTRY OF COMMERCE KEY FOR SUCCESS)

It was critically important for the newly registered Burma Trade to receive the goodwill, support and full cooperation of the British Government's Ministry of Commerce to establish official acceptance, legitimacy and accreditation to conduct business, commerce, trading, banking and financial operations in the UK. It would add enormous weight when communicating with Corporations in England, Europe, Scandinavia and the U.S. holding the hidden funds in violation of Burma's Foreign Exchange Laws. Bo Aung Din and U M. M. Gale recommended U Ohn Sein (ethnic Shan) who was the first Commercial Attaché after independence in 1948 with extensive inside connection and working relationship with the Board of Trade.

In the early fifties Prime Minister U Nu had appointed his friend, eccentric, long haired (hsan shay) U Ohn (ICS) Ambassador in London. This bachelor, vegetarian, penny-wise and pound-foolish Burmese envoy had laid off U Ohn Sein and U M. M. Gale, saying that the Embassy had too many officials. He also sold off the Embassy Building, Ambassador's residence and the Rolls Royce, all "independence gifts" from the British Government to Burma. As a result the Burmese Embassy Chancery had ended up in a shabby leased building in 19(A) Charles Street for the past ten years since 1952-53. In Burma Trade the long term investment portfolio recommended by our banks and financial planners all office and residential estates leased for Embassy officials would now be purchased by the Umbrella Organization that would replace the current Landlords under a Special Contract signed with the Ministry of Foreign Affairs and the Ministry of Defense for the Defense Attaché Office and Residential Estates. That was a sound investment and excellent business arrangement for all concerned with the State Organization owning prime Real Estate in London.

In the midst of all these discussions Bo Khin Nyo asked if I had called on Ambassador U Hla Maung (Peking) since my arrival in London several months ago. On learning that I have been too occupied to do so he suggested that we call on him together and asked U. M.M. Gale to set up the date and time. It turned out that the Ambassador was eagerly waiting to meet with us and invited all of us to a Burmese dinner at his residence that very evening. After work around 6:30 PM all four of us were driven to the residence of His Excellency and Madame U Hla Maung, in the Bentley leased for Bo Khin Nyo. He was a man of slight build, brown complexion (perhaps a hint of Indian blood), mild mannered and soft spoken in lower Burma (Southern) style. He was a classmate in university of Bo Khin Maung Galay (Bo Khin Nyo's elder brother) and colleague of Aung San and Gen. Ne Win (still calls him Ko Shu Maung). No wonder that Bo Khin Nyo, now a Member of the ruling Revolutionary Council, did not want to call on him alone. Moreover, U Hla Maung was notorious for initiating the breakup of the AFPFL Party of Aung San by imprudently suggesting that Prime Minister U Nu be kicked upstairs to be the Party Elder (Mentor) like Mao Tse-Dong in China.

He and Madame welcomed us warmly but before we even reached the formal reception room, he started whining about being kept in the dark for almost half a year. He complained that the Ministry of Foreign Affairs had not bothered to inform him about my coming to London let alone what my mission was. He found out from the "gossip and rumor channels" of London's Little Burma. That put me "in the hot seat" and that was Cairo, Egypt all over again. At that time Ambassador U Pe Kin (a Muslim and also a Colleague of Aung San), also a political appointee, wanted to know what my mission was. Obviously the Ambassadors had no clue of Bo Ne Win's penchant for secrecy compounded by his paranoia, distrust and disdain of the Ministry of Foreign Affairs bureaucrats, all Western educated and indoctrinated. Madame came to my rescue with a complaint of her own that she had been listening to his frustrations for many months and asked the butler to serve the drinks and appetizers. She definitely saved the evening for all of us.

Bo Aung Din mentioned our need for a Government Affairs Manager and interest in U Ohn Sein to fill that post. The Ambassador was all for it as they were classmates at Rangoon University and he was delighted beyond words that U M. M. Gale was already on our team and his friend was being given the opportunity to join us. He excused himself and went to his private office. In a few minutes he rejoined us for drinks and said he would bring U Ohn Sein to Burma Trade tomorrow at a time convenient to us. Bo Aung Din said, "H. E., please come around 12:30 PM and join us for light lunch." The full course Burmese dinner prepared by his official chef was enjoyed by all and Bo Khin Nyo thanked Madame for having us at short notice and the fine meal. We went to the Washington Hotel and I escorted the exhausted Colonel up to his suite and took a taxi back home to Twickenham Park. After 9:30 PM the traffic was light and it takes about half an hour's drive to get home. The next morning I was back at the hotel by 8:00 AM for a breakfast meeting in his suite to discuss issues that could not be discussed in the presence of others.

He revealed to me his concern that the Revolutionary Council Members including the Chairman were going through a very stressful time due to the very heavy load of responsibilities, very new and different in nature from Military duties because the Civil Service, Police and Government Ministries and Departments could not be managed and operated along the same "Command and Control" system which was the only way Military Officers were trained. In the Military, questioning orders from above is not tolerated. In Civil Service Administration Officers are trained to implement formulated policies from above under broad guidelines and are required / encouraged not to hesitate to discuss with superior / senior officers areas of ambiguity, or possible unintended consequences of implementing the policy. The bottom line is the Civil Service Officer Corps is required to deal with the "wide general public / population's needs", from "Law and Order to necessities of daily life" – food, water, utilities, health and administration of justice.

This huge systemic difference and wide gap in the psyche, mindset, education and training between the Military and Civil Service Corps was at the root cause of the Military Officers' frustration in not being able to make progress in the daily lives of the general population. This stark realization was setting in at all levels of the Armed Forces as well as the Civil Services but because of the extraordinary and multiple duties on their shoulders this crucial issue was being ignored and put out of sight "under the rug". However, the Communist Financial Adviser U Ba Nyain (a retired Civil Service bureaucrat) was aggressively pushing his agenda that the solution to this "Systemic Conflict / Gap" must be closed with "Political, Economic Ideology and Indoctrination" first the Military Establishment, then the Civil Services and the General Population – The Burma Socialist Programme Party Embracing the Ideology "Burmese Way To Socialism". Major tenets were adopted from Aung San's ECONOMIC BLUE PRINT FOR INDEPENDENT BURMA. I heard this from Bo Khin Nyo for the first time while having breakfast in his Washington Hotel suite in London (fall of 1962). I was lost for words. He did not tell me the source of this information but I assumed it was Bo San Yu because he was his next door neighbor and they often discussed and consulted on issues of the day.

Another matter of concern he wanted to get off his chest was the very sensitive and delicate "State Secret" of the maximum leader's overall health especially his memory lapses, short attention span and hair-trigger temper. He was quite open and said Bo Maung Lwin (Moustache) was worried sick because he was on the receiving end every morning at the intelligence briefing session. "He is not eager to see people and often conveys his instructions (orders) through Bo Aung Gyi, Bo Ko Ko and Bo Maung Lwin (Moustache) because he sees them daily and Bo San Yu is in poor health. The Military and the Government is operating smoothly under the capable leadership of Bo Aung Gyi and Bo Ne Win feels secure and comfortable to leave the country for Rest, Recreation, medical attention and a visit with his friend Marshal Tito at the end of the year." Bo Khin Nyo did not see the big boss before his departure but Bo Aung Gyi and Bo Maung Lwin (Moustache) briefed him together on all important policy issues and specific particulars to discuss with the Yugoslavia Ambassador in London.

He was cautioned not to involve U Hla Maung, the Ambassador, or any Embassy official but to have me accompany him for interpretation. Both mentioned that in their letters to me. We arrived at the office well after 10 AM. I left him with Bo Aung Din in the Boardroom and went to my office to check on the incoming cable / telex traffic and the diplomatic pouch packages delivered from the Defense Attaché's office. There was a message from Bo Maung Lwin confirming that he would be accompanying the boss, Katy, Rajoo, doctors and other attendants to London towards the end of the year for an extended stay and visits to Eastern Europe. At around 12:40 PM H.E. U Hla Maung showed up with U Ohn Sein in tow. They were very impressed and admired the office set up, the décor and the high end Danish and Italian office furniture. Our Front Desk Receptionist ushered the two gentlemen to the Boardroom where Bo Khin Nyo welcomed and greeted them. He requested that Bo Aung Din conduct the guided tour of the Office Complex and brought them first to my office and the adjoining "Secure Room" where the documents from the Union Bank of Burma would be reviewed by the new staff and utilized as legally substantiating documents of the hidden funds in the accounts of British, European, Scandinavian and U.S. Corporations.

After the tour light lunch was delivered from the Indian High Commissioner's Restaurant – mutton puff, samosas, vegetable sandwiches and the compulsory English staple, fish & chips. Bo Khin Nyo was in high spirits and suggested that an exception be made and had the bar serve drinks. I asked U M. M. Gale, the Administrative Manager, to have the appointment documents prepared before the lunch party shifted into high gear. As the party progressed we invited the other Managers and Senior Staff to join us for drinks and snacks in the Board Room and the adjoining Reception Room. Before the day ended we completed the formalities of appointing U Ohn Sein, Manager, government Liaison Department and assigned a large office space with several private rooms for his deputies and senior staff. Burma Trade U.K. Representative Office of BEDC was complete. With the Chairman visiting from Burma to launch the UK Action Plan implementation it was a rare opportunity for our Managers and Staff to meet a member of the Revolutionary Council that had taken over the reins of the Government in early March of that year and perhaps would enable the British nationals to better understand their Burmese colleagues.

I accompanied the Colonel back to his hotel to continue our one-on-one discussion of matters on his "things to do in London". It was quite apparent to me that one person he did not wish to meet was Bo Aye Maung but there was no way to avoid that because he was appointed de-facto Chairman of Burma Trade which had triggered the outburst and disapproval of Gen. Ne Win. I suggested that we have him join us during the lunch break to shorten the duration of his stay with us in the Boardroom. Bo Khin Nyo liked the idea and told me to have him come over during the lunch break. Another item of urgent importance was the West German Government's offer of a Low Interest Commercial (G to G) Loan Negotiation to build four Cargo Vessels for Burma Five Star Line BEDC Shipping Company now fully owned (Jewish Zim Navigation was kicked out) after my negotiations with the Arab League). The Vessels to be named: MS TAVOY, MS BASSEIN, MS MOULMEIN and MS MYAUNGMYA. The West German Bundes Bank Officials and Diplomats would come to London to meet with Bo Khin Nyo. He gave me the file to review and to give him my take on the case.

The next morning I called Bo Aye Maung from the hotel and advised him because of his busy schedule, the only convenient time available for meeting with Col. Khin Nyo would be for him to join us during the lunch break around 12:30 PM. He was very anxious and grabbed the opportunity saying "I will be there today and join you during lunch break". As in the hierarchy of Buddhist Monks, seniority trumps everything in the Military. A few minutes after 12 noon, the Front Desk Receptionist announced that Col. Aye Maung had arrived and ushered him to the Boardroom but he abruptly stopped in his tracks and stood at attention as soon as he saw Bo Khin Nyo who greeted him saying "Hey Bo Aye Maung, you are looking well, London must be treating you well, come, come sit here and tell me how things are with you and the family". That friendly greeting put Bo Aye Maung at ease and he joined us in munching on the samosas, mutton puffs and sandwiches. He commented that "this is the biggest and the best Burmese Office Complex in London". I noted that Bo Aung Din, U M. M. Gale and U Ohn Sein were quite tense and one after the other made an excuse to visit the rest room. To my surprise and discomfiture Bo Khin Nyo said, "All of us in Rangoon are confident that U Kyi Win Sein will achieve the same success of his Mission in the Middle East". It was reiteration of "this is our man here in London entrusted with the implementation and operation of this Organization".

# BURMESE POLITICIANS AND MARSHAL TITO OF YUGOSLAVIA

Since the days of the WE BURMAN ASSOCIATION AND THE THAKIN MOVEMENTS Burmese political leaders held in high regard and looked up to the Socialist Revolution of Yugoslavia and the rapidly rising Tito's popularity with the multi-ethnic races which came together under the Democratic Socialist banner. The loose Federation was made possible by a well thought out "Inclusive Constitution" and "Strong Leadership at the top". The proof of its mettle came to be severely tested during the period of German Nazi invasion and occupation and at the end of WWII when the Soviet Union's Communist Party attempted to take over other East European countries but were defeated by the Patriotic Forces under the strong leadership of Marshal Tito. Bo Aung San read every available book and documents in English on Yugoslavia while he was staying at the home of Colonel Suzuki in Hamamatsu. His Constitution for Independent Burma was written along the same lines.

During and after WWII the Indian Congress and Communist Parties under the leadership of Jawahalal Nehru and Subas Chandra Bose / Goshal introduced the up and coming Burmese Socialist leaders – Thakin Ba Sein (Bo Ne Win at that time Thakin Shu Maung was a member of that faction), U Ba Swe, U Kyaw Nyein, Bo Khin Maung Galay, Thakin Mya (Pyawbwe) and Thakin Tha Khin. In the early fifties, Nehru, U Nu, Sukarno, Nasser and Tito founded the Non-Aligned Movement at the historic gathering in Bandung Indonesia. Bo Ne Win sought the advice of Bo Khin Maung Galay and U Kyaw Nyein on the International Socialist Movement and he was advised to Consult and Cooperate with Marshal Tito of Yugoslavia, a highly respected world Statesman for many decades.

Bo Khin Nyo asked me to prepare a short brief prior to our meeting the Yugoslavian Ambassador in London, a close Comrade and Confidante of Tito. In the midst of going through recent historical background of Burma / Yugoslav Relations, Bo Khin Nyo surprised me by bringing up his rather shabby Indian tailored attire, both sets several years old already. He wondered aloud if his old three piece suits would not be appropriate in London especially when calling on Head of Diplomatic Missions representing the Head of State and in his own capacity as Member of the Revolutionary Council. I was lost for words and quite taken aback, ashamed and guilty for not having had the courage to suggest having a tailor from Savile Row come take measurement of the Old Colonel for a few sets of the best English three piece suits. Now that he had broken the ice, I related to him what happened to me when I was in Cairo. After about two months working with General Yaha Ramadan, he shocked me one day by announcing that "Mr. Sein, we are going to outfit you with a new wardrobe, as you will be in the company of Arab League Ministers and it is important to be impeccably attired like them. The wardrobe will be a gift (compliments of the Egyptian Presidency)". Three suits were ordered (Spring, Summer, Fall weights for Middle East climate and weather patterns).

He had the Chief Tailor of the General's wardrobe shop take my measurements and asked me to select from wads of the best British and Belgian 100% wool fabrics. He ordered three suits – Spring, Summer, Winter and All Weather complete with dress shirts, matching ties and dress shoes and socks. The old Sandhurst graduate general said, "You are now our brother and we must take care of your needs as our State Guest." He lectured and taught me that "when you are representing your Country, you must be equal to your counterparts or better". The next morning I had a very reputable tailor from Savile Row come to the Colonel's suite with samples of British wool fabrics and take measurements for custom tailored suits. We ordered three suits and one blazer with the first one to be delivered within 48 hours after the necessary "fittings". I advised him that on recommendation of Lloyds Corporate Management Consultants, Burma Trade's "Employment Benefits Package includes one-time wardrobe allowance for one year minimum service". It ensures appropriately attired employees and enhances the prestige of the Company in the business community, and loyalty and low turnover of office staff.

The Embassy of Yugoslavia was located in the best prime diplomatic enclave of Central London and impeccably maintained inside and out. In the main front lobby there was a banner hung on the wall:

EMBASSY OF YUGOSLAVIA WELCOMES HIS EXCELLENCY COLONEL KHIN NYO, REVOLUTIONARY COUNCIL MEMBER OF THE UNION OF BURMA.

The Ambassador personally accompanied by the Minister and Counsellor (the three highest diplomats of that country Accredited to the Court of St. James) waited at the main front entrance to the lobby for our arrival. Both of us were taken by surprise at the grand welcome and reception. The Embassy Protocol Officer exchanged business cards with us and conducted the formal introductions in the lobby and led the way to a very well appointed Conference Room and in good taste there were no chairs at both ends of the large table covered with green velvet and thick plate glass like the one in our office. We sat facing each other, four on their side and two on ours. Immediately the attendants came in to serve tea / coffee / cold drinks. With due consideration of the language barrier the Ambassador kindly suggested that "diplomatic formalities be waived and dispensed with" and "U Kyi Win Sein is requested to assist with interpretation". In a cocktail party setting and environment Bo Khin Nyo seemed to be quite at ease and holding his own conversing in English.

However, in the stiff formal face-to-face setting, English words were almost nonexistent and comprehension is about 40% depending on the accent of the speaker. Some Yugoslavs have that thick and heavy Serb-German accent and one needs a little time to get the hang of it. It was tedious and time consuming to say the least but both sides needed vital information to lay the groundwork for the visit of Bo Ne Win to Yugoslavia and the things (issues / matters / subjects) he wished to discuss with Tito. The Yugoslav Ambassador and his three top diplomats expected a more comprehensive briefing and information package from the Revolutionary Council Member on the Burmese Head of State's agenda and subjects he would like to explore with his host and the economic specialists of that country and their actual experience in practicing the Command Economy and the outcomes so far for the population.

From the bits and pieces and fragmented information from Bo Khin Nyo during many days of conversation, it was quite evident that he did not have one-to-one discussions with his boss and was only briefed by Bo Aung Gyi and Bo Maung Lwin (Moustache), and had also received the instruction to call on the Yugoslav Ambassador during the briefing sessions. No wonder that he did not have much to discuss with Tito's men in London. We found the three to be very polished and experienced in their dealings with foreign dignitaries with faultless courtesy and correct protocol. We were entertained to lunch in their formal dining suite and was joined by two lady diplomats – Commercial and Cultural Attachés both educated in elite British Universities. Unlike the typical Yugoslav cuisine their Ambassador in Rangoon served us many times, we were pleasantly surprised to be given "a gold trimmed Menu of the day" in English and French but the Chef's recommendation was "full course Indian Lunch or fish and chips" and it was the joke of the day. Bo Khin Nyo got a big kick out of it and went for it.

The Yugoslav Ambassador and his diplomats, in deference and courtesy to the Member of the Burmese Military Regime, opted for the same making it easy for the Chef. Apparently their Embassy had a fully equipped restaurant class kitchen. The Indian cuisine was as good as those served in the High Commissioner's basement private restaurant. During the leisurely luncheon, many of the questions were directed at me by the Ambassador and the two ladies departing from proper diplomatic protocol, inquiring how old I was and where I had learned to speak "such perfect English". Bo Khin Nyo, ever considerate and supportive, told our Yugoslav host "U Kyi Win Sein is our Chief Legal Adviser and international business projects with a Law Degree from Tokyo University". All of them could clearly notice that I was surprised and rather embarrassed by such praise in the presence of our Host by a senior member of the ruling Military Regime who was my direct superior. I quickly had to move the conversation away from me to Yugoslav current affairs and its future in Europe. Among the five of them in front of us, the Ambassador was a Serb, the Minister was a Croatian, the Counsellor was a Montenegrin, and the ladies were either Serbian or Croatian.

It was quite a surprise to them that we were familiar with their country's make-up of ethnicities. We could clearly see that they were very eager to pursue that line of conversation with us when I brought up the question of Yugoslavia after Marshal Tito. The seasoned Ambassador, probably aware that I had collaborated with their Intelligence Operatives in the Middle East, frankly admitted that the Yugoslav Federation was held together by the strong leadership of one man – Marshal Tito – and thus far there was no one they knew of who could take his place. "We are all concerned that after his demise, there is all likelihood that the Federation will shatter and disintegrate – implosion from within, outside pressure or both."

That conversation we had with the Yugoslav diplomats in London was a premonition of what came to pass some forty years or so later when President Bill Clinton and his Secretary of State Madeleine Albright bombed and dismantled the Yugoslav Federation, splintering it into NOT NATION STATES BUT CITY STATES, some like Montenegro with just a 650,000 population. America's Regime Change foreign policy was at play and at the same time legitimizing the existence of NATO and depriving the Russians of a potential ally in Europe. Yugoslavia, under Tito's leadership, was advancing rapidly as an industrialized society successfully practicing the mixed economy policy of State owned enterprises competing with private corporations and more often the Government companies would fall behind and immediately be auctioned off to the highest bidder. Failed Government Corporations were not subsidized and their Management was held responsible for the Company's failure for whatever reason (more often bribery, corruption, poor work ethics, etc) and appropriate punishment meted out in accordance with existing Laws.

It was a success story when other European countries tottered on the brink of insolvency burdened by sovereign debts to the IMF, World Bank, Export-Import Bank of America and other State Banks in West Germany and Great Britain. Marshal Tito advised Gen. Ne Win to avoid a 100% State Owned Command Economy and adopt the Yugoslav Model of a Mixed Economy. The Burmese Socialists led by U Ba Swe, Bo Khin Maung Galay (elder brother of Bo Khin Nyo) and U Kyaw Nyein were consulted in secret by Bo Ne Win, together with Bo Aung Gyi, Bo San Yu and Bo Thaung Kyi and all the Political Leaders advised him to look at the Yugoslav model and select those that were applicable to the Burmese Economic Realities and Conditions. U Kyaw Nyein and Bo Khin Maung Galay had very close personal relations with Marshal Tito who visited Burma as State Guest several times. This was the background of Bo Ne Win's plan to visit Yugoslavia and see for himself how the Mixed Economy was being managed and get counsel on the "Things to do and Things to Avoid" from the man at the top.

It was clear evidence that Bo Ne Win sought the advice and counsel of Burmese Socialist leaders prior to his moving headlong with the Burmese Way to Socialism authored by the Communist National United Front Party that for all intents and purposes high-jacked the Burma Socialist Programme Party and led the Burmese Military by their noses (including Bo Ne Win) like bullocks into disaster for the entire country. Here again to relate it in true historical perspective, Bo Aung Gyi, the #2 General of the Military, recognized as its "Economic Czar" with a track record of success, openly opposed this ill-conceived, unproven, untried and ideology-based economic policies, but Bo Ne Win in their last one-to-one meeting convinced Bo Aung Gyi that he was determined to move ahead but with a rather unintended and disingenuous compromise of "If in four years our policies fail to make progress I will hand over State Power to you".

This was the last straw for Bo Aung Gyi who frankly told the Commander-in-Chief, "Bogyoke (General), we are deciding the fate and destiny of the country and people, it cannot be on the basis of I run it for four years and you do it for four years like the Military is run. For you to have a free hand I will tender my resignation from all the positions I now hold" and he walked out of the War Room. He wrote his resignation in long hand and inserted it in an envelope addressed to Bo Ne Win and left it with his Personal Staff Officer for submission. He asked Gen. Tommy Clift to arrange a plane to fly him to MachanBaw in Kachin State to rest and reflect over what had transpired between him and the #1. The resignation letter was delivered while the Revolutionary Council Meeting was in session. According to eyewitness accounts of Bo Thaung Kyi, Bo Khin Nyo and Bo Tommy Clift, the Chairman opened the letter and stared at it for several minutes in silence with an expression of utter disbelief.

They thought someone close had died. Bo Ko Ko, the Revolutionary Council Secretary, asked, "Bogyoke (General) is something the matter?" He said, "All of you can read it for yourselves" and he barged out of the room. All were shocked except the Bo Tin Phay faction and U Ba Nyain the National United Front Financial Adviser. Now, the biggest barrier was removed from within the Revolutionary Council as well as the Military itself. However, on reaching home, Bo Ne Win summoned U Thi Han, Minister of Foreign Affairs and instructed him to immediately fly up to Machan Baw and aske Bo Aung Gyi to withdraw his resignation and return to Rangoon. Both men hailed from the same town (Paungde) and had been close friends since High School and University days. The Foreign Minister dropped everything he was doing and flew up to the Kachin State in a special Air Force plane to the great surprise of his friend. They spent three days together enjoying the clean mountain air, fresh vegetables and fruits, reminiscing on the good times of the past and discussing the primary reason of his trip ordered by the #1.

Here in the interest of brevity and proper historical record, both of them related their version of what transpired during the three days together in the Government Rest House up in the Kachin State. U Thi Han revealed to Bo Khin Nyo and me while on a visit to London and we arranged their stay at the Washington Hotel in adjoining suites at their request. At breakfast in Bo Khin Nyo's suite, U Thi Han on his own brought up the matter of his failed mission to persuade Bo Aung Gyi to withdraw his resignation. What I noted as significant was the sense of "personal guilt" he admitted suffering for not having the courage to explain the "Five National Policy Issues Bo Aung Gyi wrote on a sheet of his writing pad, explained it to him in detail and asked him to do the same with Bo Ne Win on his return to Rangoon". Should Bo Ne Win agree to those 5 National Policies, Bo Aung Gyi would withdraw his resignation.

U Thi Han told us that on his flight back to Rangoon he struggled with the task of explaining these National Policy matters to the #1. The more he gave thought to it, the more questions popped up in his head – such as: I am the only civilian in the Military Regime, would it be appropriate for me to mediate the difference of opinion of the two top Generals? How would #1 interpret this? There is a possibility he thinks I am siding with Bo Aung Gyi? Why am I playing Advocate's role? It was quite apparent that the Foreign Minister was getting "cold feet" at the prospect of being misunderstood by the #1 who had sent him in the first place but did not like the message he'd brought back and sacks him, as in the saying "the messenger gets killed because the receiver did not like the message". His plane landed in Rangoon with all these negative thoughts in his head. My immediate reaction on hearing this in Bo Khin Nyo's suite was "here is our country's Foreign Minister quite intimidated by being the only civilian in the Military Regime, thinking with his emotions and not with his intellect and rather confused as to whether it's his post or the National Policy issues that he wholeheartedly agrees with Bo Aung Gyi, his friend.

On the flip side of the coin he thought that of the Five National Policy Issues THERE WERE NONE THAT BO NE WIN COULD NOT ACCEPT. Notwithstanding what he personally thought of, he could not muster enough courage to explain them to #1 as Bo Aung Gyi requested for him to withdraw his resignation. The poor man was having second and third thoughts and definitely regretting and blaming himself and frankly telling us that he would have to live with it and take it to his grave. He said the heavy blow struck him when he told #1 "Bo Aung Gyi would not withdraw his resignation" and Bo Ne Win remarked "I never thought he would abandon us like this". Then and there he said to himself "I should have explained the Five National Policy Issues to him". Bo Khin Nyo was aghast and incredulous and told U Thi Han "Ko Thi Han, I wish you had shared your dilemma with me because I would have accompanied you to explain them to #1". At that time Bo Khin Nyo revealed the secret that Bo Ne Win had asked his elder brother Bo Khin Maung Galay and U Kyaw Nyein to persuade Bo Aung Gyi to come back and redirect the economy.

Yes, when U Kyaw Nyein came to see me in California at the request of Bo Aung Gyi, he did not say it in the same words, but said Bo Ne Win admitted his biggest mistake was Policy Conflict with Bo Aung Gyi and letting him leave the Government. The result was the Military Regime was left with unthinking "Yes Men" with absolutely no clue of what they were doing and the consequences of their actions. In fairness we must give due recognition that these men voluntarily gave their service and many the ultimate sacrifice of their lives in the fight for the country's independence from the British, then the Japanese and after independence ended up in the Military. They were not trained for "Nation Building", they were trained to take orders from above in the defense of the country. Then all of a sudden ordered to the Ministries, Departments, Civil Administration, Police Departments and Government Organizations to supervise and manage them with no training whatsoever. It was not surprising that the entire Government Machinery came to an abrupt stop.

The responsibility rests with the Commander-in-Chief, Gen. Ne Win. On this score he was made aware from within and outside the inevitable outcome of pursuing Command Economy Policies as early as the end of 1962 just ten months after the Coup in early March of that year. In all likelihood he did not grasp the gravity of going down that path because on his return to London from Yugoslavia, Czechoslovakia and Romania he did not discuss anything with Members of his Mission – Bo Khin Nyo, U Thi Han and Bo Maung Lwin (Moustache) – what they had heard and seen in three Socialist countries. In one of the dinner sessions we had in Bo Khin Nyo's suite Bo Lwin after a few drinks bluntly wondered aloud: "Bogyoke most probably did not understand half of what Marshal Tito was telling him through the interpreter and he is too proud or embarrassed (Ar-Nar-De) to repeat again what was explained to him".

To my surprise all three of them said they only understood at most 30% because the interpreter's English pronunciation was difficult to understand. I surmised that all of them came back with very little information from the "Face-to-Face Talks" and when I enquired if they had reviewed the "Transcripts in the Portfolio from the Presidential Office" they asked in unison, "What do you mean? We received packages but no transcriptions". I said it must be in the package. They had not opened it because they thought it was "Catalogues and Brochures of Socialist / Communist Propaganda". Bo Khin Nyo opened his package and asked me to check them out. There was a leather bound folio with the "English Transcript of everything that was uttered by Marshal Tito". The laughed and joked about it saying "if you had not told us we would never have opened it". Bo Khin Nyo left the "transcript for my review" and Bo Lwin said he would give his copy to Bo Aung Gyi on return to Rangoon and U Thi Han said he would review his on the long flight back home and give it to the Chief of Economic Division in his Ministry. I found the transcript to be of a very high level in every aspect: "Language, Academic, Intellectual and Factual Accuracy as a State Owned Official Policy Document". Information gleaned from the transcript was most insightful and proved its relevance and validity when I was assigned as General Counsel and Legal Adviser to the Central Nationalization and the Economic Insurgency Control Committees under the Central Security and Admistrative Committee.

Another thing that surprised me was these that three men, among the people trusted by Bo Ne Win, were quite at ease in their off-guard moment out of the country openly and frankly expressing their opinions including their severe limitations in understanding the English language. U Thi Han was very curious how I had learned several languages simultaneously and attained proficiency in both written and spoken English. I explained my very late start at age 12 when everything was taught in English. We were not allowed to speak Burmese in class and by the time of taking the Matriculation examination I was interpreter (English to Burmese) in first the Pre-Medical courses under pressure to learn and absorb medical terms and science subjects like Bio-Chemistry, Micro-Biology, Mammalian and Human Anatomy.

And by luck of circumstances when I was studying at University of Tokyo, the faculty and professors were desperately learning to master the English language as MacArthur and the Americans occupied Japan and ruled it through the General Head Quarters (GHQ) from where the the 5-Star General of the Army issued his first order to change "all street names of Tokyo and major cities from Japanese to English – A to Z, A-1 to Z-1 in that order for the the poorly educated GI to easily understand and not get lost in the cities that were flat from carpet bombing of American planes.

My Professors assigned most of their Academic Research Papers for me to write, edit, type and communicate in English with the International Institutions. It was strange and incredible that one was required to study in Japan's #1 University in English soon after Japan's surrender to the Americans in 1945. My Japanese Professors often asked me, "Hey, Sein kun, in what language are you thinking? In Burmese or English?" I was confused and puzzled because I really don't know to this day. But the three Burmese Cabinet officers – the Foreign Minister, the Military Intelligence Chief and Revolutionary Council Member – were surprised to hear what I had to tell them about my learning the English language in Japan pressed into serving the Academic Faculty as their Assistant for Research Paper writer for International Law and Relations Reviews and Publications. As a Japanese Government invited State Scholar under the Treaty of Peace and War Reparations with the Burmese Government I was placed under the care and supervision of the Law School Dean; I had no other option but to gratefully accept his arrangements.

The most significant Research and Review task assigned to me at the time by Dr. Yokota Kisaburo, Dean of Tokyo University Law School (later Chief Justice of the Japanese Supreme Court) was the "Secret Papers at General MacArthur's Head Quarters, the Pacifist Constitution and the Deliberations of the Allied Supreme Command on the Fate of Emperor Hirohito and General MacArthur's Veto of the other Allies to try him for War Crimes". I was awarded my first degree (B.A.) in International Relations and Diplomatic History and later my Law Degree (LL.B) in International Law. I was one of the few Foreign State Scholars with the distinction of being Japanese Supreme Court Chief Justice Yokota's protégé (Yokota Sensei's De-Shi). It was something that foreigners will never understand but in Japanese society it was indeed a very big deal. The mere mention of his name would open doors to the highest echelons of power anywhere in Japan. Three of my classmates went on to become Prime Ministers of Japan and many others rose to the level of Cabinet Ministers. It was incredible for me personally because in 1955 all of these friends were punching train tickets after classes to buy his next meal with the meagre earning of a few hours of work. Whereas as foreign State Scholar sponsored by two Governments, I was getting more than my Professor's monthly salary and housed in International Students' Dormitory with a Restaurant Class Dining facility.

I would often invite classmates to my dining room and have them join me for meals and they would not accept. It really surprised me at first but I came to learn later that the custom was "Dutch" – even if invited you pay for your order. In our Burmese custom if you invite someone for a meal (he / she is your guest) and the tab is on you. It is considered rude to expect your guest to pay for his/her order. After they came to understand our Burmese custom, there was no reluctance and they would happily accept my invitation. However, the next day I met them in class, they would thank me for "yesterday's treat". After a few times I had to tell them that there was no need to feel obligated. In the Burmese language, there is no "good morning, good afternoon, good evening", the greeting is always "have you eaten?". If you haven't eaten, we offer whatever food is available or go eat together at a food shop. Many years later when I left Burma and returned to Japan, many of these friends, now Ministers and Corporate Executives, would tell me quite frankly "you were very kind and always invited us to your dormitory to join you for meals regardless of the time of day".

# POLITICS OF LONDON BURMESE COMMUNITY

The Burmese community in London goes a long way back to the time of King Mindon, who sent his relatives and the famous Kin-Wun-Mingyi on a study tour of England. That had some positive change in attitudes within the King's rather large immediate family and by the time Thibaw succeeded to the Throne in Mandalay Palace there was a school for the royal family's children learning English language from a resident "white British teacher". At the time King Thibaw was rudely taken away from Mandalay, his Princesses were able to communicate with their captors as recorded in the papers of "the British conquest of the Burmese Kingdom". It supposedly helped the captured Burmese King and his family to complain to their captors about the rude and improper treatment of not addressing the King, Queen and the Princesses with their appropriate Royal Titles.

During many decades of British colonial rule the most favored Burmese elite were sent to Oxford, Cambridge and London Universities for higher training for service in the Colonial Rule of British possessions and Colonies. The most desired and highly regarded were Civil Service Examinations of the Indian Civil Service (ICS), Imperial Police Service (IPS), Indian Education Service (IES) and Indian Judicial Service (IJS). This class of educated local natives helped the British "white Colonial Service Men" rule over the entire country divided along ethnic lines. In Burma that rule lasted continuously for nearly eight decades for the entire country but for Lower (Southern) Burma well over a century. When Burma regained independence, this same class of bureaucrats became the instruments of the Burmese politicians led by U Nu that took the place of the "while British Colonial Rulers". Again the #1 preferred country to send for higher learning, for medical doctors, engineers, educators, civil service, police service, military service (Army, Air Force, Navy) and Judicial Service (Barristers) of course was England.

In March 1962 when the democratically elected Government of Prime Minister U Nu was toppled by Gen. Ne Win, the Burmese Community in London was shocked beyond belief and even more when full-fledged recognition was accorded to the Revolutionary Council by Her Majesty's Government within a matter of days after the Coup. The huge Anglo-Burmese and Karen Christian communities felt betrayed by their British supporters. The reaction in other Burmese enclaves was rather muted and did not have emotional outbursts like the Karens and the Anglos. The Official Burmese Embassy and the Defense Attaché's Offices' Burmese group were in no position to express their reaction to what had taken place back home but to await for "Official Orders" from the New Military Government or for news from colleagues or relatives back home. The strange irony was the Ambassador U Hla Maung (Peking) was a senior politician and close friend of the ousted Prime Minister U Nu and the Defense Attaché Colonel Aye Maung was caught in the act of staging a Coup with Gen. Maung Maung and exiled to London unwanted in the Military but not sacked for the sake of the ten children.

As such, the civilian Foreign Minister U Thi Han took every precaution not to appear to be the source of information to political appointee Ambassadors. Defense Attachés are directly under the Military Intelligence Chief and no one in the Ministry of Defense dared to contact Col. Aye Maung. The two Official Offices of the country were for all intents and purposes kept in the dark. They had to rely on private information sources in Rangoon which consisted mostly of rumors and speculations circulating within the various vested interest groups. The large and diverse Burmese Communities in London were practically in the dark starved of news after the take over of the country by Gen. Ne Win on March 02, 1962.

Then after several months at the end of May-early June 1962 when the Action Plan Committee received approval and authorization to launch the project in London and I was instructed to call on U San Lin, Union Bank of Burma Governor, to collect the documents from him, the first hint of the leak of the project was traced back to that source. It turned out that some senior bureaucrats in the Union Bank of Burma and the Ministry of Finance through their personal connections with Air Force and Navy officers started the gossip, rumors and speculations that the Revolutionary Council was about to embark on a monumental shakeup and changes in the banking, financial and payment systems of the political era. They missed the target completely but were partially correct. Thereafter, when Gen. Tommy Clift's man Lt. Col. Aung Din (Air Force Rtd) was rejected by Gen. Ne Win and I was nominated to lead the UK Action Plan implementation, set up and operation, the information leakage became more widespread.

A young Japanese educated Lawyer was being sent to London to set up the necessary organization to "implement the Revolutionary Council's Secret Project". This was clear evidence that despite the tight security precautions to prevent leakage, it could now be traced to Union Bank of Burma, Ministry of Finance, Air Force, Navy, Ministry of Foreign Affairs and even the Ministry of Defense. Bo Aung Gyi as Chairman of the UK Action Plan Committee was rather upset but agreed with Bo Maung Lwin's (Moustache) assessment that it would have no effect on the project's outcome as luckily it had been deflected to some minor personnel issue. Notwithstanding that the Committee members brushed off the leakage of information from several Ministries, there certainly was some feeling of being kept out of the inner circle of the "Greens". The sarcastic comments of the "Khakis and Whites" was "If the Green Lawyers did not stand a chance we are out of the question" (A Senior Major of the Judge Advocate General's Office was also rejected) by the Revolutionary Council Chairman.

Bo Khin Nyo and Bo Maung Lwin (Moustache) told me not to worry about it as Gen. Clift, Air Force Chief of Staff, was fully aware and present at the final approval session with Gen. Ne Win when Bo Aung Gyi proposed Bo Aung Din who was already in London working for a BEDC JV Company. That did not matter at all, the RC Chairman rejected that proposal and ordered that I be sent to lead the implementation – mentioning that "Marshal Tito's Adviser told him that the Yugoslav Intelligence Operatives in the Middle East praised your performance very highly". As a matter of fact Bo Aung Din revealed to me that he received a personal letter from his boss, Gen. Tommy Clift, advising him about my nomination by the RC Chairman and to fully cooperate in the implementation of the project (without giving any specifics) but mentioning about my youth and Law Degree from Tokyo University.

The various groups and factions of the London Burmese Communities were receiving all kinds of information (gossip, rumors and speculations) after more than three months of blackout. Then out of the blue news about the first official being sent to London by the Military Regime for a special project. The Defense Attaché's office knew the name from the instructions received from the Ministry of Defense regarding the many diplomatic packages to be securely kept until my arrival. However, the Burmese Embassy did not receive any information from the Ministry of Foreign Affairs on my mission. Under normal circumstances the Embassy would be informed about officials visiting or even transiting London. They did hear the news through the grapevine and the Defense Attaché office staff about receiving many diplomatic packages in my name.

Bo Aung Din was the first Burmese in London to receive official information from his Air Force Chief of the impending restructuring of the BEDC Joint Venture enterprises in the UK, Europe and U.S. advising him to fully cooperate with the Legal Adviser entrusted to implement the project and manage the operation. He then received from Bo Perry Aye Cho, Managing Director of Oppenheimer Jones Rangoon (The Head Office), a retired Air Force Lt. Colonel cautioning him to be extra careful in dealing with the young Japanese educated Lawyer nominated by the Revolutionary Council Chairman and reporting directly to Gen. Aung Gyi and his Deputy Col. Khin Nyo Chairman of BEDC under the Prime Minister's Office. I later learned that Perry Aye Cho (Anglo-Arakanese background) implicated his ex-Boss Tommy Clift warning his colleague in London what he was told (if at all) in confidence "Kyi Win Sein is the only civilian Legal Officer (Under Cover) placed directly under the Intelligence Chief for Overseas Covert Operations. He successfully pulled off the Middle East Operation negotiating with the 22 Nation Arab League lifting the Boycott and All Economic Sanctions and allowing passage of Burmese Flag Merchant Ships through the Suez Canal. In return the Burmese Government dismantled all JV Enterprises with Israel and their U.S. allies.

"Gen. Aung Gyi, the Trade and Commerce Minister and Col. Khin Nyo, BEDC Chairman, entrust all International, Legal, Financial, Banking and Contract matters to him for review before the Law Firm Sooma & Boon prepares the Original Hard Copies for their Signatures." Apparently there was "suppressed feelings of resentment within the Defense Establishment as well as the BEDC Head Office and its many subsidiary Corporations in Burma and JV Enterprises abroad. However, Bo Aung Din with many years of experience as Deputy Defense Attaché in London was aghast that a retired senior officer would divulge such classified information implicating a Serving Air Force Chief of Staff and immediately alerted his Boss who in turn informed Col. Maung Lwin (Moustache), the Intelligence Chief, who hit the ceiling. He asked Gen. Clift to quietly pursue the serious breach within the Air Force and submit his findings after questioning Perry Aye Cho and his General Manager retired Captain Kyaw Nyunt (Arakanese) from the famous Millionaire Square of Akyab (Sittwe).

The Intelligence Chief wanted to confine the serious breach of blowing the cover of an officer involved in overseas covert operations by the indiscretion of a retired senior Air Force Officer appointed in a management position in BEDC JV Corporation with a British Company. It was urgently imperative for Gen. Clift to ascertain that the "information was revealed to Bo Aung Din Only and no one else". Perry Aye Cho was questioned by Air Force Intelligence and retired Captain Kyaw Nyunt by Army Intelligence specialists. Fortunately for all concerned, especially for Gen. Clift, the two separate internal investigations confirmed conclusively that it was simply a case of "disgruntled retired officers venting steam" at the "Army Greens" for what they perceived as "discrimination" and a gesture of moral support for a fellow officer being superseded by a Civilian close to the Seat of Power. It did not go beyond Bo Aung Din and it was his good judgment and swift alert to Gen. Clift that saved the day for all concerned. If the breach of information had gone viral and official investigation launched, the consequences would have been catastrophic for many senior officers. It was a huge relief for Gen. Clift and Col. Maung Lwin (Moustache) who handled the matter without any preconceived notions and due consideration deference to the Head of the Service to handle and resolve it internally.

# UNIVERSAL PHENOMENA OF DISCRIMINATION, PREJUDICE AND JEALOUSY

When I left Rangoon in late July-August 1962 with wife Kazuko, toddler son Bob and accompanied by Lt. Col. Myo Myint, Chairman of State Timber Board, there was a great amount of accusations regarding the executive class tickets and excess baggage of the family that we were taking along. The fact of the matter was I was instructed to expedite my departure for London via Copenhagen to take care of the STB Contract and push ahead with the UK Action Plan. I was planning to ship the personal effects by sea but Bo Aung Gyi and Bo Khin Nyo said "don't waste time, just take them along with you". The reason was that at the "Wake" of Admiral Than Phay, Gen. Ne Win saw me there and asked "why are you still here?" and he told (ordered) Bo Khin Nyo "send him there ASAP". There was no way for me to spend time shipping personal effects by sea. At Mingaladon Airport departure Bo Maung Lwin (Moustache) instructed the Security Officer to take care of our departure procedures and several officers from the Ministry of Defense showed up to see us off. The Immigration and Customs officers were intimidated by the Military Intelligence Officers looking over their shoulders.

The poor Col. Myo Myint, a gentleman in every sense, was helping us with carry-on bags as well as carrying Bob asleep on his shoulders (he had just flown in from Tokyo a few weeks earlier and was tired of flying). All that went on during our departure became the subject of disparaging speculation and gossip in Rangoon starting with the large number of excess baggage charges paid by the Military Intelligence Officers. Then Col. Myo Myint carrying our son Bob and being escorted up into the aircraft front cabin by the Airport Security Officer. Who is this young fellow with a Japanese wife and baby son? Why was he given such special VIP treatment? What is he going to do in Copenhagen and London? It was hardly a surprise to learn that the Immigration, Customs and Airline personnel involved in the departure procedures are prone to talk about the day's unusual happenings to family and friends and by word of mouth spreads to others far and wide, even to London thousands of miles away.

We stopped over one night in Bangkok to connect with a non-stop flight to Copenhagen. During the long flight Bo Myo Myint talked about his Military career and his earlier education at St. Peters, Mandalay and then Rangoon University. He was briefly posted to the Defense Services Academy as an instructor and I assumed that he graduated and received his degree although he did not mention it himself. He discussed the Contract with me and said he did not get the opportunity to study Law. He was happy to hear that I started by schooling at St. Alberts and then at St. Peters, Mandalay. By the time we landed at Copenhagen I noted that he was physically exhausted and perhaps made worse by several hours of trying to make sense of the legal stuff. We checked in at the Airport Hilton and rested for the night after dinner together. The next morning after breakfast, we met the team of Executives and Lawyers from STHF in the hotel Conference Room and settled the Contract issues by terminating it and signing a Memorandum of Agreement to negotiate a New Contract at the earliest in Rangoon. Bo Myo Myint returned to Rangoon with the Memorandum of Agreement and we proceeded on to London.

After two days of rest and reunion with our favorite Aunty Eve at her home in Cheam Village, Surrey, I took the 8:30 AM express to Waterloo Station. Bo Aung Din waited at the central exit gate holding a piece of cardboard with my name on it. We shook hands and he welcomed me to London. His first comment was "you look a lot younger that what Bogyoke (Gen. Clift) told me in his letter". I noted that he did not mention anything about the communication from Perry Aye Cho, his Air Force colleague at Oppenheimer Jones Rangoon (the Head Office). We took a taxi to his office and got there in less than fifteen minutes. He ushered me to their well-furnished reception room and his secretary served us coffee. My impression of the retired Air Force officer was a middle aged man (late forties-early fifties), conservative, mild mannered and soft spoken. During our one-to-one discussion while having coffee, he said very little and was quite anxious, eager for news of the recent changes back home and the changes I was about to make for BEDC JV Enterprises in London. To break the ice and find out how much Gen. Clift (a member of the Committee) had told him in his letter I said, "Gen. Clift must have explained in his letter the general outline of our UK Action Plan Project".

He quickly responded with "he wrote about meeting you in Tokyo together with Gen. Ne Win and Aung Gyi while you were a law student there and received your Law Degree from Tokyo University and now Legal Adviser to Chairman of BEDC. He also mentioned that the Revolutionary Council Chairman nominated you to implement the project and changes and to assist and cooperate fully with you". A very clear confirmation of his experience in London as a Military Diplomat. His boss and good friend must have advised him to bear in mind that this project was initiated at the very top and the young Lawyer "is their man with full backing". That was the distinct impression I received during the first discussion with Bo Aung Din, Executive Managing Director of Oppenheimer Jones (JV) London. He introduced me to his General Manager, Mr. Hari, a Hindu Indian and Chief Accountant Mr. Magol, a Muslim Indian, both naturalized British citizens. I asked the three of them to immediately consolidate the Company's Bank Accounts and the Chief Accountant to prepare checks made out to OFFICE OF BEDC REPRESENTATIVE, LONDON for Bo Aung Din's signature.

Next, I asked Bo Aung Din to write a letter to Mr. Jones, the Chairman of JV, informing him that under directive from BEDC Head Office, he is herewith notified that per Right to Purchase the Shares of the JV Partner AT MARKET VALUE at our discretion, the acquisition will be effected at the earliest possible date. The three men stared at me in disbelief, practically speechless because they later told me "you had only met us a few hours ago". Then, the two Indian Managers dropped a bombshell. Mr. Jones, the typical Jewish businessman, a few weeks ago had ordered the two Indians to alter and doctor the account books of the Company and to keep Bo Aung Din in the dark and they would be rewarded. They apologized profusely for not telling him earlier. I assured them that their continued employment with our new organization was guaranteed. My gut feeling was they (the two Indians) most probably thought that I was somehow aware of Mr. Jones' plan of doctoring the books and to protect their jobs and future told us the plot of the English Jew to drain the coffers of the nearly century-old company.

There was very strong and persuasive evidence that Mr. Jones was tipped off by some of his cronies still working in Rangoon Head Office, alerting him that radical changes were imminent as the Revolutionary Council Government was sending "their Japanese educated young Lawyer" to London. They had no clue of the specific changes but a seasoned Jewish businessman would immediately realize the "stock buy-out option by BEDC" in the JV Agreement that prompted him to "alter and doctor the Account Books before the buy-out". However, the "Preemptive Strike" I initiated within days of my arrival in London prevented Mr. Jones from "depleting the Bank Accounts and Cash Assets" before the buy-out of his stock. The English Jew took his Burmese Government Partner "as fools and suckers that he can twist around his fingers" at will. Well, this time around he was on the receiving end forced to swallow the bitter pill by a young Japanese educated Lawyer about the age of his grandchild, as stated by the two Indian Managers. It was a devastating blow to the elderly Mr. Jones who suffered a heart attack and was rushed to hospital. Bo Aung Din on return from visiting his Chairman in hospital was himself under stress and not feeling well. I became concerned and suggested a medical check-up to sure that he had no medical problems. Mr. Hari accompanied him to the doctor's office and after examination, was found to be suffering from fatigue, exhaustion and stress ulcers. The doctor prescribed medication for the ulcers and one week rest at home. Fortunately Mr. Jones survived his cardiac arrest and Bo Aung Din recovered fully after his rest at home. It was a great relief for me that Mr. Hari, U M. M. Gale and Mr. Magol all assisted me at the Washington Hotel temporary office during the medical leave of Bo Aung Din at his residence.

The buy-out of the 49% stock from Mr. Jones was completed and the first Bank Account of the UK BEDC Representative Office was opened with Midland, Lloyds, Westminster and Chartered Banks. These four banks in 1962 served as correspondents of the Export-Import Bank of Burma and were already familiar with my Official Credentials of Legal Counsel and Secretary to the Board of Directors of the Bank. In almost a century of business in India, Ceylon and Burma, Oppenheimer Jones accumulated substantial fixed assets of prime real estate, office and residential buildings in all three countries and in London. It was common practice in those days for companies making huge profits in colonial possessions to invest in interest-bearing Royal Treasury Bonds, City of London Development Bonds, Securities, Debentures and Certificates of

Deposit (CDs) in addition to Corporate Checking and Savings Accounts in several banks.

After paying in cash for his 49% Stock, BEDC owned the Company outright and with it came the assets consisting of real estate and buildings valued in 1962 at £4.5 Million, Bonds and Securities £3 Million, Royal Certificates of Deposits £2.5 Million and Cash in three Bank Accounts £5 Million. Rowe & Co. with a much longer history of business in India, Ceylon (Sri Lanka), Burma and Hong Kong but a much bigger privately owned Scottish-Welsh Company after Consolidated Liquidation of Assets (100% BEDC Owned) netted us £11 Million After Taxes. The other long standing and well known Burma-British Companies Acquired, Consolidated in Burma Trade, the BEDC HOLDING CO., were:

Burma Oxygen, East Asiatic, Mawchi Mines, IWTB, Bombay Burma, Burma Minerals Corporation, Burma Teak and Hardwood Exports, Indo-Burma Petroleum, Burma Oil Company (BOC), Burma Shoes Co., Burma Garments, Burma Dairy & Condensed Milk Factory, Mandalay Brewery and Dalah Dock Yard and many more JV with European countries, the biggest being with Fritz Warner of West Germany that included Defense Industries. Our Law Firm Durrant, Cooper and Hambling, working in coordination with our Auditing and Financial Consultants (Mergers, Acquisitions, Diversification and Liquidation Specialists), represented our interests with extraordinary professional expertise and achieved the desired outcome for us not only in the UK but also in Europe and the U.S.A. through their Affiliates.

One need only to imagine and contemplate the enormous foreign exploitation Burma suffered under British Colonial domination for almost a century and then after gaining Sovereign Independence the AFPFL Party founded by Aung San, under the leadership of Prime Minister U Nu for a dozen (12) years did practically nothing to end the foreign domination of the country's economy, trade, commerce and industry but colluded with the local business class Sino-Burmese, Indo-Burmese, British Companies, and Anglo-Burmese Traders enriching themselves, the political class, the bureaucrats and their cronies. In 1958 for the first time in Independent Burma when the Military took over the reins of Government from Prime Minister U Nu, the Caretaker Government led by Gen. Ne Win came face-to-face with the stark and bleak realization that the country's economy, trade, commerce, industry and banking were practically in the hands and controlled by various foreign elements and without ending that state of affairs there was very little any Government would be able to achieve. Bo Ne Win's instinct at that time was to embark on taking draconian measures but Bo Aung Gyi and his moderate colleagues persuaded the Commander-in-Chief of the time constraint imposed on the Military to hold elections and hand over power back to the politicians.

It is appropriate and important for the people of Myanmar to bear in mind that the Military leaders in 1958 found themselves in a bind to undertake serious measures to bring the national economy back under the control of the Government and indigenous Burmese Nationals. That was not possible for the above reasons. The State power was handed back to U Nu after he won a landslide victory in the elections of 1960. Soon after the transfer of power, Bo Ne Win instructed Bo Aung Gyi to terminate business relationships with Israel and the WEST. Towards that end he sought the help of Marshal Tito of Yugoslavia to intercede with Gamal Abdel Nasser of the United Arab Republic (UAR) to lift the boycott and economic sanctions on Burma by the 22 Nation Arab League, the most crippling being Burmese Flag Merchant Ships barred from going through the Suez Canal. As fate would have it, I was stopped from leaving the country for good by Bo Aung Gyi, just in the nick of time and Bo Ne Win instructed him to assign the Covert Mission task to me to deal with the Arabs with the active support of Egypt and Yugoslavia. The mission was concluded successfully after 13 months of undercover negotiations with the Arab League.

It was not a surprise to the UK Action Plan Committee Members after the successful Coup on March 02, 1962, that Gen. Ne Win pushed Bo Aung Gyi, Bo Khin Nyo and Bo Maung Lwin to get the implementation in London moving ASAP. These three senior Members of the Revolutionary Council Government impressed upon me to bear in mind the trust and confidence in my capability to achieve the same success and outcome as in the Middle East Mission and they were here to render any and all support I needed in London. It was true that I had gained experience and confidence in the course of the delicate and risky covert Middle East Mission but the UK Action Plan project was entirely a different ball game and uncharted waters. Despite the extensive due diligence we covered I would still have to have to play it by ear and take one step at a time firmly and decisively without hesitation and/or procrastination that would convey a lack of confidence.

The Burmese Military leaders of that time had been through the struggles and fight for independence and resistance against the Japanese occupiers and had developed through actual in-the-field experience the motto "Do not send men into battle without FULL BACKUP". I had the full back-up from the top which lifted my morale to take on all the challenges that awaited me in London. The successful buy-outs and acquisitions of the UK, European and U.S. JV enterprises and consolidation in the holding company Burma Trade Organization representing the BEDC Head Office in Rangoon strengthened our position in the Business World of the WEST as well as their respective Governments and greatly facilitated our primary objective of retrieving the hidden funds of the Burmese politicians and their business cronies. Our Government Liaison Manager, U Ohn Sein, renewed his connections with the UK and European Business Communities and Trade Ministries and with his recommendation hired several retired senior officials who immensely helped to build trust and confidence in our organization.

The long hidden funds started to flow into our four bank accounts by the day and our Treasury and Accounts Division with the support and guidance of Lloyds Auditors and Financial Consultants monitored the bank accounts on a daily basis. Our bankers and auditors suggested that we consider investing in prime real estate instead of keeping large sums in banks yielding only minimum returns in interest. Another recommendation was to be the "Clearing Center for All Imports of the Burmese Government and Payments in Cash instead of Letters of Credit and Bank Wire Transfers saving fees and charges". Exporters pay 2-3% Cash Discount as it saves them documentation work, bank fees and charges to clear the letters of credit and Bank to Bank Transfers. That revenue to Burma Trade would be substantial and more than cover the operational overhead of the company. Our growth and diversification of business activities was spectacular in the short span of time in operation and the expansion of our full time Managerial and Specialized Staff increased to 75 including five automobiles and three drivers.

Burma Trade was the fastest growing Asian company in London and the subject of gossip and speculation in the large Burmese Community of London. However, on the flip side it became the envy of the Burmese Embassy and the Defense Attaché Office despite the fact that Bo Aye Maung was the nominal (De-Facto) Chairman of the Company. Perhaps it was not possible to dispel the general perception of a discarded and exiled Army Colonel surviving on patronage and nothing else. It was an entirely different story with the Embassy under Ambassador U Hla Maung (Peking), a senior politician notorious for his infamous role in splitting the AFPFL Party founded by Aung San. His friend and classmate at University, U Thi Han was now his immediate boss as Foreign Minister but kept a good distance because the Ambassador was a close friend of Gen. Ne Win and still called him Ko Shu Maung. It was indeed a delicate and confusing personal relationship that went back many decades and one was required to maneuver carefully not to get caught up in their petty squabbles and politics.

# INVESTMENTS IN PRIME RESIDENTIAL AND REAL ESTATE

The investment recommendation of the bankers and financial advisers was submitted to Gen. Aung Gyi, Minister of Trade and Commerce, and Col. Khin Nyo, Chairman of BEDC for authorization. We immediately received the green light to proceed with purchase of the Defense Attaché Office Building and the residences of the Officers and the Ministry of Defense Staff posted to London on Foreign Service. However, for the Embassy, the matter would be discussed with U Thi Han, Minister of Foreign Affairs and we were to wait for confirmation. The purchase of several office buildings in prime locations and residences involves specialized negotiations with Real Estate Agencies and the essential searches, inspections and certifications from licensed professionals. The purchase project was entrusted to Lloyds Property and Real Estate Division.

Ideally the owner of the present Defense Attaché's Office building would agree to sell it to the principal occupants. Lloyds' impeccable reputation and expertize worked wonders for the office building (three-stories fully occupied with tenants) as well as the six residential (Homes) including the Attaché and Deputy Attaché's residences in Wimbledon and the other four in Kingston-On-Thames were acquired. The total investment for the five-story Office Building and the (6) Residential properties in 1963 was slightly over £250,000.00. Burma Trade became a substantial London property owner with current market value in excess of half a million Pounds including the Ingersoll House, Kingsway 6th Floor (6500 Sq.Ft) fully renovated and furnished Modern Office Complex. Soon thereafter, the Ambassador, Counsellor, First Secretary, Second Secretary and Third Secretary's (5) residences were purchased. For unknown reasons the Ministry of Foreign Affairs did not approve purchase of the 19 (A) Charles Street Chancery Building. Just as well because it was very old and shabby to put it mildly.

However, there were negative repercussions for the Ministry of Foreign Affairs from the Financial Adviser U Ba Nyain complaining to Gen. San Yu, Finance Minister, that the Foreign Minister did not have "Financial Sanction from the Ministry of Finance to Authorize Purchase of the London Residences". Bo San Yu, mild, risk averse and not one to assert authority and U Thi Han, the only civilian in the Cabinet, pleaded with Bo Aung Gyi and Bo Khin Nyo to please request "Ko Kyi Win Sein to cancel the purchases for the London Embassy". I and Bo Aung Din were aghast and flabbergasted on receipt of the message from Bo Aung Gyi by diplomatic pouch. This was clear evidence of Communist Financial Adviser U Ba Nyain driving a wedge between the Army Officers and showing his total ignorance of the Business World.

Bo Khin Nyo was furious and wanted to report the issue to Bo Ne Win but Bo Aung Gyi advised against it saying "it is too petty" perhaps knowing full well the #1 himself may not fully grasp the soundness of the investment and simply interpret it as a "Squabble between three Major Ministries". He was most probably right but my take on the matter was Bo San Yu, the Finance Minister, was timid and did not exercise his prerogative to rein in the Communist Financial Adviser U Ba Nyain who technically was placed under him in his Ministry. In strict legal terms the Adviser's role is "to counsel" and the advice is not mandatory. So this Communist, at one time a mid-level bureaucrat in the Finance Ministry, was playing the role of "enforcer of red-tape" over other Government agencies pleading for "Budgets for Operation of their Departments".

It was unfortunate and regrettable that Bo San Yu, a Senior General, failed to recognize the critical and urgent need for him to exercise due control over and ensure that the Communist Financial Advisor placed under him functioned appropriately within the legally defined parameters of that Office. Ba Nyain took undue advantage of San Yu's meekness and overstepped the role of Advisor assuming the powers of the Government's "Economic Czar" exercising oversight and control over every State Institution such as Burma Railways, Burma Oil Company, and Inland Water Transport Board. He ordered that imports of coal be stopped from "capitalist countries" and diverted to Socialist and Communist countries regardless of price and quality. Burma Oil Company was forced to buy Exploration, Extraction and Refinery equipment from Romania, a backward undeveloped East European Communist country notorious for fabricating fake copies of British, American and German equipment and selling them as "genuine originals". Ba Nyain caused devastation to steam engines with cheap Chinese coal, and the petroleum industry with fake copied equipment and parts from Romania. This are just two instances of his leftist oriented policies that the Military Regime blindly followed and carried out after Bo Aung Gyi and the moderate Officers were purged from the Revolutionary Council Government.

# THE HIDDEN FUNDS OF THE POLITICIANS AND THEIR BUSINESS CRONIES

In early 1963 Burma Trade, the BEDC Representative Office, in London came to be referred in the UK, Europe, USA and generally in the WEST as the Burmese Trade Mission because our multifaceted functions included more dealings with Governments and State Agencies that worked in tandem with their Private Sector Business Corporations and Trade Associations / Federations such as the Chambers of Commerce and Industries. U Ohn Sein, our Government Liaison Executive Manager, and his Deputies played a very crucial and effective role in receiving support and cooperation in the form of "Official Reference" in communicating with the thousands of companies big, medium and small that were holding the hidden funds on their books. This was the most important first phase that established "Trust and Confidence with the Governments and the Business Communities in the WEST".

Once that objective was achieved, the Companies holding the funds came forward in droves and leveled with us on the issue of surrendering them in exchange for continuing business with Burma which went back many decades, some almost a century. These companies, in addition to the long history of business in the country, also had a deep emotional attachment to the Burmese people, the exotic cuisine, the culture, the religion and many of their ancestors actually had lived in the country and made their fortune there and returned to Britain for their retirement years and business continued with the next generation.

A legal problem arose in accepting the hidden funds from so many companies in the eyes of the Law which violated the Foreign Exchange Regulations, Overseas Payment Ordinances and the Fraudulent Manipulation (Padding /

Over-Invoicing) of Payment Documents Laws of Burma. The Burmese Trade Mission in London upon receipt of the funds was required under UK Law to not only Issue a Receipt but also A Clearance Certificate certifying that the Company in question was Clear of Any Violation of Burmese Laws and Permitted to Conduct and Pursue Legitimate Business in the Country. Our Law Firm's Senior Partner, Sir Guy Hambling, QC, recommended that the Burmese Ministry of Trade and Commerce give A Power of Attorney (In the Form of An Affidavit) to the Burmese Trade Mission "To issue for and on its behalf appropriate Legal Documents / Certifications of Clearance / Waivers as required by the UK Laws and Justice System". Sir Guy Hambling's recommendation was forwarded to Rangoon by coded telex.

Gen. Aung Gyi, the Trade and Commerce Minister, and Col. Khin Nyo, Chairman of BEDC, consulted with Col. Solomon, the Judge Advocate General, who suggested a simple and less cumbersome solution of appointing U Kyi Win Sein Legal Advisor to the Minister of Trade / Commerce with the Authority to Execute Legal Documents for and on behalf of the Minister. We promptly received the appointment confirmation by return coded telex and to await the Official appointment Original Hard Copy in the next diplomatic pouch. It was yet another surprise to Bo Aung Din and Bo Aye Maung, confirming the general perception that those in the Seat of Power of the Military Regime would not deviate from established representation channels. I later learned from Bo Maung Lwin (Moustache) that Col. Solomon was reluctant to involve the Attorney General, a civilian with hundreds of Advocates serving in his Department where the possibility of "information leakage is very high" and he wanted to avoid that risk. It was very thoughtful and considerate of the good Colonel to have suggested that course of action.

To our surprise and amazement the majority of the companies' top executives expressed genuine relief with the opportunity to rid their books of the funds they were obliged to safeguard for many years, in fact concealing from the yearly "Audits" and the "Tax Collectors". It was indeed a revelation that they were in violation of the Laws of Burma as well as their own. We followed the procedure to cross-check all the surrendered funds with the documents collected from the Union Bank of Burma, the Ministry of Finance and the Trade Ministry because they were duplicated and kept on record "For Enforcement Action at

Later Date". This aspect of the operation turned out to be very disturbing and stressful especially to me and Bo Aung Din in London and to Bo Aung Gyi and Bo Khin Nyo in Rangoon. On receipt of the funds in our bank accounts the relevant documents were sent back to Rangoon where Bo Maung Lwin (Moustache) would have his special team to track down the Company and the "Owner / Manager taken into custody for investigation and prosecution".

I was not aware of the plan to take legal prosecution after the funds were retrieved. The distressing situation was that those hundreds detained languished in hurriedly set up shacks for years because the Attorney General's Office did not have enough Prosecutors and the Justice System did not have enough Courts to handle these "Economic Insurgency Cases". Bail was refused for the detained as most were Sino-Burmese, Indo-Burmese, Chinese, Indians (Questionable Residential Status) and the possibility of absconding or leaving the country altogether was high. I was amazed at the attitude and demeanor of Bo Maung Lwin (Moustache) telling me coolly that these people knowingly and deliberately violated the Laws in conspiracy with the politicians in power at that time and expecting to get away scot-free. Now, the Government in power must send out a clear and loud message that these people would be caught and brought to Justice sooner or later.

The long arm of the Law would seek them out wherever they may be hiding. It was the typical mindset of a career Police Officer trained by the British Imperial Police at the Mandalay Police Training College during Colonial Government days. He graduated as Detective Sub-Inspector for Infiltration / Surveillance. The first job assigned to him by the Colonial Government was to monitor the activities of Rangoon University Student Union leaders, Aung San, U Nu, Shu Maung (Ne Win), Bo Khin Maung Galay, Hla Maung and others. While monitoring these student leaders he managed to infiltrate and befriend many of them fond of enjoying the life of a free-wheeling University student like Ne Win, chasing women, gambling and playing the horses. So, after WWII and the country kicked out the British Raj and Ne Win became Commander-in-Chief of the Army, he recruited his friend and nemesis to switch uniforms and nurtured him to head the Military Intelligence Service.

He rose from Lieutenant to full Colonel in a matter of years because of Ne Win and the Organization Structure based on War Emergency (WE). When the (WE) Post of Department Head is (Colonel / General, Etc) accelerated promotion to that rank can be granted by the Commander-in-Chief. Bo Ne Win recognized the value and critical importance of good intelligence taught to him by the infamous Japanese Imperial Army Intelligence School located in Nakano Ward Tokyo (Nakano Gakko as referred to in Japan). To the police detective turned Chief of Military Intelligence all the detentions, investigations and prosecutions come with the territory and it is not something one need lose sleep over. Also being raised in a traditional Burmese Buddhist family he often would invoke the "good or bad Karma" of one from past incarnations manifesting its consequences in the present life and determining one's station in society and performance of the duties that comes with it.

On hearing that Buddhist philosophy of life it occurred to me that it was a kind of vent / stress relief valve for all sufferers; in this instance the detainees and those having to perform their duty of rounding them up. However, it greatly bothered my Legal training and its core principle that detention without trial or bail is unjustified in a civilized society. I discussed this legal and moral dilemma with Bo Aung Din and as a devout Baptist he expressed deep sorrow that our action here in London was sending large numbers of people to confinement in detention centers all over the country. I suggested the idea of discussing the issue with our Law Firm and his initial reaction was they would view the matter from British legal and moral values and we may end up poking a stick in the hornet's nest. After a few days he came to the office early in the morning with the Financial Times article about the crackdown of the Chinese and Indian businessmen in Burma and denying entry visa to journalists.

He agreed with my idea to take the initiative from our side and broach the delicate subject with our Law Firm protected by the Attorney-Client privacy Agreement. It was a matter of time for the Governments concerned to seek diplomatic clarification from the Military Regime regarding the arbitrary detentions without trial. The Financial Times article triggered serious concern on the part of the companies that cooperated and voluntarily surrendered the funds into our accounts. Despite this good faith cooperation their long standing Agents, Distributors and Representatives were now being detained and prosecuted. They understood that foreign exchange laws were violated by these agents but now that their overseas principals had returned the "hidden funds" to the Burmese Government, "we expect reciprocity in the form of considering a waiver of Legal Action and Punishment".

Preliminary to inviting our Law Firm for discussions, Bo Aung Din, U M. M. Gale, U Ohn Sein and myself evaluated the progress achieved thus far and the likelihood of remaining companies reconsidering their cooperation with us because those that did resulted in actually sending their Agents back in Burma to prison. In such an eventuality our project would be stalled halfway. Our Law Firm assigned the Case to Barristers Templeton Smith and Clive Richardson to prepare a due diligent brief of the ramifications and/or repercussions of the Burmese Military Regime's crackdown on the Agents of the Western Corporations surrendering the hidden funds to the Regime's Trade Mission in London. There were no such precedents to rely on for guidance.

The Brief was an eye opener for us. The most serious and crucial observation of the brief was the "Conflict of Ownership Laws of Burma and Western Europe". Notwithstanding that under Burmese Laws these funds were "illegal" under British, European and US Laws "the Agents were Legal Owners". They had the "Legal Right" to sue the British, European and US Companies for surrendering their funds without their written permission". If not handled properly it would be like opening a can of worms and in a worst case scenario with Law Suits flying all over the world. We must definitely avoid that from becoming a reality. Towards that end it was urgently imperative that we alert Col. Khin Nyo, the Chairman of BEDC, to inform and discuss the matter with Gen. Aung Gyi and Members of the UK Action Committee.

The reaction from Rangoon was characteristic Military mindset – crucial and imperative that the fund recovery project proceed without losing momentum and advise the necessary course of action to be taken by the Revolutionary Council Government to achieve that objective. Our attorneys Templeton Smith and Clive Richardson suggested that: "Burmese Trade Mission in London, as Official Representative of the Ministry of Trade and BEDC, issue a Clearance Certification and a Waiver of Punitive Action against their Representatives in return for the surrender of the funds". In the business world of the Capitalist

Western countries there needed to be a "quid-pro-quo" which was simply – "I will surrender the funds you want in exchange for your promise not to harm my Agent in your country". This compromise resolution of the conflict would avoid the time consuming and costly litigation that in the end would only benefit the lawyers.

Such a humanitarian gesture in appreciation of receiving the hidden funds would go a long way to change the perception and improve the image of the Military Regime in the business community of the capitalist countries. Additionally it would give assurance to the companies surrendering the hidden funds that their cooperation with the Burmese Trade Mission in London would have no adverse repercussions on their Agents in Burma. However, for those already in detention centers awaiting trial, the Clearance Certification and Waiver issued by the Burmese Trade Mission would serve as evidence of their Principal's compliance with the Government's directive and gain their release from detention. This compromise resolution would benefit all concerned. The Military Regime would have saved itself the hassle of diplomatic representations accompanied by the Western Media's hype to tarnish their image. The bonus would be the closure of the over-crowded, squalid and unsanitary detention centers and the great relief on the over-burdened Justice System.

This satisfactory and happy outcome was achieved primarily because the UK Action Plan Committee under Bo Aung Gyi was focused on the main objective and fully grasped the importance of avoiding the danger of being entangled in litigations in a foreign country with uncertain and costly outcomes at best. Due credit must go to the Committee Members for backing the Chairman all the way to the Revolutionary Council Chairman. Having said that, I would be remiss if I failed to mention and stress the fact that "The UK Action Plan Committee was set up by Bo Ne Win as a covert project and restricted to report directly to him only". I am certain that had the matter been deliberated by the full Revolutionary Council the outcome would not have been the same. The project to retrieve the hidden funds of the politicians proceeded to a successful conclusion in London, Europe and the U.S.A.

# SUCCESS, MONEY BREEDS ENVY, CONTEMPT AND CONFLICT

The collection of hidden funds was cruising in high gear facilitating the buyback of stock from high value corporations such as BOC, Mawchi Mines, IWTB, Bombay Burma, East Asiatic, BPI, Mandalay Brewery, Etc. In the normal Government procedure, the Management of the Company would submit to its Minister official request for extraordinary supplemental budget (funds) in Foreign Currency for the Stock Buyback and the Minister would request the funds from the Ministry of Finance. However, the Revolutionary Council Chairman and Prime Minister Gen. Ne Win overruled the normal procedure. The reason being his "Direct Order to UK Action Plan Committee Chairman Gen. Aung Gyi, Col. Khin Nyo, BEDC Chairman and Col. Maung Lwin (Moustache), Military Intelligence Chief "That all Financial Matters of the Burmese Trade Mission in London must be Reported to Him Only". I received the Official Instruction in writing from BEDC Chairman Col. Khin Nyo in my capacity as 60% Stock Holder of Burma Trade and De-Facto Chief Executive Officer of the Corporation under UK Laws.

Therefore the funds of Burma Trade London were "Not Part of the National Treasury under Control of the Ministry of Finance and Revenue". For all intents and purposes it was directly under the control of Gen. Ne Win, the Revolutionary Council Chairman and Prime Minister. In strict legal terms BEDC from its inception by an Act of the dismissed Parliament was placed directly under the Prime Minister's Control and Management with the prerogative to name the Chairman to administer for and on his behalf – first Bo Aung Gyi and currently Bo Khin Nyo. Burma Trade (Burmese Trade Mission) being the Official Representative of BEDC in London and being classified as "Covert Operation" was most likely the justification for Bo Ne Win to confine it under his direct personal control assisted by the #2 and two senior Colonels.

The project had reached a very crucial milestone success well beyond the expectations of the selected few tasked to plan, implement, operate and manage the covert project in the Capital City of the UK. It was important for #1 to maintain secrecy of the financial affairs and status in London. Bo Ne Win's penchant for secrecy exposed Burma Trade (Burmese Trade Mission) and BEDC to accusations of illegal collection and accumulation of huge funds and concealing them from the Ministry of Finance. However, since the UK Action Plan project was initiated by the Commander-in-Chief and classified "Overseas Covert Operation" there was no way for any other Ministry to raise any question, especially after March 02, 1962 Coup when Bo Ne Win toppled the democratically elected Prime Minister U Nu and installed the Revolutionary Council Government and assumed the Prime Minister's post as well as that of the Head of State.

The collection and accumulation of the hidden funds was cruising along in high gear facilitating the acquisitions of prime real estate properties and the buy-back of stock from Joint Venture Enterprises in the UK, Scotland and Europe. While the reaction from the British and European business communities was positive, the expatriate Burmese communities, the Embassy and Defense Attaché crowd indulged in their favorite pastime of gossip, speculation and rumor-mongering based mostly on hearsay and misinformation. In the interest of truth and fairness, it must be mentioned that the traditional rivalry, feud and hostility between the Civilians (Embassy) and the Soldiers (Defense Attaché) was at its worst when I arrived in London in 1962. Bo Aye Maung, the unwanted and exiled Colonel, could not stand the Senior Politician Ambassador U Hla Maung (Peking) and a close friend of Bo Ne Win since their student days.

I was briefed by Bo Maung Lwin (Moustache) on these personal relationships before my departure from Rangoon and in observance of the Intelligence Chief's cautionary advice, I stayed away from all diplomatic functions. Despite that careful social behavior there was one I could not avoid – the Burmese Independence Day celebration on January 04, 1963 at the Embassy hosted by Ambassador U Hla Maung and attended by the selected members of the Burmese community in and around London. I decided to attend alone and have our company driver pick up me and Bo Aung Din at our homes in different locations. As a result we were late for the ceremony. Oblivious to me, I later learned to my shock and horror that Bo Aye Maung had rudely stopped the ceremony from getting started and to wait for the arrival of the Revolutionary Council Representative, U Kyi Win Sein.

On our arrival there was Bo Aye Maung, attired in full dress uniform and reeking of alcohol and escorting us to the anxious and nervous U Hla Maung and invited assembly of guests that notably stared at me with expressions of surprise and disbelief. I was taken aback and somewhat puzzled when the Ambassador almost in a whisper asked me to address the assembly. I felt things were not right and I responded firmly but with due respect that I had come to attend "Your Excellency's celebration of our independence anniversary and there was no place for me to say anything let alone addressing the gathered guests of your Excellency". I stood next to the Ambassador during his brief address and joined in the toast to the guests. After the ceremony more drinks were served and I was introduced to the Embassy Staff and their families and the elders of the Burmese community who could not restrain their curiosity and asked how old I was. Bo Aung Din came to my rescue to explain things from the perspective of a colleague as well as a longstanding member of the London Burmese and diplomatic community.

I could hardly blame anyone for my appearance because I only weighed 108Lbs, looked badly malnourished with a full crop of hair more like a High School kid. During my Middle East mission I was referred to as "the underfed Burmese". It worked well for me as no one ever suspected what I was actually doing. Strangely it was the same back home in Rangoon, especially in the Ministry of Defense where everyone was in uniform and I was the rare civilian moving around in the corridors from one office to another, often with senior Generals and Colonels and many would ask – "Who is that young civilian fellow among the top brass of this Ministry?" "He is always escorted by the personal staff officer of one of them".

The buyback of the high value JV Enterprises was deliberated by the UK Action Plan Committee chaired by Bo Aung Gyi, based on the report of Bo Khin Nyo as BEDC Chairman and responsible for overseeing and supporting Burma Trade (Burmese Trade Mission) in London. Bo Maung Lwin (Moustache) reminded the Committee of the project operation classified "Under Cover" by the Revolutionary Council Government Prime Minister and as such for other Ministries to be involved in the stock buyback plan the classification needed to be revised by the Prime Minister's Office. It was easier said than done. The entire Committee went to discuss the matter with Bo Ne Win for the acquisition of stock held by the Foreign JV Partners in the following high value Corporations critically important to the National Economy:

Burma Oil Company (BOC), (2) Mawchi Silver Mines, (3) Inland Water Transport Board (IWTB), (4) Bombay Burma Trading Corporation (BBTC), (5) East Asiatic General Trading (EAGT), (6)Mandalay Brewery, (7) Burma Oxygen Production and Distribution (BOPD), (8) Burma Pharmaceutical Industries (BPI), (9) Dalah Dockyard Dredging and Ship Building, (10) Indo-Burma Insurance Company (BIC), (11) British-Burma Timber Corporation (BBTC), (12) Inwa –Japan Pulp/Paper Industries (IJPPI).

In the interest of proper historical perspective most of the above Joint Venture Enterprises, with the exception of a few, were crafted by the British Colonial Government in the waning days of their administration with the dual purpose of "keeping and continuing their interest and influence in the key business and industries of Independent Burma" and ostensibly to assist the U Nu Cabinet to seamlessly operate and manage them upon assuming State Power. In reality the foreign partners managed and controlled these businesses for almost fifteen years with the employees made up of Anglo-Burmese, Indians, Indo-Burmese, Sino-Burmese and British Managers at the top. The Burmese that managed to get hired did minor clerical or menial work. U Nu and his Ministers, all Nationalists who had struggled for Independence with Aung San, with meagre and limited financial resources, practically used the first decade of independence enriching themselves and their cronies and left the common Burman to beg for crumbs.

It is very important for the present generation of Myanmars to know that in 1963, after 15 years of sovereignty running our own affairs, the Military Regime under Bo Ne Win was planning the buyback of stock owned by foreigners in the country's key businesses and industries with the money retrieved from overseas banks where the Burmese politicians had hidden it. In this regard, it is critical to fully understand the scope and scale of the robbery of the country's precious foreign exchange earnings on the backs of the Burmese peasants struggling with the cattle and water buffalo in the rice fields. The next question is "why was Bo Ne Win and his inner circle discussing buyback and not nationalization?".

# THE SCOPE AND SCALE OF ROBBERY AND CORRUPTION

In more than the six months of planning and preparation for the UK Action Plan project Implementation that began in late 1961, there was data and documentary evidence pointing to the existence of the hidden funds in the British, European, Swiss and U.S. Banks. But as to the actual realization of the desired outcome, there were more questions than answers. We were in uncharted waters except for the insight gleaned from the Middle East experience when Gamal Abdel Nasser nationalized the Suez Canal and the key banking, businesses and industries. It was truly an eye opener for me and those in BEDC Head Office who reviewed the comprehensive report in English that was translated into Burmese. Bo Maung Lwin (Moustache) kept the originals. The report contained information on the absolute ruler King Farouk and generations of his ancestors hiding large sums of money in Western banks while the Egyptian peasants toiled with the water buffalo in the fields and lived in abject poverty. King Farouk had more than 100 palaces; the smallest of the lot was bigger than any in Europe with gold plated faucets and plumbing.

In the interest of fully understanding the extent of our Burmese politicians' moral decay and their out of control greed, the statistical data gleaned from Union Bank of Burma recorded documents of payment for "Imports" and receipt of credit for "Exports". These documents were corroborated by "Licenses" and "Foreign Exchange Approvals / Sanctions" from the Ministry of Finance and revenue going back to the Financial year 1947-1948 when the average annual Exports of Burma was US$430 Million (+/- 3%) and the average annual Imports was US$375 Million (+/- 3%). Burma during the first decade of independence enjoyed a trade surplus of over US$50 Million annually. The country exported 3.5 Million Tons of Rice and over 750 Million Tons of Beans, Pulses, Oil Bearings Seeds, Oil Cakes and Molasses. Import licenses were generously issued with Letters of Credit to the Private Sector approved by the Directorate of Imports and Exports of the Ministry of Trade and Commerce.

The "Yard Stick for Imports Commission" was 10-15% of Invoice Value and for Private Sector Exports was 15-20% higher because of Export Incentives. This practice (system) was inherited from the British Colonial Government and the Burmese politicians led by Prime Minister U Nu since 1948 simply continued with the entrenched practice because it served their purpose of skimming off the cream from the top and some from wherever convenient. The Ministers were in the pockets of the Indian and Chinese Merchants. The intelligence reports from the Special Branch Police (SB) and the Bureau of Special Investigation (BSI) indicated that 10% of the Commissions from Imports and Exports went to the politicians and their cronies and retained on the books of the foreign companies.

Lloyds Auditing and Financial Consultants based our overall targeted figures on the information from the (3) Ministries vested with the authority to approve and sanction Foreign Payments. Lloyds simulated "a Model" on their Main Frame IBM System 360 and projected the "Expected Revenue Outcome" for the period 1948-1963 (15 years). The actual final figures far exceeded Lloyds' projections primarily because of the "interest bearing" Bonds, Securities, Certificates of Deposits, Royal Treasury Certificates, Time Deposit Debentures and sale proceeds of Real Estate that was very substantial (Interest) as most of them went back more than seven decades. Since all the cash and assets came with the "acquisition of Stock" they had to be converted to cash in the name of Burma Trade and deposited in our four British banks, a Swiss bank and Scandinavian bank. The tax burden was reduced as Burma Trade was a British Corporation. The hidden Commission Funds collected were US$700 Million and the Bonds, Deposits, Securities and Certificates were US$147 Million. It was a staggering success well beyond our wildest dreams and Burma Trade (Burmese Trade Mission) was "Cash Rich" and the Company Credit Rating jumped to "Platinum AAA+++".

In the scheme of things for a Corporation it was truly a big deal but in terms of a Sovereign Nation State it was nothing to write home about because Burma has the largest land mass in South East Asia with every conceivable resource and a very long coastline. The country was well known as the "Rice Basket of Asia" with a small population relative to its physical size. This fact was stressed by the leading economist of that day, Dr. Hla Myint, who served as Harold Wilson's Economic Adviser. Lloyds, in fact, was concerned that a sound investment plan was not in place apart from the stock buyback. Having large bank accounts that are stagnant makes no financial sense from a bean counter's perspective. We asked their investment specialists to come up with a proposal to place some of the cash in a diversified portfolio. Within a few weeks Lloyds recommended that Burma Trade consider the purchase of a "Small-Medium size British bank" and use it as "a depository of our funds" as well as for the payments of the Country's Imports and Receiving Bank for its Exports.

Another recommendation was to purchase a medium size "High Quality Hotel in London" (70-100 Rooms). It would serve as the Burmese Community Center and for the substantial number of travelers from Burma to the UK and Transiting through London to Europe and the U.S. The Lloyds' recommendation was submitted to Bo Aung Gyi, Chairman of the Action Plan Committee, and we immediately received information that the matter was being referred to Bo Khin Nyo, BEDC Chairman, to pursue the deliberations with Members of the Committee, Bo Tommy Clift, Bo Thaung Kyi and Bo Maung Lwin, the Intelligence Chief. Following this advice, we were informed in the next diplomatic pouch that Bo Ne Win would be coming for another medical check-up with his British specialists and the famous Austrian Dr. Hans Hoff in Vienna. Bo Khin Nyo would come ahead and Bo Maung Lwin would accompany the Head of State's entourage.

The proposal to invest in bank acquisition and hotel purchase was to be discussed during that time. U Kyi Win Sein was to prepare a background brief for 2nd Reparations Negotiation with Japan in the next few months. Mr. Okuda in Tokyo informed me regarding the "undercurrents" within the Liberal Democratic Party (LDP) Factions concerning the "Supplemental Reparations Payment Clause" in the Treaty of Peace and War Reparations Agreement between the two countries in 1954. Since Burma was the first country in Asia to sign such a treaty and now that Indonesia and the Philippines had received disproportionate payments in comparison to the amount Burma was paid, new negotiations were called for the supplemental payment to make up for the shortfall.

However, Burma's democratically elected Government was overthrown by the Military, the extreme Right and the extreme Socialist / Communist factions were opposing any additional reparations to the Military Regime of Dictator Ne Win, whose background was well known to the Imperial Rightists, the remnants of the Japanese Imperial Army that still held sway with the powerful Agricultural Co-Operatives (NOKYO) and the largest bloc of votes for the (LDP). Prime Minister Ikeda was under intense pressure to postpone the negotiations to a later indefinite date because his tenure as (LDP) chairman and Prime Minister would be up for election in about 18 months. According to Okuda's memo to me in English, it was a serious dilemma for the Prime Minister because he had promised the elected Government of U Nu during his State visit to Burma additional reparations payment.

Okuda was asking me to request the help of Ex-Colonel Tagami (Chief of Intelligence – Ken-Pei-Tai in Burma during WWII), who was in 1963 Chairman and Chief Executive Officer of the Japan Agricultural Bank which was the Main Bank of NOKYO. He also asked me to request the support of my Godfather's elder brother (Nagano Shigeo), Chairman of New Nippon Steel and Japan Chamber of Commerce and Industry. He also mentioned that he would be flying to Rangoon soon to privately discuss these issues with Bo Ne Win, Bo Aung Gyi and Bo Khin Nyo. Among the five Japanese Imperial Army Intelligence Officers that defected to the Burmese Military under Aung San, Okuda was the most senior and connected to the top echelon of the Imperial General Staff because he was the only son of General Okuda, Governor General of Formosa (now Taiwan) and close friends with Bo Ne Win and Bo Aung Gyi since the days when Aung San was alive. The other four (Takahashi, Yamada, Sugii, and Mizutani) were instructor Warrant Officers in the Japanese Imperial Army Training Schools where the Thirty Comrades received their advanced training after the initial preliminary basic boot camps in Hainan and Formosa. Colonel Tagami would have nothing to do with these five defectors who had betrayed the Imperial Army and collaborated with the Burmese forces fighting the retreating Japanese Army. To Colonel Tagami these five Japanese were traitors deserving the "firing squad".

## THE SCOPE AND SCALE OF ROBBERY AND CORRUPTION 179

Bo Khin Nyo arrived in London exhausted after the long flight and appeared to be rather stressed. I and Bo Aung Din met his flight at Heathrow Airport and had the Bentley driver take us directly to the Washington hotel and checked him into his suite for the much needed sleep. We instructed the driver of the leased Bentley to stand by at the hotel and returned to Burma Trade office in Ingersoll House. On the way Bo Aung Din noted that it was his third trip since my arrival in London about nine months ago and it had taken a heavy toll on the frail Colonel. Back in my private office I opened the package from Bo Maung Lwin (Moustache) entrusted to Bo Khin Nyo for secure delivery. There were three sealed envelopes addressed to me and a folder from the Ministry of Foreign Affairs Reparations Division with a cover letter addressed to Gen. Aung Gyi, Minister of Trade and Commerce and signed by U Thi Han, Minister of Foreign Affairs. On the cover letter was Bo Aung Gyi's notation – UKWS Burma Trade London for Review and perusal with Bo Khin Nyo and his initial.

In his private letter, it was all about Okuda's visit and his report on the state of affairs within the ruling LDP Party Factions and the difficulties facing Prime Minister Ikeda. I noted a misunderstanding or perhaps miscommunication by Okuda because Bo Aung Gyi mentioned about "your wife's relatives helping Mr. Ikeda and his Cabinet overcome the opposition". He also wanted to know if it would be possible for me to take time off and fly to Tokyo and join him for the negotiations or return to Rangoon with Bo Khin Nyo who would be a member of the Burmese Delegation and also Bo Kyaw Soe. If that was possible he would include my name as Legal Adviser and General Counsel to the Head of Delegation. When I read the letter from Bo Maung Lwin it was again about Okuda's visit and then I could not believe what I was reading.

He was quite blunt telling me that "this fellow Okuda seem to be counting on your influential Japanese friends and in-laws to influence the negotiations in our favor and he will take all the credit. He also is pushing for you (with #1 and Bo Aung Gyi) to be in the delegation. Think of a good reason (Excuse) you cannot be away from London at this crucial time. If the negotiations succeed he will take all the credit and should it fail he will dump the blame on you". He used a metaphor "A cow that jumps the fence will do it again". He cannot be trusted. "Destroy this the usual way." The third letter was from Bo Thaung Kyi (Ko Lay). Again, I was aghast because he wrote – "Bo Lwin came to see me and mentioned about Okuda's visit and the forthcoming negotiations with Japan and expressed his serious concerns about you being used by this Japanese "double-crosser traitor" and we don't want to see you become the scapegoat.

Colonel Thaung Kyi continued in his letter "I have privately discussed this with Bo Aung Gyi at the request of Bo Lwin and he now fully understands and appreciates the situation. Just reply that it is not possible for you to be away from London at this important time. Destroy this in the usual way." I was sure that there was a lot more that the two Colonels became aware of than the brief alert they rushed off to me through Bo Khin Nyo. I was astounded at the risk Bo Maung Lwin (Moustache) took to protect me and then went the extra mile to discuss the matter with Colonel Thaung Kyi to ensure that I got the message. It reminded me that the two of them had befriended me when I was merely a High School student in Bassein (Pathein) in 1952 and nudged me into the complicated and highly sensitive world of National Security Intelligence work. Now, eleven years later in London I was grateful that both of them were behind my back and looking out for me. I went into our secure room and put the two letters in the hermetically sealed incinerator and turned on the switch.

# RESIDENTIAL ESTATE WITH 9-HOLE GOLF COURSE FOR HEAD OF STATE

We reserved a private room at the Indian High Commissioner Office restaurant for dinner that evening. I called Bo Khin Nyo's suite around 5:30 PM and he was awake and refreshed, ready for drinks and a full course of Indian cuisine. All four of us, Bo Aung Din, U Ohn Sein, U M. M. Gale and I, would go to the hotel in our office car with driver Roger Banister at the wheel where I would join Bo Khin Nyo in his Bentley and proceed to the restaurant in two cars. While we dined in the private room, the two drivers would have their dinner in the general public area. The other three were more relaxed this time around and chatted with the Colonel after a few drinks. The conversation was very casual on generalities and consumer prices of daily necessities in Rangoon and major cities. It was quite apparent to all that he could not talk about the political issues of the country as a member of the Revolutionary Council Government. Even so, lubricated by a few pegs of Scotch he got quite a bit off his chest regarding the leftist Financial Adviser and the newly converted Socialists within the Government bureaucracy.

The next morning during our breakfast meeting in his suite, Bo Khin Nyo mentioned his meeting with Bo Aung Gyi and Bo Maung Lwin (Moustache) on the eve of his flight where the issue of security for Bo Ne Win during his extended stays in London for medical check-up, rest and recreation, and especially his favorite pastime playing golf on an exclusive public course, was raised as it had become a burden on the Royal Security Service. On almost all his visits to Britain, Lord Louis Mountbatten, the uncle of the Queen and Prince Phillip, would provide one of his estates for the Burmese General and his entourage. Now it appears that the "State House", meaning Madame Katy, was pushing for a secure residential estate for the Burmese Head of State to be on a par with other Heads of State with their own estates in and around London. Bo Aung Gyi, always very considerate and accommodating to all especially when it comes to his friend, comrade and boss Bo Ne Win, asked the two senior colonels to pursue the matter with Ko Kyi Sein in London, for the best way to comply with the needs of our Commander-in-Chief during his stay in London.

Bo Khin Nyo's account of the reparations negotiations with Japan and Okuda's visit was along the lines of Bo Lwin and Bo Thaung Kyi and I was glad that the three Colonels were on the same page. He then asked me about the idea of my joining them in Tokyo. I told him that it would not be advisable to be away from the Corporation at this crucial time, being the 60% stockholder and the Chief Executive Officer requiring his signature on large payment checks and authorizing bank-to-bank transfers. He seemed to understand my explanation and somewhat accepted it but asked me to write a Memo to Gen. Aung Gyi about our discussion and send it in the next pouch to Rangoon – a clear indication that the idea emanated from Dagon House. On the issue of secure residential estate for the #1 he broached the subject very gingerly, struggling to avoid specifics of who was actually behind the scheme. I sensed (my sixth sense) that Bo Khin Nyo and Bo Lwin were being manipulated by the wily and cunning Madame Katy, and the two hapless Colonels had gone to the good natured and compliant Bo Aung Gyi to help them placate and satisfy the #1's scheming wife who some how got wind that BEDC London was sitting on a mountain of cash and on a buying spree of prime London Real Estate.

Apparently the gossip, rumors, wild speculations and accusations were that BEDC Office London under Bo Aung Gyi's man Kyi Win Sein had accumulated vast sums of cash and was practically sitting on mountains of money, buying a posh luxurious office complex in a prime location of the city and several high end residences in Wimbledon, Kingston and Richmond – Twickenham Park along the Thames River all paid for in hard cash which had reached the ears of Madame Katy. She was making her move to ensure that she would be the first to lay her hands on some of that money in London. She would be aghast to know (if ever) that the UK Action Plan Project was her husband's and entrusted to his Selected Committee under Bo Aung Gyi. The truth of the matter was that Bo Aung Gyi had proposed Bo Aung Din (recommended by Air Force Chief Gen. Tommy Clift) to lead the project and it was her husband who rejected that and asked "where is our fellow that carried out the Middle East Operation". Bo Aung Gyi reminded him, "You asked me to have Ko Kyi Win Sein set up the Export-Import Bank and he is now helping us and the Board of Directors as Legal Adviser". "Call him back to the Ministry of Defense and send him to London ASAP for implementation of the project and provide all the support necessary." All the rumor-mongers and accusers were off-track and barking up the wrong tree. Unfortunately and regrettably Bo Aung Gyi became the scapegoat in Rangoon and I was the main subject of the Embassy and Burmese community gossip. Under such circumstances I religiously stayed away from all social functions and gatherings of the expatriate society.

It also dawned on me that #1 was most probably oblivious to this jockeying going on and no one among the handful who knew the true state of affairs would take the risk of enlightening the King with a short fuse, hair-trigger temper and memory lapses. I suggested to Bo Khin Nyo the idea of conveying to the "State Household" (meaning Madame Katy) that Bo Aung Gyi would have Burma Trade London provide the necessary "funds" for the secure residential estate for the Burmese Head of State and to advise the amount required to purchase their desired estate". I further explained to him, "Perhaps that was really what they wanted." He stared at me in silence a couple of minutes and then said almost in a whisper, "I am always amazed at you folks in the intelligence business figuring out what the other party is trying to get at."

Again, he asked me to write another Memo and send it off to Bo Aung Gyi quickly to reach him before the departure of #1 and his entourage for London. Bo Khin Nyo agreed that we needed to bring Bo Aung Din into the picture as it concerned the financial affairs of the Company. During the lunch break in our Board Room we casually informed him about providing the financing of the estate; he was wide eyed and listened in silence showing no emotion or reaction. However, later in the day he walked over to my private office and asked what amount we were talking about. I told him we have no idea yet and most likely would know during their stay this time. I advised him that I would be broaching the subject with Lloyds Real Estate specialists to tap into their "available estates on the market" and the current prices based on "mortgage and cash terms". He concurred and said that would give us the "ballpark" asking prices to start the negotiating process.

When I received Lloyds' due diligent file and reviewed the properties for sale on the market, I was amazed and flabbergasted to find several estates with 9-hole golf courses belonging to the family of Lord Mountbatten of Burma. I immediately shared the information with Bo Khin Nyo and Bo Aung Din, both commenting that there must be some kind of deal-making going on between the Burmese first family and the British Queen's uncle. As luck would have it this vital information was received just in time to caution us to steer clear of the two top families' business arrangements and confine our role simply to providing the money asked by the State Household. We would have to rely on Lloyds Auditors to advise on how to "classify the cash outflow from the Company's Books" in conformity with the "generally accepted rules and principles of accounting". The format normally followed by Ministry of Defense and Ministry of Foreign affairs was "Extraordinary Expenditure for Overseas Covert Operations".

In about a week I received a response from Bo Aung Gyi confirming receipt of my Memos and pursuant to recommendations therein he advised Bo Maung Lwin to "contact our man and discuss the money requirements for Bogyoke's (General's) secure residential estate in London". I gave the note to Bo Khin Nyo and Bo Aung Din and they seemed to be somewhat worried by their facial expressions but did not say anything. Next morning during our routine breakfast meeting in his suite, Bo Khin Nyo expressed his concern that this news would reach Rangoon sooner than later and it was not going to sit well with the newly minted Socialists in the Revolutionary Council Government. I gently reminded him that it was primarily for the security of the Head of State during his frequent visits to London. What he said next really surprised me – "I am not sure Bogyoke knows about this arrangement?" It became clear to me that the BEDC Chairman was having "second thoughts" and the repercussions within the Revolutionary Council as well as the first family. Things were getting complicated even before the whole thing started. I told the worried Colonel about the cautionary note in Lloyds' package for Burma Trade to just provide the money and stay clear from other issues of ownership, titles, management and numerous chores of running an estate with a 9-hole golf course. Lloyds' advice and guidance was based on their experience of many years with other Heads of State from Africa, South America, Central American dictators with estates in the UK etc.

More often than not, most ended up in family fights and lawsuits for ownership when the dictator loses power or was toppled and often times assassinated, and the immediate family escapes and seeks asylum in Britain. In the midst of our agonizing about the possible negative consequences, #1 and his entourage arrived and as usual was accommodated at one of the secluded estates of Lord Mountbatten of Burma. Within a matter of days of arrival, Bo Maung Lwin called to set up a private meeting with me and Bo Khin Nyo. I quickly reminded him that Bo Aung Din, being a stockholder and Managing Director, by UK Law needed to be involved in all financial matters. He grudgingly conceded "when it comes to 'Legal Issues' it is up to you to call the shots". Having started his career as Imperial Police Detective Sub-Inspector, he appreciated the need to comply with the Laws especially being in the City of London. He asked for a car to pick him up. U M. M. Gale arranged with our Limousine service to send a Bentley to the estate the next morning at 8 AM. He had a long ride alone and arrived at our office well after 9 AM.

We had a closed door meeting in our Boardroom and the wily intelligence chief appeared to be tired and under some stress because he was vague and unsure of how to proceed. Bo Khin Nyo asked him if there was any specific place the "State Household" wished to acquire or a real estate agent of their choice to provide a list on their inventory of estates on the market. He said he would try to find out and let us know. It was quite apparent that the two Colonels were avoiding mentioning Katy's name who reallywas pushing them to do her bidding. Bo Aung Din remained silent for obvious reasons. Then Bo Lwin mentioned about his discussion with Bo Aung Gyi in Rangoon who advised him to discuss with "our man" in London the best way to proceed. I sensed that he was now attempting to pass the ball to us and unless we lay down some kind of barrier now we would end up holding the bag as well as the consequences that come with it.

I mentioned Lloyds' caution that institutional ownership of an estate would involve a very high tax burden in addition to the need to hire and sign a long term management contract. Private ownership would be preferable, a lot less expensive and uncomplicated as regards ownership, registration of titles and estate taxes. Bo Aung Din mentioned that Burma Trade already has this office complex and several properties in its name and it would not be advisable to overextend the burden. The estate for the Head of State needed to be under a special arrangement acceptable to the State Household (meaning Madame Katy). Another factor Lloyds enlightened us on was the distinct likelihood that the Burmese General himself or his wife was being manipulated by those in the Mountbatten Clan to "palm off the estate with a 9-hole golf course" that was costing a great deal of upkeep money with no return. We were not privy to the compensation paid to the estate which is common courtesy to cover for estate staff, utilities, equipment, security, wear and tear and for many other facilities and services provided to the Burmese Dictator and his entourage during his entended stays as personal guest of Lord Maoutbatten of Burma.

It could also be that the British Foreign Office, the Royal Palace Protocol and the Mountbatten family was getting tired of playing host to the Burmese Dictator 3-4 times a year and decided that it was time to suggest a place of his own in London. Perhaps Katy and Bo Lwin were given a hint to that effect, or even an indirect message through personal connections the British were notorious for utilizing to soften the impact. It prompted Bo Lwin (Moustache) to broach the issue with Bo Khin Nyo for support and then together they went to Bo Aung Gyi for help. A few days later the Intelligence Chief came back with information that there was indeed an estate recommended by a close relative of Lord Mountbatten's eldest daughter. We all looked at each other with the unspoken words – "Is it coincidence that Lloyds' package included such an estate or is there more to it?" To break the silence and evaluate the evolving situation more closely I said, "As we all know too well Lloyds, a huge multifaceted British conglomerate with many Head of State clients from all over the world, is under pressure and/or obligation to not only share information but work in cahoots with MI-5 and MI-6. And these Intel-Agencies keep an eye on and monitor the activities of British citizens including the Aristocrats and the Royals."

Bo Lwin (Moustache) added that he had been concerned of this security aspect from the beginning but kept quiet for fear of being misconstrued. "I am glad you brought this up now and appointing Lloyds as Auditors and Financial Advisers was a good strategic move to have them in your corner." Now that the cat was out of the bag I asked him point blank, "Is it the estate where you are staying now?" He said yes almost in a whisper that made Bo Khin Nyo and Bo Aung Din wide eyed with expressions of disbelief. I held back realizing that I had overstepped the bounds by asking a blunt question to the Military Intelligence Chief that even his colleagues would refrain from. But the wily Colonel was in a foreign land away from his power base having to perform odd jobs for his moody boss as well as his scheming wife Katy. His focus was on getting the money and not on his powerful position. After a couple of minutes of silence Bo Lwin revealed to us the asking price for the estate, £90,000.00 – 100,000.00 (in 1963 value). I checked the ballpark price in Lloyds' package and it was fairly close with some allowance for negotiations. The price of a large detached single family home in Wimbledon was Sterling Pounds 6,5000 – 8,000.00. The defense attache's residence with five bedrooms was #7,000.00.

In terms of security and protection of the country's Head of State in a foreign country many thousands of miles away it was a very small worthwhile investment. The question now was the modality of transferring the funds to whom? To an Escrow Company Account? Directly to the Buyer's Bank Account? Directly to the estate owner? In compliance with our accounting and book-keeping requirements, Burma Trade would have one of our banks transfer, remit or issue a Banker's Check to any party and/or entity nominated by the State House Authority and the bank would debit that amount to Burma Trade Account. Again, Bo Lwin said he would advise us when the decision was reached where and to whom the funds needed to be transferred and/or remitted.

After the Intelligence Chief left Burma Trade office for the estate to be in time for the wake up time of #1, who was sleeping most of the day and awake at night, Bo Khin Nyo could not help mentioning how meekly Bo Lwin submitted to my questioning and conceded to the blunt question of in fact staying at the estate for sale. I mentioned about first meeting Bo Lwin at dinner in Bo Thaung Kyi's home in Bassein when I was a 16 year old High School student in 1952 and attending Intelligence Training at the Brigade Head Quarters. And then meeting in Tokyo with Bo Ne Win and Bo Aung Gyi. "So, we have been associated in many aspects of legal and intelligence work for many years and the level of trust and confidence is comparatively more than those in his immediate circle. "He very seldom will take exception to what I tell or ask him in direct reference my professional role of Legal Advisor and General

Counsel that you witnessed today." "Yes, I was amazed and taken aback and was surprised at how Bo Lwin accepted like it was normal routine discussion and exchange of information. He also is fully aware and recognizes that you are the first Burmese after WWII to graduate and receive a law degree from Japan's top University with the #1 and #2 Generals of the Army taking care of you at the personal request of my eldest brother Bo Khin Maung Galay. Now I clearly understand the basis of the relationships and how it works." Notwithstanding that, he asked me to write a Memo to Bo Aung Gyi informing him about the discussion and the request from Bo Lwin for £90,000.00 – 100,000.00 that Burma Trade would be complying with by transferring the amount to their designated bank, entity or account within the next few days. Bo Khin Nyo wanted to be sure that Bo Aung Gyi was in the know from the outset and tacitly approved it in his capacity as the most Senior Officer of the Revolutionary Council directly involved in approving it. However, my primary concern at that time was as 60% Stockholder I would have to "sign off" on the Stock Holder's Resolution "Authorizing the Extraordinary Expenditure for Overseas Special Covert Operations for the Revolutionary Council Government of Burma".

The other Co-Signers were Bo Khin Nyo and Bo Aung Din. Our Lead Attorney Barrister Sir Templeton Smith would prepare the documents (Including A Receipt to be signed by Representative of the Government) and also "append his Signature as Witness" as required by UK Laws. On the Auditing and Book-Keeping side, Lloyds Auditors and Financial Advisors would work closely with Mr. Magol, our Treasurer and Chief Accountant to record the outflow of the amount / amounts to comply with the Generally Accepted Rules of Accounting. It all came down to establish that Principles of Company Management and the Relevant Laws Governing its operation were observed and followed as stipulated with proper Documentation and Recorded on the Books of the Company by Certified Competent Accounting and Auditing Professionals.

All these elaborate legal and accounting measures were taken to ensure that should things go awry for known / unforeseen circumstances we would all be protected from any accusation of violating the Laws as well as from Legal Prosecution for Dereliction of Fiduciary responsibilities. Bo Lwin was reluctant to sign the receipt and asked me if there was a legal option to circumvent the receipt in any other form that would serve as receipt to Burma Trade.

We discussed the issue with Barrister Sir Templeton Smith as well as Lloyds Auditors and both struggled to find a resolution to no avail. However, Lloyds Auditors consulted with Lloyds Bank Specialists on "Transfers / Receipts / Classifications and Designations" of such transactions. Voila, Lloyds Bank came back with a suggestion that "In bank-to-bank transfers from our account in their bank" could be recorded in their Transfer Record as "To the Revolutionary Council Government of Burma Account" and a "Copy of that Record would serve as a Receipt for Burma Trade".

Normally it is only for the bank's internal record but under special circumstances, the account owner whose money was transferred can request the bank's record. Bo Lwin was excited and all smiles and said, "From tonight I wll be sleeping well; you have taken a heavy load off my shoulders." As for Bo Khin Nyo and Bo Aung Din, their comment was "You Lawyers can do amazing things". It was indeed the best desired outcome for Burma Trade Corporation as well as for those of us entrusted to operate and manage it. We were caught between a rock and a hard place, a Military Regime and the UK Laws, both with the authority and power to put one behind bars for any violation or even perceived transgressions of British or Burmese Laws.

In the case of the latter one could be held in detention on mere "suspicion of wrong-doing by the powers that be of the Military Regime". To our surprise Bo Lwin showed up at our office unannounced with his aide Captain Kyaw Zwa Myint (Johnny Lears, my classmate at St. Peters in Mandalay). Apparently #1 and Katy had their own private arrangement for the day. While Johnny was given a tour of our office complex by Bo Aung Din, Bo Lwin and I slipped out to my private office where he handed me a slip of paper with the bank account number and particulars and asked me how long it would take to hit the account after the transfer. I told him that the official letter to our bank was already drafted to include the Receivers Bank Account Number and Particulars and we (I and Bo Aung Din would sign) and have our Treasurer and Chief Accountant visit Lloyds Bank Manager within the hour and have the funds transferred. "Since it is a large amount transfer our bank Manager will call the receiving bank Manager first. It should be there within thirty minutes. Our treasurer will return with the documents of bank-to-bank transfer." I noted that it was a Swiss Bank Branch in London with the account numbers in encryption. He asked me if he could have duplicates of the documents from the bank but when I told him that he would have to sign for them he backed off. He seemed to want some evidence of the fund transfer. I sensed that the account owner (whoever it may be) may not tell him the money had been received. My Middle East experience indicated it was a distinct possibility.

I wrote a Confidential Memo addressed to Bo Lwin (Moustache) confirming that the funds were transferred to the account number he had given me this morning. I sealed it in an envelope and handed it to him and he immediately opened it and gave me a big smile. It would give him the written evidence of the funds transfer in the event of someone pulling a fast one on the Intelligence Chief. In such a high stakes deal one cannot take any chances and all possible precautions needed to be taken in advance. In fact I asked him if he wanted me to "put a hold for a few days" and he said "yes please do"; I immediately asked Mr. Magol to call Lloyds Bank Manager to "keep a hold on the funds for 72 hours". Now, whoever was withdrawing the funds would require a "Final release Order" providing "Identity to the Receiving Bank Authenticity of Account Ownership" and Lloyds Bank would receive that proof for their records and perhaps the identity of the "account owner".

Bo Khin Nyo came to our office around lunch break after receiving one of his family friends in his suite. We ordered food from the Indian High Commissioner's office restaurant and hosted a luncheon party for Bo Lwin and his aide Johnny Lears. I had the opportunity to reminisce with him about our student days at St. Peters in Mandalay. After the luncheon gathering the standby Bentley drove them back to the estate. A few days later Bo Lwin called to confirm that all had gone well and he would discuss "the details" when we got together the next time.

# OKUDA FACTOR IN NEGOTIATIONS FOR ADDITIONAL WAR REPARATIONS

I reviewed the English transcript of the Memorandum Okuda had submitted to Bo Ne Win in Rangoon who instructed Bo Aung Gyi to do the needful. Bo Khin Nyo had reviewed the Burmese transcript and when we sat down to compare notes we realized that a great amount of the crucial information was lost in the process of translation, Japanese to English and from English to Burmese. However, in the personal Memo (in English) Okuda sent to me directly there were many issues he did not mention in the one he had submitted to his friend Bo Ne Win. I expressed my concern to Bo Khin Nyo regarding these discrepancies and he wondered aloud why Okuda would do such a thing and he asked me if I had any idea. I told him that there was one reason I knew off the top of my head and it was very personal "that you may already know of" but since the national interest of Burma "is at stake it is inevitable for us to lay it on the table" at this critical time when Bo Aung Gyi will be negotiating with the Japanese as leader of the Burmese delegation representing the Revolutionary Council Government.

Since the end of WW-II the Japanese political elite in the Liberal Democratic Party that monopolized Government Power maintained a "black list" of those in the Imperial Army, Navy, Air Force and Intelligence Service (Ken-Pei-Tai) who had betrayed and defected to the enemy and caused the loss of lives of many Japanese soldiers. Okuda, a graduate of the Japanese Military Academy (Shikan Gakko), was very high on that list being the only son of General Okuda, Governor General of Formosa. He first defected to the Burmese resistance against the Japanese occupation together with Takahashi, Yamada, Sugii and Mizutani. On repatriation back to Japan after surrender to the Americans, Okuda, because of his father's position and connections, was allowed to attend Tokyo University as a special reward to succeed in upper Japanese post-war Japanese society. However, soon after graduation from the university, he defected to the American Occupiers and worked for Defense Intelligence against Reorganized Post-War Japanese Intelligence. His fence jumping character trait is well recorded by succeeding LDP Governments. Then he betrayed his friend Bo Ne Win's trust and joined Ex-Prime Minister U Nu's armed insurgency to overthrow the Military Regime. When the insurgency of U Nu ended in catastrophic failure, Okuda jumped fence again to work for the CIA and with that backing manipulated the Saudi Royal Government to appoint him Representative of Saudi Royal Airline in Japan. As such Okuda had no credibility whatsoever within the Japanese Society, especially the political and business elite.

In 1963 Okuda was working for the Burmese Reparations Mission in Tokyo as Liaison Officer with the Japanese Government and Business Community on the personal recommendation of Bo Ne Win. On the eve of negotiations with the Ikeda Government, he was wiggling his way into the crucial talks from the Burmese side through his friendship with the Prime Minister of the Military Regime because the seat of power in Japan (the LDP Party elite) would have nothing to do with a "black listed defector". In reviewing his memos the most disturbing and sinister was his arrogance and disingenuous dictate that I make a request to Ex-Colonel Tagami (Intelligence Chief – Ken-Pei-Tai in Burma during WW-II), Chairman and CEO of the Japan Agricultural Bank with influence on LDP leaders. He also said I should make a request to Shigeo Nagano, Chairman and CEO of New Nippon Steel and Japan Chamber of Commerce and Industry with tremendous influence over LDP Governments since 1946 because of Agricultural Cooperatives' votes as well as the top Japanese business, banking, financial and industrial leaders.

Both Tagami and Nagano (brothers) were my "sponsors / mentors" and "Go-Between" officially asking on my behalf the hand of my wife from her parents and the assurance to take responsibility for my future. It is a lifelong undertaking for them and I was obligated to always stay in touch and seek their counsel and guidance prior to taking any major life changing steps. In Japanese culture and society such a relationship is the ultimate "social undertaking" especially at that level and taken very seriously. You practically become a member of the family and in public you are always introduced as "my adopted son". It is almost impossible for a foreigner to fathom this very long and religious adherence to this cultural practice by the Japanese people.

I was already alerted to this sinister interference of Okuda by Bo Maung Lwin and Bo Thaung Kyi, but Bo Khin Nyo was shocked and taken aback by what he had just heard from me and wondered if the #1 was aware of Okuda's pariah status in today's (1963) Japanese society. It was quite apparent that the two impediments in the way of the forthcoming negotiations with Prime Minister Ikeda's Government was the Military Dictator Bo Ne Win and Okuda who was self-promoting his role from the Burmese side taking undue advantage of his personal friendship with the Regime's leader. Bo Aung Gyi, the delegation leader, was characteristically reluctant to ruffle any feathers especially one close to #1. However, this was no time to allow such emotional sentiments to distract and interfere with the goal of successful negotiations with the Japanese.

Bo Khin Nyo agreed with that evaluation and suggested that we include Bo Maung Lwin (Moustache) in our discussions. I called him at the Estate and he asked for the Bentley to pick him up early next morning at 7:30 AM and the three of us would have a breakfast meeting in the Suite and then move over to Burma Trade Boardroom. After receiving our input on the issue, Bo Lwin (Moustache) was forthright in telling us that #1 was aware of Okuda's difficulties in Japanese political circles and he had been cautioned by "the other four Japanese friends" to keep him "behind the curtain". The next thing he said surprised me because he suggested that I request Ex-Colonel Tagami to rein in Okuda and have him stay clear of the negotiations. He said the Ex-Ken-Pei-Tai Chief was a close colleague of General Okuda who entrusted his only son to his friend who was head of the Imperial Army Intelligence Apparatus in Burma during WW-II, more powerful than General Suzuki, the titular head of the Ba Maw Puppet Government. I was not sure if that was the appropriate thing for me to do knowing full well the Japanese hierarchy of how seniors relate to and treat juniors, and I certainly did not want to further jeopardize Okuda's precarious situation in Japan. I remained silent and did not respond to his suggestion. Both the Colonels seemed to have received the message from my silence and remarked "keep that in mind as a last resort". I was quite certain that the Japanese would not tolerate Okuda's involvement in any way, form or under any circumstances.

I expressed my view that the Japanese side, especially the Ministry of Foreign Affairs and Finance Ministry bureaucrats, would definitely reject any local third party involvement except at the highest levels like the Nagano brothers and Tagami with political clout over the LDP leadership and Okuda is nowhere near it. That was the reason for his lobbying the Burmese side with the hope and expectation of being officially included in the delegation in some capacity like an Advisor or consultant. My sources in Japan said the Japanese Government would be "extremely irritated and uncomfortable" should the Burmese elect to include him in their delegation. Here again the two Colonels suggested (instructed is more correct) I send a Memo to Bo Aung Gyi explaining all the above. I was aware that Bo Thaung Kyi and Bo Lwin had already reported to him about this.

I noted that the Intelligence Chief was playing safe knowing full well that #1 was silent on this issue up to this stage – neither for nor against, perhaps leaving it up to the delegation leader. However, Gen. Aung Gyi the #2 ever sensitive to personal matters involving the five Japanese friends of the Burmese Military Dictator was surprised by the information in my Memo and immediately responded via pouch asking Bo Khin Nyo and Bo Maung Lwin to seek the opinion of #1 vacationing in London. Both were visibly distressed to be assigned the task by the #2 to approach their moody and quick tempered boss with such a delicate and sensitive issue for his decision. I was aghast and flabbergasted when they asked me to accompany them and do the explaining because "this concerns Japanese affairs and the boss thinks highly of your degree from Tokyo University". I thought it was undisguised flattery and I was merely being used as a punching bag. However, on second thought I explained the need for direct input from the Japanese side. I would call my close friend Nakao Eiichi Chief Cabinet Secretary for his input.

I called my friend Nakao Eiichi, Chief Cabinet Secretary and serving on the Foreign Economic Affairs Committee chaired by Takeo Miki (later Prime Minister), LDP Secretary General. I called him at his residence, discussed the reparations negotiations and requested him to discuss with our mutual friend Miyazawa (Later Prime Minister) who was serving as Prime Minister Ikeda's Secretary about Okuda. Within a matter of a few hours Nakao called back and "categorically" said "better not involve any Japanese on your side". When I reported the reply to the two Colonels, Bo Maung Lwin (Moustache) was encouraged by the firm input from the "movers and shakers of Japan" and decided that he would advise #1 without mentioning names that the Japanese political leaders prefer that the Burmese did not involve any third party Japanese in the negotiations.

"In the unlikely event of #1 asking for specific clarification, then you will have to come along and do the explaining." It turned out as expected and no questions were raised but I was instructed to inform Bo Aung Gyi about it and have him confirm the members of the delegation. I drafted a memo and sent it by pouch to Dagon House in Bo Lwin's name. Three days later we received the composition of the delegation: (1) Delegation Leader – Brigadier General Aung Gyi, Vice Chief of General Staff and Minister of Trade; (2) Colonel Khin Nyo, Chairman of Burma Ecinomic Development Corporation, Member; (3) Colonel Kyaw Soe, Minister of Home Affairs, Member; (4) Nominee of Minister of Foreign Affairs; (5) Burmese Ambassador in Tokyo, Member; (6) U Hla Aung, Chief of Reparations Mission in Tokyo, to act as Secretary of the delegation. Gen. Ne Win the Chairman of the Revolutionary Council and Prime Minister approved the composition of the Burmese delegation while he was in London but asked to schedule the negotiation time and date after his return to Rangoon as well as the "Press Release".

The next critical issue of contention to be resolved by the Burmese Government under Military Administration was the additional amount of reparations to ask from Japan based on those given to Indonesia and the Philippines – US$600 Million in War Reparations and US$250 Million in grants to be disbursed in ten years. In the original agreement Burma already received US$350 Million in War Reparations and US$150 Million in grants. As such the general rule of thumb and mindset on the Burmese side was to ask for US$250 Million in War Reparations and US$200 Million in grants. These figures were well within those given to the two other countries but the advantage to the Burmese was being the first to sign the Treaty of Peace and Friendship after WW-II and the Japanese public sentiment towards the Buddhist country and the Burmese people, sheltering and saving many sick and hungry soldiers on the run, was a huge favorable factor.

In this regard the Burmese Buddhist culture and upbringing was at play and from the #1 to the delegation members were reluctant to name a hard and fast figure that the country was entitled to receive for the suffering of the people for many years. The US$450 Million target figure was based on the Indonesia and Philippines payments that the Japanese were obligated under the clause of the Peace Treaty to ensure equity with war reparations paid to other South East Asian countries. However, there were no precedents in International Law and diplomatic practice for countries to meticulously honor "Bilateral Peace Treaties and the war reparations clauses" particularly "pertaining to the amount to be paid".

Bo Khin Nyo as Deputy Leader of the Burmese delegation was concerned that Burma would have to settle for less because the country was now under Military rule and its legitimacy being questioned. Prime Minister Ikeda was already facing that problem from within his own LDP Party Rightists as well as from the opposition in the Diet. True to his gambler's instinct it was quite apparent that the #1 wanted to determine the "negotiating or bargaining figure and the bottom line settlement amounts". To achieve that desired outcome we invited our Lloyds financial consultants and several of their specialists participated in our closed door discussions with Bo Khin Nyo, Bo Maung Lwin, Bo Aung Din and myself. We were enlightened by the in depth presentation on the criteria of Bilateral War Reparations Settlements between the UK and Germany after the two World Wars and those of the thirty years European Wars.

It was truly an eye opener for the Burmese to come to terms with the reality that a defeated nation's economy does not have the capacity to pay large sums in a short period of a decade that history has taught us. Therefore it would be wise not to push hard for "War Reparations and Grants but for Low Interest Long Term Loans and Lines of Credit that will accrue more benefits to the recipient country". The most beneficial and positive effect of such a reality based approach would be less contentious bargaining resulting in a shorter period of negotiations and mutually satisfactory agreement and friendlier diplomatic relations and cooperation between the two countries. Based on this negotiation principle and criteria the Burmese Trade Mission Panel recommended the Burmese High Powered Delegation ask for Supplemental War Reparations US$250 Million, US$150 Million Grant and US$350 Million Low Interest Long Term (20-25 Years) Loans with 5-10 years Repayment Extension. On his return to London from Vienna, the recommendation brief was submitted to #1 by Bo Maung Lwin (Moustache) explaining the discussions with Lloyds financial specialists. He was very pleased with the meticulous deliberations with the British professionals and instructed Bo Lwin to forward it to Bo Aung Gyi in Rangoon. On the eve of his return to Rangoon we (Burmese Trade Mission Officers – Bo Khin Nyo, Bo Aung Din and Myself) were suddenly summoned to report to the estate at 10 PM that night. All three of us were taken by surprise and apprehensive of what was in store for us. Concerned and anxious I first called Kyaw Zwa Myint (Johnny Lears) and asked him what was the reason for this sudden order and he said there was nothing to be worried about.

He just wanted "to grant you fellows an audience before returning to Rangoon" in a gesture of thanks for "rushing the rescue money when we were broke in Vienna". Johnny just could not help himself without uttering a sarcastic comment. No wonder that he defected to Thai Intelligence within the next several months after his return to Rangoon with #1, Katy, the personal doctor and Rajoo the Nepalese Gurkha cook.

We drove to the estate in Bo Khin Nyo's Bentley and were received by the British security officer, and Bo Lwin and Kyaw Zwa Mying were waiting for us at the main house and we were immediately ushered to the living room where Bo Ne Win was seated on a huge reclining chair. Johnny opened the door for us and Bo Khin Nyo entered first and was greeted with "hey Bo Khin Nyo, when are you returning to Rangoon?". I was the next to enter and as soon as he saw me the usual "hey kaung Papun-Pu, come sit here" pointing to the chair next to his. When he saw Bo Aung Din – "hey Bo Aung Din, you have been away from Burma for such a long time, come take a seat". "Hey Bo Lwin, ask Rajoo for some coffee, tea and cakes." It was like in Rangoon, in all Burmese homes, tea, coffee and cakes are normal fare for guests at any time of day or night. He asked Bo Khin Nyo about the reparations negotiations and the briefing from Bo Lwin.

He then wanted to know the latest information we have from Tokyo and Bo Khin Nyo said "Ko Kyi Win Sein has spoken to his friend in the ruling party and to the Secretary of Prime Minister Ikeda, Mr, Miyazawa". I also mentioned that Col. Tagami is helping through his Agricultural Bank. He asked, "Is he still that influential in Japan?" I said, "He is Chairman and CEO of Japan Agricultural Cooperative Bank (NOKYO) that controls the largest votes for the LDP. "Is that so? It should be very helpful. Bo Khin Nyo make sure to brief Bo Aung Gyi about this." "Yes Bogyoke, Ko Kyi Win Sein has already submitted a memo to him." "Good, good, have some cakes." Bo Ne Win was aware of the opposition in Japan to giving additional reparations to his Military Regime that had toppled the democratically elected government of Prime Minister U Nu which signed the original Treaty of Peace, Friendship and War Reparations.

Then the conversation changed to the buy-back of stock from high value joint ventures with the British like Burma Oil Company (BOC), Mawchi Silver / Lead Mines, Inland Eater Transport Board (IWTB), Bombay Burma Timber Corporation (BBTC) and the #1 said he was shocked when informed that these companies' operations would come to a standstill in less than six months without British technical, engineering and parts support. He apparently asked Okuda and Takahashi to get Japanese help and was surprised beyond belief when told by his trusted Japanese friends that such industries could not be replaced easily from a British technical base to Japanese or any other without serious disruptions and perhaps total loss. It would be wise and imperative to continue with the original operators to support with engineering and especially essential parts until the Burmese attain the experience and capacity to produce them in Burma. He said he now fully understands the buy-back condition with 15 years of technical, engineering and parts support. "It will be a shame if we cannot do it in 15 years." This conversation took place in early 1963 in the Palace-like estate of Lord Mountbatten of Burma during Bo Ne Win's third trip to London for medical check-up and rest. Now in 2018, 55 years later, the Burmese still cannot produce parts in the country 100% to efficiently operate these and many other high value industries. It is this lesson that I wish the current generation of Myanmar leaders to take from what transpired just about a year after the Military toppled the elected Government and despite that understanding Bo Ne Win pushed ahead with the disastrous Burmese Way to Socialism.

The Japanese opposition was using it as legitimate justification and pushing hard for negotiations to take place only when democracy was restored in Burma. And that was not going to happen any time soon from the perspective of the General running the Regime and he wanted to have the easy money soon as an insurance policy against the untested political and economic policies he was about to embrace along the lines of Aung San's Blue Print for Independent Burma. It was almost a foregone conclusion that the negotiations for additional reparations, grants and loans would bear fruit with Bo Aung Gyi leading the delegation because the Japanese political and business leaders knew him well as a moderate Military Officer having a successful track record in economic development, trade, commerce and appreciation of working in cooperation with the international business community for technology, financial and banking collaboration.

The success of the UK Action Plan was attributable to the good standing and reputation of Burma Economic Development Corporation (BEDC) and the Defense Services Institute (DSI) established and led by Bo Aung Gyi from inception. We had also achieved the goal of eliminating the foreign elements in the country's trade and commerce (aggressively pursued since 1958 Caretaker Government) through acquisition of stock held by foreign partners by legal means that was highly acclaimed by the international business community that facilitated expansion of direct investment in the development of country's rich resources and related industries. The success of the reparations negotiations with Japan would be a monumental achievement for the Military Revolutionary Council Government and a feather in the cap of Bo Aung Gyi, the #2 man of the Military Regime, highly respected as a moderate and the country's "free trade, free press and facilitator of national business development advocate".

Despite the Burma Army under Bo Ne Win having no respect for democratic government, the immediate neighbors and the rest of Asia were in no mood to overtly oppose or antagonize the new Regime, evidenced by the quick recognitions extended within hours of the almost bloodless Coup on March 02, 1962. As such, after a year in power (1963), there was political stability and the economy was poised for take-off having a healthy trade surplus with major trading partners and very substantial foreign exchange reserves in the Central Bank (Union Bank of Burma) as well as in foreign banks in the State fully owned Enterprises such as BEDC and Burma Trade Mission in London, Europe, Switzerland and Scandinavia.

# BURMA NEGOTIATES FOR ADDITIONAL REPARATIONS WITH IKEDA CABINET

After his extended stay in London at the estate of Lord Mountbatten of Burma for medical check-up, rest, recreation and more check-ups in Vienna, Austria by the world famous Hans Hoff (known as the Doctor of/to the Dictators) and often derogatorily referred to as the "Head Examiner" whereby a Burmese strongman was made to stay at some Aristocrat's vacant estate for security reasons that cost a bundle so that Burma Trade Mission in London had to authorize the British bank to have their Vienna Correspondent branch to finance the entire bill of the Head of State, no questions asked. The Hans Hoff Clinic originally arranged the accommodation for the Burmese General and his entourage but the Austrian Government Security Service overruled the place as "High Security Risk" and recommended the secluded estate. Bo Lwin (Moustache) asked his aide Bo Kyaw Zwa Myint (Johnny Lears) to call Burma Trade Mission in London for necessary financial arrangements ASAP. I had our Treasurer and Chief Financial Officer Mr. Magol to call Lloyds Bank Manager to have their Vienna Correspondent Bank to provide the necessary funds to the Burmese Head of State and his entourage and debit our account. I called Johnny at the estate and advised him to contact the Vienna bank and get the cash needed and to have the Estate Management forward their invoice for all other charges to the bank.

He wanted to know if he needed to sign for it and I told him to do so, showing his passport. He sounded nervous but I assured him that "everything has been taken care of by Burma Trade Mission in London and the bank there will provide all the financial needs including cash". That brought out a sarcastic and uncalled for comment from aide Captain Kyaw Zwa Myint (Johnny Lears, my high school classmate) – "Hey Malcolm, I didn't know you fellows are that rich".

I reminded him that "when you are dealing at the Head of State level even the sky is not a limit". He thanked me "for the lecture" and added "I wish you will consider me for a job in your organization". I quickly retorted "you must be out of your mind to say such a thing" and hung up. I briefed Bo Aung Din on the call from Vienna, arrangements made with Lloyds and the conversation with Bo Kyaw Zwa Myint, and his comment was "the Austrians are notorious for their gold digging" and he suspected Hans Hoff and the Austrian Government Security Service to be "hand in glove in collusion to get a hefty kick-back from the Aristocrat's estate".

Bo Ne Win and his entourage returned to Rangoon and within a matter of days after their departure gossip, rumors and speculations went wild about the purchase of a huge secluded estate with a 9-hole golf course from a close relative of the Royal Family by the Burmese Head of State. The mainstream British and European media and the tabloids were sniffing around for the "dirty stuff" to lay it on the Burmese Dictator. The Embassy and the Military Attaché's office had no clue of what was going on and the Burmese Trade Mission itself was in the dark as to what actually transpired between Lord Mountbatten's family and the Burmese Dictator. We at Burma Trade realized the invaluable advice and guidance that our Auditors and Financial Consultants Lloyds had recommended to stay clear of any transaction for purchase / ownership / title transfer or Management role as all of the above "require legal and mandatory registration that is public knowledge". As such Burma Trade was totally in the clear and unrelated to any transaction on the estate where the Burmese Head of State stayed during his recent visit here.

Bo Khin Nyo stayed behind to wrap up the odds and ends of the many BEDC Joint Venture Enterprises with British and European partners and the consolidation of their operations under Burma Trade. Many required liquidation and several enterprises scaled down and restructured to operate as fully owned subsidiaries of Burma Trade to maintain continuity of long relationships with suppliers and manufacturers of proprietary parts for the machinery, equipment, road / river transport vehicles and boats no longer in production but many still in use and operation in Burma, and without such continued support things would come to a standstill. It was a monumental undertaking for Burma Trade Mission because many were in locations far from London – Liverpool, Manchester, Edinburgh (Scotland); some in Europe – France, Germany, Denmark and Sweden – where the Company Laws were quite different from the UK.

Our British Law Firm could not handle such affairs and referred us to their Associates and correspondents in those countries and Retainer Arrangements had to be set up for them to take care of our Legal and Business affairs. Fortunately for us all of these countries were within an hour by jet from London and a quick one day business trip was possible and be back in London by evening. Several of the companies required our special attention – like Burma – Fritz Warner in West Germany involved extensively with our Defense Industries providing latest state-of-the-art technology, engineering, know-how and specialized raw materials, parts and production equipment as well as onsite technical advisers in Burma.

The French Daggramont-Alstom was working with Burma Railways' transition from Steam Locomotives to Electric Diesel Engines. Bofors of Sweden to the Burma Navy and the Dallah Shipyard for installation of the medium/heavy equipment/armaments, operational testing of such retrofitted on Navy Vessels. The three Petroleum Oil Refineries at Chauk, Yenanchaung and Syriam were supported and supplied by the British-Burmah Oil Company under the fifteen year technical and parts Agreement that included third country procurement of exploration and drilling equipment and platforms mainly from the U.S. through their tie-up and association with Hughes Tools in Houston, Texas. Burma Trade Mission guaranteed all payments in London in cash against presentation of documents. It was the largest financial undertaking by a Burmese Business Enterprise and coordination with all the Departments and Corporations in Rangoon, and Bo Khin Nyo as Chairman of BEDC was responsible to work with the Cabinet Ministers and report to the Revolutionary Council Chairman and Prime Minister.

# DIRTY POLITICS CRACK REVOLUTIONARY COUNCIL UNITY

The success of Bo Ne Win's covert UK Action Plan Project under the leadership of Bo Aung Gyi created a mixed bag of very positive and negative reaction within the ruling Revolutionary Council Members. The moderate liberal faction heartily welcomed the news of the big success and achievements of the Burma Trade Mission and were encouraged by the buy back and ownership of the high value business enterprises vital to the National Economy. However, a small faction, mesmerized by the untried socialist command economy espoused by the above ground Communist Financial Advisor U Ba Nyain, were greatly alarmed that Bo Aung Gyi, already recognized and acclaimed as the economic brain of the Military Establishment, would be enhanced even further. This faction led by Bo Tin Phay and Ba Nyain freaked out.

To compound and add to their sense of insecurity, the success of the forthcoming negotiations with Japan under Bo Aung Gyi's leadership for more War Reparations payment would bring in several hundred millions of dollars to the already huge cash holdings in London banks. That would practically push Bo Aung Gyi up to pedestal of the country's Economic Czar. The Tin Phay / Ba Nyain half-baked socialists started a vicious campaign of character assassination by spreading disinformation and fabricating false rumors of Aung Gyi and his forty thieves sitting on a mountain of cash in London "plotting the overthrow of the Revolutionary Council Government". All of this began while #1 and Bo Khin Nyo were in London and as soon as the Ministries, Departments and Corporations were officially informed that Burma Trade mission would guarantee all National Imports Payments in London which for all intents and purposes takes away the Financial Authority from the Ministry of Finance.

Another fabricated disinformation was the alleged conspiracy of BEDC Chairman Bo Khin Nyo and Burma Trade Mission executives with Japanese political leaders of the LDP and the Ikeda Cabinet to manipulate the final amount of the supplemental War Reparations to Burma and the economic assistance by way of low interest loans and favorable repayment terms. The accusations went as far as claiming that Bo Aung Gyi himself would assure the Japanese Government and the business community that Burma would not pursue a policy of Nationalization in dealing with foreign businesses in the country and International Trade and Commerce. The rumors of such allegations were traced to the above-ground Communists within the National United Front (NUF) party whose front man Ba Nyain was pushing the Tin Phay faction in the Revolutionary Council to portray Bo Aung Gyi and the BEDC Group as opposing the Burmese Way to Socialism and an imminent threat to the Military Regime of Bo Ne Win.

On arrival back in Rangoon after the extended medical check-up, rest and recreation and visit with the world famous Austrian Neuro Diagnostic Clinic of Dr. Hans Hoff, the re-energized Burmese strongman received an earful of petty complaints of Bo Aung Gyi sending greetings to Foreign Heads of State on their Independence Day anniversary. Actually the Ministry of Foreign Affairs simply complied with diplomatic protocol as Bo Aung Gyi was officially entrusted with running the Revolutionary Council Government during the period of Bo Ne Win being officially abroad for medical treatment. In strictly legal terms and in accordance with the Ministry of Defense Command and Control Rules, all the Official Positions held by Bo Ne Win were "entrusted over to the Vice Chief of General Staff (VCGS) Bo Aung Gyi" during his official period of "Leave from his Posts" for Medical Leave in a Foreign Country.

Notwithstanding the established "official procedures" governing the "change of command at all levels" Ba Nyain, Bo Tin Phay and their harebrained lackeys persisted and continued their disinformation campaign against Bo Aung Gyi and BEDC Conglomerate, accusing the group of being a "capitalist monopoly" controlling the country's economy, trade, commerce, banking, financial and international businesses. In such an environment of animosity within the ruling Revolutionary Council Government one conspicuous factor was the deafening silence of Bo Ne Win and the majority of Members who "sat on the fence" waiting to see which side the #1 would elect to embrace. Looking back with the benefit of hindsight, this was the pivotal time when the Revolutionary Council's cohesion and unity cracked and pushed the Commander-in-Chief to side with the half-baked socialists, taking the country on to the path of Military Dictatorship and catastrophic economic decline, isolation and down graded to least developed country.

The disinformation, rumor-mongering and accusations directed at Bo Aung Gyi and BEDC Conglomerate by Ba Nyain and Tin Phay lackeys were not taken seriously by the #1 knowing full well that it was simply the whining of the sick and insecure man obsessed with the wishful desire to be named the de facto socialist ideology leader of the Army with Ba Nyain as the economic Czar of the Burmese Way to Socialism replacing Aung Gyi, the recognized economic brain of the Military establishment and perhaps of the country itself. Ba Nyain and Tin Phay faction knew full well that Bo Ne Win's UK Action Plan success under the leadership of Bo Aung Gyi and the BEDC group sitting on a mountain of cash as much as or more than all the foreign reserves held by the Union Bank of Burma (the Country's Central Bank) was greatly admired by the top Military Brass and in the "good books of Ne Win".

He was very pleased and announced to the Revolutionary Council the end of foreign domination of the country's high value economic and business enterprises, especially the buy-back of high value enterprises from the British, Jews and Europeans with the money recovered by the Burma Trade Mission. And of course the estate for him with a 9-hole golf course in the prime location close to London. Therefore it was urgently imperative from the perspective of Ba Nyain and Tin Phay to cast Bo Aung Gyi, the Minister of Trade, Chairman of UK Action Plan Project and Head of BEDC, as one conspiring to overthrow the Regime and take over the reins of Government from Bo Ne Win using the financial resources of all the money at their disposal in London managed and controlled by the Japanese-educated young lawyer. The Communists are experts at fabricating something sinister and threatening to the seat of power (Ne Win) by one closest to him. To those of us involved in the day-to-day operation of the Regime's financial assets in the West, the disarray within the ruling Revolutionary Council was alarming to say the least.

The two senior colonels Bo Khin Nyo and Bo Maung Lwin (Moustache) closest to #1 and trusted colleagues of Bo Aun Gyi expressed confidence that the two Generals at the top would not tolerate anyone coming between them because their relationship goes a long way back to Rangoon University student days and throwing their future in the Thakin Party with Aung San, U Nu, Bo Khin Maung Galay, Kyaw Nyein, Ba Swe, etc. They (Ne Win and Aung Gyi) were the closest trusted comrades and aides of Aung San throughout the struggle for independence from the British and the Japanese occupiers during WW-II. They have been through thick and thin, so going separate ways was unthinkable from the perspective of Bo Khin Nyo and Bo Maung Lwin (Moustache). That was my diary entry after several breakfast meetings with the two senior colonels in the Washington Hotel suite in London on the eve of their departure for Rangoon.

Another entry in my diary memo also noted that there was clear indication Bo Ne Win had pretty much given up on the established political elites of Burma and leaning towards the above ground Communists (National United Front) by appointing Ba Nyain Financial Adviser and accepting his proposal for wholesale nationalization of all private enterprises that Bo Aung Gyi openly opposed. This could very well be the last straw that would break the camel's back but that probability seemed to have escaped the calculus of Bo Ne Win's scheme to experiment with the untried, unproven, leftist socialist Command Economy policies espoused in Aung San's Blue Print for Independent Burma that was used as an effective bait to entice and lure #1 to weigh in on their side. The Communist strategy to drive a wedge between two top Generals of the Burmese Army was taking place right within the ruling Revolutionary Council Government.

True to his character of moderation, non-confrontation and a rational approach to "national policy issues", Bo Aung Gyi ignored the personal attacks and character assassinations let alone taking counter measures to dispute such blatant fabrications. My take on that attitude of "giving the other cheek" was utter shock and disbelief knowing full well that Bo Tin Phay was back-stabbing a colleague who had gone out of his way to bend the rules and appealed to the Commander-In-Chief to keep Tin Phay in service against the Medical Board Certifying him unfit for active service in the Army after the horrendous auto accident suffering several broken ribs, collapsed lungs and kidneys, broken right arm, brain concussion and punctured bladder. After months of hospitalized treatment in Burma and in the UK, the Military Medical Board of Colonel Hla Han (Doctor), Colonel Maung Lwin (Doctor), Colonel Ko Ko Gyi (Doctor) Chaired by Dr. Ba Than (Bo Ne Win's father-in-law) concluded unanimously that Tin Phay was "Medically Unfit for Active Military Service". Notwithstanding, Aung Gyi stuck his neck out to save him.

He persuaded and explained to Ne Win that the Quarter Master General's Department was the lightest and least stressful position in the Ministry of Defense most appropriate for Tin Phay. Senior General Staff Officers involved in the emotionally charged personnel episode quite openly stated later that Tin Phay and his wife, Daw Thein Saing, a Sino-Burmese like Bo Aung Gyi, ruthlessly exploited his soft, considerate and emotional side taking full undue advantage by appearing before him "in tears" not once but several times in his office and residence. This tear-shedding is the last desperate resort of those about to be drummed out of the Army for one reason or another. But in the case of uncouth Tin Phay, the irony and strange twist of fate or perhaps destiny, and oblivious to Bo Aung Gyi was that the QMG Department was a Brigadier-General's Post and Bo Ne Win was aghast and hit the ceiling when the Posting Order and Promotion File reached his desk for final approval and signature of the C-In-C. Bo Aung Gyi suffered yet another tongue-lashing from the #1 because he had already signed-off on the file as Vice Chief of General Staff. According to his own account this was what #1 told him: "Hey Bo Aung Gyi, look what you have done, this mother fuc...ing SOB Cripple certified medically unfit for Army Service is not only Retained in Active Army Service but promoted to Brigadier-General in QMG Post".

He dumped the entire responsibility on Aung Gyi's head and grudgingly signed-off the Tin Phay file. Aung Gyi was flabbergasted but man enough to calmly take all the abuse, anger and displeasure of his C-In-C who simply could have rejected and thrown out the file that he had done many times on other matters but did not on this one. I asked Bo Aung Gyi why he did not "withdraw the file" and his response was because "Bogyoke (General) did not ask me to". I then raised another question – why he or #1 did not prescribe or stipulate "A Qualifier" before signing the Posting and Promotion File. He asked what qualifier? I explained like "Confirmation of Promotion to QMG

Post subject to Medical Certification in six months or even 12 months (one year)". His response was "you are thinking like a lawyer – it never occurred to me the necessity of a qualifier or stipulation but now I realize that was the proper procedure in this case".

The Administrative Law (Procedural Rules of Postings and Promotions for General Staff Officers in the Ministry of Defense), a carbon copy of the British Defense General Staff Administrative Law (Parliamentary Legislation Ordinance) where it is clearly defined that it is entirely the prerogative of the "Recommending General Staff Officer" to stipulate or prescribe qualifiers as deemed appropriate and/or necessary on a Case-To-Case basis, always taking into consideration the special circumstances (If Any) of the subject officer currently or those in his Career File. Apparently because the case involved the Senior Colonel, the Judge Advocate General was not consulted by the two top Generals and the Military Secretary was merely performing the "Clerical Functions of Preparing the Documents and Submitting the File" to the Vice Chief of General Staff for "submission to the Chief of General Staff's perusal and signature".

Tin Phay and wife Daw Thein Saing's tear-shedding drama paid off well beyond their wildest dreams but to the chagrin of the Medical Board forced to revise the "Unfit to Serve to: LIGHT NON-COMBAT SEDENTARY DUTIES". It was a very huge, demoralizing blow to the top three medical doctors in uniform of the Burma Army Medical Corps – Colonels Hla Han, Maung Lwin, Ko Ko Gyi and Dr. Ba Than, Dean of the entire Burma Medical Profession and above all father-in-law of Ne Win. He was visibly disgusted with the whole affair especially the immense personal pressure on him from Bo Aung Gyi, the Vice Chief of General Staff of the Burmese Military establishment, to revise the professional judgment of the top Medical Board. For that rather out of character action he received a great amount of negative reaction from the medical profession as well as from Senior General Staff Officers lobbying to get the coveted and much desired and sought after Brigadier-General QMG post in the Ministry of Defense.

Looking back with the benefit of hindsight the Tin Phay dispute between Ne Win and Aung Gyi was a harbinger of things to come because it produced one hundred percent (100%) all round negative outcomes for both men, the military and of course the country. The sick, crippled and uncouth Tin Phay with an immobile right arm, bladder out of control and numerous physical disabilities that required continued special medical care and treatment in Burma as well as in the UK, was a very heavy burden on the Ministry of Defense. However, the shock, disbelief and disgust of those familiar with this case was Tin Phay's arrogance, bombast and demeanor that all this special consideration, care and extraordinary expense was owed to him by the Military and country for his participation in the struggle for independence. It was indeed the height of self-glorification and ingratitude, especially to colleagues who bent over backwards and went out of their way to help him, practically risking their own Military careers.

To subordinates and junior Staff Officers, he referred to himself as "Nga-Saya" (Literally translated "I am the Teacher / I am the boss"). His constant demands and need for "extra-special respect" apparently was the result of his long period of life in robes as a monk, and he never failed to mention that all his contemporaries were leading Abbots of the Buddhist religion with exalted titles of Agga-Maha-Pandita and he would have attained that position if he had stayed in robes. His psyche and delusional perception of his General rank pushed him to take undue and inappropriate liberties with female officers, groping them in his office and making sexual advances. His frequent trips to the VIP Ward of the Army hospital for overnight care became a nightmare for the medical team and nursing staff. It became such a serious problem and embarrassment that the medical team would recommend treatment abroad just to get rid of him and save the female nurse officers from his blatant groping and unwanted advances.

However, to the shock of all, that pattern of misbehaving would continue abroad regardless of location. The specialist medical professionals in the UK and France concluded that there was a clear indication of neurological factors to be looked into and thoroughly examined, such as "neuro-impairment and/or diminishment because of the near fatal auto accident history resulting in severe physical disabilities and need for continuing treatment of medical ailments". As such he was referred to the world famous Neurological Clinic of Dr. Hans Hoff in Vienna, Austria. It was a God-send gift patient for Hoff from his British colleagues and Associates who would receive "kick-back" from Hoff deposited into their secret Swiss bank accounts to avoid British tax. It was a grand conspiracy of Harley Street British Medical Specialists and their Austrian colleagues to squeeze as much money as possible out of the Burmese Dictator and his Generals.

# THE UK-EU MEDICAL SPECIALISTS AND THEIR DICTATOR PATIENTS

My encounter and experience with UK, French and Austrian medical specialists is one of awe, shock and eye-opening awareness that these highly trained medical professionals were not in the business of curing illnesses of powerful patients who sought their help but to keep them on a long leash by inflating their egos, making them feel good about themselves and squeeze as much money out of them for as long as possible. There is no standard treatment regimen in these clinics for high profile Dictator Head of State patients. Each one has to be "individually designed" to meet the special requirements of each and the first requirement to "quality and be accepted as a patient" is "reference from recognized and accredited medical institution" and "written payment guarantee accompanied by a UK/European bank reference". At the time of admission to the Clinic, "a retainer security deposit (30%) of the estimated cost" of the specifically designed treatment needed to be paid upfront by bank transfer or banker's check.

Since independence in early 1948, Burma's Cabinet Ministers, senior Government and Military officials would be sent to UK for medical treatment on Government expense and well-to-do private citizens would be given foreign exchange to cover the medical treatment costs abroad. The very first beneficiary was Deputy Prime Minister U Kyaw Nyein, whose long suffering tuberculosis (TB) was treated in London just in time as one lung was beyond treatment and had to be removed. The country at that time had healthy foreign exchange reserves earned from exports of 3.5M tons of rice, almost a million tons of beans and pulses, silver, tin, wolfram, teak and various hardwoods. However, 14 years later in March 1962 when the Military toppled the civilian government, the exports had been reduced drastically almost by half but were still very substantial in comparison to the rest of S. E. Asian countries.

Foreign exchange reserves had dwindled and the luxury of medical treatment in the UK and Europe was limited to the selected few at the top. Despite the highly restricted and protected secrecy of the UK Action Plan Covert Project initiated by Bo Ne Win, bits and pieces of information of what was being planned by the Revolutionary Council became known to senior Ministry of Defense officials perhaps by "controlled leaks" or through the collection of documents and data from many Ministries, Departments and the Union Bank of Burma relating to foreign exchange approvals for imports, overseas payments, letters of credit, bank transfers abroad, Ministry of Foreign Affairs, Ministry of Defense foreign exchange Bank Accounts to cover the expenses of the diplomatic missions world-wide (Embassies/Attachés).

On the eve of my departure for London via Copenhagen and the hectic 18 hours a day schedule of last minute meetings and never-ending briefings at Dagon House by Bo Aung Gyi and always present Bo Khin Nyo, Chairman of BEDC and Bo Maung Lwin (Moustache), Chief of Military Intelligence, to my surprise and amazement, I was instructed to call on Colonel Hla Han (Doctor), Minister of Health and Education and Colonel Maung Lwin (Doctor), Director of Army Medical Services. "They want to consult with you concerning bank guarantees abroad." I was taken aback and surprised because the UK Action Plan Mission was classified "Covert" and I was quickly cautioned by the Intelligence Chief to refrain from talking about the mission goals and simply mention that it is a Trade, Banking and Commercial Office for UK and Europe.

The two Colonels, both Army doctors, wanted to know the financial and banking resources of BEDC available to their respective organizations particularly for "payment guarantees demanded by UK Institutions of Higher Learning and Hospitals where Burmese Medical Doctors are sent for Membership Titles, fellowships and Internships at designated hospitals in UK, Scotland, Ireland and Wales". It was quite apparent that the two Senior Colonels (Doctors) were attempting to avoid having to deal with the additional bureaucracy at the Ministry of Finance – the Office of Finance Advisor U Ba Nyain. It definitely would become another gripe against Bo Aung Gyi and BEDC for encroaching on the financial authority of the Ministry of Finance under Bo San Yu a Senior General and member of the Revolutionary Council.

The writing on the wall was quite clear for BEDC – "avoid being used as a bulldozer to break down long established barriers that will inevitably lead to confrontation and turf wars". I came to know Col. Maung Lwin (Doctor) when he arrived in Tokyo as the first Defense Services Attaché after the WWII Treaty of Peace and friendship. Before departure from Rangoon to take up his new posting, defense protocol required Attachés to report to the Chief of Staff for final last minute "instructions and/or assignment". At that meeting Gen. Ne Win told him that we have our (Ye'-Baw) in Tokyo and to ask him for assistance with language and other matters and to get all the information from Bo Aung Gyi and Bo Maung Lwin (Moustache). Col. Hla Han had been to Japan several times as a member of Military Delegations led by the Chief of Staff and had met me on those trips. Knowing both the Army Medical Doctors since my student days in Japan I fully appreciated their dilemma with the Finance Ministry and their desire to get help from BEDC, knowing full well that the top management would accommodate their needs.

There was a distinct possibility that the two medical doctor Colonels gleaned some information on the UK project from their own connections with the Committee Members as well as from the several Ministries that were asked by the Revolutionary Council Secretary Col. Ko Ko to release documents, data and files classified "Restricted and Confidential". It was a difficult situation for me to figure out how much to reveal without compromising the "Covert Classification" of the project and the constant concern of being responsible for "any leakage" or worse-case scenario of blowing the Cover. I explained to the two Colonels with "a qualifier" that as far as I knew, it would take some time for BEDC to set up the financial and banking infrastructure and organization abroad with the necessary connections and correspondent arrangements in Europe. Once that was established and operational, the full spectrum of financial, banking, insurance, etc. would be available to all Ministries, Departments and State owned Corporations. I reported to the three men "Mission Control and Operation Committee" (Gen. Aung Gyi, Col. Khin Nyo and Col. Moustache Maung Lwin) and they were relieved that at least we had avoided being used by other Ministries to circumvent the overbearing and arrogant Communist Finance Advisor at the Ministry of Finance and Revenue. That was the state of affairs a few months after the Coup.

The internal frictions and dissensions at the very core of the Army's seat of power were coming up to the surface but still confined to the very few at the top and the inner-circle technocrat special Advisors. It can definitely be attributed to paranoia and obsession with keeping all things under wraps even between and among those at the very top. This practice was taught to the 30 Comrades by their Japanese Imperial General Staff mentors and the Nakano Intelligence School where elite officers are taught and indoctrinated to always bear in mind that in the "Administration and Management of Armed Forces the worst enemy is often closest to you", especially at the top echelon requiring compartmentalization of both personnel and issues to be pursued and/or discussed "strictly on a need to know basis". Aung San followed this practice when he was Head of the Burmese Armed Forces, Para-Military and the Militias, a disparate group with their own political agendas and questionable loyalty to any one entity.

Notwithstanding my many years of higher learning at top elite Japanese Universities and exposure to their body politic, I was surprised and taken aback when told after every briefing /meeting "don't tell what we discussed to so and so". It became routine parting words with whomever I was meeting – with Bo Khin Nyo he would say "don't tell Bo Aung Gyi". With Bo Aung Gyi he would say "don't tell Bo Khin Nyo". With Bo Maung Lwin (Moustache) "don't tell Bo Aung Gyi and Bo Khin Nyo". It was strange and bizarre at the beginning but with time you learn not to reveal anything, period. Everyone, even the Generals one rung below #1 and the Senior Colonels, felt insecure and seemed to have suddenly lost confidence in themselves and did not want any matter emanating from them or being the source of it, especially when it requires submission to #1. The discretion for silence, not offering / volunteering comments at official meetings unless asked by the presiding senior officer became normal behavior.

The consequence was disaster for the administrative machinery of the country – it came to a screeching stop. The affairs of the State and matters affecting the daily lives of citizens were pushed aside or completely ignored. Saving one's butt took precedence over all other things. Another very disturbing and worrisome development was the Cabinet Ministers of the Revolutionary Council Government, for reasons of ignorance, incompetence and pressure from non-cooperating bureaucracy, were seeking help and rescue from Bo

Aung Gyi, who as always could never say no and found himself involved in the affairs of every Ministry. The inevitable result was shortage of time and personnel around him. In desperation, he would grab the one closest and order them to attend totally unrelated this or that meeting and report back to him. Unfortunately or unluckily I was often the victim of this pattern. It created and caused a lot of problems for all.

At one such meeting I went to attend at the Ministry of Mines Chaired by the Permanent Secretary, I was introduced as Legal Adviser of the Revolutionary Council Office. It was going to discuss Mawchi Silver and Lead Mines, a Joint Venture with the British like the Burma Oil Company, the Government owning 51%. The Minister was taken ill and hospitalized. The Permanent Secretary, a career Civil Service officer close to retirement, was not keen on making any decision on behalf of his sick Minister or the Ministry, concerned that it could impact negatively on his retirement plans. In characteristic Civil Service tactics he was going to palm off the decision-making to the #2 General in the Revolutionary Council Government.

Reviewing the meeting agenda, I noted several sensitive issues concerning the Contract renewal of several British Executives, Engineers and Technical Staff, the Stock buy-back option and new Technical and Parts Procurement Agreement. Two middle-aged British Executives, the Managing Director and Chief Accountant were present at the meeting. Other members of the board were Permanent Secretaries of the Ministry of Finance and Revenue, Ministry of Trade, Ministry of Home Affairs, Ministry of Agriculture and Forests, the Accountant-General and the Attorney-General. It was quite apparent that all the bureaucrats wanted to avoid handling the issue of the stock buy-back and the extension of service for the British technical team.

The meeting started off on the wrong foot because the Ministry Permanent Secretary Chairman attempted to put me in "the hot seat" by requesting me to address the Board (in English) with "clarification of the Revolutionary Council Government's policy on Mineral Resources and the Joint Venture Corporation in particular at Mawchi Mines". I firmly pushed it right back to him by saying that I was instructed by General Aung Gyi to attend this meeting "as an observer" and report back to him on the proceedings and decisions taken". I also explained to the Board Members the technical correction of my position being Legal Adviser to BEDC, Office of the Prime Minister. There was gasp of Oh! and a long silence. During the lunch break with meat patties, cakes, tea and coffee, the two British Executives came over to my seat and invited me to visit them at Mawchi, well known for its excellent cool climate and ideal for golf. After the recess the meeting resumed but a decision on the agenda was postponed until the Minister's return.

The Cabinet Ministers in uniform, all members of the Revolutionary Council, ran their Ministries along the same lines of the Military Command and Control system but the bureaucracy under the Permanent Secretaries was too big and unwieldly to be managed and operated like a Military unit of soldiers, sergeants, warrant officers and commissioned officers. As such there was a huge disconnect between the Minister and his few uniformed Officers on Special Duties (OSDs) on one side and the vast bureaucracy with allegiance to the Permanent Secretary. The decision-making process is "deliberate and layered" involving review and input of many Officers and by the time it reaches the Permanent Secretary's desk the file is several inches thick and there is very little possibility of serious errors like "misrepresentation of facts, biased comments and/or evaluations" and the Ministry's judgments and decisions are highly respected as a rule.

There is no way for a General or a Colonel to grasp the depth and significance of that tried and true Management Practice and more often than not "impose the Military style top down Command Orders" with very little or no relevance to the matter in hand, resulting in delays, confusions and mountains of unsolved files affecting the affairs of State and the lives of Citizens. The unfortunate and sad thing for the country and people was that the Politicians who had replaced the British Raj since 1948 for 14 years, making no changes whatsoever, giving the bureaucrats free rein, had lined their pockets, and now in 1962 the Generals and Colonels had toppled the politicians and seized control of the country, but instead of making efforts to improve the Government efficiency they were in actual fact dismantling it and creating chaos and making life difficult for the general public.

In contrast, the Public and Quasi Public Corporations / Joint Ventures like the BOC, Mawchi Mines, Bombay-Burma, Steel Brothers, IWTB, State Timber Board (STB), Burma Oxygen, etc. were functioning normally and quite well one must say, but it was a concern that the Ministries were becoming "bottle-necks" and would very soon impact on these Corporations that required support and cooperation at the Ministerial level. The country's overall economic growth (GDP) would remain stable as long as the Agricultural Export sector continued at current levels especially the three mainstay commodities, Rice, Beans and Pulses, and Timber. Another critical factor that the Revolutionary Council failed to give due recognition to at that time (1962) was the International Business Community did not hit the panic button after the Coup as the Country's Economy and the Trade, Business and High Value Commercial Enterprises were BEDC Subsidiaries and Joint Ventures with established foreign Corporations and under the leadership of General Aung Gyi, highly regarded overseas as "business friendly" and an advocate of National Private Enterprise.

It was a huge positive factor especially in the Asian Business Community like Hong Kong, Singapore, Thailand, Malaysia, China, Taiwan, Japan and Australia. The world's reaction to the overthrow of the democratically elected Government of U Nu who had won a landslide victory just two years previously was muted and lackluster at best, as recognition of the Revolutionary Council by the immediate neighboring countries was almost immediate and the permanent members of the United Nations within days followed by the members of the UN General Assembly Members, particularly those with Embassies in Rangoon. In fact it was quite a surprise that U Nu, a highly respected Statesman and Co-Founder of the Moral Rearmament and Non-Alignment movements, was practically abandoned by the democratic leaders of the world without even a hint of concern for his personal security and his entire Cabinet placed under detention by the Military.

Despite such a glaring absence of concern for the deposed Prime Minister and his Ministers, the Military, now firmly under the control of General Ne Win, was not taking any chances and immediately retired off U Nu's son-in-law, a Lt.Colonel and U Kyaw Nyein's brother-in-law, another Lt-Colonel in the Army, with orders "not to leave the environs of Rangoon without permission from the nearest Police Station from their respective residences". The two famous top

Police Commissioner brothers Tin Maung Maung and Khin Maung Maung were also placed on "leave preparatory to retirement", a strategy used by the British Colonial Government in ensuring that the Law Enforcement apparatus remained loyal with the Heads of Department practically held as hostage. One can clearly see the hand of Colonel Maung Lwin (Moustache), the Chief of Military Intelligence who began his career as Detective Sub-Inspector in the British Imperial Police Service together with the two Police Commissioner brothers.

# CIVIL SERVICE BUREAUCRATS AND POLICE BEATEN INTO SUBMISSION

The short fuse of the Generals and Colonels did not last more than a few months after the Coup on March 02, 1962. Bo Aung Gyi, the Vice Chief of General Staff (VCGS), was entrusted with the monumental task of running the day-to-day operation and management of the entire Government machinery, and was soon bogged down with key ministers seeking his guidance and decision on critical matters – such as the Ministry of Home Affairs responsible for National Police, Civil Service, Prisons' Operations, National Fire Services, Ministry of Justice, Ministry of Transport and Communications to name just a few.

The bureaucrats with an entrenched following of loyal Civil Servants used every trick in the book to slow everything down– tantamount to sabotage. It could no longer be tolerated. The bureaucracy needed to be brought under control quickly. Bo Aung Gyi reported the urgency to the Revolutionary Council Chairman who in characteristic modus operandi set up a Secret Committee under Bo Aung Gyi to take all necessary action to restructure the Administrative Machinery. The need for secrecy was to shield the members from any distraction from within the Military, Public, Media, Clergy, Etc. The composition of the "Confidential Government Restructuring Secret Committee":

- Gen. Aung Gyi, Chairman, Revolutionary Council Member, Minister of Trade & Commerce
- Gen. San Yu, Vice Chairman, " " " Minister of Finance & Revenue
- Col. Thaung Kyi, Member, " Adjutant-General (AG), Ministry of Defense
- Col. Khin Nyo, Member, " Director of Military Training (DMT), Ministry of Defense

- Col. Maung Lwin, Member, Military Intelligence Chief (MIS), Ministry of Defense
- Col. Kyi Maung, Member, Colonel General-Staff (G-1), Ministry of Defense
- Col. Solomon, Member, Judge Advocate General, Ministry of Defense
- U Maung Maung, (Committee Secretary), Permanent Secretary, Ministry of Defense
- U Kyi Win Sein, General Counsel / Legal Advisor BEDC, Prime Minister's Office

This High Powered Secret Committee was given full authority to take any measure/action deemed necessary including but not limited to summary dismissal of Civil Service Officials considered in obstruction of Administrative and/or causing delays and such officials to be investigated for obstruction of Justice and Government operations.

It was early July 1962, in the midst of heavy monsoon downpours one late evening, I dropped by Dagon House at the entrance to the Ministry of Defense to see Bo Aung Gyi before my departure for London the next day. I ran into Bo Lwin (Moustache) at the entrance door and he asked if I had come to attend the meeting and why I had not yet left Rangoon. I told him the departure was tomorrow but the excess baggage situation needed to be resolved at check-in at the airport. He said not to worry – "I will send your friend Hubert to Kayah State Guest House to accompany you to the airport and to check you in. "I will tell Bo Aung Gyi you are here, all the best and have a good trip". Bo Aung Gyi came out from the Conference Room and without hesitation said they were holding the first meeting of the Secret Committee and walked me to the living room.

"I am glad you came as it will give me a break while Bo San Yu is holding the fort" and he gave me a wink and a wide grin. It was his sense of humor because Bo San Yu was notorious for remaining silent at such meetings. Despite the heaviest load he was carrying for the Revolutionary Council Government, he cheerfully assured me that "you have the full support of Bogyoke (General Ne Win) and we have confidence in your capability and sound judgment to make this important mission a success. We are here to give you all the support you need. Have a good flight and thank you for taking care of Bo Myo Myint". With that he stood up, gave me a hug and went back to the Conference Room to resume the Secret Committee meeting. That was the last time we met face-to-face until my return from London a few years later.

Early next morning at the Kayah State Guest House where I was staying, I noted the English newspaper Guardian (Army owned) "Headline": "Chief Secretary of the Government relieved of duties and put on leave preparatory to retirement". It was "the decapitation of the Civil Service", the senior most Civilian Officer "abruptly removed from service" no doubt by the Secret Committee. This action would send a shudder down the spine of every bureaucrat in the Government. The era of Civil Service supremacy and their exalted social status in Burma had ended. Perhaps it was a mere coincidence but it happened on the day of my departure for London where my mission was to bring to an end to the foreign domination of the country's economy and the business enterprises. To put it in true National Interest perspective it was 14 years too late for the country and the people. The politicians of Aung San's party (AFPFL) not only neglected to effect the needed changes but enriched themselves using the bureaucrats and the foreign business enterprises, sucking the economic blood of the country for 14 long years.

Later in the morning Intelligence Captain Hubert Vumko Taul showed up in two unmarked cars – Opel 4-door sedan and Land Rover for the luggage. The vehicles were equipped with wireless communications as well as walkie-talkies. He was together with me at the University of Rangoon and after graduation had joined the Army and was selected for intelligence training. He was ethnic Chin from a prominent family of that State. His uncle U Vum Kohau was Aung San's colleague and first Minister of Chin Affairs and later Ambassador. Hubert reported to me that his boss Bo Lwin (Moustache) had personally called the Mingaladon Airport Security Officer to take care of our check in, immigration and customs clearance, etc. Hubert would be with us until we were seated in the front cabin of BOAC Airline.

At the airport Major Aung Thein, the Security Officer, awaited us and escorted us to a private room in the VIP Lounge where Col. Myo Myint was already there. He greeted me, Kazuko and toddler Bob, wide-eyed and mouth agape, seeing the intelligence officers attending to the check in and departure formalities. He joined us in the private living room where coffee/tea/cold drinks and snacks were served. While waiting the Security Officer handed me a note – a message from Bo Lwin (Moustache) advising me that the Military Attaché in Bangkok would meet our flight and clear us through formalities and take us to our hotel for the overnight stopover and do the same next day for our flight to Copenhagen. The stopover and rest was arranged for baby Bob who had just made the long flight from Tokyo about six weeks earlier. We were the first group to board the aircraft, escorted by Major Aung Thein, the Airport security chief and Hubert, with Col. Myo Myint carrying Bob up the boarding ladder. The BOAC Rangoon Manager welcomed us aboard and led us to the front seats of the cabin and took leave with the two Army officers.

The Captain and Purser of the plane welcomed us aboard and pinned a wing on Bob's shirt and he was thrilled. It was a smooth, quiet 45 minutes flight to Don Muang Airport in Bangkok and we were met at the gate by the Burmese Military Attaché, who was holding a piece of cardboard with "U Kyi Win Sein and family" written on it; but Col. Myo Myint recognized him as a colleague at the Defense Services Academy when both were serving as teaching academic staff. The Attaché had the expression of surprise and curiosity as to why I was accompanied by the Colonel carrying my son. He reported to me the receipt of the telex signal instructing him to meet the flight and extend necessary help. BOAC had a limousine for us but the Attaché drove us to the Dusittani Hotel in the Embassy cars. He wanted to entertain us to dinner but I declined and suggested that he and the Colonel have a good reunion in Bangkok. Our family ordered room service dinner and did shopping in the Arcade and turned in early. Bob was up early 6 AM next morning and hungry. We ordered up breakfast and again ate in our spacious twin room. About 8:30 AM Col. Myo Myint called and said the Attaché was in the lobby inviting us to breakfast.

I went down and had coffee with the two colonels and they were very curious to find out the purpose of my being sent to London with the family. Col. Myo Myint, a well-educated man starting from Saint Peters in Mandalay as I had, recalled how he first met me at Dagon House, summoned there by his Agriculture and Forest Minister Gen. Tin Phay without any advance notice. And how he was surprised beyond belief to see a very young man introduced by Gen. Aung Gyi as "our Japanese educated Legal Advisor to BEDC at the

Prime Minister's Office". The next thing Gen. Tin Phay said jolted me – "Bo Myo Myint, Ko Kyi Win Sein will explain how the Contract with the Scandinavians can and will be terminated.

"All those "SOBs" in the Ministries, the Lawyers in the Attorney General's Office and our own Judge Advocate General Attorneys do not understand International Law enough and are just simply scared of the "White men (Myet-Hna-Phyu). Col. Khin Nyo, BEDC Chairman added, "U Kyi Win Sein has reviewed the Contract and we have authorized him to stop by at Copenhagen and meet the Scandinavian Federation and terminate it. We want you to accompany him as Chairman of State Timber Board (STB)." Then I was more stunned when U Kyi Win Sein drafted a cable/telex informing the Scandinavian Timber Federation that the Revolutionary Council Government intends to review the Contract as soon as possible with them. The next morning a reply came agreeing to meet us in Copenhagen and now we are on our way."

Yes indeed, at that meeting in Dagon House, Col. Myo Myint was visibly shaken by what he was told by the two Senior Generals and a Colonel well known to be the confidante of the #1 at the time of the attempted Coup of Gen. Maung Maung was crushed without firing a shot. He was dismayed at what had just transpired and lost for words. His Minister boss Gen. Bo Tin Phay was relieved that BEDC was going to resolve a critical legal dilemma of his Ministry that has haunted every Minister since the country's independence in 1948. Then as Bo Tin Phay was about to leave the meeting, Bo Khin Nyo raised the delicate but obvious question of why this legal issue seemingly quite straightforward as explained by our U Kyi Win Sein has lingered on for over 14 years with all the Barristers in the Attorney General's Office?

It was a loaded question aimed at the Legal Profession of the country and I would not attempt to answer or comment on it unless asked directly or officially by the Presiding Officer or Chairman of the Competent Committee. Bo Aung Gyi, fully aware of the sensitivity of the issue and the consequences in the event of the discussions being leaked out intentionally by vested interest entities, could have huge conflict of interest problems within the Revolutionary Council Government. Bo Aung Gyi was aware that this issue was taken to #1 by his wife Katy because of this contract. Regardless he went further saying that since it is a legal matter of critical importance to our national economy you perhaps know better than any one of us – looking at me. There was no escape for me to wiggle out of this being thrown at me directly.

I first had to qualify my response by clarifying that the Legal Issue was used as a justification for not tackling it over 14 years. It suited the agenda of all concerned as it was the "Goose that laid the Golden Eggs". Col. Myo Myint and the Attaché for the first time in their military career encountered the complexities of International Legal Contracts between Nation States and the Private Business Corporations and Multi-National Enterprises. Many years later when our paths crossed again, Col. Myo Myint recalled our breakfast meeting with the Military Attaché at Disit-Tani hotel in our Bangkok transit to Copenhagen in Denmark. There at the Airport Hilton Hotel conference room we met the Scandinavian Timber Federation Chairman and their Lawyers and terminated the Contract which the Cabinet of newly independent Burma's first Prime Minister had renewed and allowed it to continue operating in full force as it did under the British Colonial Government.

As officially authorized and credentialed to represent the Revolutionary Council Government I signed the Memorandum of Agreement (Col. Myo Myint, Chairman of State Timber Board as witness) with the Federation, officially terminating the Contract in its entirety and agreeing to enter into a New Contract to be negotiated in Rangoon with the Ministry of Trade and Commerce, the Ministry of Agriculture and Forests represented by the State Timber Board. The Colonel returned from Copenhagen to Rangoon with the "original hard copy Agreement" and reported to Gen. Tin Phay, the Minister of Agriculture and Forests and Gen. Aung Gyi, the Minister of Trade and Commerce. I reported via Diplomatic Pouch of the Military Attaché in London to Col. Khin Nyo, the Chairman of BEDC in the Prime Minister's Office. Mission accomplished.

From Copenhagen it was a short flight to Heathrow Airport in London and the weather mid-summer was rather warm in the day but getting chilly after sunset. We went through immigration and customs fairly quickly and took a full-size taxi to our favorite Aunty Eve's house in Cheam Village, Surrey. She and husband Uncle Maurice eagerly awaited our arrival. The last time

I saw both of them was in Maymyo (now Pyin-Oo-Lwin) nearly 15 years earlier, soon after independence in 1948 when Uncle Maurice, the last British Chief Conservator of Forests, was on his farewell tour of the country before proceeding to British Guiana as Deputy Governor-General, the #2 official of the British Colonial Government of the small Island. He retired from Colonial service many years ago and settled in a single family detached spacious house with a fenced backyard rose garden in Cheam Village, Surrey with his beloved wife Eve.

It was a great reunion for me as Mom was the eldest adopted daughter of Ivan Nicholson before Aunty Eve was born, becoming her closest beloved younger sister. When they left Burma with Aunty Eve's two sons Peter and Paul from her previous marriage to Edward Reynolds, Uncle Maurice's subordinate in the Forestry Department, I was in the 5th Standard (grade) at Saint Alberts English High School, about 13 or 14 years old. Now in 1962 my real age was 29 but with reduction of 3 years to get admission in the 1st Standard (grade) at the Catholic Missionary School my official age was 26. However, since I only weighed 105 pounds and with a full head of hair my appearance to a stranger was a kid in grade school or at most a Junior High School student. Aunty Eve was elated that I had elected to put up at her home instead of a hotel in the City and she was curious about my official mission goals in London. Her motherly instinct was to be the substitute mother for her beloved big sister Hnin who had written several letters to her since my assignment to the UK Special project was announced to the immediate family several months earlier.

Uncle Maurice, the typical Oxford Don with over three decades of overseas Colonial Civil Service at Senior Levels of Management and Administration in Burma, had difficulty lecturing his strong-willed Anglo-Burmese wife that her nephew Malcolm was not the young teenager she had known since his birth but an official of the "Military Government that rules Burma now and he is on Official Assignment representing that Government". It reminded me of the time I was in Cairo, Egypt when Aunty Kitty, Mom's close friend in American Baptist Mission (ABM) School who was childless, went all out to "mother me" to the surprising extent of telling me to move in to her huge official residence of the UN UNICEF Chief of Africa Dillon Singh, her husband.

In London it was more difficult and delicate because Aunty Eve was Mom's younger sister and she happened to be our favorite Aunt who always stayed with us despite the cramped space, and slept on the deck chair or on the camp cot in the corner of the room, whereas poor Uncle Maurice had to stay alone at the posh Government Circuit House for touring officials. Now in Cheam Village, we immediately contacted the real estate agencies close by to get an apartment in a secure location and within a week or ten days found a two bedroom apartment in Twickenham Park on the bank of the River Thames, close to Richmond Bridge train station, and moved into it.

Before leaving Aunty Eve's house I asked her what she would like to do most and without hesitation she said "I want to visit a beauty salon that I have not been to since Maurice retired". I gave her thirty pounds and told her to go have a good time and she gave me a big hug. When Uncle Maurice found out he jokingly told me "Malcolm, don't spoil your Aunt, I am a poor retired Government Servant" and I told Aunty Eve in his presence "whenever you feel like going to a beauty salon don't hesitate to let me know". I was surprised to learn later that retired overseas colonial service personnel were not treated equally compared with the home service employees in the Colonial Affairs Ministry attached to the Prime Minister's Office.

There was widespread resentment, even at the highest levels where Uncle Maurice belonged that he was treated shabbily when returning to Britain in retirement. Only then did I fully understand the British Society's status classification term "one's station in life" which is a well-defined one in the UK as it was then. In the Legal Profession I was involved in depth – "A Solicitor's role and function was clearly defined and limited in scope and always subordinate to a Barrister".

# ESSENTIAL INGREDIENT FOR RAPID ECONOMIC GROWTH

However, as an official of the Revolutionary Council Government Legal Advisor to the highest National Economic Development Corporation in the Prime Minister's Office, I was accorded equal accreditation and recognition by the UK Legal Profession. The British political and educated elite, with over a century of global empire building experience and colonial rule in the Middle East, Africa and Asia, was very well practiced in dealing with newly independent States, especially its ex-colonial possessions like Burma. And despite the more than usual age disparity for one in such a senior official position, I was always received with correct and proper courtesy of regard and respect accorded to an official of a Sovereign Government by the British Foreign Office, the Board of Trade (Ministry of Trade) and the Bar Association of the UK in London.

The British Academic Institutions of Higher Learning such as the London University King's College, Imperial College and the School of Oriental and African Studies where many Burmese had completed the highest scholastic studies, welcomed me as the First Head of the Permanent Burmese Trade Mission headquartered in London with offers of support and assistance in every possible way. One of the proposals and invitations was for me to participate in the Special Private and Exclusive Seminar Discussion project under the auspices of the London School of Economics led by the prominent Burmese economist Dr. Hla Myint on the subject of State Controlled Command Economics. Being private and exclusive the qualification for participants was Senior Government Officials nominated by the Ministry of the Government of that country. The duration was three months, 3-times a week and the fees were three hundred pounds sterling and very steep, even for Governments.

In my case Colonel Khin Nyo, Chairman of Burma Economic Development Corporation, Office of the Prime Minister, Revolutionary Council Government signed the official nomination and sponsorship letter and certification for Corporate Counsel and Head of Burmese Trade Mission in London. Dr. Hla Myint at that time was also Economic Advisor to Harold Wilson the Labour Party Leader and Prime Minister of the British Government. His seminar format discussions were very well received and immensely popular because many of the newly independent countries in Asia and Africa were stumbling all over in search of a workable economic model to raise the living conditions of their ever increasing populations. Dr. Hla Myint stressed the critical importance for political leaders and senior government officials to bear in mind the population's dependence on the land for survival and livelihood for past centuries and therefore the agriculture sector needed to be given top priority and the necessary resources allotted in the Nations' Fiscal Policies and National Budgets.

The first and most politically difficult task would be to take the bull by the horn and tackle Land Reform with determination and resolve to liberate the tenant peasant from the clutches of the wealthy blood-sucking landlords. Without such drastic and revolutionary land reforms instituted to transform and empower the peasants into landowners, farmers producing agricultural products for the export industry and domestic consumption, the nation's economy would not develop quickly. This drastic measure was taken by the U.S. occupation government under General of the Army, MacArthur in Japan in 1945 which became the driving engine of the miracle economic growth of the country that was totally bombed to the ground by American carpet bombing. The Japanese peasants overnight became landowners thanks to MacArthur and produced bumper crops, thus gaining immense financial and political power to the extent of determining the future outcome of democratic elections in Japan at the Local and National levels.

However, land reform is easier said than done in any country, even in Burma ruled by the Military for more than half a century. General MacArthur succeeded because the country was on its knees and the previous Emperor-God was at his mercy. The American General had the power to over-rule his allies and impose the Constitution drafted under his direction on the country and fortunately for the Japanese people he was a well-read man on the country's history and culture, and his personal desire and vision was to lead them on to the path of a Parliamentary Democratic Nation. A rare opportunity indeed for a career military officer who rejected outright the proposal of the allies to dismantle and abolish the Emperor System and rule the Japanese islands as an American Colony. But after MacArthur's disgraceful downfall and departure from Japan at the hands of President Truman, the American political elite turned the island nation into its puppet in Asia that continues to be the same to this day, after more than sixty years, in 2018.

# THE DICTATOR AND THE AFPFL PARTY BREAKER AMBASSADOR

His excellency U Hla Maung (Peking), the first Burmese Ambassador to the People's Republic of China in 1949, was Aung San's close friend since their student days at Rangoon University and comrade-in-arms in the struggle for independence from British colonial rule. He joined the Thakin Party together with politically active Student Union members and activists such as Shu Maung (later Gen. Ne Win), whose ambition to become a medical doctor did not materialize because he could not pass the tough entrance examination to the Medical Course. When Gen. Aung San discarded his uniform and launched the PFPFL Political Party towards the end of WW-II with U Nu, Bo Khin Maung Galay, Ba Swe, Kyaw Nyein, Thakin Tin and Thakin Tha Khin, U Hla Maung was an inner circle member together with Bo Aung Gyi (later Gen. Aung Gyi) and U Thi Han (later Foreign Minister, the only civilian in the Revolutionary Government in 1962).

As such in the Burmese political arena he was senior to Ne Win and both addressed each other Ko Shu Maung and Ko Hla Maung even after the March 02, 1962 Coup. He was known to be the "quiet, behind the scenes mover-shaker and manipulator". In one of the infamous private meetings of the AFPFL Party big-wigs at the residence of U Ba Swe, acting Prime Minister while U Nu took leave of absence from Office and was away on pilgrimage to Buddha-Gaya in India and Ceylon (now Sri-Lanka), Ambassador U Hla Maung at that gathering also attended by Generals Ne Win and Aung Gyi, casually suggested (OR allegedly proposed) that Ko-Gyi Nu (big-brother) be allevated to the role of Party Elder like the Chinese Communist Party did with Mao Tse Dong.

When that casual talk at a private gathering reached the ever suspicious and insecure cohorts of U Nu (Thakin Tin and Thakin Tha Dun) it was misconstrued as Ba Swe, Kyaw Nyein, Bo Khin Maung Galay and the two Army Generals were plotting to kick the Prime Minister upstairs permanently. When the naïve and vulnerable U Nu's plane arrived at the gate, Thakin Kyaw Dun went on board and advised him that Thakin Tin in hospital wanted to see him right away. The sick Deputy Prime Minister informed the travel weary leader that a plot was underway to oust and push him upstairs as Party Elder. U Nu reacted in typical (Saturday-born characteristic) temper and demanded that Ba Swe hand back the Premiership to him immediately, well before the 18 months period publicly announced when he took leave of absence for rest, pilgrimage and meditation. Parliament immediately voted and restored the Premiership back to U Nu.

This hasty, emotional and arbitrary action based solely on Thakin Tin and Kyaw Dun's information shocked the AFPFL leadership because nothing could be farther from the truth and the sincere intent of U Hla Maung, knowing full well his friend's interest in writing and meditation than in politics and governance. Notwithstanding, the human nature of emotions and egos took the better of the AFPFL Party leaders that eventually led to the split – Nu – Tin (Clean AFPFL) and Swe – Nyein (Stable AFPFL). The Party-Breaker stamp was imprinted on Ambassador U Hla Maung forever but strangely enough he still enjoyed the trust and confidence of Prime Minister U Nu and continued serving as his Ambassador in London, and Bo Ne Win kept him on after the Coup and was quite friendly when we met his flight at the Queen's Royal lounge at Heathrow Airport – saying "Ko Hla Maung you must be used to cold places like London and Peking by now?" "No, Ko Shu Maung, I suffer a lot from more than half a year of intense cold".

*L-r Kyi Win Sein, author, Colonel Khin Nyo and U Thaung Win in Calabasas home of Mal Sein 1989*

*L-r Colonel and Mrs Khin Nyo with Bob, Sayoko, Kazuko and Mal Sein at Calabasas home of the Sein family*

*At Geihinkan Japanese Govt Guest House with Taku Yamazaki, Chief Cabinet Secretary and California Delegation*

*Author Mal Sein with U Kyaw Nyein, Deputy Prime Minister*

*With Taku Yamazaki, Chief Cabinet Secretary of Japan and California Mayor's Delegation*

*With ex-Prime Minister Toshiki Kaifu*

*With Mr Okuda, friend and comrade of General Ne Win and top Burmese military officers*

*Father and Mother's Wedding Photo*

*U Sein (Harry Maung Sein) in uniform of Excise Inspector*

*Back row, standing L-R: MaMa Sein, 1st daughter, Kyi Win Sein, 3rd son, Kyaw Htun Sein, eldest son, Thawda Sein, 4th son, Myo Myin Sein, 2nd son, MiMi Sein, 2nd daughter. Seated L-R: U sein, Father, U tin, Maternal Grandmother, Daw Hnin (Rose Nicholson), Mother. Front row, sitting on floor L-R: tin Htoo Sein, 5th son, Cho Ko Ko Sein (Henry), 7th son, Tin Htet Sein, 6th son (younger twin brother Tin Htoo Sein)*

Kyi Win Sein and U Kyaw Nyein,
Ex-Deputy Prime Minister

California State Central Valley Mayor's Trade delegation to Japan: L-R: Rene Gonzalez,
Mayor tom Olson, Taku Yamazaki, Chief Cabinet Secretary of Japan, Mal Sein, General
Counsel, Mission Leader, John DeWeerd, City Economic Development Manager

Last visit with our favorite aunt in Cheam Village, Surrey. Back row kneeling L-R: Sayoko Sein, Kazuko Sein and Robert Sein. Seated L-R: Evelyn Nicholson (Mrs. Eve Taylor), Kyi Win Sein (Malcolm)

L-R: Kazuko Sein, Daw Hnin, Mother, U Sein, Father, and Kyi Win Sein

# MISFORTUNES NEVER COME SINGLY, ALWAYS IN WAVES

The woes of Bo Ne Win and his inner circle began with the unexpected and sudden departure of Bo Aung Gyi from the Revolutionary Council, the Army and all the key Government Positions he held and ran for over a decade. He was head and shoulders above anyone else in the military hierarchy and more than just merely the "right-hand man of Gen. Ne Win". When U Thi Han got cold feet and could not muster enough courage to present the five key issues of contention that Bo Aung Gyi wanted Bo Ne Win to shelve for at least four years so he would withdraw his resignation, Thi Han never mentioned anything about Bo Aung Gyi's proposal to Gen. Ne Win except that he had failed in his mission and Bo Ne Win's comment was "I never thought he would abandon us like this". On hearing this lament of Ne Win it dawned on U Thi Han the huge error of judgment he had committed. To me and the two Senior Colonels it was clear evidence of how much Gen. Ne Win had relied on Gen. Aung Gyi and now expressing his true feeling of loss and being abandoned by a close friend, comrade-in-arms and colleague who helped build the Modern Professional Military Institutions of Burma together with Gen. Maung Maung. Now both have left him with "incompetent yes men" to rule the country under "Command Economy".

He confessed this to Bo Khin Nyo, Bo Maung Lwin (Moustache) and me in the Washington Hotel, London, not conveying Bo Aung Gyi's political and economic proposals because he was afraid of being accused by Bo Ne Win of "acting as Advocate of Aung Gyi's Political Agenda for the Country". U Thi Han was never able to forget or forgive himself for thinking with his emotions of being misunderstood by Ne Win rather than the unity, stability and future of the country. In all fairness this is perhaps the inevitable outcome you are serving a Military Dictator.

On further reflection on this issue by the two powerful Colonels of the Revolutionary Council and the lone Civilian Foreign Minister of the Military Regime, I noted with surprise that all three agreed that "there was nothing in the five key national issues that Bo Ne Win could not accept judging from his deep feeling of being abandoned by one on whom he has relied for sound, rational and sincere advice and guidance since their activist days for independence. As proven later by events and passage of time, that was the pivotal time when Bo Ne Win realized the enormity of his personal loss and doomed Military Regime. He was going to be left with no one of that stature to deliberate, discuss and decide on "National Issues" on an equal basis with him because all the rest were way too junior in rank as well as political status and would not dare to express their true feelings to the almighty Commander-in-Chief and now the Dictator.

As the youngest civilian man among the three Senior Cabinet Officers of the Revolutionary Council Government in the Washington Hotel Suite in central London, it was quite apparent to me that the moderate elements in the Revolutionary Council had lost their leader and there was no one in sight to fill that vacuum. Then there was an abrupt change of mood among the three middle-aged men in their mid-fifties. Bo Maung Lwin (Moustache), the Military Intelligence Chief, with his British Imperial Police Detective Training and experience turned to me and said, "I have known you since your High School days in Bassein (Pathein) when you were recruited and worked for Col. Thaung Kyi, the Irradaddy Delta Region Combined Military Commander. I don't need to impress upon you that what we discussed here today must be confined between the four of us only and all of us know that you have been entrusted by the Revolutionary Council Chairman with the most delicate and difficult covert project in UK and Europe."

Needless to say, I was stunned and taken aback to put it mildly, but my training and field operational experience was telling me that the "wily intelligence Chief" was merely using the diversionary tactics that all four in this room would suffer dire consequences in the event of any leakage. I was glad that my instinct or sixth sense prompted me to remain silent and keep my mouth shut as I was taught "If you are uncertain or unsure, say nothing". Silence is golden indeed. Then, the Intelligence Chief turned to Bo Khin Nyo and in no uncertain terms said this is now time for him to step into the void and bravely pick up the mantle of leadership of the "moderate and silent majority in the Revolutionary Council". The poor man was visibly shocked and taken aback by the sudden and rather aggressive push by the much feared Chief of Military Intelligence well known to be the "eyes and ears" of #1 and not to be taken lightly especially in matters of this nature. Bo Khin Nyo without any hesitation dismissed the idea and emphatically said there was no way he could step into the shoes of Bo Aung Gyi let alone fit into them.

Moreover, there were more senior officers like Bo San Yu, Bo Thaung Kyi, Bo Chit Myaing, Bo Sein Win, etc. Regardless, U Thi Han was in agreement and support of Bo Maung Lwin's idea said "Ko Khin Nyo, as far as I remember #1 always assigned you to be Bo Aung Gyi's Deputy in key important organizations like BEDC, BOC, Burma Railways Board Chairman and this London Burma Trade Mission to be the Chief Coordination Revolutionary Council Member reporting to Trade Minister and Prime Minister". From that perspective of important and critical assignments entrusted to him by #1, it was indeed an accepted fact that he was groomed to be the one capable of assuming the responsibilities from Bo Aung Gyi and managing the operations with the least disruption and loss of confidence by the huge Executive Boards of the enterprises and the Business Community at home and overseas.

It was a very daring and risky move by the Intelligence Chief and the Civilian Foreign Minister to express their personal and sincere feelings to a friend and colleague Bo Khin Nyo to step up to the plate and pick up the bat, but the "Gentleman Colonel" (as referred to by Katy, #1's wife), was not convinced that he was the man to lead the "Moderates in the Revolutionary Council". My take on that crucial discussion was that the three middle-aged men owed everything to Bo Ne Win, of who and what they were up to that stage in their entire life and very much intimidated and cowed into submission and there was no taste or intent to consider themselves on the same level never mind discuss National Political issues and direction of the Country. Paramount in their mind was to be absolutely loyal to the Dictator and subservient to him at all times.

I really and truly felt the "Generation Gap"; I was officially in my late twenties and the three men were in their early to mid-fifties and despite the fact that

I had known Col. Maung Lwin (Moustache) since my late teens since 1952 and Col. Khin Nyo and U Thi Han since the mid-fifties in Tokyo as a student entrusted to the care of the top Military brass by Bo Khin Maung Galay (Elder brother of Bo Khin Nyo and Deputy Prime Minister at that time), I found myself to be the "Odd young fellow" among the inner-circle middle-aged men of General Ne Win's Military Regime. Looking back over sixty years it was simply fate and destiny that determined the career path of association that I did not seek or plan to be trained in covert intelligence work by the Military in the Ministry of Defense. Circumstances and those in the seat of power controlled and decided what I would learn, for whom I had to work and where I would be sent to carry out the orders of my superiors in the Military that now ruled the entire country.

In fact I mention it here because in the fall of 1960, soon after our son Bob was born, I decided that this was the time to quit and leave the country before getting too deeply involved which would make it extremely difficult or impossible for me to resign from my Official Positions in BOC and Legal Advisor to BEDC Chairman, let alone going abroad to start a second career. Many expressed surprise I was not punished for rash actions of being "away without leave", disobeying orders to report for duty (Officer Training) and to top it off abruptly resigning from a responsible position in BOC without informing Gen. Aung Gyi the Chairman of the Board.

That was exactly what happened. Twenty-four hours before my flight to Hong Kong when I ran smack into Gen. Aung Gyi and a bunch of Colonels in the foyer of Rowe & Co. and was practically grabbed by his aides, pushed into the car beside him and taken to his office in the Ministry of Defense. I was practically a prisoner at his mercy. In a way I was lucky because the Intelligence Chief had all "exit points" alerted already and his men would have caught me at the Airport the next day. After receiving a rather friendly scolding, more like complaining about my youthful indiscretions, the good General announced in the presence of Col. Maung Lwin (Moustache), Gen. Tommy Clift, Col. Thaung Kyi and Col. Khin Nyo that "you are assigned to Lead a Covert Mission to United Arab Republic (Of Egypt and Syria). Bo Thaung Kyi, Bo Lwin and Bo Khin Nyo will brief you fully on the specifics and details of the Mission Objectives.

As of now you are attached to and Appointed to the Office of BEDC Chairman Office of Prime Minister as Legal Advisor. This is a high risk assignment and since your wife and son are in Tokyo, I suggest that they remain there during your assignment in the Middle East. This top secret project was worked out by Marshal Tito of Yugoslavia, President Nasser of UAR and our Bogyoke (Gen.) Ne Win. You are selected to lead this very important and sensitive mission because of your Special Intelligence Training and particularly the Law Degree in International Law from Tokyo University. You will have our full support at all times and we counting on you for a successful outcome" that will hopefully lead and enable us to end Foreign Domination of our National Economy, Trade and International Commerce.

One aspect of the psyche and mindset of the Military leadership under Gen. Ne Win was their paranoia, obsession and deep mistrust of the "Burmese Upper-Crust Society" particularly those with Western education domestically (Christian Missionary Schools) and more so those with degrees from British Institutions of Higher learning like Oxford, Cambridge, London University, Harvard and Yale in the U.S. and Sorbonne in France. It was a lot more intense and serious than what I had known and experienced before my close personal relationship, association and involvement in the Military's core belief and most sensitive discipline that only "a carefully selected few are nurtured and groomed for special tasks and assignments".

Col. Thaung Kyi who was the one to recruit me when I was his next-door neighbor and final-year High School student and he pushed me into the "Intelligence Business" of Col. Maung Lwin (Moustache), the Chief Spook of the Burmese Military; these two Senior Colonels always stood by me and privately confided to me that "Bogyoke (General) Ne Win has a very high impression of your education and successfully graduating with Degrees from Tokyo University because all the Senior Instructors of 30 Comrades in the Japanese Imperial General Staff Headquarters were from that University. You are the first and only Burmese after WW-II to achieve that distinction and award of a (B.A.) and Law Degree and he is very proud that Bo Khin Maung Galay placed you under his care to have you in the Ministry of Defense. Bear that in mind always because like it or not your fate is sealed. There is nothing we or you can do about it as far as we can see. However, look at the positive side of the situation – you will always be secure and well protected in any task or assignment entrusted to you". It proved to be accurate and true up to the very end.

When it became certain that he had lost Bo Aung Gyi it was urgently imperative to "re-shuffle the second tier of the Military Leadership and the Cabinet of the Revolutionary Council Government". The two significant changes were the promotion and elevation of Bo San You to Army Chief of Staff and Vice Chief of General Staff (VCGS), the Military posts vacated by Gen.Aung Gyi; Bo Tin Phay was moved from Minister of Agriculture and Forests to Minister of Trade and Commerce; Colonel Ye Gaung, CEO of Agricultural Research and Development Corporation (ARDC) was promoted to Minister of Agriculture and Forests. What ensued after this major reshuffle was "speculation, rumors and interpretations" according to one's ambition, each faction's agenda and wishful thinking especially by National United Front (NUF) Financial Advisor and their man in uniform Gen. Tin Phay. This faction and Nga-Saya's hare-brained goons prematurely celebrated and claimed that "their Saya-Gyi" (Big Teacher) had taken over the role of Economic Czar that Aung Gyi held and therefore he was now the #2 next only to the maximum leader. A huge delusional wishful thinking that would backfire big time and soon.

A very fatal error of judgment especially by those claiming to be in the inner circle of Nga-Saya. From the perspective of Gen. Ne Win, Tin Phay was retained in service because of Aung Gyi's stubborn intervention against the rules of conduct and his (Chief of Staff's) personal objections and the official written Certification of the Military Medical Board. Moving Tin Phay to Trade Ministry was simply "expediency, damage control and political strategy" playing for time to find out the extent of the damages that would emerge as a result of Aung Gyi's unexpected and abrupt departure. The clear evidence of this tactical move was the "little noticed Order Appointing Colonel Khin Nyo Full-Time Chairman of BEDC (replacing Bo Aung Gyi) in the Prime Minister's (Revolutionary Council Chairman) Office". 65-70 Subsidiary Corporations (including Burma Trade Mission London and those under it) are in effective control of BEDC and that Post was deliberately EXCLUDED from Ministry of Trade, out of Tin Phay's reach and jurisdiction and DIRECTLY under Bo Ne Win's control.

# ANOTHER BOMBSHELL DROPPED FROM OUT OF NOWHERE

A few months after the departure of Bo Aung Gyi, an event more ominous and dangerous suddenly took place perpetrated from within the "core of the Colonel Maung Lwin's (Moustache) innermost staff assigned to serve the Commander-in-Chief as his Personal Aide". Captain Kyaw Zwa Myint (Johnny Lears), at one time my classmate at St. Peter's in Mandalay, was nurtured and groomed by the Intelligence Chief and elevated to the elite Head of State's Personal Staff rumored to be the favorite of Madame Katy for his proficiency in the English language and performing all kinds of odd jobs including but not limited to placing bets at the local London "horse and dog betting houses" for her husband whenever they were in London. On such days he would first come to my office with a note from Col. Lwin (Moustache) asking me to "give some cash" to Johnny to place the bets on the horses and dogs selected by Gen. Ne Win.

This Captain Kyaw Zwa Myint (AKA Johnny Lears) turned out to be "A Mole" of the West handled by the Thais (as confirmed later by the Official Inquiry Commission). It was an elaborate plan for violent Regime Change of eliminating the Revolutionary Council at one of its meetings where Johnny had "security clearance for free entry" being Military Officer Aide to #1. The prelude and "Test Run" to trigger the sinister plot was the "delivery of certain Codes and Keys" to the Thai Military Attaché at a cocktail party at the Residence of a Western Ambassador in Rangoon for a certain amount of cash in U.S. Dollars (US$35,000.00 as later confirmed). It so happened that the particular "Codes & Keys" delivered at that party was in the form of a Burmese Classical Song that needed to be memorized and the Thai Military Attaché was humming it on his several trips to the "wash room". That unusual and strange behavior was noted by one of "our plants" present at every such cocktail party and immediately reported to the "Operative Officer attending the Party" who immediately left the party and alerted the Intelligence Chief Colonel Maung Lwin (Moustache) who rushed to the Ministry of Defense.

Johnny was no fool; he knew at once about the "disappearance of the Operative Officer from the Premises" and realized that there was no time to waste. He drove in a hurry to John Grey's(also a classmate at St. Peters) house and asked him to drive in John's car to the Catholic Missionary in Gyobinkauk, the "white Catholic priest there being the West's mole in contact with the KNU insurgents". When Bo Lwin got to his Office it was indeed Johnny Lears, the only officer with access to that "Song". Everything was changed and the man-hunt was on. The code itself was useless now but the defection and escape of an inner-circle intelligence officer was a huge and irreparable blow to the Intelligence Chief who would have to report the defection to Gen. Ne Win first thing in the morning. I believe #1 received the news from his most trusted Senior Colonel in the Ministry of Defense with great shock and disbelief but without the characteristic burst of anger and foul language. His order was to hunt him down to the ends of the earth and the "place of apprehension shall be his grave" (in Myanmar Tway-Yar-Thin-Gyaing Dar-Ma-Saing).

The Karen insurgents did get him across the border and delivered him to Thai Intelligence but within a matter of weeks, he was viciously stabbed in their "safe house" and barely escaped with his life after multiple surgeries. The Thais were aghast and came to the conclusion that there was no place in Thailand safe enough from the "Burmese" and Johnny Lears was sent off to Australia for good. It shocked the Thais beyond belief that the Burmese carried out their act right in their "safest house under their noses". Johnny Lears and John Grey's immediate families were rounded up and detained together with the White Catholic Priest of Gyobinkauk.

Bo Ne Win's personnel problems had just begun. He was aware that he would no longer be able to retain Col. Maung Lwin (Moustache) as Military Intelligence Chief after such a devastating betrayal by an inner circle Army Intelligence Officer serving as Personal Aide to the Head of State. He had lost his #2 just a few months earlier and now he was about to lose his Intelligence Chief. He consulted with Gen. San Yu, the new Vice Chief of General Staff, Col. Thaung

Kyi, the Senior Colonel assigned with the task of "overseeing" the Navy, Col. Kyi Maung (Zat-Laik), the Colonel General Staff and privately with Col. Khin Nyo, the marginalized but still Chairman of BEDC in the Prime Minister's Office. The one who received the "consensus" nod was Senior Air Force Col. Chit Khin (Ethnic Karen Baptist) who had been assigned to serve as Deputy Intelligence Chief whenever Bo Lwin was on Foreign Missions with Bo Ne Win or as the Prime Minister's Military Advisor. Bo Chit Khin was familiar with the Intelligence Apparatus already.

I received the advance alert to these "imminent changes" from Col. Khin Nyo, Col. Thaung Kyi and of course Col. Maung Lwin (Moustache) whose future was still up in the air. I was also pleasantly surprised to receive a private note from Bo Kyi Maung (Zat-Laik) the Colonel General Staff advising me that the "issue of Burma Trade Mission London" was being discussed by #1 with Gen. San Yu, Bo Khin Nyo, Bo Maung Lwin and Bo Chit Khin. Bo Tin Phay and the Financial Advisor U Ba Nyain "were excluded from all these discussions". Very critical and significant news for me in London especially coming from the #3 man in the Ministry of Defense. With this important input I was able to decipher #1's next move would be Burma Trade Mission London and its future knowing full well the agenda of Tin Phay, Ba Nyain and their leftist goons to lay their hands on the huge "cash and recently bought back High Value Corporate Assets from the British, Europeans, Scandinavians and the U.S. surrogates Israelis".

# LEFTIST FACTION EMBARKS ON DISMANTLING BEDC CORPORATIONS

While the Commander-in-Chief was occupied putting his new team in place and consolidating his power base in the Military and the Revolutionary Council Government, the above ground Communist Ba Nyain, the Financial Adviser, not fully understanding the inter-personal relationships of the top Generals and Colonels made a very critical premature error of judgment. With Aung Gyi gone and the much feared Maung Lwin (Moustache) on his way out, it was time to push his cronies in uniform – Tin Phay, the new Trade and Commerce Minister, Kyaw Soe, the Home Minister and the naïve ignorant fatty Col. Than Sein, the Central Security and Administrative Committee (SAC) Chairman to embark on a sweeping "purge of BEDC Company Executives" on trumped up Charges of "Mismanagement, Abuse of Authority, Corruption, etc, etc." and set up the Nationalization Committee under SAC with fatty Col. Than Sein as Chairman, Tin Phay, Trade Minister and Kyaw Soe, Home Minister as Members. Strangely enough, Gen. San Yu, the Finance and Revenue Minister and #2 after Bo Ne Win, was conspicuously left out most likely because of his close personal relationship with Aung Gyi.

This massive and ill-conceived plan (Vendetta is perhaps more appropriate) was to wipe out the legacy of Aung Gyi as well as to tie down the Revolutionary Council Government in the messy business of prosecuting the thousands of Company Executives overwhelming the country's already inadequate Justice System. It became quite apparent that during the critical personnel reshuffle at the top, Bo Ne Win was caught flat footed by the manipulations of his Financial Advisor Communist Ba Nyain when his 2 key ministers and the SAC Chairman did his bidding. Many BEDC Executives, Officers and even mid-level staff were detained filling up jail cells all over the country and new detention centers had to be set up like Army Camps and make-shift barracks. At the peak of this massive purge and vendetta more than 5500 were detained.

# THE SHOCK AND UNEXPECTED PUSH-BACK CAME FROM BURMA TRADE LONDON

The misinterpretation by Bo Tin Phay and his goons was that he was given the Trade Ministry of Aung Gyi and therefore as the new boss he was free to dismantle what he inherited from his misconceived enemy. What simpletons and idiots they were. He was given the Trade Ministry but Bo Khin Nyo was retained as BEDC Chairman in the Prime Minister's Office, the deliberate strategic move of #1. Additionally, unbeknownst to most, I received specific instructions (Orders) from Col. Maung Lwin (Moustache), Military Intelligence Chief, "To report all Banking, Financial, Audit, Legal Management and Operational Affairs of Burma Trade Mission ONLY TO THE OFFICE OF THE REVOLUTIONARY CHAIRMAN". Even Bo Aung Gyi and Bo Khin Nyo were not aware of this (Order) conveyed to me by #1 through Bo Maung Lwin (Moustache). The London Action Plan Project was initiated by Bo Ne Win himself and entrusted to Bo Aung Gyi for Management and I was nominated to implement and lead the operation of the BEDC Representative Office and Chief Executive Officer (Majority Stock-Holder of Burma Trade Mission) with orders to report "directly to the Revolutionary Council Chairman".

Finally, the Bo Tin Phay wrecking crew felt confident enough to take on the most successful BEDC Enterprise outside the country in London. One morning Lt. Commander Maung Maung Khin, the Assistant Defense Attaché, came to my office and hand delivered a package from Col. Kyi Maung (Zat-Laik), the Colonel General Staff. After I had a chat and coffee with the Commander, I opened the package in our "Secure Room". In the note he mentioned that Bo Maung Lwin (Moustache) and Bo Chit Khin had asked him to send the information to me in his name as the two of them were in the midst of going through "change of Command procedures".

The message concerned the Trade Ministry (under Gen. Tin Phay), the Home Ministry (under Col. Kyaw Soe) and Security and Administrative Committee (SAC under Col. Than Sein) "in collusion" were going to "issue orders to close BEDC Office in London and Ordering my immediate return to Burma by Special Plane purchased in Holland with Captain, Crew and Security Detail will be sent to escort" me and my family. "Both of them (Bo Lwin and Chit Khin) will also be discussing the same with Col. Khin Nyo and Col. Ko Ko in #1's Office. I will keep you informed on further developments". Coming from the #3 man in the Ministry of Defense things must be coming to a head for all concerned especially the remaining BEDC Organizations targeted for elimination. However, in strict "Legal and Administrative Terms", the Trade, Home Ministry and SAC did not have "Any Official Jurisdiction" over Burma Trade Mission in London, as it was in the first place A COVERT OVERSEAS PROJECT INITIATED BY THE REVOLUTIONARY COUNCIL CHAIRMAN entrusted to a "Committee of Senior Officers under Gen. Aung Gyi, the Vice Chief of General Staff (VCGS)".

Within a week of the message from Col. Kyi Maung I and Lt. Col. Aung Din received orders from the Ministry of Trade (Signed by Order of the Minister By the Deputy Minister) to return to Rangoon immediately and report to the Minister of Home Affairs Col. Kyaw Soe. The soft and mild-mannered retired Air Force officer Lt. Col. Aung Din panicked and practically freaked out and became incapacitated for several days requiring medical care for his high blood pressure and related heart problems. To be honest, I myself despite the advance alerts was surprised at the abrupt and extreme action of the recall and involvement of the Home Ministry, a clear indication of arbitrary action of certain detention and prolonged investigation "without bail".

After Col. Aung Din recovered from his medical problems and somewhat regained his composure, I explained to him my personal evaluation of the Order issued by the Ministry of Trade under Bo Tin Phay directing us to report to the Home Ministry under Col. Kyaw Soe as being out of normal procedure and in "Contravention with the Direct Orders and Guidelines from the Revolutionary Council Chairman's Office on the Covert UK/Europe/USA Action Plan project and Management/Operation of Burma Trade Mission London". I expressed my strong view that Col. Khin Nyo, Chairman of BEDC in the Prime Minister's Office, our Direct Superior, was not aware of this Order and this "Circumvention" was deliberate to test and force Bo Ne Win's hand in this crucial matter of how far he would go to protect and keep out intruders into his "Covert Project In London". It is a direct challenge to his Order to report Directly to his Office Only. My take on the matter is "Tin Phay / Ba Nyain / Kyaw Soe" plan to destroy everything quickly while the #1 is preoccupied with "change-over" in Military Intelligence Service Command and before his attention on London. Establish the "Fait Accompli" that BEDC and Burma Trade Mission London is closed, a done deal. It is up to us to Legally Circumvent their attempt and push back, forcing them to deal with the Revolutionary Council Chairman.

Col. Aung Din, worried sick and quite confused, said, "U Kyi Win Sein, what you have just explained to me is well beyond my level and experience in the Air Force strictly taking orders from above and carrying them out the best of my ability without raising any questions. I have no legal education nor background like you and that is why I confess it is beyond me this time. Please understand that I am not in any way questioning your evaluation." At that juncture it dawned on me that the good Air Force Colonel was finding it very difficult to understand let alone accept the notion that this young lawyer was in fact "Questioning the Authenticity and Validity of the Ministry of Trade Order whereby it had no Prior Authorization from the Revolutionary Council Chairman, in fact was in Direct Violation of his Orders".

On hearing this interpretation, Col. Aung Din became visibly alarmed and said, "I would hate to be the ground on which two buffalos are going to fight." I responded with the sincere intent to relieve and give some comfort to his distress. "Col. Aing Din, you are much too generous in depicting Bo Tin Phay as a buffalo whereas he is merely a goat and Bo Ne Win Win is an elephant." He burst out laughing and said, "You have a strange sense of humor at a time when our future is at stake." Fully aware of his moderate and soft attitude to life in general, I stressed to him that "Burma Trade Mission in London is very special and unique in every respect especially the Legal and Fiduciary responsibilities imposed on the Stockholders and Directors under UK Laws. That is now our first primary Obligation to Fulfill and then to have the Revolutionary Council Chairman to Officially designate (Nominate) to Whom he wants us to transfer

Ownership of Burma Trade Mission in London in Accordance with All Relevant UK Laws and City of London Corporation Ordinances as well as Accounting and Auditing Rules.

"Towards that end I am going to request Sir Guy Hambling, Barrister Templeton Smith and Solicitor Clive Richardson for an urgent consultation at our Office Board Room or in their Chambers. In the meantime I will immediately inform Col. Khin Nyo about this Order from the Ministry of Trade and request further guidance and instructions. I will respond to the Ministry of Trade after our consultations with our Lawyers and the official response and guidance from Col. Khin Nyo, our Direct Superior in the Prime Minister's Office". Col. Aung Din appeared to be relieved after hearing the general outline of our response based entirely on the realities we face here in London and the political expediency back in Rangoon that we must confront after satisfactory and successful resolution of transferring ownership of Burma Trade Mission to Bo Ne Win's personal nominee. This would be the critical period of "buying time" for us as well as forcing the "vested interest parties" (Factions) in Rangoon to "Reveal their Hand and Their Clout or the Lack of it in the Military Regime under Dictator Bo Ne Win".

We had several very open and frank consultation sessions with our Law Firm wherein Sir Guy and his colleagues categorically confirmed that "To all intents and purposes and as far as the UK Laws are concerned the duly Incorporated and Registered Burma Trade Limited is owned by the Stockholders of the Company (60%) of the Fully Paid Outstanding Shares issued to U Kyi Win Sein, residing at Haversham Close, Twickenham Park, Richmond. However, since the Said Shares have been "assigned to BEDC in Burma by special arrangement between the parties" such impediments need to be removed in the event of disposing/transferring Shares to Another Party. Solicitor Clive Richardson will immediately have the appropriate Stockholders Resolution Passed for the Said (60%) and the (40%) held by U Aung Din as required by the Byelaws of the Corporation calling for an Extraordinary Stock-Holders Meeting".

I also requested that our Law Firm provide us with a written Certification (Brief) on the Stockholders, Directors and Executives of the Company, their Legal and Fiduciary Responsibilities when disposing / transferring / selling

Outstanding Stock to be in Strict Compliance of all the Relevant UK Corporate and Security and Exchange Laws as well as Labor Laws governing the Rights and Benefits of the Company's Employees. With Burma Trade Mission's large financial assets in the UK, Europe, Swiss and Scandinavian Banks, the Fixed Property Assets and numerous Certificates of Deposits and various Time Maturing City and Treasury Bonds it was estimated conservatively to take six to ten months to complete the Legal Transactions in Compliance with all the UK and Local Corporate Laws and Ordinances Governing the Transfer of Corporate Ownership, Registration with Competent Central and Local Government Jurisdictions.

While this was going on in London, we received a response from Col. Khin Nyo confirming that he was not informed about the recall order and shocked to receive the news from us. He now had also found out that the Trade Ministry (Tin Phay) had officially asked the Home Ministry to take action on our return to Rangoon for dereliction of Official Duties, Negligence, Disobeying Official Orders and Corruption. He added that it was a deliberate attempt to undermine and grab power from him (BEDC) to carry out their vendetta against Bo Aung Gyi's group. He would report about it to #1. Needless to mention, this was real bad news for us in London and I was not sure if Bo Khin Nyo had enough fight left in him to effectively make the case with Bo Ne Win and if his colleagues in the Revolutionary Council would rally and provide the support he badly needed. It was becoming quite clear that we in London must stand firm on our Legal and Fiduciary Responsibilities and expose their "Orders" having No Jurisdiction Over Burma Trade and BEDC London Representative Office Being Under the Prime Minister's Office".

With that frame of mind I responded to the Trade Ministry Recall Order that under UK Laws I and Col. Aung Din are "Legally Obligated to Manage the Company and Transfer to Nominated Entity" which would take six to ten months' minimum time to Complete and Comply with all Relevant UK National and Local Government Laws. The Certification (Brief) from our Law Firm was attached to the response. Copies were sent to Bo Khin Nyo (BEDC), Chairman in the Prime Minister's Office and Bo Maung Lwin (Moustache) and Bo Chit Khin in the Military Intelligence Department by Diplomatic Pouch from the Military Attaché's Office. As usual and true to his character, Col.

Aung Din was concerned and worried that my short and curt response based entirely on Legal Grounds of my "Still being a Legal Adviser to (BEDC) in the Prime Minister's Office" would be interpreted as "Disobeying Official Orders and Challenging Bo Tin Phay" by his goons and cause more trouble for us in the event we ended up in prison on return.

However, from my perspective the Revolutionary Council Chairman would not allow the Ba Nyain – Tin Phay faction control over the Action Plan Project that he himself initiated and entrusted Bo Aung Gyi and his closest aides – Bo Maung Lwin (Moustache), Bo Thaung Kyi, Bo Khin Nyo and kept Bo San Yu now his #2 involved from the outset, but deliberately excluded Bo Tin Phay and his no-brain blind followers. Now that the project had succeeded well beyond expectations of anyone there was no way his gambler risk-taking instinct and character would tolerate anyone grabbing it from under his nose. My sixth sense also told me that was the reason he was keeping Bo Khin Nyo as BEDC Chairman in his (Prime Minister's) Office and prolonging the official departure of Bo Maung Lwin (Moustache) as Chief of Military Intelligence Chief and of course selecting an Air Force Colonel, Chit Khin, an ethnic Karen Baptist to take over from (Moustache) to ensure absolute loyalty to him only and other "Army (Greens) with Motives and Agendas" would find it difficult or impossible to approach and cultivate the Intelligence Chief in any way to do their bidding.

It was classic Japanese Intelligence indoctrination of Bo Ne Win at Nakano Gakko (Kem-Pei-Tai) School, "your most dangerous enemy is the one closest to you" and all precautions and preventive measures must be in place at all times. At this stage it is no longer a case of Ba Nyain / Tin Phay going after Aung Gyi and BEDC. It is delusional Tin Phay / Kyaw Soe and naïve fatty Than Sein becoming the tools of Communist Ba Nyain in attempting to invade the exclusive turf of the Military Dictator who will not tolerate any such intrusion leave alone the "Cripple" as Ne Win refers to Tin Phay. Ba Nyain has overplayed his hand and exposed his real intent to create dissention within the Revolutionary Council forcing Ne Win to take punative measures against the empty heads in green uniforms. Characteristic Communist tactics and strategy setting up one against the other – this time three inconsequential Officers but in Powerful Official Positions.

There was several weeks of silence from Rangoon without any reaction to my response to the recall order from the Ministry of Trade. Col. Aung Din was on tenterhooks because our immediate superior Col. Khin Nyo had also not informed us of the outcome of his report to the #1 and he was assuming that things did not go well. I tried to cheer him up by saying that "No news is good news" but he was in no mood to accept my positive thinking. At long last the dry spell of communication from Rangoon was broken by a package from Col. Maung Lwin (Moustache) delivered to me by Commander Maung Maung Khin, the Assistant Defense Attaché who joined us for coffee and a brief chat in our Boardroom and returned to his office.

# THE DICTATOR AND THE PRETENDER TO HIS THRONE

In the sealed package were several sealed Official Envelopes – Directorate of Military Intelligence, BEDC Chairman, Prime Minister's Office, Colonel General Staff, Ministry of Defense, Chief of Naval Staff, Ministry of Defense. In his letter Col. Maung Lwin (Moustache) said Gen. Tin Phay the Trade Minister was in a state of shock and furious that "this young Japanese Educated upstart Lawyer" not only had the audacity to rudely disobey his order to return but to lecture the Trade Ministry on the UK Laws as well as questioning the legitimacy of his authority. He (Nga-Saya) has taken this rebuke very personally because he was under the impression that "Bo Aung Gyi's previous domain is now under his control". "What further action he can or will take will become clear after Bo Khin Nyo reports to #1 on your recall order and the future of Burma Trade Mission which I think will take some time for him (#1) to decide because I assume he will ask the Judge Advocate General and the Attorney-General their Legal Opinion." I was rather surprised that the outgoing Intelligence Chief was brief and direct to the point. To me the hint that the Attorney General and the Judge Advocate's involvement was a very positive sign for us confirming the validity of the Legal position we have taken.

The letter from Col. Khin Nyo was quite subdued and frank in explaining that he was shocked to be deliberately left out when he was assigned the task of Supervising, Management and Control of Burma Trade Mission by #1. Therefore, he had to think through carefully before reporting the serious breach of "Command-and-Control" procedures. After a few days he consulted and solicited the assistance of Col. Maung Lwin (Moustache), Col. Thaung Kyi (the original Members of the Action Plan Committee) and Col. Chit Khin to accompany him in the meeting with #1. At the meeting Col. Ko Ko, the Revolutionary Council Secretary, was also in attendance taking memos and minutes of the discussions. According to the letter, Gen. Ne Win, the maximum leader and now the Dictator, showed clear signs of surprise and irritation at the attempt by one he considered "A medically unfit Cripple" to move against an overseas project that was initiated by himself and the nerve to overstep and circumvent his procedural orders.

The next comment in the letter was baffling and a hint of uncertainty and wavering on the part of #1 with regard to "what urgent order to forestall the recall in the light of the response from Burma Trade Mission". At that juncture, Bo Khin Nyo raised the UK Legal requirements and the Certification (Brief) attached to the response letter. Bo Ne Win instructed Col. Ko Ko to summon the Judge Advocate General Colonel Solomon and the Attorney General to immediately come to the meeting. Both arrived one after the other, understandably with a nervousness and trepidation as to their future in the Military Regime. They were asked to review our Law Firm's Certification (Brief) and to give their Legal Interpretation and opinion as to its authenticity, validity and effect on Burma Trade Management. Bo Khin Nyo commented that the two top lawyers of the country had cold sweat on their brows and took some time to fully digest the contents and import of its meaning and the Legal constraints imposed on Management.

The Attorney General, a civilian, was now smack in front of the country's Military Dictator and his Senior Colonels including the Judge Advocate General who was also uncomfortable facing the Commander-in-Chief eyeball to eyeball. The explanation in Bo Khin Nyo's letter was vague but I assumed that the two top lawyers were not sure what the boss wanted to know about my response to the Ministry of Trade, the attached legal brief and where to begin. Observing the tension and discomfiture of all at the table Gen. Ne Win asked, "Bo Solomon, from what you have just reviewed, what is our young fellow (Kaung-Lay) in London telling us?" "Bogyoke, he and the Law Firm are explaining that as major stockholder (60%) of the company he cannot return to Burma immediately as it will take 6-10 months to transfer ownership to officially nominated entity or person according to UK National Laws and Local Company Laws of London City. He is required to discharge his Legal and Fiduciary responsibilities before leaving London.

"This young fellow owns 60% of the shares? How did that happen?" Bo Khin Nyo reminded his boss: "Bogyoke instructed us to have U Kyi Win Sein to be the major stockholder and control of the company because of Bo Aye Maung and Bo Aung Din being retired Air Force officer." "Yes, now that you mention it, I remember receiving that explanation from our fellow when I was in London. Bo Solomon, is the legal situation as stated by the Law Firm?" "Yes, Sir, I am very sure because it is a highly respected Law Firm in the UK and the Senior Partner Sir Guy Hambling is the Queen's Counsel (QC) as we can see on their Letterhead" showing it to #1. "Now it is quite clear that our young fellow (Kaung-Lay) is reporting to us the real true situation he is facing there in London. Is that not what this is all about?" Col. Solomon and the Attorney General concurred saying in unison, "yes, Sir, that is correct". To the great relief of the two lawyers #1 thanked and excused them from the meeting. Both were ushered out of the War Room.

Apparently the Dictator strongman of Burma seemed to have grasped the seriousness and gravity of ownership of Burma Trade Mission in London entirely in the hands and under the control of the Japanese educated young Lawyer. The next part of Bo Khin Nyo's letter indicated that #1 wanted him and Bo Maung Lwin (Moustache) to make a quick trip to London ASAP to discuss the issues thoroughly (Face-to-Face) how best the transfer of ownership to the officially nominated Entity or Person (Not mentioned) could be achieved without a hitch. The letter ended with – more to follow as soon as further developments and / or Orders are received from above. There was no doubt in my mind that the wily Military Dictator had taken over the control of "Burma Trade Mission File" and placed it directly under his personal Command.

The next letter was from Col. Thaung Kyi. He was more direct and blunt having known me since my teens – having nurtured, mentored and guided me like a big brother he wrote "Bo Tin Phay, Ba Nyain and their Thugs are out to get your Head and have Officially asked the Home Ministry in writing to detain you on return to Rangoon. I am of course concerned about your personal security and that of your Japanese wife and son. However, Bo Lwin (Moustache) himself is in deep trouble but still very much around and his already nominated successor Bo Chit Khin came to see me privately. They informed me that Bogyoke (General) wanted to see me to ask about you. So, all three of us went to #1's office and he was expecting us as Bo Ko Ko reported to him that we are on our way. I was surprised that he started out by telling us that he first met you in Japan attending Tokyo University as Ko Lay (Bo Khin Maung Galay) asked him to look after you. He said after you returned with a degree in International Law he put you in JAG but U Lun Baw and Bo Aung Gyi assigned you to other places like BOC. The other day Bo Khin Nyo reminded me that I assigned him to the UK Action Plan Project after his very difficult mission with the Egyptians, Middle East Kalars (Indians) and the Yugoslav Government that was completed successfully. Bo Aung Gyi also reported that he set up the Export-Import Bank.

"The Yugoslav Ambassador has high praise for his work in the M.E. The UK Action Plan project is also very successful. Bo Thaung Kyi, how well do you know him? I told him that we were neighbors in Bassein (Pathein) when you attended High School and I recruited you for special undercover intelligence training and work since 1952 and introduced you to Bo Lwin – who then explained that Kyi Win Sein is the only civilian that completed all phases of Undercover Intelligence Training while still a High School Student. He is highly praised by our Foreign Counterparts (Egyptians, Yugoslavs and Syrians) for successful outcomes. Then the Dictator asked the "Bomb Shell Question to the three Senior Colonels". What is your evaluation that he will betray us? Bo Thaung Kyi answered first. "I know him well, since he was 16-17 and his entire family very traditional Bama Buddhist middle class, 7 brothers and 2 sisters.

"His character is very strong and cool under stress because he beat Bo Aung Zin in the Irrawaddy Division Golf Championship Match when he was just 17. Bo Lwin then added that "Kyi Win Sein was educated in Japan's No. 1 Tokyo University and received his B.A. degree and LL.B. degree in International Law and I know personally that his Legal Opinions are highly respected among other Lawyers including our own Bo Solomon". It became clear to the three Senior Colonels that the "trustworthiness of this young fellow" (Kaung-Lay) in London was weighing heavily on the Military Dictator of Burma. He now faced the hard reality that he must handle this matter with extraordinary care as this young fellow holds all the cards in his hands and without his willing cooperation all could end up in total loss to the country, the people and of course the Dictator." Reality set in and all present, including the Dictator came to the conclusion that confrontation, intimidation and Orders will only aggravate the young lawyer.

Col. Thaung Kyi's letter concluded with "It could very well be that all the good deeds (Karma) of your previous incarnations have provided you with the "protective shield of the KING" in this world who himself will have to appeal to your personal sense of loyalty to country, people and family to amicably resolve the Burma Trade Mission London ownership transfer issue". The letter from the Colonel General Staff Kyi Maung (Zat-Laik) mentioned that Ba Nyain – Tin Phay and their cronies were furious and had started a disinformation campaign that "Kyi Win Sein has betrayed the country and rejected the Trade Minister's order to return to Burma". However, Bo Ko Ko, Secretary to the Revolutionary Council, privately informed him that #1 had now effectively taken over the matter after receiving the report from Bo Khin Nyo, Bo Maung Lwin (Moustache), Bo Chit Khin, JAG Bo Solomon and the Attorney General.

He also indicated that Bo Khin Nyo and Bo Lwin "will visit you soon". Bo Kyi Maung noted that Bo Ko Ko seemed quite puzzled because #1 did not take any action or order the cancellation / reversal of the recall issued by the Ministry of Trade. Perhaps it was deliberate strategy to keep other Ministries out of the loop and in the dark until the appropriate time determined by him. The letter also confirmed that the dismantling of the BEDC Group Companies in Burma was about done and the only one alive and standing firm was Burma Trade Mission London which was beyond the reach of the Ba Nyain – Tin Phay wrecking crew. Considering the developments of the past several days they would never reach it because the elephant had stepped in front of them. In characteristic Japanese Intelligence style, the Burmese Military Dictator was playing close to his chest keeping his confidante and most trusted Bo Maung Lwin to be with him until his plans for Burma Trade Mission were decided and in place. Despite the obsession with secrecy I was alerted to and tipped off that Bo Maung Lwin (Moustache) would be assigned to a Diplomatic Post as Ambassador in a European country close to London at least for the next 12 months while the Burma Trade Mission ownership transfer was going on. Great importance attached to it. It is also a clear indication that #1 is personally interested in the final outcome.

# AMBASSADOR ROPED INTO PLAYING PROXY FOR DICTATOR FRIEND

While the two colonels were preparing to make the long trip to London, the Ba Nyain – Tin Phay people in the Trade and Home Ministries somehow got wind of Bo Ne Win's sessions with the Intelligence Colonels, Solomon of JAG and the Attorney General and desperately scrambled around to find out what had transpired but without any success. All were tight lipped knowing full well the consequences that await the whistle-blower. Rumors, innuendos and wild speculations spread out of control in Ministries and the vast bureaucracy about the young Japanese Lawyer who reported directly to #1 through private personal connection that prompted him to hold the urgent meetings with the Senior Colonels and the Attorney General in the War Room. The Tin Phay / Ba Nyain group for the first time came to the stark realization that the young lawyer in London was nominated by #1 and their interpretation that he is Bo Aung Gyi's man was dead wrong and now they will have to contend with the most powerful man in the country that can have catastrophic outcomes for all concerned.

Then I received out of the blue a letter (with Singapore postmark) from my elder brother Kyaw Htun Sein (Ivan) informing me that he, the parents and the entire family were worried sick from hearing "all the bad, negative and horrible things about you. The latest that you are deeply involved and embroiled in the "power struggle of the factions within the Military" and if true he, the parents and the family "implore you to stay out of it". He also wrote that at the urging of Dad and Mom he tried several times to contact Col. Thaung Kyi and Col. Maung Lwin (Moustache) but neither responded. There was no way for them to do so for obvious reasons. I was saddened and distressed that the elderly parents and family were now innocent victims but under the given circumstances there was nothing I could do from London to allay their worries and concerns – not even reply in a letter via normal mail sure to be intercepted by the Home Ministry.

However, when the Ministry of Foreign Affairs issued diplomatic passports to the two colonels and the information reached the Home Ministry (responsible for issuance of Ordinary and Special Passports) for Record and Registration and the British Embassy in Rangoon for Diplomatic Visa Stamp, the news was out that Bo Ne Win was sending them to discuss the issues face to face with the young Lawyer and report back to him on agreed arrangements. By that direct arbitrary intervention from the Head of State's Office, Bo Tin Phay the Trade Minister, Bo Kyaw Soe (the stooge) Home Minister and Ba Nyain the Communist Financial Advisor were stopped in their attempt to take control of Burma Trade Mission in London and its huge cash, financial assets, bank accounts, interest bearing British Treasury Bonds and the fixed Real Estate properties in the UK and other cash accounts in Europe, Scandinavia and Swiss Banks.

Col. Aung Din (40%) and myself (60%) stockholders with Board of Directors and Share Holders Resolutions terminating the Assignment of Shares to BEDC Head Office were the two (100%) clear Burma Trade Mission London owners under UK National and Local Laws. That legal fact and reality was causing the inflammation of stomach ulcers of frail Col. Aung Din and, at times, to bleed, requiring frequent medical attention by Specialist Physicians of Harley Street recommending that the patient needs long leave from work for the body to respond to treatment. Another thing that was bothering him greatly became strongly expressed in his desire to transfer the (40%) Shares in his name to me, releasing him from all the Fiduciary burdens of holding the stock. I advised him that the BEDC Chairman Col. Khin Nyo would have to authorize and approve such a transfer and it was very unlikely for him to agree without first clearing it with Bo Ne Win who had signed off on the current arrangement after consultation with Bo Aung Gyi at that time. After hearing the above reminders and clarifications from me Bo Aung Din backed off. I was relieved and happy he did because I was witnessing daily that the stress and pressures of the situation was taking a very heavy toll on his health and I wanted to prevent further deterioration and if push came to shove I was prepared to "stick my neck out" and take over his (40%) Shares because in strict legal terms there was no big deal as (60%) majority Stock Holder Controls the Company in any event.

We asked U Maung Maung Gale to reserve 2 suites on the same floor at the Washington Hotel and went to meet their flight in the full size Bentley at Heathrow Airport. I noted that Bo Aung Din was already showing signs of uneasiness at the prospect of meeting 2 senior Army Colonels famous for their proximity to #1. Being a retired Air Force Lt-Colonel serving overseas with a young Lawyer assigned by the Revolutionary Council Chairman to lead the Special Covert Project in the UK was having an adverse effect on the psyche of an Air Force Officer caught up right in the middle of the Army Commander-in-Chief's UK Action Plan Project. I fully understood and sympathized with his feelings and all that he had to put up with and with a sincere intent to relieve his stress I shared some pertinent and permissible inside information I had received earlier from my sources, the most crucial being the future of Burma Trade Mission London was now effectively in the hands and under the control of Bo Ne Win and the 2 Colonels arriving today were sent by him to discuss the issues with us face to face.

I also revealed to him the attempt by Ba Nyain – Tin Phay gang to lay their hands on Burma Trade London and being thwarted by #1 but in a very strange and open-ended way because he did not go far enough to cancel or reverse the Orders issued by the Trade and Home Ministries. "I am going to ask the 2 Colonels about this as a top priority." Bo Aung Din stared at me wide eyed with the demeanor and expression of – I understand that you have been informed all about it in advance. I expected him to raise some questions but to my surprise he refrained from it. Despite the long flight with a refueling stop at Tehran, Bo Khin Nyo and Bo Lwin came out quickly and quite fresh and alert – perhaps the First Class comfort, good food and best booze greatly helped. Both were as usual very casual and comfortably chatting with me in the car.

The four of us sat face to face in the two rows of sofas at the back of the Bentley with a raised coffee table in-between and the driver served us soft drinks before he hit the road. On the way to the hotel there was only small talk like Col. Thaung Kyi and Bo Kyi Maung send their greetings and remembrances to you. We checked them into their respective suites and both wanted a few hours of sleep in a regular bed. I left the direct phone number of my office and asked them to call when they woke up and were ready, to come to our office or dinner (depending on the time) at the Indian High Commissioner Restaurant private dining room. We returned to our office in the Bentley and on the way I suggested that we invite U Maung Maung Gale and U Ohn Sein to join us for dinner to welcome the two Colonels and the three of them to become acquainted with the guests. I felt strongly that all the Managers need to be involved in discussing the future of the company that they have all worked hard and contributed to is success.

It was about 5:30 PM when I received the call from Bo Maung Lwin (Moustache) well rested and ready for leisurely cocktails, appetizers and full course Indian dinner. Bo Aung Din and the two Managers took a cab to the restaurant and I went to the hotel in the Bentley to pick up the 2 Colonels and join the three waiting for us. We had the Ambassador's suite, private bar with bar-tender and an adjoining dining room. Drinks and a full range of Indian appetizers freshly cooked in the kitchen were served and it gave the other 3 Burmese long-time residents of London to get to know the two Senior Army Officers representing the Dictator. Greased after a few drinks things became relaxed and conversation was flowing freely but I noted that politics was avoided by all. Dinner was served Indian style with all the dishes laid out on the table including the rice, naans and Indian bread (chapatti and puri). The food was superb and immensely enjoyed by all especially the two Colonels who must have been tired of the high end onboard English cuisine served by BOAC, the preferred Airline of the Burmese Government since independence in 1948.

Bo Aung Din and I accompanied them back to the hotel and then proceeded home in the Bentley as it was leased for the duration of their stay in London. The next morning at 8:00 I was at the hotel and we ordered breakfast in Bo Khin Nyo's suite during which I was briefed and brought up to date on the events that led to the meetings with #1 who had ordered them to London to meet with us and work out an arrangement for the transfer of Burma Trade Mission London ownership to the Official Nominee who would be named after our discussions with our Law Firm, Lloyds Accounting and Auditing and the Main Bankers. At the beginning I noted that both of them were dancing around the Legal issue of (60%) Shares in my name and (40%) in Bo Aung Din's name, apparently trying to avoid being overbearing because they mentioned being reminded by Colonel Solomon the Judge Advocate General and the Attorney General that as far as UK National and Local Company Laws are concerned Burma Trade Limited is owned by U Kyi Win Sein as Majority Stock Holder and U Aung Din the Minor Stock Holder.

They also stressed that the two top Burmese Legal and Justice Officers expressed concern regarding the termination of the Stock Assignments to BEDC Head Office uncertain about the intent and motive behind that action taken by Burma Trade Mission Board of Directors and Stock Holder's Resolutions. This was the first clear confirmation that the two Legal Officers back in Rangoon had cautioned the two Colonels to tread carefully and handle the matter with utmost care because without the full voluntary cooperation of the two Stock Holders especially the majority owner U Kyi Win Sein, there was NO LEGAL LEG TO STAND ON ON THE GOVERNMENT SIDE to force the issue in UK COURTS OF LAW THAT NOT ONLY FAVOR THE STOCK HOLDERS BUT SHIELD AND PROVIDE ALL THE PROTECTIONS.

Up to this stage of our breakfast meeting, I was all ears trying to remain calm and figuring out what their boss had ordered them to achieve in their discussions with us. Thus far they were telling me that their "Legal Professionals concur with what our British Lawyers have certified in writing and that they understand and accept the reality of the situation and in a rather vague and round-about way asking for our cooperation". Without responding or commenting I suggested that we proceed to our office and include Bo Aung Din in our discussions but the wily intelligence chief said we needed to get to the core issues between the three of us before involving the retired Air Force officer. This was clear confirmation to me that they most likely had been advised by the two top Legal Professionals in Rangoon to ascertain that notwithstanding the UK Legal Rights and the Protections my loyalty to Country, People and Family was Intact and to secure my commitment first. Once that was clarified and confirmed Bo Aung Din's (40%) stock position would be rendered moot and less critical to the overall ownership transfer issue.

Frankly I was surprised and rather irritated by the attitude and demeanor of the two Army Colonels towards the retired Air Force Lt-Col. Aung Din whom

I had come to know to be a very decent human being of high moral values and integrity of the highest order. The superiority mindset of the Army against the Navy and the Air Force was on display right in front of me and I strongly felt the obligation to make a statement of record that Bo Aung Din from the very first day of our meeting had cooperated fully and extended all the help and guidance to me in setting up Burma Trade Mission London from the ground up and was an invaluable asset of our Management Team. Despite his very long residence in London his loyalty to the Burma Air Force and his patriotism to Country and People had not diminished as far as I had noted thus far. It dawned on the two Army Colonels that I was making my position very clear to them that Bo Aung Din's (40%) Stock position and his Management Status must be given recognition and due respect. Under normal circumstances I would not have taken such a liberty of standing toe to toe in deliberating such crucial issues involving high policy and senior Military Officers but both Bo Khin Nyo and Bo Maung Lwin (Moustache) were on their way out and most likely on their last assignment of their boss Bo Ne Win. Failure was not one of their options.

They were not the self-confident inner circle Colonels I had known just a few months ago. They were subdued beyond belief and understandably so because they were in uncharted waters dealing with business matters about which they knew very little. Bo Maung Lwin (Moustache) having known me since my High School days in Bassein (now Pathein) revealed to me that Bo Ne Win had discussed about me with Col. Thaung Kyi who categorically guaranteed that he was very confident that I would never betray Country, People and Family under any and all circumstances. He most probably felt that mentioning Col. Thaung Kyi's involvement was important at this stage, being the senior Army Commander who had befriended the young and naïve High School student and introduced him to the complicated world of Military Intelligence, National Security and the ever increasing foreign interference in Burmese domestic affairs by sending their agents under the guise of "educators, technical advisors, exchange scholars, cultural researchers, Christian Missionaries to infiltrate and mingle with local communities and report to their handlers at their Embassies in Rangoon, their Information Libraries permitted to operate in other Cities".

It was indeed a very clever and astute strategy on the part of the Intelligence Chief as it reminded me of how and where it had all started and the depth and extent of my involvement with the Military leadership of the country that had brought the two Colonels and myself to the Washington Hotel suite in London to discuss how to amicably resolve the ownership transfer of the country's enormous financial, trade and fixed property assets in the UK, Europe, Scandinavia and Switzerland. It was very clear to all three of us that Bo Ne Win the Dictator was extremely concerned when advised by the two top Legal Professionals in Rangoon that "Everything hinges on the ethics, integrity and loyalty of one person that holds 60% of the Company's Shares and without his voluntary cooperation the options available to the Burmese Government are very few and none of them are good to get the desired outcome. It is therefore absolutely imperative to approach the delicate personal issues with extreme care – "not to antagonize the person holding all the cards". That is the position that all Dictators dislike most but one that Bo Ne Win the "Gambler and risk taker" was fully aware of when he brought in Col. Thaung Kyi whose honesty, morality and integrity he respects very highly. Only one other person received Bo Ne Win's high regard – Bo Aung Gyi.

# MESSAGE FROM THE FOOTHILLS OF THE HIMALAYAS TO LONDON

After U Thi Han flew back to Rangoon from Machan-Baw in the Kachin State located practically at the foothill of the Himalayas, tranquil, up in the clouds and peaceful, Bo Aung Gyi continued his stay at the Government Guest House meditating and reflecting on his long political and Military service to the country and the consequences of his abrupt resignation from the Revolutionary Council and all the high positions he occupied second only to Gen. Ne Win. With so many pressing things on his mind it was remarkable that he recognized the critical importance of BEDC's most successful UK Action Plan Project entrusted to him by Bo Ne Win. As Head of the Management Committee in the Ministry of Defense and Trade Minister, he knew full well the specifics of the hidden funds recovered and now safely secured in the bank accounts of Burma Trade Mission London, managed and controlled by the Officer Lawyer nominated by the Committee and approved by the Revolutionary Council Chairman and Prime Minister Gen. Ne Win. The primary concern of Bo Aung Gyi was the misconception of those in the Military allied with Bo Tin Phay that they were deliberately excluded from National Policy-Making bodies by him not knowing that all Members in such Committees and Bodies without exception were hand- picked by #1 himself and assigned the task of leading them to Gen. Aung Gyi.

After his abrupt departure and Bo Tin Phay replacing him in the Trade Ministry, the above-ground Communist Financial Advisor Ba Nyain exploited the situation by inflating the already huge ego of the new Trade Minister by proclaiming him as the "New Economic Czar" as well as pushing his leftist agenda to dismantle BEDC as being the capitalist business model under Aung Gyi. That line of blatant misinformation and outright Communist propaganda was an attempt to further drive a wedge within the Military leadership was swallowed hook, line and sinker by the naïve Tin Phay and his hare-brain goons oblivious of the fact that BEDC is 100% State Owned and Placed directly under the Prime Minister by an Act of the deposed Parliament that Bo Ne Win elected to retain after the Revolutionary Council Government assumed State Power on March 02, 1962, appointing Bo Khin Nyo Chairman because Bo Aung Gyi was tasked to run the day-to-day Administration and Management with all Cabinet Ministers (All in uniform except U Thi Han the Foreign Minister) reporting to Vice Chief of General Staff, Ministry of Defense.

Misled into the fantasy world by the Communist Financial Adviser, (Nga-Saya) Tin Phay was on cloud-nine believing that he was now the "New Economic Czar" and his top priority was to destroy the "Economic and Business Empire" of Aung Gyi in Burma and lay his hands on the "Mountain of Cash and Financial Assets accumulated in the Bank Accounts of Burma Trade Mission in London". The destruction of BEDC Corporations back in the Country went on unabated and we (Bo Aung Din and myself) in London were informed by colleagues, friends and family that we would be next to be sent to the infamous Insein Prison just outside Rangoon.

# URGENT ADVICE AND GUIDANCE TO AVOID PAR-KAIK NAR-KAIK

Bo Aung Gyi did not get his peace of mind in the foothills of Himalayas for long. The disinformation, rumors and wild speculations in Rangoon that the young Japanese educated Lawyer in London had refused the Trade Ministry order to return immediately and report to the Home Ministry somehow reached him and he was greatly distressed and at the same time believing in his guts that "he is not this kind of person" "unless antagonized, intimidated and provoked" like the time he pulled his gun on the Israeli in retaliation for the personal insults that he considered unacceptable under any circumstances. I received Bo Aung Gyi's very short letter sent all the way from Machan-Baw in the Kachin State expressing his distress and grave concern at the vendetta against him personally and at the cruel and arbitrary detentions of the BEDC Company Executives and the unjustified destruction of the country's Trade and Business assets.

What he wrote next in the short note shocked and surprised me greatly: "Bogyoke and I had full confidence and trust in you at the time of entrusting you with the difficult UK Mission and I have full faith and trust in your judgment at this very difficult time but my brotherly advice is please avoid "Par-Kaik Nar-Kaik" as our saying goes because it will only do harm to all concerned". I reflected on this message alone for several days telling myself "here is a man with an uncertain future who departed from the #2 position of the country's power elite and sending me a personal note of brotherly advice to avoid confrontation and confirming his belief that I will make the appropriate and proper judgment". Years later he told me that he and the UK Action Plan Committee Members initially were concerned to learn that "you appointed Bo Aye Maung the Defense Services Attaché Chairman of Burma Trade and Bogyoke (Gen. Ne Win) hit the ceiling with disbelief and anger. To calm and placate this sudden outburst and consternation of #1 I proposed sending Bo Khin Nyo immediately to look into the matter of the reason behind your decision to put Aye Maung in that position. It was like a thunderbolt to all of us".

The speculation was this uncouth Army Colonel, notorious for misconduct, falsification of funds and a loose cannon participating in the foiled Coup of retired Gen. Maung Maung, had bullied his way into that seemingly important position. Upon receipt of Bo Khin Nyo's report from London by diplomatic pouch, explaining that under extraordinary and extenuating diplomatic and UK Legal conditions that the Law Firm recommended having the Defense Attaché in London be in that position as the New Corporation Burma Trade London will be the Representative of BEDC, the Economic Arm of the Revolutionary Council Government of the Country. I shared this report from Bo Khin Nyo with all the Members of the Committee and the unanimous consensus was Bogyoke (#1) would understand and accept the explanation especially the Law Firm's clarifications that "it is a Symbolic rather than Executive position without Any Voting Rights in both the Board of Directors and Stock Holders Meetings and no shares issued to him".

Bo Aung Gyi said he and the Committee Members in Rangoon, Bo Thaung Kyi, Maung Lwin (Moustache) and Tommy Clift, went to the War Room to meet #1 and submitted Bo Khin Nyo's report from London the English original, Burmese translation and the attached Board of directors and Stock Holder's Resolutions. Colonel Solomon, the Judge Advocate General, was called in to explain the Legal Documents. Bo Solomon commented that under these legal constraints, limitations, current conditions and circumstances, he was certain that our Yebaws (Comrades) in London elected to move forward along the lines recommended by the Legal Team which was the safest course of action in setting up a brand new Business Corporation in the UK. Bo Lwin, the Intelligence Chief, suggested the option to replace Bo Aye Maung but Bo Ne Win shot down that idea saying "the New Organization just started their work in a foreign land and it would look bad and disorganized to all concerned just make sure that (SOB) is not given any Executive and Financial Authority". It was clear evidence that he wanted our mission in the UK to succeed.

I disclosed the main points of Gen. Aung Gyi's letter to Bo Aung Din sent all the way from Machan-Baw in the Kachin State per kind assistance of Gen. Tommy Clift who dispatches a special Air Force plane up to the Hill Station once a week with essential supplies and the two Officer pilots also serve as "special mail carrier". The Air Force Chief himself was already on his way out but asked to stay on a while to help incoming Chief of Air Staff to get the hang of the top job held by Clift for more than a decade. I believe it was Col. General Staff (Air) Thaung Dan who received training in Japan during WW-II by the Japanese Imperial Air Force. Bo Aung Din, a senior Air Force Officer close confidante of Tommy Clift, commented that this new leadership would definitely weed out the remnants of the Burma-British Air Reserve Officers who had retreated to India and received their training there where Selwyn Khin and Clift were assigned to "Battle of Britain air defense of London". It was indeed the end of the generation of British Burma Air Force officers that built the infrastructure of the Defense Services (Air).

Strangely enough, and as fate would have it, I was with Col. Maung Lwin (Moustache), a relic of the British Imperial Police Detective whom the Colonial Government had assigned to keep tabs on the Student Union leaders of Rangoon University and political activists including Shu Maung (Ne Win and Aung San), now his boss was making every effort to get my commitment of loyalty and full cooperation. Bo Khin Nyo on the other hand was a product of the Burmese Nationalist Independence movement with his elder brother Bo Khin Maung Galay a close colleague of Aung San and one of the first Deputy Prime Ministers (the other was U Kyaw Nyein) in U Nu's Cabinet since 1948 was treading carefully and left the probing to the wily Intelligence Chief. Both were perhaps surprised and wondering why after nearly three hours of discussions during breakfast in Bo Khin Nyo's hotel suite I had not said much, let alone the answer they had sought without seeming to be overbearing from their position of power back in Burma but irrelevant in London and both of them seem to be aware that I was not going to be rushed into anything.

It was indeed a very leisurely private breakfast meeting with several refills of the coffee pot by a waiter-cum-chef taking charge of the Mini-Kitchen and serving us in the "living room". It was almost 11 AM and I suggested we resume our discussions again in the Boardroom of Burma Trade Mission with Bo Aung

Din and continue through lunch. Our Bentley chauffeur drove us to Ingersoll House in Kingsway and we were taken up to the sixth floor by Executive Guest elevator (Lift) and our receptionist ushered us to the private lounge adjoining the Boardroom. Bo Aung Din joined us for a brief break in the lounge and the two Colonels asked for soft drinks and plain water as the many cups of coffee (caffeine) was taking effect on them – perhaps causing mild dehydration. I left the three Colonels and went to my office to check on the urgent telex and cables and referred to other Managers to respond and went back to the lounge to rejoin the three still engaged in mundane casual chat, apparently preferring to discuss substantive issues in the presence of all "All Stock Holders". I noted that from Bo Aung Din's facial expression.

A light lunch of the usual mini-sandwiches, meat puffs and Indian samosas was served with coffee, tea and soft drinks and in the relaxed atmosphere I casually mentioned the message received from Bo Aung Gyi in the Kachin State, which surprised all three of them, especially Maung Lwin (Moustache) who stared at me wide eyed and mouth agape with a questioning expression of "through whom did he send it?". Normally all such messages came through him. Without mentioning specifics I said his message stressed the importance of cooperation and the need to avoid "retaliation, vengeance and confrontation" which in the end will not benefit anyone but be harmful to all concerned especially the country's Economy and Trade. Bo Khin Nyo asked when I had received the message and what was my initial reaction? I said it was a few days before their arrival and I had shared the information with Bo Aung Din, who looked at me puzzled but not saying anything.

I assumed that he was playing it safe realizing his "Air Force status" facing two Army Senior Colonels and a Japanese educated young Lawyer assigned to lead the UK Mission by #1 who gave him a wide berth and practically Carte Blanche Executive Authority as far as Burma Trade Mission was concerned. No one ever imagined that a situation such as this would arise within a matter of a year of successfully launching the UK Action Plan Project to recover the hidden funds stashed away in the banks in Britain, Europe, Scandinavia and Switzerland. The strange irony was that the strong, uncompromising Military Dictator found himself right in the middle of a dilemma of his own creation because he was the one who had ordered Bo Aung Gyi to "pull out our Tokyo

University educated fellow in the Judge Advocate General's Department (he assumed) tasked with setting up the Export-Import Bank of Burma to lead the UK Project. He was also the one who ordered "our fellow to be the Majority Share Holder of Burma Trade's (60%) of the Stock".

In all fairness Bo Ne Win never ever dreamed that Bo Aung Gyi would abruptly leave him with second / third rate officers used to taking orders and following the leadership and guidance of the #2 General. Now, the fact of the matter and stark reality was that Bo Aung Gyi is gone and his nemesis and detractors Communist Ba Nyain and Cripple Tin Phay (Nga-Saya) were meting out their vendetta of destroying the successful BEDC Group of Corporations in Burma and making the bold attempt to lay their hands on the last and biggest pie of them all in London. For some reason the Dictator did not raise a finger against the blatant idiotic dismantling of the BEDC Companies in Burma owned by the State, but apparently he was not going to allow them to get close to Burma Trade Mission in London – he was going to take charge personally. However, that was easier said than done because "his (Japun kaung-Lay) young Japanese fellow now holds all the cards in his hands with (60%) majority Stock of the Company and protected by UK Laws". The Burmese Military Dictator, a notorious gambler and risk-taker, this time found himself with no cards in his hands and worse was the "serious caution by the two top Legal Professionals of the country that recourse to Litigation should be the last resort as the outcome would not be favorable". U.K. Corporation Laws protected the majority Stock-Holders.

I again for the 2nd time raised the importance of Bo Aung Gyi's message from the Kachin State not to engage in back-biting and to avoid confrontation and his confidence and good faith that we would make the proper and appropriate judgment. I noted that my mentioning it again gave the wrong impression, especially to Bo Maung Lwin (Moustache) who commented that "Bo Aung Gyi must have received some input from Rangoon that made him very concerned that you" (looking at me) "would not accept anything coming from (Nga-Saya) or Ba Nyain". I told him that is the disinformation already being spread that I have disobeyed the Trade Ministry Order to return immediately and report to the Home Ministry. From reliable sources I have been branded disloyal to the country and a defector by that group. I said I was not concerned by such unfounded accusations as my primary responsibility is here in London to ensure that whatever we are required to do, it must meet all the requirements of UK Laws under any circumstances.

Up to this stage Bo Aung Din for reasons of his own elected to be a mere observer but my take on his silence was the 2 Colonels were directing their probing questions to me stressing the fact that #1 discussed with Col. Thaung Kyi my background and the chances of "taking matters into his own hands and cutting off all ties with Government, Country, People and Family". Oblivious to them I was guided by the input from Colonel General Staff Kyi Maung (Zat-Laik) who had served under Col. Thaung Kyi and a close personal friend of Col. Ko Ko, Secretary to the Revolutionary Council Chairman and "privy to the innermost decisions and inter-actions of #1 with top Military Officers" on matters of this nature". I was also aware that the 2 Colonels were themselves already marginalized and most probably on their last mission before being pushed out or exiled out of sight and away from the seat of power.

I could clearly see that Bo Aung Din was deeply concerned, not knowing the reason for my taking a rather "Rigid Legalistic Position" and obviously skirting the Commitment, Guarantee and Pledge of Absolute Loyalty that Bo Maung Lwin (Moustache) and Bo Khin Nyo wanted to hear from me. Bo Ne Win sent the two of them because the Order issued by Trade Minister Bo Tin Phay had been ignored by the young Japanese educated Lawyer controlling the affairs of BEDC Burma Trade Mission in London indicating that Trade Ministry had no Administrative Jurisdiction over it by Order of the Revolutionary Council Chairman and Prime Minister that all UK Action Plan Project Matters must be reported to him directly by the Chairman of BEDC placed in his Office. By that firm response it was made very clear that I would only observe and honor the Original Order of the UK Action Plan Project Committee Selected by Bo Ne Win himself. For the sake of brevity I reminded Bo Maung Lwin (Moustache) and Bo Khin Nyo, and both stared at me with mouths agape and surprised.

Bo Aung Din was now in a state of shock and disbelief witnessing the 2 Senior Colonels speechless at the young Lawyer boldly establishing the fact that Burma Trade London was the brainchild of Bo Ne Win and as such it was our responsibility to adhere to his Official Directives concerning the present status and future of the Organization. I had no desire nor intent to engage in any argument with the Colonels who had been like big brothers (except Bo Aung Din) for over a decade working closely on special International Projects of the Caretaker Government and the Revolutionary Council Government. However, at this critical juncture I strongly felt the urge and the need first to stand my ground to protect the unique position of being the (60%) outright Majority Stock Holder of the British Corporation and all the UK Laws protecting such ownership status.

The difficulty for me was to avoid giving the impression to the three Colonels, very much older in age and of course in Official Military Rank, but being the "The only Legal Professional Entrusted with the task by #1" (The Strongman Military Dictator) was ever present on their psyche and I have always been treated with due courtesy, high regard and respect for my contribution on Legal Issues and in my Official Capacity of General Corporate Counsel to the BEDC Chairman in the Prime Minister's Office. Some would even go as far as to say that "The General Counsel's Position being a very Special Professional and Technical Status" is not comparable in any sense, is like apples and oranges. I never paid any attention to such gossip and was never concerned about rank perhaps because from very young High School age I was exposed to, trained and nurtured by high ranking Military Officers. As such I was never intimidated by rank or status of any kind like – Colonel, General, Admiral, Minister, Ambassador, Bishop, Cardinal, Etc. I also did not make a big deal of whatever my Official Status was at any given time because I was required to carry several Business Cards.

The wily Intelligence Chief, whose British Imperial Police Detective Training and experience enabled him to figure out from where the other party was coming, used his police tactics asking me "Hey Kyi Win Sein, the three of us here are soldiers and not a Lawyer like you and since we are all in this together I want you to advise us the best course of action you would like to take here in London that we can report back to Bogyoke (General) in Rangoon". This was a clear sign to me that he and Bo Khin Nyo were not going to take any initiative of their own and not dwell on complicated legal, corporate and financial issues that they knew nothing of and only wished to report back to #1 the best course of action recommended by Burma Trade Management. I suggested that we invite our Law Firm Senior Attorneys to join us at their earliest convenience and guide us on the best course of action to pursue that would meet the requirements of UK Laws. U Maung Maung Gale, our Board Secretary, immediately contacted Barrister Clive Richardson to request the attendance of his Senior Partners Barrister Templeton Smith and Sir Guy Hambling. He came back with the confirmation that they would come the day after tomorrow.

That left us, Bo Aung Din and myself, to cover some of the issues of mutual concern especially the firm stand insistence on our fiduciary responsibilities of Stock Holders and Directors of the Corporation and the Legal Obligation to the employees to ensure that their rights are protected. I explained to him my strategy to have the Revolutionary Council Chairman and Prime Minister nominate the "Entity, Person or Institution" for us to transfer / handover the Ownership / Affairs /and Responsibilities of Burma Trade Mission in London" other than "A Ministry, Department and/or Government Board / Committee". In our present situation it was critically imperative for our vital interests (Security and Future) to deal directly with the Seat of Power and not the Surrogates. As luck would have it, Bo Ne Win's agenda coincided with ours in excluding his Surrogates' involvement in this matter. In considering our current position and that of the Government in Rangoon we here in London held all the Cards in addition to having UK Laws and Justice System protecting British Corporate Stock Holders. This advantageous circumstance and position of strength was NOT our making and apparently the Legal Professionals in Rangoon fully recognized and accepted it as fact and reality. I went as far as disclosing that "my inside sources" confirm that they would deal "along the lines proposed and acceptable to us". Bo Aung Din was visibly relieved to hear that and said he now understood and appreciated my approach and the reason that Bo Khin Nyo and Bo Maung Lwin (Moustache) were subdued this time because they are under pressure to deliver a positive outcome acceptable to Burma Trade Mission Stock-Holders and Management as well as to the strongman Dictator Bo Ne Win.

I stressed to Bo Aung Din that the two Senior Army Colonelsare in uncharted waters and their given bottom-line mission goal was to explore with us the resolution that would meet all the requirements which we faced here and entity

/ person that we consider acceptable and appropriate to meet all the Legal and Fiduciary Responsibilities of the Corporation. Bo Aung Din asked if there was any entity / person I had in mind and I quickly reminded him that it would amount to and be construed as "Conflict of Interest" for the Management of the Corporation especially the Majority Stock Holder to even hint at the prospective nominee. He looked surprised and thanked me for bringing up the matter and reminding him to remain silent on the issue. Perhaps for the same reasons the Colonels had so far not mentioned any party, but actually I was quite sure they and their boss had so far no idea who to nominate. It would be interesting to see what our British Lawyers had to say and their recommendation who the Burmese Military Dictator should nominate to assume responsibility for the management of Burma Trade Mission.

# A GAMBLER WITH NO CARDS IN HIS HANDS TO MAKE A PLAY

In my sincere gesture to Bo Aung Din that we are in this together by fate and destiny, I mentioned to him that Bo Ne Win was notorious for his addiction to gambling, womanizing and penchant for taking risks that some would not think of. I mentioned a book I had once read about a gambler "without any cards in his hands to play" and the Psychiatrist Author of the book wrote "At such a time in dire straits a Gambler almost always turns to his long time personal friend who would not turn him down whatever the circumstance". I believe that this was such a time for #1. On examining the options available to him more closely, by mere force of instinct and proximity there was a high possibility that the most convenient and logical move would be to recall Bo Aye Maung, the Defense Services Attaché in London already serving as Honorary Chairman of Burma Trade and replace him with someone like Bo Khin Nyo, already marginalized and on his way out. He once served as Military Attaché in New Delhi, India.

The only negative was that his long Military Career and family background might interfere with his (Bo Ne Win's) personal agenda, which was quite clear by his quick action in stopping Tin Phay and Ba Nyain in their tracks to lay their hands on Burma Trade London. We are caught between a rock and a hard place but there was absolute certainty that Bo Ne Win, the strongman dictator of Burma, was weighing his best approach to wrest control of Burma Trade Mission in London from the hands of the young lawyer and a retired Air Force Officer. Replacing the exiled and discredited Aye Maung with another Colonel purged from the Revolutionary Council to hold his bag and serve as his surrogate with such high stakes involved could have negative repercussions from within the Military establishment still going through the trauma of Bo Aung Gyi's abrupt departure. Bo San Yu who took over the #2 position of

Vice Chief of General Staff (VCGS) was a soft and docile person, not quite big enough nor willing to grow and fit into the size simply because he did not have the deep and widespread following, high regard and respect of the Military establishment that Bo Aung Gyi enjoyed as one of the Original Founders of the Army. From that perspective it was very unlikely that Bo Ne Win would nominate an Army Officer. Bo Aung Din concurred with my evaluation, mentioning that he would have ordered Bo Lwin (Moustache) to take over soon after Bo Aung Gyi vacated all his Official Positions. His message from the Kachin State to "avoid retaliation and to compromise" was prompted by the harsh personal vendetta perpetrated against him and the BEDC Group within the country but perhaps aware that doing the same to Burma Trade Mission in London "would not be that simple in a far-away Country and the possibility of outright rejection by the Japanese-educated young Lawyer fully versed in UK-European Legal Systems and in Complete Control of the Corporation in every aspect of its Operation and Management". The news of my refusal to return immediately as ordered by Trade Minister Bo Tin Phay also reached him via the weekly Air Force supply plane.

# THE BRITISH LAWYERS LAY DOWN THE ROAD MAP AND GUIDELINES

The conference with the 3 Senior Partners of our Law Firm (DURRANT, COOPER & HAMBLING) took place in our Boardroom and was expertly led and guided by Sir Guy Hambling in a very relaxed format with generous time allowed for Official Translation to Burmese by U Ohn Sein, Government Affairs Manager for the benefit of the 2 Colonels. The Legal Team laid out the Fundamental Fiduciary Principles that must be observed and followed by the Stock Holders and Directors of the Corporation.

1. Transparency
2. Must avoid even the Appearance of Conspiracy
3. Compliance with all Laws, Ordinances of Central and Local Jurisdictions
4. All the Books of the Corporation to be opened to Registered and Certified Accounting Firm to be in accordance with Recognized Standard Principles of Accounting and Book-Keeping
5. All Banking Accounts to be opened to Auditors
6. All Banking and Financing Arrangements / Agreements / Contracts to be disclosed to Law Firm / Accounting Firm / Auditors
7. All Real Estate / Fixed Property Titles, Mortgages and Financial matters thereto to be disclosed to Accounting Firm / Auditors
8. All Bonds, Debentures, Certificates of Deposits (CDs), Treasury Bonds to be disclosed
9. Executive Compensation, Stock Options, Benefits, Bonuses to be disclosed to Auditors
10. Employee Compensation, Social Security, Benefits to be disclosed to Auditors
11. Extraordinary, Contingency Funds, Bank Accounts, Entertainment Funds to be disclosed

12. Corporate Taxes, Property Taxes, Contribution to Employee Pension Funds, Reserve Funds for Severance Compensation, Insurance Costs for Accidents / Fires, And Catastrophic Force Majeure Acts of God – Earth Quakes, Storms Floods, Acts of Government, Riots, Political Turmoil / Instability / Coups, Etc.
13. All such actions taken by the Company's Management must be Authorized and Approved by The Resolutions of the Board of Directors and the Stock Holders properly recorded as Stipulated in the Bye-Laws of the Corporation.

It was indeed a long list that must be meticulously followed one at a time, guided each step of the way by the Lawyers, Accountants, Auditors and Bankers. The conference adjourned to be resumed after the lunch break. The caterers from the Indian High Commissioner's Restaurant set up a Buffet Lunch in our Reception Room and adjoining Lounge and we had our Wet Bar open with a Bar Tender serving drinks from the Full Collection including English Draught Beer. Our Managers joined us for a leisurely and relaxed break with exotic light Indian food served together with assorted meat puffs, hamburgers and desserts, coffee and tea. It was a full course affair and our Lawyers enjoyed it immensely, especially the time to get acquainted with their special client and the 2 powerful Colonels from the Burmese Military Regime. It was the first time for them to participate in a formal Professional Consultation Conference with a team of British Barristers in London guiding the Management and Stock Holders of Burma Trade the critical importance of Transparency and the Compliance of UK Corporate Laws and Ordinances.

The Conference resumed after the long lunch break. Barrister Templeton Smith explained at length the serious consequences of any breach or non-compliance, especially for Burma Trade being owned entirely by Foreign Citizens known to be associated with and closely connected to the Military Regime of Burma that had recently toppled the democratically elected Government of that country which was a British Colony until 1948. That political background and reality was crucial in this case and could not be ignored because many UK and European Companies with long ties of Trade and Commerce could through their elected Members in Parliament "raise questions on Burma Trade's Legitimacy as well as its Status and Functions in London Representing the Military Regime". Without

Transparency such eventuality was a distinct possibility but with everything out in the open it was unlikely for anyone or any entity to pursue such action. The other pitfall to avoid was to satisfy the Central and Local UK Registration Authorities which could order Foreign Owners from leaving Britain until their Legal and Fiduciary Responsibilities were fully met to the Satisfaction of All the Competent Jurisdictions Governing Corporations owned by Foreign Entities.

It was an eye opener for all of us to realize that one person or a single company could take us down that path and cause untold trouble for a long time with unknown outcomes. Therefore, it was incumbent upon us (Burma Trade Mission Management and Stock Holders) to ensure that the "Legitimate Successors of this Corporation" would undertake in writing to honor and comply with all the responsibilities and obligations explained hereinabove by Barrister Templeton Smith. We made every attempt to ask the legal team to give us their idea or even a hint as to the entity, person or organization for the Authorities in Rangoon to nominate but true to their Professional Ethics and Pledge not to cross that Red Line, our efforts did not bear fruit. It was entirely a matter for the Burmese Military Dictator to nominate whomever he wished to "Accept the Transfer of Burma Trade Mission Ownership in its entirety and all the Responsibilities and Obligations that come with it". The Conference with our 3 Attorneys ended on that note. The 3 Colonels without any academic Law education confessed that it was beyond them to make any comment. After the Lawyers left, Bo Khin Nyo and Bo Maung Lwin (Moustache) insisted that they needed to at least have an idea of "who we (Bo Aung Din and myself) think would be acceptable to take over the burden from us". Their dilemma and fear was #1 had sent them to London to find out "who would be acceptable to Burma Trade Management, especially the Major Stock Holder because I refused to return immediately as ordered by Bo Tin Phay the Trade Minister". Simply put I was the bad fellow, the traitor and disloyal young Lawyer as portrayed by the Communist Ba Nyain and his harebrained Army goons. Bo Aung Din was distressed, feeling isolated and still not quite sure of going all out with the young Lawyer "who without hesitation responded that immediate return was not possible". He probably felt a milder roundabout reply would have been more appropriate and better all-around but didn't express it to me. But now, Bo Khin Nyo and Bo Lwin (Moustache), their time in London running out and still without any definitive answer to report back to their anxiously waiting boss, asked me to come early next morning to the hotel and join them for breakfast. It was a desperate time for the 2 Colonels. It is now urgently imperative for them to get an indication from me who would be acceptable to take over the ownership and all the legal and fiduciary responsibilities.

I arrived at the hotel 7:30 AM the following morning and ordered breakfast room-service for 3 in Bo Khin Nyo's suite and we started talking about yesterday's conference with the 3 British Lawyers and their rigid, professional, uncompromising attitude. I could not help but note that both men had aged and were quite subdued since the last time I saw them together with #1 in London. The situation this time was radically different with Bo Aung Gyi gone from the seat of power but still unable to make a clean and complete break with concern for those far away in London. I casually raised again the message from the Kachin States and this time Bo Lwin (Moustache) asked "what do you think was his primary concern?". Knowing full well the personal vendetta against him and the dismantling of BEDC Corporations in Burma and the detention of its Executives by Ba Nyain and Tin Phay, his concern judging from the message was the distinct possibility of "an all out retaliation by Burma Trade London being the only Group Company beyond their reach". That would be disastrous for all concerned.

He asked us to avoid back-biting and confrontation that would have a huge negative impact on the Country's Economy and International Business Relations as well as the Diplomatic repercussions with the UK, U.S. and European Countries. However, that eventuality had been averted by direct involvement and handling the matter from the Office of #1 where the BEDC Administration was officially placed under the Jurisdiction and Control of the Prime Minister. This affirmation of fact put Bo Khin Nyo in a very embarrassing and uncomfortable situation being the current Chairman of BEDC tasked with the responsibility for Burma Trade Mission in London by Bo Ne Win himself. Notwithstanding, Ba Nyain and Tin Phay ignored all of this and arrogantly issued the Order for our immediate return to Rangoon and report to the Home Ministry. Now, it dawned on the two Colonels that IF "Kyi Win Sein had meekly submitted and capitulated to that order all would have been over and we would not be here" commented Bo Lwin (Moustache). I do not know why he made that comment and I did not respond to it.

Bo Khin Nyo was gentleman enough to say "U Kyi Win Sein, I must thank you for standing up for BEDC and saving its dignity". I said my primary objective was to "end the intrusion and involvement of Ba Nyain and Tin Phay in Burma Trade London Affairs" pushing the Case to the Highest Office of the Military Regime because it was Dictator Gen. Ne Win who had initiated the Project in the first place and entrusted the rest to Bo Aung Gyi. With his unexpected departure from the "Seat of Power", it was imperative for me to be dealing with that "Seat of Power" and not relegated to be manhandled by lower level functionaries (Ministers) without any decision-making authority and in all cases incompetent to make any policy decisions "without the Green Light from the Dictator". I could see that coming as clear as daylight after Bo Aung Gyi's departure. BEDC Enterprises were successful because the top man had trust and confidence in his Professional Aides giving full reign and freedom of action and full support at all times. Bo Ne Win recognized that leadership quality and always entrusted business, trade, commercial, financial and banking to BEDC and the outcomes speak for themselves; and of course Burma Trade Mission London was one of the extraordinary achievements overseas and the envy of all other Ministries and Departments of the Government. Bo Ne Win, the strongman Military Dictator of the country, knowing full well the extent of Burma Trade London's very substantial financial assets from the private and personal reports of Bo Maung Lwin (Moustache), the Intelligence Chief and Bo Khin Nyo, Chairman of BEDC directly under the Prime Minister's Office, sent two of his closest and most trusted Colonels in the Military establishment to London, with the task to ascertain and find out from the young Lawyer the appropriate and acceptable Entity, Official, Institution that the Management could safely hand over Burma Trade in its entirety in accordance with the UK Laws and Ordinances.

Bo Aung Din was on tenterhooks because the Colonels had been with us for over a week and there was still no indication from Burma Trade Management as well as the British Lawyers and one could clearly discern that things had reached an impasse as far as nominating the candidate to take over responsibility, management and operation of Burma Trade Mission London. Time and patience was running out for the two Officials but exercising restraint because of the "serious warning" from the top Legal Professionals of the Country "to avoid Antagonizing and Provoking the young Lawyer" owning (60%) Shares of the Company and Protected by UK Laws. I later learned that they were advised in very definitive terms that "without his voluntary cooperation there is absolutely no way to regain ownership and control of the Company". Up to this point in our discussions I had not expressed by personal opinion one way or another except to mention the message received from Bo Aung Gyi in the Kachin State.

I interpreted the message sent all the way from the foothills of the Himalayas by the concerned man who until a few months ago was the #2 General of the Military Regime, as a reminder of the UK Action Plan Project that was initiated by Bo Ne Win and placed directly his control with Bo Khin Nyo and Bo Maung Lwin (Moustache), the Intelligence Chief assigned to support and monitor the operation of the Burma Trade Mission London entrusted to the Tokyo University educated young Lawyer pulled out from the Export-Import Bank of Burma by his order and nominated to implement, manage and operate the Covert Project of the Revolutionary Council Government. Knowing full well that Bo Tin Phay would not get the #2 Vice Chief of General Staff (VCGS) the "Power Base of the 3 Military Services" given to San Yu instead. Desperate, frustrated at being bypassed again, he lashed out at any and everything achieved by BEDC under the leadership and guidance of Bo Aung Gyi during his long tenure as Economic Czar of Burma.

His guidance to cooperate fully was accepted and understood by Bo Aung Din and myself as being with BEDC Chairman Bo Khin Nyo in the Prime Minister's Office having Exclusive Jurisdiction over Burma Trade Mission London. Therefore the order from the Ministry of Trade was "Out of Administrative Procedure / Order, Irrelevant and Invalid" to say the least. My endeavor was to impress upon the 2 Colonels this arrogant and blatant transgression and power-grab by Bo Tin Phay and the Communist Financial Advisor Ba Nyain. My hope and expectation was for them to report this to #1 for him to be aware of what was being perpetrated by the two right under his nose. Bo Aung Din cautioned me not to push too far on these delicate inter-personal issues at the top of the Military Regime. I knew where he was coming from, particularly the inadvertent misinterpretation by the 2 Army Officers that Burma Trade Management was asserting its position of strength and entertaining ideas of pursuing an independent path of their own. That is the worse nightmare scenario warning of the two top legal professionals in Rangoon and Bo Ne Win the strongman Dictator of Burma want to avoid that that outcome at all cost.

Bo Aung Din's thinking and mindset was understandable because he was not aware that both were on their last mission, already marginalized and pushed out from the "inner circle of power" around the Dictator – Bo Maung Lwin (Moustache) with the defection of his Aide, Captain Kyaw Zwa Myint (Johnny Lears), and Bo Khin Nyo with the sudden departure of General Aung Gyi. His long Military career and position in the Revolutionary Council was uncertain with the Tin Phay thugs and Communist Ba Nyain digging all kinds of dirt on him for alleged abuse of power and corruption all trumped up to throw him into prison. How far the Dictator would protect him remains to be seen. Moustache Maung Lwin, according to my information, would get a better deal from the boss – exiled to Bonn, West Germany as Ambassador for a time to erase the ugly defection affair of the Anglo-Burmese intelligence officer who had betrayed his trust and brought him down from the powerful Military Intelligence Chief position. For obvious reasons and regretfully I could not share the "inside information from Rangoon" with Bo Aung Din. It was unfortunate and regrettable but there was absolutely nothing that can be done to relieve his sense of insecurity.

The disinformation and character assassination campaign back in Burma was escalating in "official circles" that Bo Aung Gyi's men in Burma Trade Mission London, the young Lawyer with a Japanese wife and retired Senior Air Force Officer as Deputy Defense Attaché at the Embassy had betrayed their country and disobeyed the Order from the Minister of Trade to return to Burma. These two Officers were controlling and managing the BEDC Representative Office in the UK and all its Joint Venture and Subsidiary Companies in Europe, Scandinavia, Switzerland, USA and the Defense Industries JV Corporation FRITZ WARNER in West Germany. The Ministry of Trade was coordinating with the Home and Foreign Ministry to take appropriate official action against the two Officers. This was a deliberate attempt to sabotage the Mission of the 2 Colonels sent to London by Bo Ne Win to work out and find the best resolution for the future of Burma Trade Mission and BEDC Representative Office in London. And of course the intent and wishful thinking of the campaign perpetrators was to push us over the edge and commit the cardinal sin of open defiance and defection, seeking asylum and protection of the UK Government under the Geneva Conventions as well as the British Corporation Laws Protecting Stock Holders.

What Bo Tin Phay, the Trade Minister, the sickly Bo Kyaw Soe (with a short memory) and Ba Nyain, the Communist Financial Advisor, did not know or perhaps did not care was that Bo Maung Lwin (Moustache), the Military Intelligence Chief and Bo Khin Nyo, BEDC Chairman, had known me since I was a High School student as well as during my studies at University of Tokyo in Japan. They were more like big brothers to me and in fact it was Bo Khin Maung Galay, the elder brother of Bo Khin Nyo, as Deputy Prime Minister and Chairman of Foreign State Scholarship Board who practically forced me to study International Law in Japan after WWII. With such a relationship history and the fact that Bo Ne Win had nominated me to lead the UK Action Plan Mission, this gave me gave me some allowance and slack to take liberties in freely speaking my personal opinion as well as my Professional Advice as official Legal Counsel to BEDC as well as being the General Counsel to the Ministry of Defense.

Human nature being such, especially the Government bureaucracy, there was wild speculation and false rumors that the "young Japanese educated Lawyer must be related to one of the Generals or Colonels to be given special treatment and position at Official Meetings of top Senior Officers of the Ministry of Defense, particularly the Vice Chief of General Staff Gen. Aung Gyi, Colonel Khin Nyo, BEDC Chairman, and the Military Intelligence Chief Colonel Maung Lwin (Moustache). It seems this young Lawyer is with them at almost all meetings". Under such extraordinary circumstances I meticulously had to honor and observe the general rule to "keep my distance" and not intrude into their official space both physically as well as to strictly confine my involvement in the deliberations "On Legal Issues", on subject matters referred for my perusal, such as banking, financial, overseas trade, diplomatic issues, foreign business representatives in Burma, Embassies in Rangoon, etc. It was indeed a monumental task, being the only one educated "In the East" as those with Western Education (Barristers, British, U.S. French, Germany, Ph.Ds) were all on the "Suspect List" of Bo Ne Win. His psyche and paranoia with the "Axe Handles of the West" was more than one can imagine – all were untrustworthy and would do the bidding of their "White Thakins (Masters)". Notwithstanding that his preferred destination for medical treatment, rest and recreation was London – perhaps because the Queen opened her Royal Lounge at Heathrow and Lord Mountbatten of Burma would have him stay as his guest at one of his many estates with a 9-hole golf course close to London. All that convergence of favorable situations and circumstances (the good Karma) put BEDC London in a protected position of strength to counter those on the war-path to destroy us.

It was critically important for us to ensure that the nominee to accept responsibility for Burma Trade Mission London would be named by Bo Ne Win himself and not by any of the surrogate ministers – particularly Bo Tin Phay, out to destroy BEDC after taking possession of all the money and locking us up in prison. He had already got away with doing exactly that to all the Corporations in Burma and its Executives thrown into detention on trumped up charges. Col. Kyaw Soe, the sickly, naïve and weak Home Minister, and Col. Fatty Than Sein, the powerful Chairman of Central Security and Administrative Committee, were bullied into doing so by Tin Phay and Communist Financial Advisor Ba Nyain. As such it was very important that we (Bo Aung Din and myself) maintained the direct link to Bo Ne Win facilitated by his personal interest and involvement in determining the future of Burma Trade Mission London.

Luckily it finally dawned on Bo Aung Din the existential threat that awaited us in Rangoon without this direct linkage to the maximum leader and Dictator of Burma. He called me late one night and expressed his understanding and appreciation of my taking a firm stand in presenting "our position" to the two Army Colonels. He confessed that he could not do such a thing with the Senior Colonels as they were notorious for being thin-skinned and intolerant of arguments by subordinates and junior officers. But "with you I was surprised to see them subdued and they did not say much, perhaps realizing that you are a Certified Lawyer Qualified to dispense Legal and Professional Counsel". I told him that he was very generous in giving me more credit than I deserve. "Well, U Kyi Win Sein, let me just say that it is quite clear and evident to all here in the London Burmese Embassy and Community at large that you have a very unique and special relationship with the top Military leadership in Rangoon, being the only Lawyer educated in Japan after WW-2 under the personal care and nurtured by the #1 and #2 of the Army." I then suggested he join us for breakfast in Bo Khin Nyo's suite at 8 AM. He was hesitant at first and not too keen but later agreed to be there in the hotel lobby and to wait for me.

"My ex-boss Gen. Tommy Clift was greatly impressed by your maturity, polite humble manners, Academic Certifications from Japan's #1 University and Professional Credentials. He also mentioned in his letter that you helped him and all the VIP Military Delegations to Japan earning the enviable nickname "Our Comrade Yebaw" in Tokyo then and now "Our Comrade Yebaw in London" by the Chief of General Staff and the entire top echelon of the Ministry of Defense. All senior officers sent to London for medical treatment are advised by #1 on their report to him before their departure "In case you need any help contact "Our Yebaw in London" and seek his help – before you leave this office ask Bo Ko Ko for all the information how to contact him". Usually as a matter of normal procedure Col. (Dr.) Hla Han, Director of Military Medical Services and his Deputy, Col. (Dr.) Maung Lwin, would advise the same with all the information including my residence phone number." My bedside phone would ring at most unearthly hours 2, 3, 4 AM.

I made it my personal duty to attend to all the needs of these Generals and Colonels far away from home in failing health and more often than not "short of funds" and without hesitation Burma Trade would step in and take care of the "Payment Guarantee". Time permitting I would accompany the patient on the day of the surgical procedure and wait for the "outcome report of the Surgical Team" and make sure that the patient is back in the post-surgery ICU. Among the many that I recall was Col. Aung Zin, Central Region Commander and my golf nemesis in Pathein (in the 1953 Irrawaddy Delta Championship Match), who was sent to London for surgery on his prostate cancer, Col. Kyi Maung (Zat-Laik) Colonel General Staff, Ministry of Defense for prostate cancer, Col. Thaung Kyi, Chief of Naval Staff for Kidney and Liver problems, Col. Hla Han, Director of Military Medical Services for Cardio-Pulmonary treatment and of course the notorious Gen. Tin Phay with multiple medical and psychological ailments that played right into the hands of and down the money making alley of the late Dr. Hans Hoff of Vienna, Austria.

The next morning four of us ordered room service breakfast to be served in the dining room of Col. Khin Nyo's suite and we continued our discussion, focused this time on the nominee's qualifications and credentials that would meet the requirements of UK Laws and be acceptable to the authorities of the Central and Local Company Governing Bodies. This was a sensitive and delicate territory to get into as it would be highly inappropriate particularly for Burma Trade Management (Bo Aung Din and myself) to even be indicating their preference of the candidate. We carefully avoided going down that path. However, the wily Intelligence Chief, sensing that no one was going to stick his neck out, broke the ice asking "Ko Khin Nyo, what do you think about U Hla Maung the Ambassador here who is a long time close friend of Bogyoke (General)?". "Yes, Bo Lwin, that is true and he is also a close friend and colleague of my elder brother Bo Khin Maung Galay and Bo Aung San." Bo Aung Din interjected with "Ambassadors are not permitted to get involved in commercial enterprise by the Geneva Diplomatic Rule and Protocols".

I quickly added "should he be the nominee of the Head of State a special Waiver could be negotiated with the British Ministry of Foreign Affairs for U Hla Maung to serve as "Caretaker" for a transitory period". This was the first time in over a week of their arrival that a possible candidate acceptable to both parties was identified. Bo Khin Nyo suggested reporting to #1 immediately via diplomatic pouch. We proceeded to our respective Office Suites and left the two of them in the Boardroom to draft their report. It was completed in about an hour, sealed in an envelope and addressed to the Secretary of the Revolutionary Council, Col. Ko Ko, marked Confidential and Urgent Attention. We had our chauffeur deliver it to the Defense Attaché's Office and Bo Lwin called Bo Aye Maung to send it by Special Pouch. It was indeed a relief to all of us because the ball was now in #1's court.

We just had to wait for orders from Rangoon – hopefully soon. A few days later orders came for the Colonels to inform U Hla Maung of Bo Ne Win's desire to have him accept responsibility of Burma Trade Mission London as Caretaker and necessary communication with instructions from Foreign Minister would be sent soon. The two Colonels were to discuss full details with Burma Trade Management and U Hla Maung and report fully to the Chief of General Staff on return to Rangoon.

NOTE: DO NOT INVOLVE DEFENSE ATTACHÉ OFFICE AND STAFF AS WELL AS EMBASSY STAFF. STRICT CONFIDENTIALITY TO BE OBSERVED AND REPORT ONLY TO THE REVOLUTIONARY COUNCIL CHAIRMAN'S OFFICE TO THE ATTENTION OF THE CHIEF CABINET SECRETARY, COLONEL KO KO.

It was quite clear to the four of us in London that H.E. U Hla Maung, a political insider starting from the Thakin Party movement and a close friend and Comrade-in-Arms of Ne Win, Aung Gyi, Kyaw Nyein and Bo Khin Maung Galay in the underground operations against the British Colonial Government, and now serving under the Military Dictator, would have to obey the orders of his immediate boss, the Foreign Minister U Thi Han, also a close friend since Rangoon University Student Union days. From my own personal perspective he would be the ideal nominee for us to work with, being the Official Representative of the Military Regime as well as a personal friend of the Dictator. Moreover, being a complete outsider totally removed from the covert UK Action Plan Project from the outset, the possibility of having an agenda of his own was not only remote but his official and personal loyalty to the Dictator would be enough pressure on him not to stray from the transitory Caretaker role and also serve our (Bo Aung Din and myself) critical need to be dealing directly with Bo Ne Win. And of course it would remove Tin Phay, the Trade Minister, and Communist Ba Nyain, the Financial Advisor, from dealing with us in London. The Ambassador would have to rely entirely on the good faith cooperation of Burma Trade Management, especially the costs of engaging a reputable Law and Accounting / Auditing firms of his own to conduct and coordinate "Acceptance of the Transfer from Burma Trade of its Stock ownership, Management Responsibilities, Assets, Banks Accounts and Employees".

Another huge advantage and benefit would be the British Ministry of Foreign Affairs having a very friendly and cordial working relationship with Ambassador U Hla Maung would in all likelihood elect to remain silent and refrain from looking at it as a breach of Diplomatic Conduct by a Head of a duly accredited Embassy. It could also be construed as acceptance by the British Government authorities of what the Burmese were doing with their commercial and business affairs in London. In fact our lawyers told us that the

Arabs, Africans, South and Central American Ambassadors and their wives were involved in things a lot more inappropriate and flagrant than what we Burmese planned to do. For the British it was a minor issue to raise and not worth the risk of alienating the strongman Military Dictator of Burma.

# THE POLITICIAN-TURNED AMBASSADOR AND THE ARMY COLONELS

I noted with surprise that the two Senior Colonels of the Revolutionary Council Government, knowing full well the personal relationship of their Dictator boss and Ambassador U Hla Maung, and the delicate task at hand to "officially inform / assign to him the extraordinary responsibility to take over the Ownership and Management of Burma Trade Mission in London under the direct orders of General Ne Win the Head of State" when even at the highest level of political power structure the first human instinct was to push it off to someone else close by, no matter how inappropriate it may seem. It was also strange and amusing to me that the two senior Army Officers were in a dilemma over how to deal with the Ambassador notorious for being the "power-broker and instrumental in the break-up of the AFPFL Party founded by Aung San".

They did not tell me outright or order me, but hinted broadly that "perhaps I contact and request of U Hla Maung to join us for a luncheon briefing at Burma Trade Mission Office". I definitely was uncomfortable with that idea because that practice of "Relaying Orders from Above in the Military Chain of Command" was to ask Senior Officers to attend briefing sessions. I wanted to avoid the inordinate gossip and fabrication of false information like "That young Japanese educated Lawyer of Burma Trade summoned the Ambassador to his Office". The reader must be reminded of the huge divide between the remnants of the colonial entrenched bureaucracy and the Military Regime in power just a little over a year with ingrained "mistrust of the Western Educated elite that make up the bureaucracy". On the same token and along the same lines, their bias and prejudice against those educated and trained in the East was truly beyond the pale. This segment of Burmese society looked upon the independence movement of Aung San and the 30 Comrades as "political opportunists" and made all-out effort to organize the politicians to their side soon after the departure of the British in 1948. It was a huge success for a decade until 1958 when the political parties were at each other's throats and the Military emerged as the only Burmese Institution with Stability and Discipline, and Parliament was pressured to transfer power to Gen. Ne Win, the Chief of General Staff to save the Union from disintegration. However, in 1962, he took over the country in a bloodless Coup and set up the Revolutionary Council Government.

Now in late Spring of 1963 after the parting of ways with Gen. Aung Gyi, the only man with political, military and moral stature to stand his ground and speak to Ne Win as friend, colleague, comrade-in-arms and fellow founders of the Army, there was no one to fill that vacuum and Bo Ne Win found himself all alone at the pinnacle of Political Power unchallenged and the Era of Military Dictatorship began in Burma. His top priority as maximum leader of the country was to ensure that almost all of the hidden funds of the politicians successfully and legally retrieved by Burma Trade Mission London, a BEDC Corporation under the leadership of Aung Gyi, would be to hand over to his trusted personal friend U Hla Maung and also Ambassador of Burma to the Court of St. James. Colonel Khin Nyo, the Chairman of BEDC in the Prime Minister's Office, and Colonel Maung Lwin, Military Intelligence Chief, must now relay the order to the Ambassador that official orders were on the way from his immediate boss Foreign Minister U Thi Han to that effect. They would return to Rangoon and report the "success of their special mission to London".

I was fully aware of the need to have a good working relationship with Ambassador U Hla Maung as majority (60%) Stock Holder of the Corporation and for all intents and purposes the OWNER according to the Laws of the UK and the City of London Company Laws and Ordinances. The Colonels were not too keen on meeting the Ambassador and I later learned that U Hla Maung shared the same feeling because as Revolutionary Council Members of Cabinet Rank, they were senior in status to Ambassadors. To save and reserve my Official Status of Legal Advisor to BEDC and CORPORATE COUNSEL TO BURMA TRADE MISSION, LONDON, I suggested that since they had not met him on this trip, I would invite him to a Private Dinner at the Indian

High Commissioner Office restaurant where we could discuss in complete privacy. I also proposed that U Ohn Sein, our Government Affairs Manager, and U Maung Maung Gale, our Board Secretary and Administrative Manager, be included since they had previously served in his Embassy and would be most helpful to him now in the uncharted task of transfer procedures.

I asked U Maung Maung Gale to write a formal invitation (under my signature as Legal Advisor to BEDC and Representative Office in London) and requested U Ohn Sein hand deliver it to the Ambassador who personally recommended his service in Burma Trade. For that act of observing correct protocol and courtesy, U Hla Maung reciprocated in kind despite the huge difference in our ages. Bo Aung Din, U Maung Maung Gale and U Ohn Sein went ahead in the company car to the restaurant and I accompanied the Colonels in the Bentley. During the 15 minute ride to the restaurant, Bo Lwin (Moustache) surprised me by saying that "as majority Stock Holder and Legal Advisor of the Company you outline briefly the Legal procedures that need to be followed and we will stress that from the outset the original UK Action Plan Project was approved by #1 and the implementation, operation and management was entrusted to you in your Official Legal Advisor Position to BEDC in the Prime Minister's Office".

He also stressed that I must report "Only to The Office of the Revolutionary Council Chairman, for the Attention of Colonel Ko Ko, Secretary of the Chairman". It dawned on me the gravity of the burden put on me. I also noted with concern that Bo Khin Nyo remained silent while Bo Lwin did all the talking. When the three of us walked into the reception room adjoining the Formal Dining Room, U Hla Maung greeted the Colonels and myself rather formally with due respect and our Burma Trade colleagues with drinks in hand waved for the bartender pushing the serving cart with drinks and appetizers. I could not help but note that I was the odd young one among six other Burmese men of middle age, most likely in their mid-fifties and I in my late twenties (27). Bo Lwin (Moustache) was in his element and he loves the cocktail hour. After a few drinks there was a great deal of chatter and I overheard several times my name being mentioned to the Ambassador by Bo Lwin and Bo Khin Nyo. I did manage to get across all the essential steps to take immediately and U Hla Maung without hesitation told me that he would have to rely 120% "On you as both Colonels stressed to me that your help and guidance as majority

Stock Holder would be most important and I look forward to working closely with you". That was the beginning of my close working relationship with U Hla Maung (Peking).

I assured the very concerned Ambassador that the entire Management Team of Burma Trade – Lt.Col. Aung Din, myself, U Ohn Sein and U Maung Maung Gale – would be with him every step of the long way and not to worry but we must not rush, as time was essential to achieve the outcome we desired. He said "I have heard a great deal about you from various sources and now I am going to going to find out for myself the most frequently mentioned talk, or call it gossip in the London Burmese Community, that has reached our Embassy "hiring the very best and most expensive Legal Firm led by leading Queen's Counsel (QC), Lloyds Chartered Accountants and Auditors; employing the best Managers, staff and compensation / benefits on British Corporate Scale". U Hla Maung said he was rather skeptical when he first heard about "this young Burmese Lawyer's very aggressive style and the extraordinary speed of setting up Burma Trade until I saw with my own eyes when I brought U Ohn Sein to your office to officially join the Management Team".

The Ambassador, having many years of diplomatic experience in major countries, was very careful and deferential to the two Senior Colonels and expressed his concern on the question of his diplomatic status and the possibility of a negative reaction from the British Host Government. Bo Aung Din quickly assured the worried U Hla Maung that a transitory Caretaker role would not pose any problem to the Host Government according to the "inside contacts" of our Law Firm in the British Foreign Office (Ministry of Foreign Affairs). That effectively closed any wiggle room for the Ambassador to opt out of the new additional task that he would have to assume. I also raised the question of the immediate need for him to engage a Law Firm and Accounting Firm of his own to work with ours in the long transfer process. All such costs and related expenses would be borne by Burma Trade. I advised him that should he elect to have our Law Firm select Firms of equal standing for him, it would save a whole lot of protocols, procedures of "References, Banking and Credit checks, and Retainers".

It is quite acceptable and normal for one reputable Law / Accounting Firm to recommend or refer a Client to their "Colleague in the London Bar Association" to work in tandem with them on such a case as this. U Hla Maung was glad and relieved to hear that and asked me to request Sir Guy Hambling to refer him to one of his colleagues in the London Bar Association. We were referred to ARCHIBALD, BLACKSTOCK, CUNNINGHAM AND WILSON, a very old and well known Law Firm headed by Sir Roger Wilson, QC (Queen's Counsel) and the Accounting / Auditing Firm PRICE WATERHOUSE, both with impeccable track records of strict adherence to the accepted rules of Accounting, and they were hired to assist and guide the Burmese Ambassador in his new responsibilities as Caretaker of Burma Trade London. The retainer fees were high even by London standards – £4,500 each from which all costs, fees and expenses would be defrayed and replenished as needed by Burma Trade. U Hla Maung was in a state of shock and disbelief at the very high cost but calmed down when advised that in dealing with the country's foreign trade and commerce the best Legal and Accounting support and guidance must be available on call and could not be compromised under any circumstances as hundreds of millions were involved and there was absolutely no room for errors. The Ambassador said he was in uncharted waters and at this stage of his career and age it would take some time to fully comprehend and grasp the complexities of his new job. He expressed personal thanks and appreciation for our staying on the job as long as needed for him to gain enough confidence and then take over all the responsibilities from Stock Holders (myself and Bo Aung Din), and the two principal Executives leading the Management of Burma Trade Mission, London.

Before their departure for Rangoon the two Colonels wanted to have a private chat with me. I went to the Washington Hotel at 8 AM on the day of their flight late in the afternoon from Heathrow International Airport. We ordered breakfast service in Bo Khin Nyo's suite and had a leisurely conversation for several hours until lunchtime when Bo Aung Din was going to join us. Bo Lwin (Moustache) in his usual characteristic casual demeanor revealed that on return to Rangoon he would be handing over everything to Bo Chit Khin, Air Force Colonel, and begin the preparations and briefings to assume the Ambassador's post in Bonn, West Germany. He said that with a wink and a grin as if saying "you probably know that already", a clear indication that even at the very top of the intelligence hierarchy information seeps out, especially when the Ministry of Foreign Affairs is involved – having to inform first the West German Ambassador in Rangoon and then the Burmese Embassy in Bonn to seek acceptance of the new Envoy. There was no way to keep it under wraps. Bo Lwin was quite at ease to personally let us know that his long tenure as Chief of Military Intelligence would come to an end on his return to Rangoon.

Bo Khin Nyo said Burma Trade London was the only BEDC Organization standing intact and functioning normally whereas all the many others in Burma had been nationalized and dismantled despite the fact that the Government already owned them. He sadly lamented that through fate and bad karma he was presiding on a pile of rubble and debris as Chairman of BEDC in the Prime Minister's Office. He continued that this agony and pain would endure until the time Burma Trade's ultimate fate was determined by the #1. I interjected that it would be at least six months or perhaps a year depending on Ambassador U Hla Maung's timeframe, comfort and confidence to accept full responsibility in writing and sign all Legal Documents of Release witnessed by Senior Lawyers of London' two leading Law Firms and Accounting / Auditing Firms. On our way to Heathrow International Airport Bo Lwin (soon to be U Lwin) said he would contact us as soon as he settled in Bonn as Burma's Ambassador. He also promised to give a full report to Colonel Thaung Kyi "who will be anxious to know how you are getting along in London". Looking back with the benefit of hindsight it was a significant milestone in my personal relationship with the notorious Military Intelligence Chief I had first met at dinner in Col. Thaung Kyi's house in Bassein (now Pathein) in 1952. And since then the long, close association and involvement in the Ministry of Defense "Special Covert Projects in the Country and Overseas".

The next morning after the two Colonels' departure, Ambassador U Hla Maung called to confirm that he had received official instructions from U Thi Han, Foreign Minister, to fully cooperate with BEDC Legal Advisor and Representative U Kyi Win Sein and Burma Trade Managing Director U Aung Din with regard to "The Affairs of the Company and its future Management". He said he would come over to discuss with us the details and plans to move forward. I invited him to join us for light lunch at around 12:30 PM. I informed Bo Aung Din of my conversation with the Ambassador and he was surprised that the Revolutionary Council Chairman's Office was moving quickly on this matter. Just at that time I received a package delivered from the Defense Attaché's Office Diplomatic Pouch Officer. The confidential message was from Colonel General Staff Kyi Maung (Zat-Laik) informing me that Colonel Thaung Kyi, Chief of Naval Staff, had instructed him to convey it through Military Intelligence Pouch to Defense Attaché London. The message was: "Hmu-Gyi (Colonel) Thaung Kyi in his meeting with the Chief of General Staff confirmed full Trust and confidence in your Professional Qualifications, Management Capability, Moral Integrity and good judgment in implementing the Policy Directives of the Revolutionary Council Government as conveyed and discussed by Bo Khin Nyo and Bo Maung Lwin with you in London in your Official Position of Legal Advisor and Representative of BEDC in UK, Europe, Scandinavia and USA. Report all matters to Colonel Ko Ko, Secretary to Chairman of Revolutionary Council Government. Wishing you good health and Regards, Bo Kyi Maung". This message was heart-warming to know that I had friends at my back.

It was a categorical guarantee by Col. Thaung Kyi to #1 that my loyalty to duty, country and patriotism was absolute and solid as far as he was concerned, having known and nurtured him personally including Special Intelligence Training since his High School days. I shared this information with Bo Aung Din who stared at it for several minutes with an expression of disbelief. He then said in an afterthought, "Col. Thaung Kyi definitely is a very courageous person and a straight shooter to give the Chief of General Staff of the Armed Forces such a firm and absolute assurance on a person's loyalty to duty, country and people is unquestionable."

It made me realize the enormous risk and heavy burden that Col. Thaung Kyi had taken upon himself to stand squarely behind me at the most critical time when the Military Dictator was unsure and wavering as to the loyalty of one entrusted to his care by Bo Khin Maung Galay. And he himself had given direct Commission in Judge Advocate General Department and assigned sensitive covert missions overseas and was now seeking reassurance from one of his trusted Colonels reputed to be the strict disciplinarian of the Burma Army. The #1 got what he asked for and was pleased with the arrangement in place. Col. Thaung Kyi elected to send the message through the Colonel General Staff who had served under his Command and introduced him to me when he was sent to London for medical treatment and we became good friends.

He was sent to London for treatment of prostate cancer and arrived exhausted from the long flight and depressed. Before departure from Rangoon senior Military Officers were required to call on (report to) the Chief and Vice Chief of General Staff in the Ministry of Defense. Gen. Ne Win told him to contact "Our Yebaw in London" for any help he needed during his stay and to get the contact information from "Bo Lwin or Bo Ko Ko on your way out". Bo Aung Gyi and Bo Lwin told him not to worry about anything – "just contact our man for any help you need" and gave him "handwritten introduction memos" to me and all the information including my residence phone number. He called me one late afternoon as soon as he was settled in his hotel room. I inquired about his condition and learned that he was tired but very excited and could not wait to get together. I advised him of receipt in today's pouch information about his coming from Bo Lwin and to rest up as our chauffeur would pick him up and bring him to our office around 4:30 PM.

He arrived about 5 PM and was ushered to the reception room. When I walked in through the Boardroom Bo Kyi Maung stood up and I complimented him that the nick-name Zat-Laik (Actor) was a very apt one and it was perhaps not too late to change careers. He laughed heartily holding my hands and said he really was surprised at how young I looked because when Bogyoke-Gyi (General Ne Win) said "our Yebaw in London" and Gen. Aung Gyi said "Our man" his expectation was to meet someone of their age – "this is truly a surprise and I must apologize for not doing my homework and for saying it to your face". I told him not to worry about it because it has been the same since my first meeting with the Generals in Tokyo in 1955. He said "your reputation of high achiever in international missions is often mentioned by our superiors in the Ministry of Defense". I informed Bo Aung Din on the intercom that Col. Kyi Maung was with me and invited him to come and meet him and join us for afternoon tea.

I was taken aback when he walked in – always proper and correct in observing "protocols of greetings" stood at attention on entering the room and Bo Kyi Maung was quick to get up and rushed to the door and grabbed Bo Aung Din's hands and put him at ease. Of course in the Military rank trumps everything and here was a full Colonel (G-1) in the Ministry of Defense occupying the #3 position of the Burma Army and a Lt. Col. of the Burma Air Force greeting a senior Army officer with due respect, especially this being their first meeting. It was quite evident that the two Colonels, about the same ages but from different services of the Military and different cultural and religious backgrounds, were tense and very formal in their conversation and it took some time for them to settle down and converse informally in a relaxed manner like regular friends. Perhaps because of my exposure very early in life (high teens in High School) to high Government and Military Officials – Regional Commissioners and Military Commanders and later as State Scholar in Japan to Colonels, Generals and Cabinet Ministers – I may have developed perhaps unconsciously a psyche to accept them as seniors, elders, teachers, brothers, uncles and was always at ease to meet and be in their presence without any intimidation or fear.

Military politics being such there was no mention of the Defense Services Attaché Col. Aye Maung being exiled to London by Gen. Ne Win for his part in the attempted Coup by Gen. Maung Maung exiled to Israel as Ambassador. Col. Kyi Maung did mention that Lt. Commander Maung Maung Khin, the Assistant Defense Attaché, had met his flight at Heathrow and checked him into his hotel. I asked him if he was comfortable at that hotel and he said being there for only one night he was not yet sure. I told him if for any reason he was not at home there to let us know and we would move him to the Washington Hotel where we have an open account and all our VIP guests are put up during their stay in London and it is close to our office. He thanked us and appreciated that offer. He mentioned again that both Gen. Ne Win and Aung Gyi had told him "contact our man in London for any help you need during your stay".

We had dinner at the Indian High Commissioner Restaurant together with U Ohn Sein and U Maung Maung Gale and Bo Kyi Maung greatly enjoyed the excellent food and the new Burmese friends in Burma Trade. His special request to me was to accompany him to the appointment with the Specialist Doctor to discuss the treatment procedures and I assured him that I would be glad to go along with him. In all such cases of VIP Military patients coming to London for medical treatment the suffering of the patient was compounded first of all by being all alone in a foreign land, limited language capability to communicate with doctors, nurses and hospital caregivers, especially with personal and privacy issues like defecation in bed-pan and insertion of catheter, etc. They were used to getting their way in the Military Hospitals at home such as insisting on attendance by Commissioned Officer male nurses only. In London hospitals such special accommodation was out of the question and the patient goes into deep depression with a false sense of deprivation, hopelessness, resignation to fate and makes a desperate attempt to "hang on to the closest Burmese for everything like a drowning person".

This was the common factor with all the VIP patients whom I was asked to accompany by the top brass in the Ministry of Defense in Rangoon, and more often than not directly by the Directorate of Defense Medical Services, because the Col. Hla Han (Dr.), the Director and Deputy Director Col. Maung Lwin (Dr.) personally knew me since the time I was studying at Tokyo University when they visited Japan with Military Missions led by Gen. Ne Win, Aung Gyi, Tommy Clift or Admiral Than Pe. As such my presence in London establishing and operating Burma Trade Mission had evolved into a multifaceted help and resource center especially for the Ministry of Defense, the Seat of the Revolutionary Council Government. A role that evolved by necessity and not envisaged in the original UK Action Plan Project. As a Buddhist I accepted these unexpected encounters as my fate (Karma), "that our paths crossed in a faraway land where I happen to be and they had come with great expectations and hope to have their serious illnesses cured and return healthy back to their country and anxiously awaiting love ones". Many of them enjoyed the benefit of medical treatment in London and resumed their duties in the Ministry of Defense or Regional Commanders, the ranks that qualified for treatment abroad.

However, more than two decades later, in the mid-eighties, Bo Aung Din showed up in Southern California. His younger daughter, Betty, had married a Marine Guard at the U.S. Embassy in Rangoon, and her husband was transferred back to the Marine Base near San Diego and he was visiting them on his way to join his son Billy in London. I drove more than a hundred miles to the Base for a reunion with Bo Aung Din, Betty and her two toddlers. He was in failing health but did not specify the medical condition. He complained bitterly the suffering he and his children went through in Burma and how fortunate and lucky for you that "the Army Goons were afraid to touch you because the #1 knows you well since your student days in Japan and the Military Intelligence knows you are one of his (Japan Pyan man). I also learned that we were not detained because of your position".

Bo Aung Din continued, "I wanted to tell you before I leave this world, how much I regretted not accepting your sincere and most generous offer for me to stay behind in London. I owe you an apology for suspecting that your offer was a lure into a trap, as my mindset and perception was preoccupied with your (Legal Adviser) Official Position in the Ministry of Defense. Additionally, your close personal connection to Bo Ne Win, Bo Aung Gyi, Bo Maung Lwin (Moustache) and Bo Khin Nyo, four most powerful Army Officers of the Revolutionary Council. I did not realize at that time that it was because of your close personal and working relations with them that you confidently offered me the opportunity and I turned it down. I learned later from my Boss, Bo Tommy Clift (Air Force Chief), the message he sent you to extend any help for my private and personal plans."

It was a strict basic rule to avoid any mention of "sources and/or names" at all times. I was very happy and appreciated his sincere effort to tell me face-to-face that I was "on the level" with him, two decades previously and he blew it and paid a heavy price. That was the last time I met Bo Aung Din and his daughter Betty at the family quarters in the U.S. Marine base near San Diego. He was looking forward to settling down in London with his son Billy. After all, that was the place where he spent the best time with his entire family including his beloved wife and mother before their passing. It was his home and he went back. The final phase of the transfer process to the Ambassador was complicated, stressful for all concerned and delayed several times because H. E. U Hla Maung could not reconcile himself with the reality that he would be the sole legal owner of Burma Trade, operate and manage the Company until the time Rangoon decided what to do with it. He insisted that all payments due to the Law and Accounting Firms of both parties were settled before he signed the final transfer documents. I privately advised him to continue the services of our Law and Accounting Firms and additionally to involve them in the day-to-day operation and management of the Company on agreed "Management and Consulting Fees" until further instructions from Rangoon. He felt more comfortable with that arrangement. The Attorneys and Accountants would be at his disposal any time he needed their advice and guidance.

The Senior Partners of the Ambassador's Law Firm and the Auditing Team completed the review of the Legal Documents of Transfer, the Company's Bank Accounts in the Main Banks, the Stock Transfer Certificates and the Official Acceptance by the British Registrar of Company Stocks and Debentures. The Title Transfer and Official Records of the Interest Bearing Bank of England and City of London Treasury and Development Bonds and the Notarized Release Certificate for Bo Aung Din and myself. The Attorneys, the Accountants, the Auditors, all the Executives and Senior Staff assembled in the Conference Room for the Official Signing Ceremony. The Principal Signatories and Witnesses were:

- His Excellency U Hla Maung, Ambassador Extraordinary and Envoy Plenipotentiary of the Union of Burma, representing the Revolutionary Council and Government.
- Colonel Aye Maung, Defense Services Attaché, and Honorary Chairman of Burma Trade Ltd.
- Lt.Colonel Aung Din (Rtd. Burma Air Force), Managing Director, Burma Trade Ltd.
- U Kyi Win Sein (General Counsel and Legal Adviser, Ministry of Defense), Chief Executive Executive Officer, Burma Trade Ltd., London, U.K.
- U Maung Maung Galay, Secretary of the Board of Directors and Administrative Manager, Burma Trade Ltd., London,
- U Ohn Sein, Executive Director & Manager Government Affairs Department

His Excellency signed all the documents in the presence of all the Executives and Senior Staff of the Corporation, each of the designated signatories signed above their respective names as required by U.K. Law, and the required number of "Official Copies" were ordered to be archived in permanent binders to be secured in the Custody of the Principals involved. It was undoubtedly the most thorough and professional handing over of a private business enterprise to a serving Ambassador in a foreign country. No stone was left unturned in the Auditing of the Company's fixed and current financial assets, the bank accounts, revenues and incomes from various sources to establish that the company was managed according to Law and beyond reproach and any wrongdoing.

Looking back with the benefit of hindsight, U Ba Nyein, the Economic and Financial Adviser, and Bo Tin Phay, the Trade and Commerce Minister sent their henchmen Auditors to London. It was an attempt to "find fault and punch holes in the transfer" but they returned frustrated and grudgingly conceded that the "transfer to H. E. U Hla Maung was done professionally and waterproof for all intents and purposes". The missing money in the "Current Account Cash flow" the Ambassador refused to disclose (by prior personal request of Bo Aung Gyi to avoid "finger pointing and back-biting").

It became intolerable after eight months of interrogation after our return to Rangoon. All the original receipts of the missing money was given to U Ba Nyein in the presence of Bo Chit Khin, Military Intelligence Service Chief (MIS) and both immediately delivered them to Bo Ko Ko, the Secretary of the Revolutionary Council. The missing money was attributed to Bo Aung Gyi and Bo Khin Nyo but it boomeranged back to Bo Tin Phay and his cronies. Bo Ne Win hit the ceiling and was furious. "Hey Ko Ko, call that cripple to come immediately." Bo Ne Win threw the receipts in front of Bo Tin Phay with the question: "How dare you accuse Bo Aung Gyi and BEDC to be Ali BaBa and the Forty Thieves? Who is the real thief that points the finger to the other? Get out of here."

Bo Tin Phay left the Chairman's office distraught, but, lacking moral principle and personal respect, did not resign. In addition, with all that anger and outburst, Bo Ne Win did not fire Bo Tin Phay from service. Bo Chit Khin was asked to explain the circumstances and from whom he had received the receipts (the smoking gun), perhaps thinking that it came from H. E. U Hla Maung in London. However, on learning that after more than eight months of interrogation about the missing money, he said, "U Kyi Win Sein gave me the receipts. Ko Hla Maung wrote to me about the good work handing over everything to him by this young fellow and concerned for his future on return to Rangoon. Those mother f….ing SOBs are bullying this fellow. Keep him in your foreign Economic Security and Embassy Control Unit. The Egyptians, the Yugoslavs, the British and Ko Hla Maung confirmed to me the successful results. Report to me if those idiots continue to mistreat him." Fortunately, I was assigned to be the (Undercover) Officer on Special Intelligence Duty position in the Ministry of Defense by the Chairman, secure and out of reach from the abuse and bullying of the goons under Bo Tin Phay and the vengeance of U Ba Nyein.

However, to protect the undercover position, Bo Chit Khin and Bo Than Sein, Chairman of the Central Security and Administrative Committee, appointed me Legal Adviser to the Nationalization Committee. It was "Officially Classified as a Diversionary Post" in the Confidential Appointment Order copied only to the Office of the Revolutionary Council Chairman and to Bo Chit Khin, Director of Military Intelligence Service, Ministry of Defense.

Ambassador U Hla Maung invited Bo Aung Din, U Maung Maung Galay and myself to his residence for a very private farewell dinner after the signing ceremony and buffet lunch with the Attorneys, Auditors, Officers and Staff was over. It was a very informal and relaxed evening where opinions and personal concerns could be expressed openly and freely, especially after a few cocktails. Bo Aung Din was worried about the immediate future of himself and his three children brought up in the London school system. I noted that the Ambassador went out of his way to stress that in his entire career as Burma's Ambassador, it was the first time for him to be entrusted with such a magnitude of the country's financial assets, and "a private business Corporation that you established in the name of BEDC".

He said: "This is a huge achievement for you personally, and more importantly, your loyalty to the country, the honesty and transparency of handing over to me in such a professional manner are unprecedented. It is highly commendable, and I am very proud and appreciate your helping me to receive everything in perfect order. Return home proudly and without worry, the truth of your excellent work and achievements here are on record and will be a model for generations hereafter." With those kind words of praise and encouragement, our two families took the short flight to Amsterdam the next morning. We were met at Schiphol International Airport by the Captain and crew, including three cabin attendants (MIS Men) to escort us back to Rangoon.

The Pilot and co-pilot were Air Force Officers assigned to run the Union of Burma Airways and, aware that Bo Aung Din was their senior officer, were deferential and respectful. The three cabin attendants mentioned that they had seen me many times in the Ministry of Defense in the company of their Ex-Chief and were very attentive to our every need in addition to carrying our son Bob and all the luggage. Of course, in reality, we were now essentially their captives. We checked into a high-end downtown Amsterdam hotel where everything was prearranged for our arrival from London. The rooms were very comfortable, and the Captain advised us to feel free to order anything from Room Service and sign for it.

After breakfast the next morning, we were informed that the brand new Fokker Friendship High-Wing Turbo-Prop had not passed several final delivery "Inspection Tests" and departure would be delayed a week. We asked the Captain to wire Rangoon requesting permission to take another airline flight to save time and related costs of staying a week at the hotel. The request was denied, insisting that we wait a week and return as planned by the special flight.

After a week of rest and sightseeing in Amsterdam, we finally took off across Europe at rather low altitude and slow speed because the plane was new and this was its first long transcontinental maiden flight. It landed at Athens, Greece in the afternoon for the stopover and we checked in at a downtown hotel. We had some daylight hours to take in a few sights and returned to the hotel for dinner with the Captain and the crew. Apparently, for the first 30 days of regular operation (running-in period), the plane needed to strictly observe the altitude, load, flight time and speed limits. Our next overnight transit stop was the oil rich Island of Bahrain in the Persian Gulf ruled by a very wealthy Arab Sultan.

The hotel management and staff were all Indians, and the restaurant served very good authentic Indian food. The next morning after a leisurely breakfast, we were on our way to Karachi, Pakistan, the final stopover. We checked in at the airport Hilton Hotel and had another Indian food dinner. Our flight arrived in Mingaladon Airport the next afternoon at around 3:30 PM local time. It took three stopovers and one day for the small plane to fly from Amsterdam in Holland to Rangoon. The plane taxied to the terminal, and we did not see any other aircraft, just a few vehicles. As soon as the aircraft engines stopped, the door opened and an Air Force Major (Thein Maung) came aboard, introduced himself as the Chief Security Officer and welcomed us back to Burma, and enquired if we had had a good flight. The reception was contrary to the rumors that we (Bo Aung Din and I) would be taken to Insein Prison.

As a matter of fact, I had prepared my medications, toiletries and some clothes in a small bag and instructed Kazuko to contact the Japanese Ambassador and ask for his assistance to go back to Tokyo with Bob to her family and wait there for my contact. Now, the situation was entirely different and the Major informed me that my friend U Ye Kyaw Thu was waiting to take me home. It was a great surprise and truly a relief. The Major took care of the Immigration and Customs procedures within about 30 minutes and after taking the address where I would be staying he advised that a car would be sent the next morning to that address.

On the way to my family home, Ye Kyaw Thu told me that the Chief Security Officer Major Thein Maung (his cousin) had told him the arrival date and time of our flight and the "planned arrest". However, one hour before arrival, all the extra security personnel and the arresting party were withdrawn by order from the Military Intelligence Service Chief (MIS) Ministry of Defense and instead to assist and ensure all clearance procedures. I was very grateful and appreciated the kindness of Ye Kyaw Thu to meet our flight on advice of his cousin. My Dad, Mom and family were surprised when we got to the small apartment because they had heard the same rumors as we did in London and therefore no one had showed up to meet our flight. All were intimidated and too afraid they would become implicated in my affairs. It was the lowest point of my entire adult life in Burma.

That was the true state of my immediate family's psyche and mindset because there was nothing the family could do without any connection to the "seat of power". I was the only one with that connection and I would have to maneuver my way within the power structure of the Government and get the guidance of officers in the Military that knew me well since my High School days and had helped me get this far in my career. My eldest brother Kyaw Htun Sein (Ivan) and his wife Ma Khin Than kindly shared their small two-bedroom apartment in Yankin diagonal to our parents' place. We at least had a roof over our heads, shared meals and started life all over again from scratch.

# VENDETTA & INTERROGATIONS OF OVERSEAS FUNDS

Early next morning at 7:45, a car came to pick me up and drove me to the Oppenheimer Jones Office Building on Merchant Street. I was ushered to the conference room on the third floor, and Bo Aung Din was already there with three officers (a Lt.Colonel, a Major and a Captain) from the Military Intelligence Service (MIS). The senior officer, in a very courteous and polite manner, told us not to go out of Rangoon without permission and every morning a car would come to bring us here to our Office Rooms now being prepared. He requested our cooperation in answering questions raised by the Government. I waited several minutes for Bo Aung Din to say something, but he kept quiet. Obviously, he was under great stress.

I asked the Lt.Colonel to give us in writing what he had just told us. He wanted to know the reason why I needed it in writing. I explained to him that his orders amounted to "putting us under house-arrest" and "since my wife is a Japanese Citizen, I am obligated to inform the Japanese Embassy in Rangoon to protect and take care of her and our son to return to Japan". He was visibly uncomfortable and taken aback by what I said. He promised to report my request to higher authorities and inform me the next day. I also informed him that my wife would need to extend her stay visa as a dependent of a Government Official (Legal Adviser in the Ministry of Defense), which was her status before our departure for London.

As Senior Military Intelligence Officer, fully aware of my background (and Bio-Data), he became quite nervous in the presence of two junior officers observing their leader losing confidence, unsure of himself, as if being questioned by a superior. I could not help noticing Bo Aung Din's expression of surprise at my demeanor and attitude in dealing with the three MIS Officers. The phone rang, and one of the officers answered and received the message that the two office rooms were ready. We all proceeded to the office rooms on the same floor of the Conference Room across on the other side of the building. Three large individual office rooms in a row with the middle room already occupied (MIS Staff).

Our offices were sparsely furnished, bare minimum Executive Teak Desk, Executive high back chair and two armed chairs in front, wastebasket, hanging hook racks on the wall, and telephone. We were introduced to our personal attendants (actually guards, checkers) sitting outside our office's entry doors. The room between the two offices with all kinds of listening (snooping electronic) devices and the technicians operating them. Our offices were probably set up hurriedly for purposes of interrogation. They told us to feel free to ask the attendants for tea, coffee, soft drinks, water, lunch, light snacks, newspapers, etc.; in reality though, we were being confined to our Offices the entire day for the interrogators to come in any time to question us. At least, we were not under lock and key. That was our consolation the next day after arrival back in Rangoon from London, restricted and practically under house arrest but not in the infamous Insein Prison. While having lunch in my office, Bo Aung Din expressed his concern that taking a hard stance could be detrimental to our immediate welfare and invite a harsh response. He wanted to know if there was any special reason for my pushing them back. I explained to him about the Airport security officer telling Ye Kyaw Thu the order from the Ministry of Defense to withdraw the (MIS) Detention and Arresting Unit one hour before arrival of our special plane and to assist in all clearance, immigration and customs procedures at Mingaladon was clear evidence that the "order came from very high above most probably from the seat of power".

My interpretation of this last-minute order from the Ministry of Defense not to arrest and detain us on arrival likely came from the Revolutionary Council Chairman's Office (Concurrently Minister of Defense). No General Staff Officer below that had the authority to countermand and terminate a detention and arrest order at the last minute of being carried out. I wanted to impress upon the (MIS) Officers the need to strictly observe and follow proper legal procedures in imposing restrictions on our legitimate rights as citizens and Government Officials.

It would also serve to remind them that the highest authority had already intervened on our behalf and there would be serious consequences for improper and/or inappropriate handling of the case. Bo Aung Din did not say anything and stared at me with the expression of "I hope your interpretation is right". We had carried out the instructions of the Government to the letter as evidenced by the certifications and release letters signed by Ambassador U Hla Maung, who was under Orders from Bo Maung Lwin (Moustache), Ex-MIS Chief, to forward all the Transfer Documents to the Chairman of the Revolutionary Council immediately upon completion. He is now Ambassador in Berlin.

The next morning in the Conference Room with the three MIS Officers, the Lt. Colonel informed us that my request for what he had told us yesterday in writing was not compulsory, and he was authorized to confirm that we were not under detention or arrest. Additionally, for visa extension and stay permit of Mrs. Kyi Win Sein, all required assistance with the relevant Ministries and Departments would be arranged by their staff. The (MIS) staff on reasonable advance notice would also arrange any travel out of Rangoon. He in addition stressed that because of our very important overseas responsibilities for BEDC, the authorities would like to take our depositions on many matters concerning the many Enterprises and Corporations in the U.K., Europe and the U.S.A. It became clear to me that Bo Chit Khin, the new MIS Chief, was under orders from Bo Ne Win's office to treat us in a civil manner. It also meant that U Ba Nyein, Bo Tin Phay and his BSPP socialists would no longer be able to use and influence the MIS to do their bidding, at least in our case. Apparently, the official confirmation of our legal status by the Lt. Col was welcome news to Bo Aung Din and thereafter he appeared to be more relaxed and comfortable with the MIS Officers. Earlier that morning, he was under stress and worried sick at the thought of detention and house arrest. That dark cloud was no longer hanging over our heads.

He explained to them the highlights of the transfer procedures, the documents, the certifications and the releases signed by Ambassador U Hla Maung in accordance with the instructions from the then MIS Chief Bo Maung Lwin (Moustache). The Lt. Col said he did not know anything about that order and therefore was unable to comment on it. However, I suggested to him that it would facilitate matters for all concerned, especially his agents, to obtain the complete "transfer folder" from the Ambassador as it contained the entire documented history of BEDC operations, enterprises and corporations in the U. K., Europe and the U.S.A. My strategy was to maneuver the MIS towards Ambassador U Hla Maung, whose strict order was to forward the "whole package to the Revolutionary Council Chairman ONLY".

I was sure that Bo Chit Khin would not dare to approach the Ambassador for the package. Bo Maung Lwin (Moustache) certainly would have briefed him and cautioned him to exercise extra-special care in the matter as Bo Ne Win himself ordered the transfer arrangement to Ambassador U Hla Maung. Anyone poking their nose or even sniffing around would suffer dire consequences. I received several notes from Bo Khin Nyo, Bo Tommy Clift (Air Force Chief) and Bo Maung Lwin (moustache) to take meticulous care and ensure proper transfer and handing over to Ambassador U Hla Maung. "That would be in your best personal interest." I knew exactly what they meant in those cautionary notes to me before their departure from the Ministry of Defense.

Without the transfer package and any clue of what had transpired in London between Burma Trade and Ambassador U Hla Maung, the MIS was at a loss where to begin their interrogation. Several weeks went by reading newspapers, magazines and talking in my office or Bo Aung Din's room. Friends and colleagues would visit us occasionally, and "our attendants" would have them register and sign in the "visitors book", and most did not come back the second time. We did have to fill out "our personal history profile" consisting of a dozen pages as well as those of all siblings, father and mother's immediate families. I had seven brothers and two sisters, father, mother, a Japanese wife, uncles and aunts. I spent many weeks filling in the forms. Once they had reviewed the completed personal and family history profiles, the questioning phase started.

A young lieutenant and a Warrant Officer would come around 9:30 AM three times a week and asked all kinds of questions; some were trivial and bizarre, concerning personal, private and family matters. The Warrant Officer took notes on a clipboard and carried packets of paper in a shan shoulder-bag. I was a heavy smoker at that time and consumed two or three packs a day. The ceiling fan was not good enough to get the smoke out of the room through the two windows, and a new table fan was brought in by the MIS officers and placed on the sideboard. It made breathing much better, but the humidity and temperature remained high (37-40C) and very uncomfortable, to say the least.

A wall-mounted air conditioner no longer functioned. Bo Aung Din was going through the same suffering. We took a very bold step and requested that they replace the air conditioners with functioning ones, without any expectation of compliance. However, to our surprise and delight, new air conditioners were installed immediately and our life in the interrogation rooms became more bearable. It was yet another clear indication that the MIS was making every effort to ensure that our "complaints" did not go beyond them. At this moment in time, there was no doubt in my mind that the transfer package was safely in the hands of Bo Ne Win, and no one dared to approach him or even raise any question on the matter. It was, at the present time, urgently imperative for him to make his move before the level below him became aware of what had been handed over to Ambassador U Hla Maung by the two BEDC men under direct orders from the supreme ruler through his Intelligence Chief.

Ambassador U Hla Maung was kept holding the bag until his close friend, the supreme boss of Burma, decided what he wanted to do with the huge cash and assets accumulated by the BEDC under the leadership of Bo Aung Gyi, Bo Khin Nyo and Bo Maung Lwin (Moustache). All three had been pushed out of the Military. The two executives responsible for the success of "The Action Plan" and the smooth transfer to the Ambassador according to his orders were now back in Burma with complete knowledge of the "contents of the transfer package". The MIS was merely going through "the motion" of interrogation because they had no clue about what had transpired in London and were afraid of broaching the subject with us without prior approval from the Prime Minister (Bo Ne Win), under whose jurisdiction BEDC was Administered by an Act of the dismissed Parliament. Notwithstanding the recent national events and developments, the Administration and Control of BEDC has always been under the Jurisdiction of the Prime Minister or his nominee. The Action Plan itself was set up by order of Bo Ne Win under a Committee led by Bo Aung Gyi, the then BEDC Chairman nominated by the then Prime Minister U Nu. After the March 02 Coup, Bo Khin Nyo was nominated Chairman by Prime Minister Bo Ne Win with orders to report to Bo Aung Gyi, the Vice Chief of General Staff (VCGS).

The Committee Members included: Bo Than Phay (Navy Chief), Bo Tommy Clift (Air Force Chief), Bo Maung Lwin (Moustache), Military Intelligence Chief, Bo Khin Nyo, Director of Military training, Bo Thaung Kyi (Deputy Chief of Navy) among others. I was concurrently assigned to the Committee (from the Export-Import Bank of Burma) as International Law Adviser. After the Coup on March 02, 1962, I was sent as TRADE REPRESENTATIVE by the Revolutionary Council to implement the Action Plan and consolidate all BEDC Enterprises and Corporations in the U.K., Europe and the U.S.A. under one Private Commercial Organization (BURMA TRADE ENTERPRISES) in London.

Bo Chit Khin, the new MIS Chief and his senior staff officers appeared to be unaware of the "Ad-hoc groups" set up by the Commander-in-Chief in the Ministry of Defense made up of selected officers tasked to deal with "special operations" only and disbanded thereafter. No records remain, except in the memory of those directly involved. It was the "Modus Operandi" of Bo Ne Win, which he adopted from the Japanese Imperial Staff Command Practice and his training at the Nakano Intelligence School on the Eve of the Imperial Army's invasion of Burma with the 30 Comrades leading the newly formed Burma Independence Army (BIA).

The subjects of interrogation became personal and directed at individuals with the passage of time as well as the rank of the interrogator – a Captain and a Senior Warrant Officer taking the notes. They wanted to know how much money was given to Bo Aung Gyi, Bo Khin Nyo, Bo Betrim Barber (Navy), Bo Tommy Clift (Air Force Chief) and Bo Than Phay (Navy Chief), and where that money was hidden. The firm and emphatic response from both of us was "absolutely none". The same question was repeated countless times and response was the same. Then, they wanted to know the total cash and assets handed over to Ambassador U Hla Maung. We told them to get the information from the Ambassador because of the "Confidentiality and Non-Disclosure Clause" in the Certifications and Documents of the Transfer Package that was ordered by Bo Maung Lwin (Moustache), Ex-Chief of Military Intelligence to be forwarded to the Chairman of the Revolutionary Council only. Upon hearing the response, the Captain backed off. It was clear evidence that the Economic and Financial Adviser U Ba Nyein, Bo Tin Phay and his BSPP Socialists could not get the transfer package from the Ambassador despite their pressure on the Foreign Minister, U Thi Han. It also was an indication that they pressured Bo Chit Khin, the MIS Chief, to get the information from us. So far, we have held them off successfully.

All the cards were in the hands of the supreme leader Bo Ne Win. In the meantime, we continued to suffer our ordeal in our guarded office rooms repeatedly answering the identical questions with the equivalent answers, smoking more cigarettes. We clearly noted that the MIS was frustrated, perhaps even more than us because of the severe limitations under which they had to operate and the extraordinary precautions they had to take in the daily interactions with us. It was risky and very high stakes business for all concerned. A mistake, and that could end one's career and land one in prison for a long spell. Many executives of BEDC Corporations were incarcerated.

The moderate and elite military senior officers continued to be marginalized, retired off or those speaking openly about their personal opinions detained and interrogated. The regime was intolerant and ultra-sensitive to dissent, especially from within the Military, the Police and the Civil Service. Our interrogation continued as usual but now an Army Major was team leader. Their primary focus was still on the total cash in the British Banks, the convertible interest bearing assets and the real property and estates handed over to Ambassador U Hla Maung in London. U Ba Nyein and Bo Tin Phay desperately wanted to know the contents of the entire transfer package but at the same time were afraid that the Supreme Ruler would misconstrue their intent in poking their nose in the matter directly under the jurisdiction of the Prime Minister's Office. Moreover, the fact that Bo Ne Win was keeping the package close to his chest for this long period was an indication of having his own personal disposal plan.

Our consistent response was "the Non-Disclosure Agreement in the Transfer Documents" prevents us from disclosing and they (the MIS) need to get it directly from the Ambassador or have him give us a legal waiver or release in writing permitting unconditional full disclosure of the Transfer Package Documents. Several weeks passed, and it was clear that the Ambassador did not comply with their request, or it might be that they (MIS) were afraid and did not ask him at all. The latter was more likely. However, U Ba Nyein, the

Economic and Financial Adviser, did not acquiesce to reality and pursued a combination of bureaucratic and political strategy of soliciting the help of Bo San Yu, the Finance and Revenue Minister, and Bo Than Sein, the Chairman of Central Security and administrative Committee as well as the Nationalization Committee. He had been a bureaucrat in the same Ministry before joining the ranks of the National United Front. This devious move was typical communist tactics to sow seeds of doubt at the top of the Government Ministries.

U Ba Nyein advised the Finance Minister that the BEDC cash and assets in London needed to be incorporated in the National Treasury Account and subsequently in the Financial Year Budget after Auditing conducted by the Accountant General's Auditing Team to be sent to London. To Bo Than Sein, an Official Notification was served to Regularize the Nationalization of BEDC Corporations. However, the fatal flaw in the strategy of the Economic Adviser as well as Bo Tin Phay, was their "cast in concrete certainty" that Bo Aung Din was the protégé of the Air Force Chief and U Kyi Win Sein was Bo Aung Gyi's Man.

Oblivious to them was the fact that the Action Plan to retrieve and recover hidden money overseas by the politicians and their Sino-Burmese, Indo-Burmese business cronies was Bo Ne Win's plan based on Bo Maung Lwin's (Moustache) report and the Egyptian Covert Operation success. Bo Aung Gyi was entrusted to lead both projects. Bo San Yu was personally close to Bo Aung Gyi and a bedroom was reserved for him at Dagon House, the Official Residence of Bo Aung Gyi. Bo Than Sein was Adjutant General and then Colonel General Staff, always in "the loop" of activities (Projects) "initiated by Bo Ne Win" and managed by Bo Aung Gyi.

Now, when Bo San Yu and Bo Than Sein received U Ba Nyein's policy recommendations, they immediately, almost by instinct, saw "red flags". Both consulted Bo Chit Khin, the Intelligence Chief on the matter of the "policy recommendations" proposed by the Economic Adviser, and he confirmed that the matter was in the hands of the Boss and was not aware of any action taken yet. Concerning the BEDC funds and assets overseas (in the U.K. and Europe), Ambassador U Hla Maung received custody from the two officers as instructed by the Prime Minister and both had since returned with written certifications of satisfactory receipt by the Ambassador. Bo San Yu and Bo Than Sein were aware of the "Action Plan" from the outset, who had initiated it and personally selected the Committee members to assist Bo Aung Gyi, one of whom was Bo Maung Lwin (Moustache), Chief of MIS at that time and I was seconded (from BOC) as Legal Adviser of the Committee. All the senior Army, Navy and Air Force Committee members were no longer in the Ministry of Defense. The only civilian involved from inception, planning, implementation, organization set-up, operation in London and transfer to Ambassador U Hla Maung was now back in Burma and not allowed to leave Rangoon without prior permission. They were under interrogation and protected by the Military Intelligence at the same time by the direct countermand from the Ministry of Defense withdrawing the arrest on arrival by special flight at the Mingaladon Airport.

The Ministry of Home Affairs under Minister Bo Kyaw Soe issued the Order at the official request of the Ministry of Commerce and Trade under Minister Bo Tin Phay. They were going after Bo Aung Gyi's men in BEDC. The two from Burma Trade London would be their final big catch together with all the overseas funds, assets and real estate. Their plan was over-ruled at the last minute by the intervention of the Commander-in-Chief who had his own agenda. My good friend (Tennis) U Maung Maung, Deputy Secretary of the Ministry of Trade and Commerce (elder brother of Bo Ko Ko, Revolutionary Council Secretary) made a surprise visit to my room during the lunch hour. He told me in strict confidence that Ambassador U Hla Maung had sent the transfer package addressed by name to Bo Ne Win through the diplomatic pouch.

In the covering letter, he expressed his appreciation of the exceptional help and cooperation he had received and the professionally audited transfer he had accepted from the two executives, the cash, assets and titles of all the properties. He also stated that the two officers had returned as instructed by special plane despite the information from BEDC Rangoon Office that arrest and interrogation order had been issued by the Ministry of Commerce and Trade. Bo Ne Win received the package in the afternoon of the day the special flight was scheduled to arrive. He was infuriated by the information and ordered Bo Ko Ko to check with Bo Chit Khin, the Intelligence Chief, what actually was going on and to cancel the arrest plans and have the order terminated. It confirmed what the Airport Security Chief told his cousin, Ye Kyaw Thu the day of our arrival.

Now, the picture became very clear that our fate took a dramatic and positive turn by the letter of Ambassador U Hla Maung to the Revolutionary Council Chairman Bo Ne Win that he received just in time. The new aircraft failing the final delivery tests and the subsequent one-week delay in Amsterdam probably was preordained from above that saved us. That was the firm belief of Bo Aung Din, a devout Baptist. When I received the information from U Maung Maung, I sighed in relief with the realization of the Ambassador's extraordinary effort to inform the Head of State the dire fate awaiting the two officers on arrival and the cancellation at the last moment. It was indeed a big sigh of relief because from this stage onwards, our tormentors would have to contend with an answer to the ultimate authority of the country.

We gratefully appreciated the Ambassador's intervention on our behalf with his friend who responded with immediate strong action. This information, we learned later, was passed on to the senior Ministry of Defense officers through the usual secure channels, because I began to receive contacts from much-unexpected officials of the Ministry. Such as, U Maung Maung, the Defense Secretary and Bo Kyi Maung (Zatlaik – Actor), the Colonel General Staff who had succeeded Bo Than Sein, the Chairman of the Central Security and Administration Committee and the Nationalization Committee. It was encouraging, and a very reassuring indication that officers in positions of influence in the defense establishment were certain there was no need to hesitate or exercise discretion in contacting me for personal reasons.

U Maung Maung, the Defense Secretary, wanted to receive first-hand information about his younger brother U Maung Maung Gale. Bo Kyi Maung had come to London for medical treatment, and Burma Trade provided all the assistance he needed at the request of Bo Khin Nyo and Bo Maung Lwin (Moustache). The medical treatment was successful and he fully recovered. We became good personal friends, and he wanted to reciprocate the help we had extended to him during his long stay in London. He was a truly decent and sincere man, and we had a highly enjoyable reunion. U Maung Maung has not seen his younger brother since 1947. He thanked me profusely for looking after his brother and appointing him Manager of General Affairs when the Burmese Embassy and Rowe and Co. employed him in clerical positions only.

I reminded U Maung Maung that his brother had graduated from Rangoon University in 1947 when I was in third standard (3rd grade), and he only needed "two dinners" to graduate as Barrister and be called to the English Bar. He was well qualified for the position, and I truly appreciated his cooperation, guidance and support. I did not do anything special. I was the one who had gained from his experience and insight into the British system, its culture and business practice. He was the scion of the British Crown knighted Sir Maung Ba family in Colonial Burma and a highly respected Permanent Secretary (BCS Senior Branch) of the Ministry of Defense. However, he was fully aware of the Burmese community rumor mill in London which went wild with negative reaction and was openly critical of employing Burmese laid off by the Embassy to Managerial Positions in Burma Trade. I confess that Bo Aung Din did mildly express his reservations but quickly supported the appointments when Bo Khin Nyo confirmed that it was in accordance with the "terms of reference of the Action Plan Implementation Director and (Legal Adviser)" to set up the Umbrella Organization in London as deemed necessary by the circumstances on the ground. The critical and negative rumors were manifestation of the colonial mindset and I had learned to ignore them a long way back in my High School days in Mandalay and Bassein (now Pathein).

We received information that Bo Ne Win's team led by Ambassador Maung Lwin (Moustache) that included his wife Katy, and a cousin (younger brother) had gone to London and discussed with U Hla Maung and the Firm of Attorneys concerning the package in his custody. Under British Law, the Ambassador was the lawful Owner and essentially, with all rights to dispose of them in any way or form that he wishes. The Attorneys would ensure correct legitimate procedures and applicable Documentation; Registration with Local and Central Government Agencies through relevant channels was completed. In fact, that was the outcome of the team's visit. U Hla Maung transferred certain parts, portions or percentage of the package to the team (specifics and details unknown).

The balance (specifics unknown) transferred to the New Management of Burma Trade, the Ministry of Trade and Commerce and the Cash, Financial Assets to the Ministry of Finance and Revenue (details and specifics unknown). The primary principals in the episode have all passed on, but I recall vividly that U Hla Maung retired soon after the transfers were completed. On his return to Burma, he elected to convey information to me through reliable and secure mutual friends for the protection of all concerned. In one of them, he did confirm the visit of the team and the help and guidance of our Law Firm that had "stood by him at all times". That said a lot to me. It clearly meant that Sir Guy Hambling, Barrister Templeton Smith and Barrister Clive Richardson continued to protect our interests and stood by the Ambassador after our departure.

What transpired in London was confirmed by the dramatic turn in the line of questioning by our interrogators. An Army Major, Khin Zaw, was leader, and he began asking for the missing money in the final financial documents. Apparently, the Law Firm ensured that the accurate Payments and Receipts documents were included in the Package transferred to the Ministry of Finance and Revenue by the Ambassador. We told the MIS major that the missing money involved extraordinary and discretionary disbursements of the Management and could not be disclosed. That response aroused their suspicion that there was more money hidden in secret Swiss bank accounts or some in Europe. The Major focused his questioning on the missing money and insinuated that there was more money hidden considering the large cash, assets and bonds in the folder received from the Ambassador. From "their perception of large", it was evident to us that Ambassador Maung Lwin's (Moustache) team took whatever they wanted and handed over the substantial balance amount to the Government. We were now dealing with basic human nature of disbelief, greed and suspicion. If BEDC gave up this large amount, they must have hidden some for themselves. That line of interrogation and insinuation continued for several weeks.

We tolerated and endured several more months of the monotonous daily interrogations and at times intimidations, veiled threats as well as rewards for cooperation (giving the information they wanted). After almost eight months of questioning, I told Bo Aung Din that this unjustified treatment had gone on too long, and I was not going to take it anymore. He expressed concern but did not object. The next morning, I informed Bo Khin Zaw, the MIS team leader, that I would not answer any of his questions, and I must talk to Bo Chit Khin immediately. He was shocked and visibly shaken. He left the room with his Warrant Officer. Both returned after about an hour and inquired if I was feeling all right. He also wanted to know the reason why I was refusing to cooperate. I told him Bo Chit Khin was the only one I would talk to on the question of the missing money. I asked him to arrange the meeting at the earliest possible date.

Two days later, Bo Khin Zaw escorted Bo Aung Din and I to Bo Chit Khin's office in the Ministry of Defense at around 9:00 AM. The reception was very polite and courteous with coffee/tea and cakes served as soon as we took our seats in front of his desk. We engaged in small talk for the first few minutes to break the ice. He then asked the reason for wanting to see him so urgently. I told him that we wanted to disclose to him the information on the missing money that his agents had been asking us for nearly eight months. He smiled broadly, and his expression brightened as I handed him a large brown unmarked envelope together with a file folder. I explained that it contained all the relevant records, signed receipts and original notes on the missing money.

He reviewed the contents very closely for about five minutes and his expression dramatically changed to concern and worry. His composure dissipated and he was lost for words. He sat frozen in his chair, silent and staring beyond the two of us sitting in front of his desk. It felt like eternity. When he finally regained his composure, he stammered and confessed that he could not handle this matter. He asked us to accompany him to meet U Ba Nyein, the Economic and Financial Adviser in the Ministry of Finance and Revenue. He ordered his aide to notify that office that he was on his way. It was a short drive from the Ministry of Defense to the Ministry of Finance and Revenue in the old Secretariat Complex.

We were ushered into the Economic Adviser's office and noted that he was sipping from a small teacup, typically for plain Burmese tea. The three of us sat in front of his desk, and the host offered no tea, which was very unusual. Burmese protocol requires the host to have visitors join in having the tea together. Later, we learned that the teakettle on his desk contained not tea but his favorite alcoholic drink. He was a hardened alcoholic and incapable of functioning without it in his system.

Bo Chit Khin handed over the folder and the envelope to the Economic Adviser and briefly explained the nature of the contents. While opening the folder and envelope, he sarcastically remarked that it would have helped all concerned if the information had been received earlier. We noted that as he was reviewing the contents, he was sobering up quickly and soon his expression was that of a very distraught man. He wanted to know the reason for our not disclosing earlier. I countered his question with "do you really want to know the reason?". He was taken aback by the question. He looked at Bo Chit Khin as if asking, "What do you think?" There was no response.

U Ba Nyein said almost in a whisper that he would like to know the reason. I told him that Bo Aung Gyi sent me a message all the way from Machanbaw to London to avoid "Parkait Narkait" (– Bite Cheek Bite Ear) and to cooperate fully with the Government without involving personalities. Bo Aung Din and I had respected and honored this guidance from Bo Aung Gyi, but we had been treated like criminals for the past eight months without any justification whatsoever. I asked him bluntly, "How could you do that to us?" I also told him firmly that I would use every means at my disposal to inform the truth to the highest authority in the country.

Both sat in their chairs stunned at what they heard. U Ba Nyein in a roundabout way said he was sorry to hear about our suffering and promised that the Burma Trade case was closed as far as he, and his office, was concerned. He requested Bo Chit Khin to immediately close the interrogations and arrange our reinstatement in the appropriate Ministry or Department. We noted that Bo Chit Khin did not respond to that request. He was fully aware that the information must be immediately forwarded to Bo Ne Win's office. A few days later, U Maung Maung, the Senior Deputy Secretary of the Ministry of Commerce and Trade told me that U Ba Nyein had gone to Bo Ne Win's office soon after we left his office and handed over the folder and envelope to the Supreme leader in the presence of Bo Ko Ko, the Revolutionary Council Secretary. That was the end of Bo Tin Phay's influence and subsequently his military career. Bo Ne Win also asked Bo Chit Khin to ensure that "there shall be no ill treatment of the two Burma Trade Officers" and to keep the "young fellow" in Economic Insurgency Suppression Department (National Intelligence Bureau) under the Military Intelligence Service. He came to my temporary office alone and informed me of the orders from "your Aphay-Gyi" and new job assignment.

I told him that I did not wish to serve in any of the jobs and requested that he arrange for me to leave the country. He was aghast at my attitude and bluntly told me that he was not going to risk his neck to tell Bo Ne Win that I refused to accept his orders. We would both be in serious trouble, he warned. His brotherly advice was, obey his orders and accept the job assignment and several years in the future get his permission to leave the country. He promised to help at that future date IF he survived in the Chief of Military Intelligence position. Overall, it was very decent of Bo Chit Khin to come up with a compromise resolution in my personal interest, avoid upsetting the big boss, and pursue the safe path for now and the immediate future.

He told me that the Economic Insurgency Suppression Department of NIB was the "Undercover Operation" and a diversion position in the Ministry of Commerce and Trade would be included in the Official Government Gazette for Public Knowledge as required by Law. The general public identity would be the Trade Ministry Position only and the "Undercover Operation Positions" would be Classified and undisclosed at all times. That was the outcome after eight months of suffering at the instigation of U Ba Nyein, the Economic Adviser, Bo Tin Phay and his harebrained Army cronies. I realized the nature of the unsavory work I would have to carry out for the Regime as well as becoming the scapegoat for the harsh "extra-judicial measures" in suppression of economic insurgency perceived (real or imagined) by BSPP and the Military.

On the personal, family and living arrangements, I requested that Bo Chit Khin arrange government-housing quarters but he said living in close proximity with other Government Officials would not be appropriate for obvious reasons. I needed to live in the general community with normal and ordinary neighbors as a government employee. He advised me to find a house for rent. Luckily for me a two-bedroom cottage in Pyidawaye Avenue, off Gaba-Aye Road next to Bagyi U Sein's house was vacant and the owner agreed to lease it to me. Bo Chit

Khin was very happy with the location as it was close to a main road and also to Boundary Road MIS Office Complex.

In late spring 1964, we moved in quickly and settled down to life in Rangoon and Robert (Bob) was admitted to Saint Augustine School on Inya Road, a few miles away. Kazuko was teaching at the Japanese School but soon worked for the Japanese Embassy. Bo Chit Khin was informed, and he said there was no problem. In fact, it was good to have one of our own inside a foreign Diplomatic Mission in Rangoon, in the event that the need arises to counter-check and verify "our own sources". That eventuality did arise a few years later and produced the desired outcome for both Governments. Within a few months of our living in our new home, Kazuko conceived our second child, and life became more complicated and hectic with pre-natal medical care at the Seventh-Day Adventist Hospital located outside the entrance to the Ministry of Defense.

It was at this time that something unexpected and extraordinary happened, that one only reads in religious literature and stories of birth and rebirth in Buddhist Mythology. I shared the good news of the second child with Bagyi U Sein, and was truly surprised and taken aback when he said he was expecting to hear it from me. I asked him how in the world he knew of it. He told me that his mother had appeared in his dreams and told him she would be reincarnated as a daughter in the family of a relative living next door, but that she would not be too long in his life, as she must go far away. I could not believe what I heard because he was not a religious man by any measure and was very well-known in the Burmese Journalist, Political and Diplomatic Community as a "hard drinker" who loves his alcohol well and was not known to believe in such Buddhistic beliefs. He was telling me something very profound in Buddhist philosophy, with a very large percentage of the Myanmars believing in the reincarnation concept.

Yes indeed, his dream did materialize on July 06, 1965; Kazuko gave birth to a baby girl under extremely difficult and complicated political circumstances. However, despite the dire state of national affairs and chaos in the health care system all help essential to bring the baby into the world came to the rescue at the right time. It was a wet and rainy evening around 8 PM when out of the blue my friend Duwa Maran Jala showed up, umbrella in hand. While conversing with Maran, Kazuko had her first contraction. I called my eldest brother Kyaw Htun Sein (Ivan) who came over in his huge old Buick. We all three got into the car (leaving Bob with the maid) and drove to Seventh-Day Adventist Hospital in front of the Ministry of Defense. The gate was closed, and the security guard reminded us that the hospital had been nationalized a day ago and told us to take the patient to the Government's Dufferin Childbirth Hospital, notorious for poor facilities and overcrowding. Maran, a Catholic, suggested that we rush to a Missionary Hospital in South Okklapa satellite town where he was known to the nuns. We got there just in time and with the help of Maran, Kazuko was admitted at around 11:30 PM and wheeled on a stretcher directly to the delivery room.

Within about 30 minutes, a nun came to the waiting room, took me to the delivery room to see our daughter, and promised to move the baby and mother into a private room. Thanks to my late brother Ivan and my friend Maran, everything worked out well that rainy night when Sayoko was born. Early the next morning I informed Bo Chit Khin about the problems I had had the previous night and complained to him about the rejection at Seventh-Day Adventist Hospital despite the advance deposit I had paid for the delivery and private room. He advised me to take a week off from work and to let him know if I needed any help. When I arrived at the hospital, Kazuko and the baby were in their private room with a nurse in attendance.

When I went out of the room, there was an American standing at the door of the next room and with outstretched hand he introduced himself as Henry Byroade, the U.S. Ambassador in Rangoon. He had had the same problem at Seventh-Day Adventist Hospital last night and ended up in South Okklapa Catholic Missionary Hospital too. I asked Henry how many children he had and the answer surprised me "three of hers, two of mine and one of ours and with the new one just born would make it six". We met every morning for five days and became friends. He was a retired Brigadier General of the U.S. Army and had married the daughter of General George Marshall (renowned for the Marshall Plan redevelopment of Europe after WWII).

When I went to the office after the morning hospital visits, I received a note from Bo Chit Khin that the American Ambassador's wife was in the next room to Kazuko's at the same hospital. Apparently, it was a cautionary reminder to avoid inappropriate conversation with a foreign diplomatic head of mission. After five days in hospital, mother and baby were discharged to go home. That same day, the Catholic Missionary Hospital in South Okklapa was nationalized. The nationalization frenzy of the BSPP was gaining momentum, and the country was becoming a Socialist Security State backed up by the Military. Two weeks after the birth of our daughter, Bo Chit Khin (a Karen) called me to his office and in the presence of two other officers asked me several questions about Duwa Maran Jala. And he then revealed to me that he had defected and crossed the border into Thailand with the assistance of the Karen Insurgents and joined the leadership of the Kachin Independence Army. All my answers corroborated with their surveillance folder information on Duwa Maran Jala that included his visit to our house that fateful night and the drives to the two hospitals and my brother dropping off Maran at his home after 1 AM that morning. I had to go through the same ordeal when Ye Kyaw Thu, Tin Maung Win and his father U Win (Ex-Ambassador to USA) crossed the border into Thailand with the assistance of the Karen Insurgents. U Win suffered a heart attack during the long trek through the malaria-infested tropical jungle and had to be buried along the wayside, as Army units were hot on their heels. They crossed over into Thailand and joined U Nu's doomed rebellion to overthrow Bo Ne Win.

The daily work environment at the Ministry of Commerce and Trade where one of my offices was located and another at the Myanmar Export-Import Corporation right next to the U.S. Embassy Chancery was tense, uncomfortable and stressful to say the least. All the officers and staff, regardless of rank were not permitted to meet visiting businessmen from abroad except in the designated Conference Room with another officer and an official interpreter / translator taking memo of every word of the conversation and recorded on tape as well, at a humongous cost of money, time and manpower. It was a daily nightmare of bureaucratic red tape; an unimaginable amount of paperwork had to be signed and approved despite the painful calluses on my fingers, in addition to attending meetings and listening to tapes and reading stacks of transcripts for hours, often late into the night.

The economy was spiraling down under the BSPP Socialist State controlled People's enterprises, and the agricultural production dwindled to such an extent of causing rice shortage – unthinkable in a country known as the "rice bowl of Asia". Exports fell and foreign exchange reserves were exhausted; import of medicines and essential machinery and spares were reduced to the lowest survival levels. The health care system was in chaos and there was untold suffering, especially among children and the elderly. The ideology based experiment of social engineering forced on the people by the above ground Communists, and the Military was dragging the country down to ruin. It was clear even at that early stage. Marshall Tito of Yugoslavia, British Socialist Prime Minister Harold Wilson and Chancellor of the Exchequer Cunningham were aghast and sent private emissaries to gently persuade Bo Ne Win to change course and not to make the same mistakes they had done in their State controlled Command economies. At that time, Prime Minister Harold Wilson's Economic Adviser was Dr. Hla Myint (Ex-Burmese), a highly respected economist and recognized expert on Socialist economies in British and European academia. At the outset of implementing the "Hidden Funds Recovery Action Plan" in London, we did receive invaluable guidance from him through the personal request of Bo Aung Gyi and U Kyaw Myint Lay, the first Burmese Economics Professor in Rangoon University.

In March 1962, the Revolutionary Council approached him to guide the country's economy but citing old age (he was in his eighties) he suggested (not recommended) Ba Nyein because Hla Myint had left the country as both studied under him. Before passing away U Kyaw Myint Lay expressed deep regret and confessed to close friends that suggesting the alcoholic (ahyet-thamar) for economic adviser was the biggest mistake (maha-ahmar) of his life. He lived to witness the horrendous nationalization excesses of his student U Ba Nyein and the half-baked Socialist Bo Tin Phay. It took the country back to primitive Banana Republic existence and created a huge black market smuggling parallel economy along the long borders with China and Thailand. All the armed ethnic insurgents greatly benefited from "safe passage taxes", extortions and setting up their own smuggling operations. It also made the Army regional Commanders more powerful War Lords at the top of the "food chain". The Chinese Communists and the Thai border troops made their own local deals with the smuggling rings (later consortiums) and made huge amounts of quick money. Extraordinary, elaborate and advanced monitoring and surveillance systems were acquired, put into operation to "keep an eye" on all foreign missions in the country 24/7, especially in Rangoon. Bo Chit Khin advised me of the new additional task assigned to my office: to review the English and Japanese "voice intercepts" with a team of specialist staff to assist with the transcriptions, report preparation and record keeping.

The information gleaned from the intercepts was shocking to put it mildly. It was no surprise that diplomatic missions were engaged in spying, infiltration and cultivating "moles" within the key Ministries and Departments. However, the Americans and British were blatantly abusing their diplomatic status and plotting destabilization and "Regime Change" as their primary foreign policy objectives in Burma. The intercepts revealed that the level of arrogance, hypocrisy and disrespect for the host Government by the WEST was unbelievable. The Military Regime and its intelligence services under Bo Chit Khin (MIS) and the Regional Commands under Bo Kyi Maung (Colonel General Staff) took extraordinary pro-active measures against the "foreign interference" in the internal affairs of the country and along the border regions.

The Americans and the British stepped up their exploitation of the ethnic insurgencies through the Thai political and military channels to widen and exacerbate the divisions with the majority Burmese. The World Bank, IMF, Asian Development Bank and OECD, the instruments of American led "unified Western Regime change policy" started a disinformation and denigration campaign with all kinds of "reports and papers" on Burma's economy and predictions of dire consequences and the country close to becoming a "failed state". The U.S. went as far as pressuring the Japanese Government to stop giving Official Development Aid (ODA) to Burma. Post WWII Japan, ruled mostly by the Liberal Democratic Party (LDP), made up of Dynastic Families and their business cronies were totally subservient to American dictates on their Foreign Policy.

It was a humongous undertaking in terms of cost, human resources, time and the inevitable intrusion and harsh punitive actions taken against the collaborators on a nation-wide scale. Looking back half a century in hindsight, it was the most uncomfortable and stressful period of my life in Burma. It compounded my stress factors with a Japanese wife working in her Embassy and the sensitive job assignment and simultaneous tasks I had to carry out in close proximity with the enforcers of the regime's security policies on the economy, international trade and foreign interference in the internal affairs of the country. On purely personal terms, my immediate superiors, Bo Chit Khin, the Military Intelligence Chief, and Bo Than Sein, the Chairman of the Nationalization Committee treated me very well with respect, consideration and courtesy. Many executives of BEDC Corporations were laid off summarily, detained without charges for years because they worked for Government owned Trade and Commercial enterprises under the leadership of Bo Aung Gyi (the derogatory slur was – Ali BaBa and the forty thieves).

Many wondered why the two from Burma Trade London did not suffer the same fate despite their high profile management roles in the consolidation of all BEDC Joint Venture Enterprises in the UK, Europe and the USA. Those without a clue of the truth circulated wild speculations, innuendo and rumors of betrayal, whistle blowing and throwing the entire BEDC group to the wolves. Oblivious to them was that the Action Plan was Bo Ne Win's covert project for control of politicians' hidden funds in the West. Bo Aung Gyi was entrusted with the task of implementation, operation and management of the project. Only a selected few in the Ministry of Defense knew of the project planned well before the March 02, 1962 Coup.

Bo Than Sein was Colonel General Staff at that time and selected to attend some of the planning sessions. Bo Chit Khin revealed to me that he only knew of the project when Bo Maung Lwin (Moustache) briefed him on the special international projects and handed over the job to him. I am certain that this memoir will be the first time to reveal the true background history of so much speculation on what transpired in London and who was actually the prime mover behind it. It was and is so blatantly cruel and unfair to assign blame on the late Bo Aung Gyi who discharged his responsibilities with absolute honesty, highest moral integrity and loyalty to his country and the Tatmadaw to the very end of his life. Despite the fallout with Bo Ne Win on "national policy and direction of the country", his personal regard for the man remained intact and he communicated openly to urge change of direction and to a great extent Bo Ne Win accepted them.

Bo Ne Win on his part confessed to U Kyaw Nyein how much he regretted the departure of Bo Aung Gyi from the Army and blamed himself for allowing misunderstanding to creep into their relations. Politicians of all stripes and colors recognize that Bo Aung Gyi and Bo Maung Maung reorganized, restructured and modernized the ragtag undisciplined groups of Militias, Union Military Police, Red Flag, White Flag rampaging armed mercenaries into a professional military institution of the country and actually anointed Bo Ne Win, first the Commander-in-Chief and later the paramount ruler of the country. That historical fact must not be swept under the rug and it is incumbent upon the current leaders of the Myanmar Military to accept and recognize the accomplishments of these leaders that built the bedrock foundation of today's Tatmadaw.

This fact and reality were not lost on him when he found himself left with the likes of sick and crippled Bo Tin Phay, half-baked socialist U Ba Nyein and yes-men in green from his 4th battalion promoted to general staff officer ranks for blind loyalty to him but little else except brutal suppression of dissent from any quarter. Nation building and governing was not part of the education and training Bo Ne Win received in Japan together with Bo Aung San. The middle echelon of the Imperial General Staff in Tokyo promised to help establish a Burma Army to Aung San, but the top brass did not fully endorse that project for the immediate and long terms and one can now discern the reasons why Gen. Suzuki, the father of the Burmese Army, was quickly recalled back to Tokyo.

It would be considered the final goal when Japan's Great East Asia (Minami Kikan) objective was achieved, and its power and control of the region consolidated. Therefore, the 30 comrades were given basic military training, guerrilla warfare, long-range penetration and intelligence operations to assist the Imperial Army's invasion of Burma. However, at the strong insistence of Bo Aung San, the Burma Independence Army (BIA) was organized in Siam (now Thailand) where blood was drawn from their arms, and the thirty pledged their eternal vows of loyalty to each other and to fight to liberate the country from the British colonial rule. Many young Burmese, on hearing the news, crossed the border into Siam, joined the swelling ranks of the BIA, and quickly marched into Burma to chase the already retreating British towards the Indian border.

The underground organization networks greatly helped the BIA to bond with the people and establish it as bona fide, as Burma's National Liberation Army. Many of the undercover movement leaders such as U Kyaw Nyein, Bo Khin Maung Galay, Bo Ne Win, U Hla Maung, Bo Sein Hman, Bo Aung Gyi, Bo Thaung Kyi among many others, contributed to the effort to liberate the country from British colonial rule as well as the resistance against Japanese occupation. The Burmese Military had come a long way and in late 1965, Bo Ne Win was ruling the country all by himself having alienated or purged his long-standing political colleagues and comrades-in-arms such as Bo Maung Maung, Bo Aung Gyi and Bo Khin Nyo. Even Bo Maung Lwin (Moustache) had to be sent away to Berlin as Ambassador.

Nation-building and national development went out the window. His full time preoccupation was security within the Military, within the Country and Security against foreign interference in internal affairs and the intensifying Regime Change schemes of the West. The U.S., Britain, France, India, Thailand and even Tito of Yugoslavia were openly assisting U Nu's insurgency to overthrow the Military Regime. Bo Let Ya, Bo Hmu Aung, Bo Set Kya, Bo Yan Naing (thirty comrades), Bo Tommy Clift and Okuda, the only officer among the five Japanese who defected to the Burmese resistance against the Japanese Army now joined U Nu. True to his tenacious character, Bo Ne Win dug in his heels to crush all the opposing forces working to remove him from power by every means, including but not limited to armed rebellion in collaboration with the more than 20 ethnic armies engaged in combat with the Military for over two decades.

The most important and critical component of the strategy to defeat and crush the multifaceted opposition forces was the intelligence services under Bo Chit Khin. However, some aspects of the functions and operations were under Bo Than Sein, the Chairman of the Central Security and Administrative Committee (CSAC) and Bo Kyaw Soe, the Minister of Home Affairs. Under such threats to National Security, I was drawn into other areas beyond the already heavy burden of "foreign missions and suppression of economic insurgency" tasks. Such as co-opted to serve as Legal Adviser to the Nationalization Committee chaired by Bo Than Sein, and the International Tender Committee chaired by Bo San Win, the Deputy Minister of Commerce and Trade.

The Chairman and Military Officers on the Committees, with very poor understanding of the English language, had no clue of the international tender documents' contents placed in front of them on the conference table. The civilian bureaucrats and technocrats on the Committee representing other Ministries pursue the safest policy of "silence and self-preservation". Until and unless the Chair directly addresses the question at them, not a word would be uttered. It was the paranoia and fear of being on record of having said something that would later be construed as "questioning official policy" or outright dissent. It was clearly the manifestation of the Command and Control Military Culture clashing with the Civil Administration Culture of established Protocols and Procedures (according to the "rule book").

In addition, of course the personal discomfort of the elite Civil Service Bureaucrats forced to take orders from the Army Officers whom they considered poorly educated and many with monastic education only (Phon-Gyi-Kyaung-Tha). On the contrary, I had worked for Bo Thaung Kyi and Bo Maung Lwin (Moustache) since my High School days in Bassein (now Pathein). Furthermore, the continued relationship with the Military leaders during higher studies in Japan, so it was not a problem for me to work in close proximity with Army, Navy or Air Force Officers in Burma or in foreign countries. My association with the Military began from the young age of about 17 in 1951-52 and in 1965 (14 years later), I was the odd and perhaps the youngest civilian educated in Japan with a Japanese wife serving the Army Regime in several Ministries. As a result, my job description in official circles became a subject of wild speculations and all kinds of rumors spread after the Committee proceedings because the Chairman and Secretary of the Committee would ask me to remain behind with them in the Conference Room.

For the Certification of Validity and Authenticity of the International Tender Documents duly approved and Authorized by the Committee for Worldwide Distribution through Burmese Diplomatic and Trade Missions overseas, Foreign Embassies and Trade Representative Offices in Rangoon and directly to Foreign Suppliers and Manufacturers. The Chairman gave me the responsibility to sign the three categories of international tenders, (1) Worldwide Tender, (2) Limited Tender and (3) Proprietary Tender to Original Patent Owner/ Manufacturer and to Manufacturer under License and/or Sub-Contractor as

Officer on Special Duty (OSD) / Legal Advisor to the Committee. The duly validated, certified and approved international tenders would be delivered to the respective requisitioning Ministries, Departments, State Corporations and Municipalities in desperate need of the items from abroad.

The Civil Service Bureaucrats, the foreign trade representatives, and their local employees ran amuck bribing and striking deals under the table from clerical staff to the Head of Department level (Retired Senior Army Officers) in State owned enterprises. The situation was getting out of control, rendering the Government's tender system meaningless. Additionally, the scale of the bribery and corruption was alarming and intolerable even by third world standards. Oblivious to the general public and the bureaucrats, an emergency meeting of the Economic Insurgency Suppression Committee was convened in the Ministry of Defense.

It was attended by Bo Chit Khin (MIS/NIB Chief), Bo Kyaw Soe (Minister of Home Affairs), Bo Than Sein (Chairman, Central Security and Administrative Committee), Bo Kyi Maung (Colonel General Staff) and Bo San Win (Deputy Minister of Commerce and Trade), all senior Military Officers. Three civilian officers, U Maung Maung (Senior Deputy Secretary, Ministry of Trade), U Ba Yi, Inspector-General of National Police and myself as Officer on Special Duty/ Legal Adviser of the Committee.

Many pages of irrefutable evidence on the long list of those involved were reviewed and there was unanimous consent for necessary investigation / interrogation under detention. However, the list included six Japanese Trade Company Branch Managers: Mitsui Trading Co., Mitsubishi Trading Co., Sumitomo Trading Co., Marubeni Trading Co., C. Itoh Trading Co., Nichimen Trading Co. I was in the hot seat as all eyes were on me, fully aware of my Japanese wife and my education in that country. Bo Chit Khin and Bo Than Sein wanted to know the legal status and I explained that Foreign Trade Representatives do not have any diplomatic immunity and are subject to the laws of the host country. In this particular case, there was clear and irrefutable evidence of violation of the laws and appropriate action was called for. The Committee approved the order for the detention of six Japanese Branch Managers.

I had to endure most of the blame-game and finger-pointing when information leaked (probably by a Committee Member with an agenda) and quickly spread that "the Japun-Pyan Legal Advisor" had recommended the detention of the six Japanese Branch Managers, several hundred government employees and many Japanese companies' local staff. Recently retired Senior Military Officers were among those arrested the evening of the Committee meeting. The Ministry of Commerce, Trade, and Corporations under it suffered the largest number arrested (450), such as the Agency Corporation, the Import Corporation; followed by Ministry of Health (Medicines, Pharmaceuticals, Medical Equipment and supplies, etc.,), Ministry of Education (Books, Paper, Educational Supplies), Ministry of Transport and Communication (Vehicles, Airplanes, River Craft, Automobile Spares and Tires, etc.) and other Government Departments.

I returned home around 8:00 PM after a fried rice and fried noodles dinner in the Conference Room with Bo Chit Khin, Bo Than Sein and Bo Kyi Maung. All three were concerned about the ramifications of detaining the six Japanese nationals and wanted to be prepared for the immediate reaction from the Japanese Embassy and the Ministry of Foreign Affairs. I suggested that U Thi Han, the Minister of Foreign Affairs, be informed immediately on the matter. Bo Chit Khin asked his aide to locate the foreign minister and get him on the secure line in the Conference Room. Within minutes, the phone rang and he apologized for calling at this hour and told him what had transpired and then hung up the phone. Apparently, the civilian foreign minister was shocked at what he just heard and lost for words, or perhaps thought it would be best to receive the information without any comment considering that the Military Intelligence Chief was on the other end of the line.

That night (more accurately early next morning) around 1:30 AM there was knocking at our front door downstairs, and my heart started to pound inside my chest. I thought my luck had run out, and they were here to get me. I went to front entry door and asked, "Who is it?" A faint voice answered, "Chida, please let me in." I opened the door and my friend Chida from Nichimen came in with a sigh of relief. I did not see his car in the driveway, and he explained that the car was left at the street corner, and he had walked from there, aware that he was being tailed. He apologized profusely for risking my personal security, but said he was desperate and at the end of his rope.

All six Japanese Branch Managers were taken away by the police after searching the houses, and the families were in a state of shock. A meeting of the Deputy Managers and Embassy Official discussed the situation and did not know what to do, except to ask Tokyo for guidance. I was certain that their "local staff" must have received information from their "moles" because I detected in Chida's conversation the insinuation that I was aware and knowledgeable about detaining the Japanese. I explained to Chida that at this stage there was absolutely nothing I or any other person could do to gain the release of the six Japanese, except the paramount ruler. And there was no one who would dare to take the matter to him.

He desperately asked for my guidance on what he should do. Off the top of my head, I suggested that he contact his Head Office in Tokyo to contact Takahashi or Mizutani and request them to fly to Rangoon and appeal to Bo Ne Win for the release of the Japanese Branch Managers. I told Chida not to tell anyone that I suggested the idea, especially to Takahashi and/or Mizutani. Chida left saying that he was going to his office to send the telex to his Head Office in Tokyo. Early next morning I dropped in to Bo Chit Khin's office and informed him what had transpired at my house and he told me not to worry because it was natural human reaction to seek help in times of trouble and despair, especially in a foreign country. The MIS was aware of Chida's visit to my house.

He told me that U Thi Han, the Foreign Minister, had called to ask for information with regard to the details and particular laws violated by the arrested Japanese executives and wanted to know if compliance would help or complicate matters. I explained to him that the specific transgressions of law after the arrests, the determination of laws violated becomes the exclusive jurisdiction of the Chief Prosecutor in the Office of the Attorney General. However, it would appear to be premature and inappropriate to respond on legal questions from the Foreign Minister when a decision to indict and prosecute was pending. He was visibly relieved to hear the explanation but told me to be in contact with Bo Solomon, the Judge Advocate General and the Attorney General's Office.

A week later, Takahashi arrived from Tokyo and contacted me through Chida of Nichimen for a meeting to discuss the matter. I was shocked by his indiscretion, rejected the request for a meeting, and immediately informed Bo Chit Khin who said, "You made the proper response of not seeing him" and better not during his entire stay in Rangoon. In the meantime, I received a call from Bo Thein Maung, Lead Counsel and Aide to the Judge Advocate General, with a request to attend a special meeting in their Department. Bo Solomon called the meeting to discuss and respond to questions raised by the Office of the Revolutionary Council Chairman concerning the arrest of the six Japanese executives. Two Government Prosecutors from the Attorney General's office participated in the discussions together with Bo Thein Maung and several of his colleagues, chaired by Bo Solomon. The Ministry of Foreign Affairs was absent from the meeting.

The Prosecutors, true to their profession and character, were more than eager to drag the six Japanese nationals before a Judge of the appropriate court of Jurisdiction and throw the book at them. Seek an indictment and proceed with the prosecution. I explained that the special good relations between the two countries were at stake and prolonged litigation would seriously damage them. The best solution in the "national interest" would be to "arrange a mutually agreed deportation with the Japanese Embassy" and avoid further embarrassment to both countries. Litigations are always messy with unintended consequences and outcomes. To quickly end the crisis should be the objective and stop the agony of both countries.

Bo Chit Khin joined the meeting and, after deliberation, it was agreed that the "recommendations of the Judge Advocate General meeting minutes be conveyed to the Revolutionary Council Chairman's Office post haste".

A day later, special agents took the six Japanese from their detention location to the airport where their Embassy Official awaited in the diplomatic lounge. After a brief rest and immigration procedures they were taken aboard a flight bound for Tokyo by Airport security officers accompanied by the Japanese Embassy official. Their families remained in Rangoon for several months to wind up their affairs and returned to Japan to join their deported husbands.

The impact of the arrest and deportation of the Japanese on the foreign business community in Rangoon and other major business centers such as Mandalay, Bassein and Moulmein was huge. It was the beginning of the exodus of Indian and Chinese enterprises from Burma. The Indian Embassy made desperate attempts to protest on behalf of the Indian business community but to no avail. Frustrated, the Indian Ambassador Admiral Katari, a retired Vice Admiral of the Indian Navy, demanded an audience with the Head of State. The Foreign Ministry Army Officer on Special Duty casually told the British Dartmouth Naval Academy graduated Indian Navy retired flag officer "General Ne Win does not see Ambassadors", oblivious and ignorant of International Law and Diplomatic Protocol giving full-fledged Ambassadors the right to an audience with the Head of State. Whether the audience is granted is entirely another matter.

Admiral Katari was flabbergasted at the casualness of the response to his demand, a very serious diplomatic situation and the Burmese dismissed it out of hand. He demanded the rejection "in writing because my Prime Minister will not believe me". Again, the Burmese Foreign Ministry official responded with, "I shall convey your demand to higher authorities." The Indian Ambassador left the Ministry of Foreign Affairs angry and frustrated. He instructed his Military Attaché (active service Colonel) to inform his "contacts in the Ministry of Defense" of Katari's snub at the Ministry of Foreign Affairs. Bo Chit Khin called me early in the morning at home and asked me to drop by his office on my way to work.

He wanted to ascertain the International Law stipulations, and the diplomatic protocols on the issue and half-jokingly added that one could not expect a green uniform to have any clue of international law. I explained to him that the Indian had every right and being ignorant of the law would not serve as an excuse to deny the right. Is it that serious? Yes indeed, absolutely. In history not too long ago, it would have been considered an insult and grave provocation, a cause for war or at the minimum, a war ship would be dispatched. However, in the 20th century, we could get away without serious consequences.

How about his demand to give him in writing? Perhaps he asked for it to protect himself and his diplomatic career and complying would probably resolve the issue. Later that day U Thi Han called Bo Chit Khin to discuss Admiral Katari's demand and was informed about the Military Attaché's complaints to him; the Foreign Minister was surprised and realized the seriousness of the Indian Ambassador's demand for a written response. He was also given the clarifications on international law that he had received in the morning from me and the justification in complying with Admiral Katari's need for a response in writing. The Indians were given the written response from the Ministry of Foreign Affairs to convince their Prime Minister, Indira Ghandi, that the Burmese Dictator rejected her Ambassador's demand for an audience with him.

The Indian Foreign Ministry was in a state of shock that the Burmese had had the audacity to put in writing their country's rejection of the generally accepted norms of International law and Diplomatic Protocols. The Burmese Ambassador in New Delhi had to endure the scorn of the Indians. It did not matter one iota to the Burmese Military Regime in Rangoon. It continued the pressure on the Indians to get out of Burma, and many did. The Chinese also left in droves to Thailand, Singapore, Hong Kong and Taiwan. The economy tanked, and agricultural production fell to the lowest level in the country that exported millions of tons of rice, beans and pulses, fish products, teak and other hard wood. That led to unimaginable mismanagement and rampant out of control corruption. The shelves of the "people's stores" were empty but bribing the manager and staff would bring out the goods from storage behind the store. Now, after the collapse of the economy, the country's moral fabric was breaking down. True to its character, the Regime's response was sweeping nationwide arrests and detentions. The jails overflowed with "enemies of the people", corrupt bureaucrats and dissidents opposing the Regime.

The Security State and its control apparatus was operating on overdrive at full capacity covering every threat to the Regime, real, actual, perceived or imagined. The surveillance, monitoring and intercepts expanded and increased to unprecedented levels and specialist staff and office space added to scrutinize, filter, analyze, evaluate and compress actionable counter measures to be taken by the "Field Commanders and their Active Operating Units". The West, led by the U.S., was using the Thai Military Intelligence Services and at times the Indian Military Intelligence to infiltrate, recruit and plant moles in the Regime's

Ministries, Departments and State-Owned enterprises. Most were detected and appropriate action taken to disable and/or eliminate the threat.

The consequences of his hard-and-fast lifestyle during his youthful days and the stresses and strains of his political/ military career and age were catching up on him fast. It became apparent to those near and around him daily such as Bo Ko Ko, the Revolutionary Council Secretary, and Bo Chit Khin, the Military Intelligence Chief. The heightened security vigilance and the verification procedures required daily meetings at the Ministry of Defense tea breaks and casual conversations about "the old man / #1's" health condition would come up such as, shortened attention span, forgetful, easily irritated, short-tempered and dozes off even on one-to-one briefing sessions.

We kept hearing such episodes of the #1 more often than before. He was well known for his photographic memory, one of the attributes for the Japanese selecting him for training at the Imperial Army Intelligence School at Nakano. The instructors at that School gave him nicknames, elephant (extraordinary memory) and snake in the grass (indistinguishable from environment and strikes first). His Japanese mentors evaluated him very accurately as evidenced by his record of accomplishment in eliminating all competitors to the top military post and then seizing political power from the Prime Minister on the verge of replacing him in early 1962.

Party cadres with less than high school education were in command of local security and administration functions, and it was like having the fox guard the chicken coop. The political and social engineering of the BSPP turned out to be the "great leap backwards". The worst fears of Bo Aung Gyi and his moderate colleagues such as Bo Khin Nyo, Bo Maung Maung, Bo Maung Lwin (Moustache) happened. Bo Ne Win realized what was happening to his regime and the country, but he was trapped in his own political experiment, implementing Bo Aung San's "Blueprint for Burma", written while staying at General Suziki's (Bo Mogyo) house in Hamamatsu, Japan. He carried that enormous burden of guilt of the disastrous failure to the end of his life.

History would judge him harshly for his rejection of sound and rational counsel from his closest comrades-in-arms and the paranoia of the threat to oust him from power. That psyche and mindset ruled out number (2) and number (3) in the scheme of succession in his Regime. Therefore, he never nurtured nor recognized anyone to be any number. There were self-appointed naïve pretenders like Bo Tin Phay tolerated and kept on in service merely to do his bidding of keeping the poorly educated officers that rose from the ranks in line. However, a new generation of officers produced by the Defense Services Academy (DSA), and the fresh crop of Officer Training School (OTS) graduates with university education were coming up the ranks.

It was a direct result of the restructuring and modernization implemented by Bo Aung Gyi and Bo Maung Maung decades ago. It is incumbent on present day military leaders (Bo Min Aung Hlaing and his contemporaries) for the need to reflect seriously on the true perspective of their evolutionary process and pass them on to the next generation. As far as I remember, Bo Ne Win made some effort in instructing Bo Saw Maung to update the "Tatmadaw Evolutionary History" perhaps urged by his wife (Daw Ni Ni Myint, Professor of History), but it was too little besides too late. In the earlier attempt to update the history of the 30 comrades in the mid-seventies, Daw Ni Ni Myint sent her Assistant History Lecturer at Rangoon University to Japan (Daw Khin Myint) for the purpose. She carried letters to me from Bo Ko Ko and his elder brother, my good friend U Maung Maung, requesting my assistance to help her access the Japanese Military Archives. Nakasone (Senior), a close friend, was Defense Minister at that time. The updated documents were among those that Bo Saw Maung sent me through Bo Khin Nyo in late summer of 1989. He carried them back with him to Burma in early 1990. I trust that future Military leaders and historians will review them again and disseminate their perspective to the next generation of Myanmar Academia and Military leaders.

Time was passing by fast and the aging process was catching up with all, including but not limited to those in the seat of power and the defense services, the Regime's main pillar of support. Key senior officers such as Bo Kyaw Soe (Home Minister), Bo Than Sein (Chairman of Central Security and Administrative Committee), Bo Chit Khin, MIS Chief and Bo Kyi Maung, Colonel General Staff (G-1) were going through treatment for one illness or another compounded by the stress and strain of the enormous responsibilities of their respective offices. The decade of the sixties was ending (1969), and during a lunch-break of a meeting, Bo Chit Khin, unexpectedly, asked if I was still thinking about leaving the country. Initially, I was surprised, but on second thought recalled his promise several years ago to help me leave some time in the future.

He was very philosophical speaking like a Baptist preacher citing the universal truth of "we are not getting any younger and must follow the body's timetable". Apparently, he was telling me that he would not be in the present post for too long. I told him that before leaving the country, I have a personal wish to visit Bo Aung Gyi and his new family in Maymyo (now Pyin-Oo-Lwin). He stared at me with an expression of disbelief, but did not reject it as insane or out of the question. He said he would privately discuss it with Bo Than Sein, the Central Security and Administration Chief. Months went by with absolutely no indication whether the matter was ever discussed. I thought I had pushed the envelope too far and crossed the "red-line".

In early March 1970, however, after a late-afternoon meeting of the Economic Insurgency Suppression Committee, Bo Chit Khin casually told me that he had flown to Maymyo last weekend to see Bo Aung Gyi carrying a message from Bo Ne Win, offering him the Ambassador post in Washington D.C. He spent many hours talking about old times, which both enjoyed enormously. However, he did not accept the offer on the principle that he could not in good conscience represent the policies of the regime abroad that he had opposed and spent seven and a half years in prison. Bo Chit Khin said half-jokingly, "Maybe you can do a better job of persuading him to change his mind."

He also revealed his discussion with Bo Than Sein about my plan to make a trip up north to Maymyo and visit with Bo Aung Gyi. He was rather surprised the reaction was positive but expressed concern for security because I was taking the entire family in the Chevrolet Bel Air purchased at the auction of foreign embassy vehicles left in Government Custody. Senior Government Officials had the priority and the privilege to select the top condition vehicle in advance and "through appropriate official channel" have the Auction Committee to reserve and transfer ownership title to my name.

I was advised to see Bo Than Sein with my travel plans well in advance of the trip. I went to see him with my itinerary three weeks before the long drive in early April. He instructed his Central Security Staff to issue an official Movement Order with my Ministry of Defense (ID), photo of the vehicle and copied to all Security and Administrative Committee (SAC) Offices along the Rangoon-Mandalay-Maymyo driving route with instruction to render all necessary help and assistance upon request. It was a very thoughtful arrangement on the part of Bo Than Sein. He did not tell me, but I had the distinct feeling that Bo Chit Khin told him everything.

It helped greatly along the way when I needed to fill up gas when the gasoline stations were closed or out of gas. The Army Officers on duty at SAC offices filled up the tank from their standby stock (free of charge) because they had received a copy of the "Official Movement Order" from Central (SAC). At Maymyo, the SAC Chairman and Commandant of the Defense Services Academy, Bo Khun Nawng arranged accommodation for the family at a fully furnished single-family house near the Railway Station belonging to the Baptist Bishop of the town. The housekeepers, servants and cooks made our stay very comfortable and pleasant. I had the opportunity to meet Bo Aung Gyi practically undisturbed except for his newly born baby daughter (Thin Nwe Aung) just one month old. One day, we both took care of the baby while Mu Mu, his wife, went buy groceries at the bazaar for our lunch on the rather old bicycle.

During our conversations, he did mention that Bo Chit Khin had come with the offer from Bo Ne Win to accept the U.S.A. Ambassador post. He felt "Ah-Nar-De" to Bo Chit Khin but there could be no compromise as long as his health permitted him to earn a living on his own to provide for his family. I asked him to accept it for the sake of the baby, the wife and to be out of the country for a few years perhaps would be good for him personally and the family. He lovingly stared at the sleeping baby and said, "No, Ko Kyi Win Sein; I cannot do that and be at peace the rest of my life on this earth. I understand and appreciate your concern, especially because you are one of the very few who treated me like a real brother and friend at all times regardless of my official status and extended support and assistance when I needed them most. I know very correctly that Ko Lay (Bo Khin Maung Galay) requested Bo Ne Win to take care of you while you were studying in Japan where I and senior Military Officers came to know you well.

"On your return from Japan I proposed, and Bo Ne Win appointed you directly to Judge Advocate General Department in the Ministry of Defense with a Commission. Your successful missions in Egypt with their Military and Yugoslav Intelligence and of course, the U.K./Europe/USA Action Plan / Burma Trade was a great achievement admired and appreciated by all including Bo Ne Win. Many BEDC people did not know your real background and history of your true personal relationship with me and Bo Ne Win.

"The others who knew were Bo Lwin (Moustache), Bo Thaung Kyi, Bo Khin Nyo and Bo Tommy Clift."

Our conversations and discussions in Maymyo covered the 15 years period from 1955 to 1970. He said many times that I was the only one to contact him when he was in Machanbaw all the way from London, and he wanted to know who had helped me in Rangoon. I revealed to him that it was "Bo Lwin and Bo Tommy Clift that made sure you got my message regardless of the risks involved". He was truly pleased and happy to hear from me that his two colleagues honored and appreciated the importance of my message to him from London.

Bo Aung Gyi, by nature, was a very soft-spoken and mild-mannered person. This persona contradicts the steely mindset and resolve to maintain his belief and the principle, and will not compromise for the sake of political expediency or self-interest. Perhaps this inflexibility came from his Accounting School education – rigid, systematic and correct method of managing "numbers and figures that never lie". He was kind, considerate and patient, but he could not accept inconsistent, deviant and "flip-flop attitude" especially from those in responsible positions.

He was the first senior Burmese Military Officer to attend the British Imperial Staff College and then followed by Bo Kyaw Zaw, Bo Maung Maung and Bo Aung Shwe. Such advanced training abroad helped greatly when Bo Aung Gyi as Vice Chief of General Staff (VCGS) and Bo Maung Maung as Director of

Military Training (DMT) spearheaded the restructuring and modernization. From the Government side, Bo Khin Maung Galay, the Deputy Prime Minister and Minister of Finance and Revenue that allocated the required funds to the Ministry of Defense to establish a professional Military Institution. It is incumbent upon the present Military leaders to fully understand and appreciate the monumental efforts made by these pioneers that laid the pillars and the solid foundation on which the present day Tatmadaw proudly stands today.

On my return from Maymyo after the water festival and New Year holidays in Mid-April 1970, I had lunch with Bo Chit Khin and Bo Than Sein after the meeting of the Economic Insurgency Suppression Committee, and both were keenly interested to know if Bo Aung Gyi had changed his mind about the Ambassador post in the USA. Upon hearing that it remained unchanged, they were concerned about his livelihood (Sar-Wut-Nay-Yay) and welfare of his new family and baby. I mentioned to them his plan to start a "fruit preservation business and a tea shop / restaurant" and both expressed shock and amazement, especially the teashop plan. He was one of the founders and number-two man of the Tatmadaw, and it would be beneath his dignity to run a teashop or a restaurant. A few days later, Bo Chit Khin said to me, "(Your Sayagyi) was greatly saddened by the news and instructed me to give whatever help was essential for Bo Aung Gyi to start his new business plans." He knew his friend, and ex-colleague would do anything to survive on his own. As such, it would be best to provide the necessary help to get him started on his way. All things being said and done, at the end of the day, he would not totally abandon his long-standing friend and ex-comrade-in-arms in the struggle for the country's independence from British colonial rule and resistance against Japanese occupation.

The workload and environment were expanding into new areas, particularly the surveillance, monitoring and intercepts of foreign missions and individuals' domestic agents. Preemptive actions on "locals" increased countrywide. The Americans, the British, the Australians, and the French in collusion with the Thais and the Indians continued with their scheme for "regime change" despite the discovery and elimination of their ill-conceived, poorly planned and inept execution by their "local recruits" and more often than not exposed before it reached "first base".

Bo Ne Win convened a meeting of his regional and field commanders to come up with an all-out assault plan to defeat and decimate the BCP forces on the Chinese border and simultaneously wipe out the BCP in the Pegu Yomas. The Burmese Army went to work and fought the BCP and their Chinese advisers, volunteers, their Wa and Kachin Independent Army allies. It took a few years and heavy casualties but the BCP and their allies were defeated to the shock and disbelief of the Chinese Communist Party and the Liberation Army. The BCP never recovered, and its Army ceased to exist to this day. Their Chairman, Thakin Than Tun, was killed and his dead body captured by troops under Bo Saw Maung's Command. Bo Ne Win flew by helicopter to view the corpse of his Communist friend and ordered him to be buried after full traditional Buddhist Rites. Bo Ne Win scolded Bo Saw Maung for celebrating Than Tun's death but later explained to him and his officers that he was also a patriot who had fought the British and the Japanese. However, he and the BCP were misguided by Communist ideology and did what he thought was good for the country. The Tatmadaw fought, defeated, killed and captured his body, but there is nothing to celebrate about his death. He was a nationalist independence leader. The country lost a patriot.

Bo Saw Maung confessed that he was concerned about his Army career after the scolding, but his fears were unfounded. On the contrary, his promotions accelerated, and he reached the very top and saved the country from an abyss by a Coup and restored Law and Order on 18 September 1988. He ruled the country as Chairman of State Law and Order Restoration Council (SLORC) and Head of State until his retirement due to ill health. He was succeeded by Bo Than Shwe, who restored a democratic civilian rule in 2011.

He and Bo Maung Aye deserve credit and true admiration for setting aside their "personal aspirations", pushing through the parliamentary elections and selecting Bo Thein Sein, President to run the country and begin the compromise and inclusion process with National League for Democracy (NLD) and the ethnic minority groups. Bo Min Aung Hlaing was selected as Commander-in-Chief to lead the Military and so far has lived up to the high expectations of his peers, colleagues and the country at large. Military leaders of neighboring countries have received him with high regard and respect. It is critically important for the present leaders of Myanmar to proceed with the democratic process one-step at a time and not to heed the "drum beat from outside" to dance to their tune. The contemporary example was when the USSR collapsed, under Gobarchev misled by the deliberate lies of the West that NATO would not expand "one inch beyond unified Germany" and today in 2014 openly dragging Ukraine into the EU and NATO.

The next year's (1971) water festival and Burmese New Year long holiday season, I drove up to Maymyo with the family under the same arrangement by the central "SAC" and stayed at the same house of Baptist Bishop U Aung Hla who had moved to Rangoon for the summer months. Bo Aung Gyi was settled with his family in a cottage on Circular Road with two (MIS) agents keeping an eye on his activities and visitors. The two agents stopped me at the gate and asked rather gruffly, "Hey, who did you come to see?" I countered with the question, "Whose house are you watching? Don't you fellows know who lives in this house? Here, keep this card, and give it to whoever ordered you to watch this house." I gave them my Ministry of Defense ID card (in Burmese and English). Both hurriedly opened the gate for me. When Bo Aung Gyi opened the door and saw me, his first question was, "How did you get past the two thugs at the gate?" He had a big laugh on hearing how the two hurriedly opened the gate for me on seeing the card.

I tried again to persuade him that staying out of the country a few years as Ambassador would enable him to reflect on the future of the country in a free and relaxed environment together with the family "without anyone watching over him like it is now". It did not work. His position was unchanged from last year. However, he did concede that should Bo Ne Win give up power to Bo San Yu, he would serve in any capacity because his trust and confidence were in the good soldier unlike the soldier-politician. It appeared to me as strange and dreaming that Bo Ne Win would even think of such a thing in his dreams as evidenced by his modus operandi of "not having a number two in his scheme of Military leadership".

I also had a distinct feeling that Bo Aung Gyi wanted to separate himself from other ousted Colonels and Generals such as Bo Maung Maung, Bo Aung Shwe, Bo Chit Myaing and Bo Aye Maung who all meekly and gratefully accepted Ambassador and Military Attaché posts abroad. In that regard, Bo Aung Gyi definitely stood alone with the distinction of maintaining his personal dignity and refusing the "carrots offered by Bo Ne Win after the stick of years in prison". Self-respect and principle was not something he would sacrifice for social status and material benefit. At the same time, he still considered Bo Ne Win a friend and comrade in arms and would not participate in any attempt or scheme to overthrow his regime by resorting to violence; apparently referring to ex-prime minister U Nu's misguided armed rebellion halfheartedly supported by the U.S. CIA, elements of the Thai Military and Indian Intelligence. He was very sure that it would fail because the Burmese Military establishment was well organized and led by dedicated "commanders in the field" from Company to Tactical Division and Regional Command levels.

His evaluation and prediction of the outcome were right on target. It was a disastrous failure where Bo Let Yar, the ex-defense minister and signatory to the British-Burma (Let Yar-Freeman) Defense Pact at the time of independence in 1948, died in Karen National Union territory in the midst of confused retreat from assault by Army units. All who knew him were saddened by his violent demise in the jungle. On the other side of the coin, one must ask the rhetorical question "what was Bo Let Yar thinking at the time of his fateful decision to join U Nu's infamous group to overthrow Bo Ne Win's regime?". I have yet to receive a coherent answer to this day, over half a century later. However, from the outcome that the world knows now, it was an unthinkable judgment error on the part of the Ex-General and Defense Minister. He paid the ultimate price with his life. May his soul rest in peace and incarnate to a better existence.

On my last day in Maymyo, I told Bo Aung Gyi my intention to leave the country for the future of my two children who would have no prospects of a good education and career options in Burma. He understood the situation very well but was concerned that some might prevent me and lay barriers in the process of getting the release. He kindly offered to write a personal letter to Bo Ne Win explaining my situation, the desire to leave the country and requesting his permission and necessary help. Then, on second thought, he suggested that I write directly since "he knows you well since your student days in Japan and your missions to Egypt and London were initiated by him". He was confident the outcome would be positive. He asked me to stay in touch wherever in the world I happened to be living. Should things change for the better for the country and for him, he would like the opportunity to work together again. He also told me to see Bo Khin Nyo before I left. On my return to Rangoon from Maymyo, the work environment became more politicized with retired Army officers indoctrinated at BSPP "learning and training centers" were posted to Ministries, Departments, State Enterprises and Corporations.

The Economic Insurgency Suppression Committee was working overtime and the surveillance; monitoring and investigation data was alarming, involving officers from the very top to clerical levels. Because the perpetrators were retired senior military officers as well as BSPP Party Cadres, taking legal action against them became a "political hot potato". It became a huge dilemma for Bo Chit Khin (Chief of MIS), Bo Than Sein (Chief of SAC) and Bo Kyaw Soe (Home Minister), the key members of the Committee because every single law in the books had been blatantly violated, and urgent action was called for. The matter was submitted to Bo San Yu (VCGS), the Finance and Revenue Minister and BSPP Vice Chairman of Central Committee and Bo Thaung Kyi, Central Committee member responsible for Party Discipline. Bo San Yu, true to his character was as usual cautious, but Bo Thaung Kyi was straightforward in advocating that the "rule of law must be enforced" OR the Laws abolished. "One cannot have it both ways, especially when we, the Military are governing the country."

The matter (the buck) reached Bo Ne Win's desk, and it stopped there for a few weeks. According to later accounts, he agonized at the prospect of these officers going to prison and being prosecuted for the criminal violation of the Laws and the abject failure of the BSPP Indoctrination Program to transform them into political leaders to lead the country on the path to a socialist paradise. Instead, the entire schemed backfired. The BSPP transformed these officers into the biggest thieves of the Socialist Military Regime, many times worse than the AFPFL politicians, the BEDC's Ali BaBa and the forty thieves.

In the closed-door Central Executive Committee Meeting presided by Bo Ne Win, the Law and Order Enforcement advocate and diciplinarian Bo Thaung Kyi prevailed. Nationwide, a few thousand were rounded up in the middle of the night and taken away to detention prisons and camps set up hurriedly. The jails overflowed with "economic insurgency detainees" who would languish under very poor and intolerable conditions for years because the "already understaffed and overburdened Justice System" could not cope with the thousands of cases to be prepared for prosecution in the few courts with presiding Judges. The morale of the civil service and government employees plummeted to the ground with the administration and enforcement of Law and Order under the control of BSPP Cadres from Village to Divisional levels.

Inevitably, the BSPP local leaders essentially made up entirely of retired military personnel came into conflict with the newly promoted Regional Commanders unwilling to share power and the scarce resources within their territory. A brand-new power struggle emerged and the Ministry of Defense and BSPP Party Central Executive Committee, both under the Control of Bo Ne Win, were at a loss as to how to defuse the conflict before the situation got out of hand. The realization of systemic failure set in at the mid-levels in the Military Establishment, particularly at the District and Divisional Levels, the basic administrative centers responsible for the security and general welfare of the population. The new system was dysfunctional and the two power centers of the country (the Military and the political party) were at loggerheads struggling for ultimate and absolute control over each other.

The Regime of Bo Ne Win was unravelling and playing the delicate balancing act would only exacerbate the already explosive confrontation in the regions that required urgent resolution from the top. A generational change in leadership of the Military was taking place throughout the country and the Ministry of Defense summoned the Regional and Tactical Division Commanders to Rangoon for an emergency conference presided over by Bo San Yu, the Vice Chief of General Staff (VCGS) as well as the number two Party Boss. Conflict resolution at the grassroots level between the Military and the Party was in reality an internal problem of the retired officers changing to civilian clothes and taking up influential positions in the party and control over all administrative powers of the Government.

Territorial Military Commanders pushed back hard, which surprised the Ministry of Defense General Staff that left Army Chief of Staff Bo San Yu with the only option to weigh in on the side of his territorial Commanders, the core power base that the Regime could not afford to alienate. It was a critical game changer and turning point for the Myanmar Military establishment to realize that "the new generation of officers would not simply roll over and surrender control" to any political entity, including one led by their Ex-Commanding officers. Organizational and structural changes proposed up the chain of command and kept on the back burner regained priority, were quickly implemented and the Officer Corps Commission and promotion system based on the archaic War Emergency (WE) system scrapped and promotions to Brigadier-General and above instituted in the system.

The long and untouchable policy of Bo Ne Win to limit the number of "generals" in the Military no longer could be practiced, and he accepted the reality of the generational change. Accelerated promotions beginning from the top Vice Chief of General Staff (VCGS) Bo Ne Win approved Bo San Yu to "Full General". Subsequently, Bo Tun Tin, Kyaw Htin, Htin Kyaw and Bo Tin Oo were promoted to full general rank. Territorial and Tactical Division Commanders were promoted to Brigadier and Major Generals respectively.

The Department Heads in the Ministry of Defense received promotions to the rank of Lt-Generals. The Air Force and Navy officers were promoted to equivalent general staff ranks. Now, with so many Generals in the Military establishment, Bo Ne Win, the Commander-in-Chief, rejected his own promotion to Field Marshall. Because of the stigma on that rank, Bo Saw Maung was the first to be elevated to the brand-new rank of Senior General. As a token of respect to Bo Ne Win, the rank he refused to accept (Field Marshall) was removed from the Military Army Ranks. It is still observed to this day. Bo Min Aung Hlaing, the current Commander-in-Chief, was promoted to Senior General soon after Bo Than Shwe selected him to take over his post in 2011.

In the middle of December 1971, as the Christmas season was approaching, Bo Chit Khin revealed to me that he was having health problems without specifying what it was and that he was seriously considering retirement on medical grounds, if the big boss would permit him to do so. He was certain that I would also have to get permission from your "Saya-Gyi" to leave the country since no one would dare to accept "your resignation, leave alone approving your passport for travel abroad". I told him about Bo Aung Gyi's offer of writing a letter to Bo Ne Win on my behalf and then suggesting that I write to him directly. He fully agreed and advised me to take that route. Additionally, he said, "Let me know if you want me to deliver it, or wish to do so through your own channel." He was very kind to offer his help but was understandably being cautious for obvious reasons. I thanked him and promised to keep him informed about my plans.

I consulted with Bo Thaung Kyi about my plan and he fully appreciated the reason for my wanting to leave the country and was prepared to help in every possible way. He also agreed that writing directly to Bo Ne Win was best as it would save time and remove all barriers. He kindly offered to deliver my letter and personally explain my situation to Bo Ne Win. He was the first man to involve me with the Burmese Military and always treated me as if I was his real younger brother. He reminded me to visit his home and to wish good-bye to (Saya – Dr.) Bo Lwin (Trade Minister), Bo Hla Han (Education Minister) and Bo Khin Nyo before I left Rangoon.

In early January 1972, soon after the New Year holiday season, I wrote to the big boss requesting his help and permission to leave the country for medical treatment at Tokyo University Hospital. In the letter, I briefly mentioned the treatment I had received and torment suffered after returning from London despite carrying out orders to hand over Burma Trade to Ambassador U Hla Maung and return to Burma by special plane. Within a matter of a few days, U Maung Maung (Tennis), the older brother of Bo Ko Ko, the Sectretary of the Revolutionary Council, came to my office. He informed me that the big boss "hit the ceiling" after reading my letter and asked his brother to find out "which mother f....ing son-of-a bitch" was tormenting this young Japanese fellow (Japun Kaung-Lay). Soon after, Bo Chit Khin told me the same story and added that he had received the green light to help with official procedures and documentations for the family's departure for Tokyo. Passport Official and camera operator from the Ministry of Home Affairs came to our residence with all the necessary forms to be completed and signed and he took photos for my Passport and Certificate of Identity for Robert (Bob) and Sayoko (Mar Mar Gyi). The Home Ministry official promised to bring the Passport and the Certificates within a few days, together with the approved Departure Forms. However, a surprised and unexpected family complication developed in the Home Ministry. The Deputy Secretary and authorized officer to "sign all

Passports and travel documents" at that time was U Tha Tun, brother-in-law of my eldest brother (Kyaw Htun Sein). He not only delayed signing my Passport and the Certificates of Identification for the two children, but also informed my brother that I was about to leave the country. Obviously, he was not aware of the arrangements.

For obvious reasons, I did not want the family to know until the last moment. It created unnecessary misunderstanding in my family as well as with the family of my brother's wife. It was out of the question for me to disclose what was really going on. I did confirm my plan to leave the country and asked my brother to request his brother-in-law to expedite issue of the Passport and the certificates "as I wish to avoid using my sources to have him do it". While the delicate family conversations not to offend each other were going on, the Ministry of Defense was upset at the delay and asked U Pu, the Deputy Inspector-General of Police (Special Branch) of the Passport Division, in the Ministry of Home Affairs to explain the delay.

It gave U Pu no other option but to reveal that it was on the desk of U Tha Tun, the Deputy Secretary, the past two days. Early the next morning, Bo Chit Khin called me at home and asked me to pick up U Maung Maung (Tennis) and swing by his office. We went in his car to the old Secretariat Complex and went to U Tha Tun's Office; he jumped up from his chair on seeing the Intelligence Chief walk into his office followed by U Maung Maung (always in trousers and tie) and myself. With characteristic sense of humor and soft-spoken jovial style, U Maung Maung informed his nervous (junior colleague in Burma Civil Service) friend the reason for our unannounced visit: "Ko Kyi Win Sein needs his Passport and Travel Documents for his children." He took them out from his top desk drawer, signed them in our presence, and handed them over to me. Bo Chit Khin thanked U Tha Tun for his cooperation.

That night, my brother called to tell me that his brother-in-law had complained bitterly to him saying, "Your young brother showed up unannounced with a powerful Army Officer and bullied me to sign his Passport." My brother was upset with what I had done and said, "you should not do such a thing to anyone," oblivious that it was not my doing and out of my control to say the least. The family's perception and instinctive inclination was to assign the blame entirely on me, not having any clue of what my real work assignment was in the Government. My parents wanted to know the reason for suddenly leaving the country with the entire family. In the midst of my problems with the many brothers and sisters, the bureaucrats in the Home and Defense Ministries for an official record advised Bo Chit Khin the need to obtain "a Certificate from the Medical Board recommending treatment abroad". It would regularize the required official procedure for approval to have medical treatment overseas.

Bo Hla Han, the Minister of Health, requested Dr. Ko Ko Gyi (Professor of ophthalmology) Chairman of the Medical Borad to convene an emergency meeting with Members Dr. Khin Maung Win (Professor of Pathology), and Dr. Hla Myint (Professor of Medicine) and issue the required certificate of Recommendation for treatment abroad. Apparently, Bo Chit Khin wanted the official procedures completed and recorded to allay any speculation and inappropriate rumors from within the bureaucracy. It was a preemptive precautionary move to establish bona fide Government records, diverting attention away from where the authorization actually originated. Additionally, he advised me to stay away from Thailand at least for five years.

Several days before departure, I made arrangements to send two new bicycles recently received from Tokyo by air, electric heaters, warm clothing and blankets to Bo Aung Gyi up in Maymyo as his Bel Air was "on jacks" for lack of tires. I offered to leave my "Bel Air" with him, but he would not accept saying, "You have done for me more than anyone while I was in office as well as when I left the Government when all avoided and stayed far away. Ko Kyi Win Sein, I greatly appreciate your sincere friendship and please keep in touch wherever in the world you may be."

*Standing L-R: General Aung Gyi, General Maung Maung, General tin Phay, Aide to Generals. Seated L-R: ADC to Generals*

*Bo Khin Maung Galay, Deputy Prime Minister and General Ne Win*

Burmese Student Union Japan 1955, SEATED L - R : Saw Mya (CEC Member), Kyi Win Sein (CEC Chairman), Tin Maung Htwe (CEC Member), Aung Soe (CEC Vice Chairman); STANDING L - R: Hla Win (CEC General-Secretary), Duwa Maran Jala (Foreign Student Affairs), Ko Ko Gyi (CEC Vice Chairman), Hla Myint Oo (CEC Treasurer), Nyein Maung Zan (CEC Member) (CEC = CENTRAL EXECUTIVE COMMITTEE)

ASIA YOUTH ASSOCIATION (ASJIA SEININ-KAI) L - R: Visvalingam (Ceylon), Carlos Romulo Jr. (Philippines), Raja Kumara Swaminathan (India), Yoshio Hayashi (Vice Chairman), Kensaburo Fujisawa (Chairman of Association and CEO of Fuji Steel Co.), Kyi Win Sein, Burma & President of International Students' Union Japan), Madame Fujisawa

# Biodata

## EDUCATION / ACADEMIC CERTIFICATIONS / DEGREES / AWARDS

1. University of Rangoon 1953... 1954, I.A. (Intermediate of Arts)
2. Osaka University of Foreign Studies
   (Japanese Language and Culture, 1955, State Scholar Under Burma-Japan Treaty of Peace, Friendship and WWII Reparations).
3. Tokyo University of Foreign Studies
   (Japanese Language, Culture, Japan-Asia Relations).
4. B.A., LL.B. University of Tokyo, School of Law
   (Jurisprudence, International Law, 1956)
5. LL.B. (International Law & Relations)
   Waseda University Tokyo, School of Law 1957-1959.
6. Senior General Staff Officer Strategic Studies
   (National Defense University, United Arab Republic by Special Invitation of the Minister of Defense, 1960).
7. Special Award of Yugoslav Minister of Defense for Multi-National Strategic Alliance And Intelligence Collaboration.

## CAREER PROFILE:
1. Direct Commission Appointment by Commander-in-Chief in Judge Advocate General Department, Ministry of Defense, Burma (1959).
2. Nominated by Deputy Prime Minister for Executive position in Burma Oil Company (1959 -1960: Regional Marketing Manager, South Burma.
3. Burma / United Arab Republic (Egypt-Syria) Yugoslavia Strategic Alliance Middle East Project: Resident Representative of Ministry of Defense, Cairo, Egypt (1960-1961).
4. Corporate Counsel and Secretary to Board of Directors: Export-Import Bank of Burma (1961-1962).
5. Legal Advisor to Chairman, Burma Economic Development

Corporation (BEDC - 1962) Office of the Prime Minister, Rangoon, Burma.
6. Special (Action Plan Project) Operations in U.K., Europe, U.S.A., Restructuring of Economic, Trade, Commerce, Finance and Banking: Legal Counsel, Chief Executive Officer and founder of Burma Trade Corporation, London, U. K. (1962-1964).
7. Judicial Advisor (Classified): Economic Insurgency Suppression/Control Committee, Directorate of Intelligence Services, Ministry of Defense (Concurrently) Legal Advisor (Classified): Foreign Residents' Activity / Movement Control Group (Central Security and Enforcement Division), Ministry of Defense, Rangoon, (1965 -1972).
8. I was permitted to resign from Government Service for Medical Treatment in Japan by approval of Gen. Ne Win, the Revolutionary Council Chairman and Head of State in February 1972.

www.ingramcontent.com/pod-product-compliance
Lightning Source LLC
Chambersburg PA
CBHW071328190426
43193CB00041B/923